Sustainable Marketing

Visit the *Sustainable Marketing* Companion Website at
www.pearsoned.co.uk/emery to find valuable **student**
learning material including:

- Multiple choice questions to test your understanding
- Weblinks to relevant, specific internet resources to facilitate in-depth independent research
- Links to video material of key Sustainable Marketing campaigns.
- Additional examples and case studies

Sustainable Marketing

Barry Emery

PEARSON

Harlow, England • London • New York • Boston • San Francisco • Toronto • Sydney
Auckland • Singapore • Hong Kong • Tokyo • Seoul • Taipei • New Delhi
Cape Town • São Paulo • Mexico City • Madrid • Amsterdam • Munich • Paris • Milan

Pearson Education Limited
Edinburgh Gate
Harlow
Essex CM20 2JE
England

and Associated Companies throughout the world

Visit us on the World Wide Web at:
www.pearson.com/uk

First published 2012

© Pearson Education Limited 2012

ISBN 978-0-273-72328-8

British Library Cataloguing-in-Publication Data
A catalogue record for this book is available from the British Library

Library of Congress Cataloguing-in-Publication Data
Emery, Barry.
  Sustainable marketing / Barry Emery.
    p. cm.
  Includes bibliographical references and index.
  ISBN 978-0-273-72328-8 (pbk.)
  1. Green marketing. I. Title.
  HF5413.E474 2012
  658.8'02--dc23
                              2011040028

ARP impression 98

Typeset in 10/12.5 Book Antiqua by 73
Printed and bound by Ashford Colour Press Ltd., Gosport

This book is dedicated to Angels, my wife,
whose constant support has made this project possible.

Contents

Preface   xi
Acknowledgements   xv
Guided Tour   xviii

Part 1 Marketing for sustainability: people, planet, prosperity   1

1 Sustainable marketing   3

Chapter objectives   3
Dilemma part 1: Behaving responsibly   4
Sustainable marketing   5
    Conventional marketing revisited   7
    Moves in the right direction   11
    Environmental marketing variants   15
    The foundations of sustainable marketing   20
Defining the parameters of sustainable marketing   23
Summary   27
Case study: Hans Merensky: ahead of the times   28
Dilemma part 2: Behaving responsibly   30
References   31

2 The backdrop to sustainability   36

Chapter objectives   36
Dilemma part 1: Who decarbonises first – business?   37
The backdrop to sustainability   38
    The habits of a lifetime   38
    Business cannot be *as usual*   41
    Approaches to sustainable development   58
Summary   61
Case study: Muji – less is more   62
Dilemma part 2: Who decarbonises first – the consumer?   63
References   64

Part 2   Understanding the nature of consumption
and consumer behaviour   67

    3   Understanding attitudes towards consumption
and sustainability   69

        Chapter objectives   69
        Dilemma part 1: Is there a sustainability crunch?   70
        Understanding attitudes towards consumption
        and sustainability   70
            The nature of consumption   71
            When attitudes do not match behaviour   78
            The risk of sustainability   85
            A citizen's act of faith   88
        Summary   90
        Case study: 360 Vodka   91
        Dilemma part 2: Is there a sustainability
        crunch?   93
        References   95

    4   The evolution of sustainable segmentation   98

        Chapter objectives   98
        Dilemma part 1: Back to nature?   99
        The evolution of sustainable segmentation   100
            The evolution of human needs   101
            Understanding segmentation for sustainability   104
            Towards a better understanding – Defra
            pro-environmental behaviours 2008   108
            Simplicity versus materialism   113
        Summary   118
        Case study: Time to think outside the bottle   119
        Dilemma part 2: Nature makes a comeback   122
        References   123

Part 3   Marketing as an agent of change   125

    5   Motivating behavioural change   127

        Chapter objectives   127
        Dilemma part 1: The bottom line   128
        Motivating behavioural change   129
            The challenges beyond the threshold   129
            Changing norms of behaviour   131
            A framework for change   140
        Summary   148
        Case study: The carrot, the stick and
        the plastic bag   148
        Dilemma part 2: The bottom line   152
        References   153

6 Reconciling product sustainability   157

   Chapter objectives   157
   Dilemma part 1: The slow rise of ethical fashion   158
   Reconciling product sustainability   160
      Designing the sustainable product   161
      Packaging the sustainable product   171
   Summary   178
   Case study: Recycling (mis)behaviours   179
   Dilemma part 2: The slow rise of ethical fashion   183
   References   184

7 Addressing supply chain sustainability   188

   Chapter objectives   188
   Dilemma part 1: The certification of sustainability   189
   Addressing supply chain sustainability   190
      Sustainable procurement   191
      Impacts along the supply chain   197
      Forget global, act local   202
   Summary   209
   Case study: Source4Style   210
   Dilemma part 2: The certification of sustainability   212
   References   212

8 Communicating sustainability   216

   Chapter objectives   216
   Dilemma part 1: Aga and a sustainable future   217
   Communicating sustainability   218
      Getting it wrong   219
      Getting it right   228
      Labelling   232
   Summary   237
   Case study: Getting it right and wrong at the same time   238
   Dilemma part 2: Aga and a sustainable future   242
   References   244

Part 4 Implementation   247

9 Managing sustainable change   249

   Chapter objectives   249
   Dilemma part 1: Bad for business, good for you   250
   Managing sustainable change   250
      The people corner   251
      The business corner   254
      The government corner   258
      Towards a framework for consolidated change   261
   Summary   272
   Case study: Adnams – sustainable brewing for the
   21st century   273

Dilemma part 2: Good for business, bad for you   277
References   277

10 The future for sustainability: Raising the game, changing the game   280

Chapter objectives   280
Dilemma part 1: Nine billion sustainable lifestyles   281
Raising the game, changing the game   281
   Not nice at all   283
   Over the next decade   289
Summary   299
Case study: Unilever and global sustainability   300
Dilemma part 2: One sustainable lifestyle   303
Epilogue   304
   A decade of reluctant or whole-hearted engagement?   304
   Low- and zero-carbon (LZC) homes   304
   Electric cars   305
   The rise of the nimby   305
   Marketing and sustainability – ideal partners   306
   Employment opportunities   306
References   307

Index   310

Preface

> Treat the earth well: it was not given to you by your parents; it was loaned to you by your children. We do not inherit the earth from our ancestors; we borrow it from our children.

Wisdom from the ancient American Indians

Welcome to Sustainable Marketing

The inspiration to write a book can come from many sources. My initial inspiration resulted from findings from an as yet unpublished piece of research written by my wife.[1] As a by-product of her research on the positioning of food by country-of-origin she highlighted the public's growing concerns with the social and environmental impacts of food imports. This acted as a catalyst for my own research and the realisation that my beloved subject of marketing was getting left behind the times when compared to the growing intensity of the sustainability agenda. I realised that the discipline of marketing should not ignore the challenge of sustainability but embrace it, and so this book project started in order to address this gap in marketing practice. After all, a true marketer does not see difficulties but opportunities.

To become truly sustainable in our business activities and in our lifestyles marketing will have much to contribute during the next decade although some still see marketing to be at odds with sustainability. It is a common assumption that marketing and sustainability are heading for a conflict of interests because marketing is about selling more while sustainability is about consuming less. But marketing is essentially about making businesses work as efficiently as possible, so it is surely well-placed to facilitate the transition to more sustainable development and negotiate change between all the stakeholders involved.

The former US Vice-President, Al Gore, eloquently summarised the extent of the change required to incorporate sustainability into our business systems.[2]

> *The age of sustainability has arrived, but now we must drive it fully through our economic system. To do so, markets will have to continue to evolve to take into account the full environmental and social externalities of business. . . . This shift will require nothing less than a complete change in mindset – one that views our planet as a long-term investment, rather than a business in liquidation.*

If we are going to live sustainably almost everything we know and take for granted will experience some sort of change, particularly as consumers, from the way we live our lives as inhabitants of the planet (become true custodians of nature) to the way we consume goods (consume to live rather than live to consume), from the way we consume energy (we might end up generating our own energy supply) to the way we obtain our food (we might end up growing our own!).

The pressing issue of sustainability is ubiquitous; all we need now is a range of solutions to match the challenges. Sounds simple enough, and indeed many of the possible solutions are not too difficult, but the scale of the change required must not be underestimated. I am optimistic that such changes can take place and that marketing has a key role to play in establishing sustainable business practice and sustainable consumption patterns and sustainable lifestyles as the norm.

Much of this text has already been tried and tested in the classroom and is designed to allow students to learn through practice and deepen their knowledge and understanding through investigation and research. The great variety of exercises allow for individual, pair and group work and may also be developed as assignments, projects and potential dissertation topics. The text is suitable for both undergraduate and postgraduate students who wish to explore the influence of sustainability on marketing practice.

Distinctive features

- *Dilemmas*: sustainability presents marketers with difficult choices and even though sustainable alternatives are desirable they are not necessarily straightforward and marketers will have to learn to balance conflicting interests.

- *Snapshots and cases*: mini-insights give quick-fire examples of sustainable issues, and broader cases highlight good practice and the many challenges that remain.

- *Apply it*: an opportunity to apply theory to practice using the concepts, frameworks and models of each chapter.

- *Researching sustainability*: the ability to research is an essential skill for a marketer and these exercises allow students to gain depth of knowledge.

- *Professional practice*: a chance to develop the kinds of skills and know-how expected of professional marketers such as presentations and pitches.

- *Getting started*: handy hints to set students on the right path for some of those more challenging exercises.

- A book-specific website with a variety of supporting material and extension activities for students and lecturers.

A book in four parts

Part one: **Marketing for sustainability: people, planet, prosperity**
Establishes the origins and key features of sustainable marketing in comparison to conventional marketing practice and explains sustainability within a contemporary business context

Part two: **Understanding the nature of consumption and consumer behaviour**
Examines the consumer's relationship with consumption in order to understand the deep-seated attitudes of consumers towards consumption and their potential predisposition towards more sustainable behaviour

Part three: **Marketing as an agent of change**
Highlights the vital role marketing plays in achieving behavioural change among consumers as well as emphasising the changes in marketing practice required to help business adopt more sustainable practices

Part four: **Implementation**
Explores how sustainable marketing might be implemented and the role of the different stakeholders within the network of the sustainable business. This part also looks at the future challenges presented by the sustainability agenda.

About the author

Barry Emery is Senior Lecturer in Marketing and researcher in sustainability marketing at Birmingham City University, specialising in behavioural change. After over a decade of experience in the prestigious Colegio San Ignacio in Barcelona, Spain, he returned to the UK to focus his career on marketing education passing through University College Birmingham and The University of Northampton before taking his present post at Birmingham City University.

References

1. Emery, A. (2007) *An analysis of consumer perceptions of country-of-origin positioning: an evaluation of the use of authentic and simulated country-of-origin positioning.* Unpublished dissertation, University College Birmingham, Birmingham, UK.

2. Gore, A. (2008) Foreword to Hart, S.L. (2008) *Capitalism at the Crossroads: Aligning Business, Earth and Humanity,* 2nd ed., Harlow, Prentice Hall, xxv–xxvi.

Acknowledgements

We are grateful to the following for permission to reproduce copyright material:

Figures

Figure 4.2 adapted from *Green and Ethical Consumers UK*, Mintel International Group (2007); Figure 5.3 adapted from A Value-Belief-Norm Theory of Support for Social Movements: The Case of Environmentalism, *Human Ecology Review* Vol. 6 (2), pp. 81–97 (Stern, P. et al. 1999); Figure 5.4 adapted from Constructing a theory of planned behavior questionnaire (figure: schematic representation of the theory), *http://www.people.umass.edu/aizen/pdf/tpb.measurement.pdf*, p. 1 (Aizen, I. 2006); Figure 6.3 adapted from *A guide to evolving packaging design: A summary of the packaging life cycle* Waste and Resources Action Programme (2009); Figure 7.4 adapted from Purchasing must become supply management *Harvard Business Review*, Vol. 61, 5, pp. 109–117 (Kraljic, P. 1983); Figure 9.5 adapted from *Household Food and Drink Waste in the UK (Figure B)*, Waste & Resources Action Programme (2009) http://www.wrap.org.uk/downloads/Household_food_and_drink_waste_in_the_UK_-_report.e294c4d0.8048.pdf; Figure 9.10 adapted from *MINDSPACE Influencing behaviour through public policy – The practical guide* Institute for Government (Dolan, P. et al 2010) p. 9, http://www.instituteforgovernment.org.uk/images/files/MINDSPACE-practical-guide.pdf; Figure 10.2 from 'World Footprint', http://www.footprintnetwork.org/en/index.php/GFN/page/world_footprint/, Global Footprint Network, 2010 National Footprint Accounts; Figure 10.3 from Millar, J. (2010) Resource efficiency support from WRAP: Slaughtering and animal by-products industries EBP Seminar: 29th September 2010 presentation by Josephine Millar, Project Manager-Retail Supply Chain Team.; Figure 10.4 adapted from *Capitalism: As If the World Matters*, Earthscan (Porritt, J. 2007) p. 255.

Tables

Table 1.6 adapted from *'Enter the Triple Bottom Line' in Henriques, A. and Richardson, J. (eds) The Triple Bottom Line: Does it all add up?*, Earthscan (Elkington, J. 2004) pp. 3–6; Table 2.1 from Measuring endorsement of the New Ecological Paradigm: A revised NEP scale *Journal of Social Issues*, 56 (3), pp. 425–442 (Dunlap, R. E., Van Liere, K. D., Mertig, A. G., & Jones, R. E. 2000); Table 4.3 from *Roper Green Gauge Survey*, Roper Starch Worldwide (2000); Table 4.4 from Shades of Green Environment, Ethics & Causes in a Downturn, GfK Roper Consulting Presentation at Organic Exchange, Porto, October 2008., Gfk Roper (Chiarelli, N. 2008); Table 4.6 adapted from Sustainability: consumer perceptions and marketing strategies, *Business Strategy and the Environment* 15 (3), pp. 157–170. (McDonald, S. and Oates, C. 2006); Table 5.2 adapted from Do better at doing good *Harvard Business Review* Vol. 74, 3, pp. 42–54 (Rangan, V.K., Karim, S. And Sandberg, S. K 1996); Table 5.5 adapted from *Big Pocket Guide Social marketing*, 2nd ed., National Social Marketing Centre (2007) p. 50, http://www.nsmcentre.org.uk/sites/default/files/NSMC_Big_Pocket_Guide_Aug_2007_2.pdf; Table 6.4 adapted from *Public Attitudes to Packaging 2008*, Ipsos MORI (2008) p. 3, http://www.ipsos-mori.com/Assets/Docs/Publications/sri_environment_INCPEN%20summary%20report_271108.pdf; Table 7.2 adapted from *Well dressed? The present and future sustainability of clothing and textiles in the United Kingdom*, University of Cambridge Institute for Manufacturing (Allwood, J.M., Laursen, S.E., Malvido, C., and Bocken, N.M.P. 2007) ISBN 1-902546-52-0, 84 pages; Table 7.3 adapted from *MSC: Commercial Commitment Growing Worldwide* Marine Stewardship Council (2010); Table 8.1 adapted from *Selling sustainability seven lessons from advertising and marketing to sell low-carbon living*, National Endowment for Science, Technology and the Arts (Bhattachary D., Angle, H. 2008) p. 6, reproduced by pemrission of the publisher and the authors; Table 8.2 adapted from *Sustainability Issues in the Retail Sector*, Ipsos MORI (2007) p. 29; Table 8.3 adapted from *Green expectations: Consumers' understanding of green claims in advertising*, Consumer Focus (Yates, L. 2009) pp. 4–5, http://www.consumerfocus.org.uk/assets/1/files/2009/06/Green-expectations-single-page.pdf; Table 9.1 adapted from *Warwickshire County Council Contract taking part in Sustainability week 2005 by making pledges*, Carillion (2005) p. 2, http://www.carillionplc.com/sustain_2005/assets/documents/2005%20-case%20records%20in%20PDF/CR_2005_Roads_pledges_warickshire_sustwk.pdf; Table 9.4 adapted from *MINDSPACE Influencing behaviour through public policy – The practical guide*, Institute for Government (Dolan, P. et al 2010) p. 6, http://www.instituteforgovernment.org.uk/images/files/MINDSPACE-practical-guide.pdf; Table 9.6 adapted from East Green – the first carbon neutral beer from the coast, *http://adnams.co.uk/beer/east-green-%E2%80%93-the-first-carbon-neutral-beer-from-the-coast* (Hibbert, E.); Table 10.1 from 'The ten One Planet Living principles', http://www.oneplanetvision.org/one-planet-living/opl-framework, The One Planet Living framework was developed by BioRegional and WWF.

Photographs

The publisher would like to thank the following for their kind permission to reproduce their photographs:

(Key: b-bottom; c-centre; l-left; r-right; t-top)

44 The Global Footprint Network. 45 Raureif GmbH. 50 New Zealand Ministry for the Environment. 52 With the kind permission of Responsible Travel. www.responsibletravel.com. 77 The Affluenza Exhibition 2009, created and organised by Hege Sæbjørnsen (www.hegesaebjornsen.com) Art direction: Iskra Tsaneva, Design; Chris Clarke. 78 Corbis: Boris Roessler / dpa. 82 Pearson Education Ltd. 91 McCormick Distilling. www.mccormickdistilling.com. 122 Image courtesy of The Advertising Archives. 175 TerraCycle: Christopher Crane. 176 Reproduced with the kind permission of Société des Produits Nestlé S.A.. 177 Image courtesy of The Advertising Archives. 212 ©Fairtrade www.fairtrade.org.uk. 217 Image courtesy of The Advertising Archives. 223 Image courtesy of The Advertising Archives. 232 Ecolabel: Ecolabel logo provided courtesy of UK Ecolabel Delivery (b). Reprinted with the permission of The Timberland Company: (t). 233 Daniel J Edelman Ltd: (b). Federal Environmental Agency, Germany.: (t). 234 The Carbon Trust: (b). 235 The Carbon Trust. 238 Lindsey Gardiner: For the Department of Energy and Climate Change.. 239 Lindsey Gardiner: For the Department of Energy and Climate Change (t, b). 242 goodillustration.com: Bob Venables for the Department of Energy and Climate Change (l, r). 257 St James Ethics Centre, Australia.. 295 courtesy of E.on: (t). www.joeharrison.co.uk: (b). 303 BioRegional Development Group. 304 BioRegional Development Group.

All other images © Pearson Education

Every effort has been made to trace the copyright holders and we apologise in advance for any unintentional omissions. We would be pleased to insert the appropriate acknowledgement in any subsequent edition of this publication.

Guided Tour

The **Dilemma** boxes separate out controversial themes helping stimulate discussion and debate regarding possible pitfalls. Each dilemma also comes with Discussion Questions to help test your understanding.

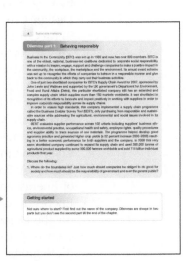

Not sure where to start? These handy **Getting Started** boxes which accompany many of the discussion questions and exercises will help you on your way.

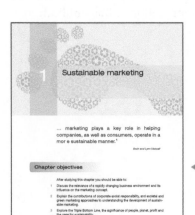

Each chapter concludes with a detailed **Case Study** which will test your knowledge of Sustainable Marketing theory by applying this to well known marketing companies from across the globe.

Chapter objectives open each chapter and enable you to focus on what you should have achieved and help structure your learning.

The **Snapshots** are an invaluable resource and demonstrate how Sustainable Marketing theory is applied in a number of business contexts.

The **Apply It** feature encourages you to read around the subject and find new examples.

The **Researching Sustainability** boxes provide handy insights into market research techniques which you could use for your own research.

The **Professional Practice** feature puts you in the shoes of a employee at a number of national and international companies.

PART 1

Marketing for sustainability: people, planet, prosperity

1 Sustainable marketing

> ... marketing plays a key role in helping companies, as well as consumers, operate in a mor e sustainable manner.[1]
>
> *Borin and Lynn Metcalf*

Chapter objectives

After studying this chapter you should be able to:

1 Discuss the relevance of a rapidly changing business environment and its influence on the marketing concept.

2 Explain the contributions of corporate social responsibility, and societal and green marketing approaches to understanding the development of sustainable marketing.

3 Explore the Triple Bottom Line, the significance of people, planet, profit and the case for sustainability.

4 Define the concept of sustainable marketing.

5 Indicate the differences between conventional marketing practice and the sustainable marketing paradigm.

Dilemma part 1:   Behaving responsibly

Business in the Community (BITC) was set up in 1982 and now has over 800 members. BITC is one of the oldest, national, business-led coalitions dedicated to corporate social responsibility with a mission to inspire, engage, support and challenge companies to make a positive impact in the community, the workplace, the marketplace and the environment. Its annual award scheme was set up to recognise the efforts of companies to behave in a responsible manner and give back to the community in which they carry out their business activities.

One of just two shortlisted companies for BITC's Supply Chain Award for 2007, sponsored by John Lewis and Waitrose and supported by the UK government's Department for Environment, Food and Rural Affairs (Defra), this particular shortlisted company still has an extended and complex supply chain which supplies more than 180 markets worldwide. It was shortlisted in recognition of its efforts to innovate and impact positively in working with suppliers in order to improve corporate responsibility across its supply chains.

In order to ensure high standards, this company implemented a supply chain programme called the Business Enabler Survey Tool (BEST), only purchasing from responsible and sustainable sources while addressing the agricultural, environmental and social issues involved in its supply chain.

BEST evaluates supplier performance across 102 criteria including suppliers' business ethics, environmental practice, occupational health and safety, employee rights, quality procedures and supplier ability to trace sources of raw materials. The programme helped develop good agronomy practice and generated higher crop yields (a 22 percent increase 2000–2006) resulting in a better economic performance for both suppliers and the company. In 2008 this very same shortlisted company continued to expand its supply chain and used 390,000 tonnes of agricultural product supplied by some 300,000 farmers worldwide and sold 715 billion individual products that year.

Discuss the following:

1. Where do the boundaries lie? Just how much should companies be obliged to do good for society and how much should be the responsibility of government and even the general public?

Getting started

Not sure where to start? First find out the name of the company. Dilemmas are always in two parts but you don't see the second part till the end of the chapter.

Sustainable marketing

Concern over the ethics of business, social responsibility and the environment was once thought to be a passing fad, encouraged by a minority of activist organisations and confined to the margins of society. Now, not a single day passes without these topics appearing before the general public. Governments regularly debate and legislate on these issues, pressure groups openly voice their opinions and take their own actions, more and more product advertisements contain more sustainability-focused messages, and businesses are beginning to take measures of their own, changing the way they conduct their operations from the beginning to the end of their supply chains. Without doubt, sustainability now forms part of the everyday consciousness of the consumer, government and of business and its presence is likely to be permanent.[2]

Accordingly, consumers themselves are altering their purchase habits as they cope with a new consumer vernacular made up from words and phrases they had not used before such as *natural, organic, fair trade, free range, ethical, eco, biodegradable, recyclable, environmentally friendly, green, carbon neutral, carbon footprint, socially responsible.*[3]

But there have been many changes in marketing in the past, which have not created so much fuss. For example, in 1980, professor of marketing Leonard Berry wrote in a seminal article that the marketing of services was different from product-based marketing, highlighting how marketing professionals needed to change and adapt their practice in order to deal with the various characteristics of the services industry.[4]

So why is the change to sustainable marketing so much more significant?

Its significance comes from the fact that sustainable marketing is not another offshoot or an alternative branch of thought or practice running alongside what is often referred to in this text as *conventional* marketing. Nor is sustainable marketing a mere cosmetic exercise. Sustainable marketing has to become the new mainstream, standard and conventional way of marketing, as there are no longer any more alternatives. And before you think this marketing author is some sort of dark-green marketing extremist you would be wrong. This marketer loves his conventional marketing and is as happy as anyone when he sees how a good marketing plan delivers what it is supposed to do and he also loves consuming . . . but it is time for change in marketing practice, there is no avoiding it.

There are physical limits to consumption and the global consumer has already overreached these limits. The advent of mass markets has given profits to business but has resulted in consumption on a scale never experienced before. Constant economic growth and consumption fuelled by a rapidly increasing global consumer class is no longer (and never really was) sustainable. The desire for economic growth has been a constant during the last century and marketing has been complicit in its pursuit, as have governments and politicians. This was because it was thought that economic growth would create wealth for everyone and improve the quality of life of the world's population.

However, this has not been the case. Not everyone has gained access to the quality of life enjoyed by many in the developed nations of the world, millions still live in poverty and the world population continues to grow at a rapid rate putting more of a strain on the planet's finite resources and its ability to renew its natural ones. Without doubt, the use of natural resources to produce goods has had a dramatic effect on the planet. Non-renewable resources such as oil, metals and minerals are running out at an increasing rate, while any new discoveries are rapidly swallowed up by the emerging economies of the world, such as China, India and Brazil, in pursuit of their own economic growth. Renewable natural eco-systems have also suffered: the depletion of fish stocks, the loss of arable land, extinction of species, pollution and climate change are just some of the consequences of the way humankind has chosen to consume and live, particularly over the last century. That is not to say that growth has not provided progress and quality of life at all; it has for many people. Technology has made life easier and more comfortable for many and life expectancy has increased in many countries, but such great benefits have not been evenly distributed around the world and they have all come at a cost, quite often at a cost to those countries that are least well-off in terms of wealth and quality of life.

It is time for significant change, to leave behind the short-term thinking of conventional marketing and embrace a truly long-term vision of the future with sustainable marketing. However, sustainable marketing sounds something of a contradiction in terms, since marketing encourages consumption and it is overconsumption that has caused the problems in the first place, it might be difficult to see how marketing can now achieve the opposite. But there are good reasons to believe that marketing can form an important part of the solution.

First, marketers have the potential to change businesses from within. They are well-positioned to communicate internally with management and other business stakeholders regarding the need to incorporate environmental, social and ethical considerations into all the activities of the organisation to make sustainability part of the business fabric rather than just an add-on.[5]

Second, the pervasive nature of marketing has resulted in it becoming central to all aspects of modern life. Political parties make use of marketing as do NGOs, charities and opinion leaders. Political parties that advocate sustainability have had a presence in Europe for some time and even the UK saw the election of its first Green Party member of Parliament in the 2010 general elections. Marketing can therefore be used to influence these groups of stakeholders and encourage them to promote and spread the adoption of sustainable practice in society.

Third the consumer-facing aspect of marketing will also be an important element of the solution. In part, sustainability can only be achieved through a change in the consumption habits of the general public. And beyond just their purchasing habits people will have to change their lifestyles as well, adopting new routines such as recycling, composting and changes to travelling methods. Sustainable marketing has a key role to play here. Because the principal role of marketing has been to understand, influence and change consumer behaviour, the discipline of marketing is ideally placed to achieve such behavioural changes among the population and move them towards following sustainable consumption patterns and adopting a more sustainable general lifestyle.[6]

It is perhaps fitting that the practice of marketing, responsible in part for unsustainable consumption, should be used to reverse this trend, although it must be emphasised that the sustainable marketing environment is both complex and challenging for the marketer. Sustainable marketing practice covers a multitude of economic, social and environmental issues and problems which are interlinked and overlap, often making sustainable marketing solutions intricate and holistic in nature.

In this chapter, the background of traditional, conventional marketing is revisited in order to understand the significance of the changes that have occurred over time, broadly tracing the developments from corporate social responsibility to societal and green marketing movements leading to the advance of sustainable marketing practice. The chapter ends with a discussion of the broad characteristics of sustainable marketing, which will be commented on in more detail in later chapters and highlights the main differences with more conventional marketing thought.

Conventional marketing revisited

Leaving to one side the splintering of marketing approaches that have appeared over the years for the moment (e.g. green marketing, societal marketing, viral marketing, guerrilla marketing, etc.) an appreciation of marketing basics helps us to understand the significant changes that are occurring in marketing as a result of the growing influence of the sustainability agenda from all quarters. Sustainability issues are modifying the relationship between business organisations and the business environment they exist in. The relationship between the business organisation and the consumer is also changing and the sustainable marketer needs to learn how to address these situations in order to be successful.

When earlier standard definitions of marketing from professional bodies and academics are compared, they appear to have differed very little. Satisfying customer needs while making a profit for the business forms the central premise of past conventional marketing definitions. Such definitions are still included in most modern marketing texts and the key concepts and terms used, such as *need, want, benefit* and *stakeholder,* are as valid today as they were then. These are core concepts within marketing, which have become all the more significant as we move towards fulfilling the demands of the sustainability agenda.

Table 1.1 shows how definitions of marketing have developed in more recent times to take into account the changing demands of the business environment, although none fully embrace the demands of the sustainability agenda.

Despite the movement towards sustainability, marketing is still driven by the tenet of satisfying consumer needs. A need refers to the difference between a consumer's actual state and their own ideal or desired state, and it is when this difference is sufficiently pronounced that the consumer becomes motivated

Table 1.1 Definitions of marketing

Then	Now
Marketing is the management process responsible for identifying, anticipating and satisfying customer requirements profitably.[7]	The strategic business function that creates value by stimulating, facilitating and fulfilling customer demand. It does this by building brands, nurturing innovation, developing relationships, creating good customer service and communicating benefits. With a customer-centric view, marketing brings positive return on investment, satisfies shareholders and stakeholders from business and the community, and contributes to positive behavioural change and a sustainable business future.[8]
A social and managerial process by which individuals and groups obtain what they need and want through creating and exchanging products and value with others.[9]	The marketing management philosophy which holds that achieving organisational goals depends on determining the needs and wants of target markets and delivering the desired satisfactions more effectively and efficiently than competitors do.[10]

enough to do something to satisfy this need. Needs can be related to both physical and psychological functions such as hunger and thirst or self-esteem, and become translated into wants, that is, a desire for a specific product which will satisfy a need in a particular way. Wants are culturally and socially influenced and while consumers will share the same needs on many occasions, for example the desire to be entertained, this need may take the form of very different wants for different people, for example the desire for entertainment may be equally satisfied by a Lady Gaga live concert or a trip to see the Liverpool Philharmonic Orchestra.

The introduction of the consumer-centred marketing concept from the 1960s onwards was in response to the limitations of the previous company orientations (which were all essentially product-centred orientations – the production concept, product concept and selling concept). The realisation that consumers did not buy products but, in fact, bought benefits, produced a significant change in the practice of business, which gradually relied more and more on researching and understanding consumers' needs and wants and the benefits they sought as a result of the act of purchase. Essentially, a product will provide the consumer with a benefit when it satisfies a need or a want, therefore we buy clean floors not vacuum cleaners, we buy the ability to write not pens and, we buy oral health not mouthwash, dental floss, toothpaste and toothbrushes.

Marketing helps facilitate the process of exchange without which businesses cannot thrive. Exchange can take different forms. For example, citizens give their vote to a political party in exchange for policies from that party, which they will find beneficial or favourable to their circumstances. However, we understand that the most common type of exchange is that of the consumer giving money to a business in exchange for products or services. Exchange is central to the marketing concept; business cannot function if the potential for exchange does not exist; that is, if there are no desirable products to satisfy consumers' needs and wants and if those same consumers have nothing to offer for them in return.

Apply it: Persil Small and Mighty

Understanding the consequences of marketing as a process of exchange is important in the sustainable environment. Sustainability has altered the conventional cost–benefit exchange relationship, creating a more complex connection between product and perceived benefit as well as modifying the consumers' perspective on price, the value exchanged and what is gained in return.

Sustainability brings potential social, ethical and environmental benefits in addition to those the product may have previously relied on. The marketer must decide which benefits to communicate to consumers and whether to highlight sustainable benefits above conventional ones, provided that they will be valued by the target market. Such tactics may also allow the marketer to differentiate the products from the competition and attract new markets. For the consumer, adopting a more sustainable purchase habit also carries consequences. In some cases, the sustainable purchase may be more expensive for consumers than its non-sustainable equivalent, leaving the consumers to trade off their sustainability concerns against the increased cost of purchase.

In more recent times energy companies have competed on price, encouraging consumer defections with the promise of a better deal on electricity and gas prices. However, as energy prices in general have risen, making competition on price much more difficult, numerous energy companies have switched their communications to greener messages and by competing on sustainability they can excuse price rises to the consumer or at least make them appear more palatable.

Table 1.2 shows how the use of communicating benefits for marketing is evolving as more products turn to emphasising their sustainable credentials.

Table 1.2   The evolution of benefits

Product	Conventional benefit	Sustainable benefit
The Co-operative Bank	I have reliable financial services	I support ethical financial practice
EDF Energy	I heat and light my home	I want to use sustainable energy sources
Waitrose	I shop in a quality supermarket	I support local suppliers I protect our wildlife
Lenor	I have soft fresh-smelling clothes	I reduce pollution through less packaging
Innocent	I have a healthy drink	I support the ethical treatment of suppliers from the developing world

▶

Investigate the Persil product **Small and Mighty** from Unilever. Explain how and why the product has been developed as a sustainable brand between 2007 and 2008. What products from the same or similar category are going through a similar transformation? Find some more examples you can add to create your own table comparing conventional and sustainable benefits. How does the Persil brand portray itself now? Has their sustainability message continued to evolve?

Product	Conventional benefit	Sustainable benefit
Persil – Small and Mighty		

Not sure where to start? Go to the 'Getting started' section below and the online resources.

Getting started

1. Start at the Unilever website (www.unilever.com) – what information does the company provide?
2. Try some practitioner sources. If you visit www.brandrepublic.com you can access a number of titles simultaneously. Here is the beginning of one article to get you started.

Unilever to push core brands   G. Charles Marketing, 12 February 2008

Flora, Persil, Surf and PG Tips will be among the most heavily supported Unilever brands in the UK, according to the company's strategy for 2008.

Speaking at Unilever's fourth quarter and annual results presentation, UK chairman Dave Lewis said innovation and marketing had a key role to play in tough economic times. The planned UK activity links into some of the global strategies that the company has adopted for its brands, based on vitality and wellbeing, sourcing and sustainability, and . . .

---

3. Try looking at Creative Club (www.creativeclub.co.uk) to find more examples of marketing communications for the brand.

Sustainability issues have been discussed for many years and, although it probably seems like a more recent phenomenon, there are a number of precedents to sustainable marketing which should be highlighted as moves in the right direction. Societal and social marketing movements both have links to sustainable marketing, as does green marketing, while corporate social responsibility (CSR) activity provides us with examples of a more concerted and organised effort from business to address the broader issues of sustainability.

Moves in the right direction

This section is not an attempt to draw a family tree of marketing thought and establish causal links between events and the appearance of different marketing movements. To do so would suggest an almost pre-planned sequential journey for marketing theory and distort marketing history, which has developed on a more ad hoc basis over the decades, often as a result of influences from outside the pure marketing sphere. Sustainable marketers Frank-Martin Belz and Ken Peattie only highlighted as significant for the development of sustainable marketing those marketing approaches which did more than just adjust or refocus existing marketing thinking and practice in an effort to gain efficiency. They signalled those approaches which substantially challenged the accepted views of the time and proposed a strong alternative in their place for marketing.[11] For the purposes of this discussion, corporate social responsibility, societal, social and green marketing movements all deserve some analysis to understand the nature of sustainable marketing.

Corporate social responsibility

Issues of ethics, social responsibility and sustainability in business have moved from marginal to mainstream and we can no longer say that the business of business is purely business.[12] The business of business now has to be much more concerned with moral principles, business has to be seen as a defender of the society it serves, as an investor in the community that provides its suppliers, employees and consumers and be seen as a driver of environmental sustainability and as a protector of the natural environment.

Corporate social responsibility predates the sustainable marketing movement. Many years before the term CSR ever existed, corporate philanthropists with their family-run businesses such as Cadbury, Lever and Rowntree had shown that businesses could be organised in ways that were profitable and that benefited others, particularly employees and the local community. To a certain extent it could be said that corporate social responsibility has appeared under many different guises over the decades, each representing a different stage in its evolution, changing as society has changed, although not at the same pace.[13]

In simple terms CSR addresses a company's relationship with all of its stakeholders[14] and is commonly defined as 'a commitment to community well-being through discretionary business practices and contributions of corporate resources'.[15] It has been used to address internal issues such as employee relations and health and safety at the workplace, as well as external issues such as the relationship with the local community, suppliers' rights and working conditions in the supply chain and consumer rights.[16]

Small and medium-sized enterprises (SMEs) are becoming an important channel for delivering CSR initiatives in the developed world where SMEs are often the principal employers in the country, as in the case of H.J. Berry mentioned below. SMEs are also playing their part in CSR in the developing world, as in the case of Hans Merensky, mentioned later in this chapter, and some sustainable development organisations such as Fairtrade tend to concentrate on SMEs in such nations. Their competitive advantage rests in adopting successful CSR strategies which comes from the unique relationship they tend to enjoy with the local communities.[17]

Furniture maker H.J. Berry has continued for five generations in the same family and location since 1840, founded on respect and fair treatment for employees, community and environment.[18] Based in the small village of Chipping in Lancashire, H.J. Berry has not sacked an employee in over 60 years, it supports the local community including the Parish Council, local churches and schools, as well as the local wildlife organisations and the Lancashire Woodland Project. It has planted and continues to manage its own woodlands with over 20,000 trees, providing work for the local community in the maintenance of the woodlands. Its furniture is made from 95 percent Forest Stewardship Council (FSC) certified wood, all lubricants and oils are eco-friendly, as are packaging and marketing communication materials. A low pollution boiler provides heating and energy for manufacture, and no waste is sent to landfill. The company was recently classified as carbon neutral by the Carbon Trust and that in fact it had been neutral since 1994. Future plans include an incubator centre for sustainable entrepreneurs and being self-sufficient in green electricity.

Much larger organisations have also successfully established their business along lines of corporate social responsibility. The Body Shop positioned itself as socially, economically and environmentally responsible from its inception and other companies have followed in its footsteps, such as the cosmetics brand Lush, the ice-cream brand Ben and Jerry's and the dairy products company Innocent. Other companies not originally established as sustainable enterprises are converting to sustainability over a period of time, such as Marks and Spencer.

Multinational companies engaged in corporate social responsibility can find themselves in difficulty even when trying to do good. Many of their CSR initiatives will be genuine and virtuous, yet CSR is often fraught with ambiguity particularly with multinationals.[19] Their extended supply chains across developing nations and extensive product portfolios are difficult to control and can easily expose multinationals to criticism.

For example, Unilever's Dove brand's largely web-based Campaign for Real Beauty encourages vulnerable young teenage girls to be positive about their physical appearance and shun unnecessary attempts to conform to artificial, stereotypical, media-fuelled beauty. However, while the company takes the moral high ground through the Campaign for Real Beauty, for its Lynx brand Unilever chooses to depict a contradictory female role model. In one campaign the Lynx website featured a fictitious female rock band, the Bom Chicka Wah Wahs and the band's video was viewed more than a million times on YouTube. One singer from the band says in a false biography on the site that she abandoned her ballet career for lingerie and pole dancing.[20]

But as one report put it, by elevating the ethical credentials of one product to hero status, as in the case of Unilever's Dove, the company runs a greater risk that attention will focus on the integrity of its remaining products, which may be regarded as a portfolio of villains in comparison.[21] Even the Dove brand has not escaped criticism, not only for its hypocrisy in comparison to the Lynx campaign but also due to its use of palm oil as an ingredient in its products, supplied by companies who are cutting down rain forests in Indonesia to produce the oil. Greenpeace parodied Dove's famous Internet Onslaught advert with its own to highlight the environmental problems caused by the creation of palm oil plantations.[22]

Old CSR versus new CSR and the sustainable paradigm

Corporate social responsibility was not originally intended to be used as a means to establish sustainable business and sustainable development and therefore 'old CSR' has received much criticism. The roots and motivations of corporate social responsibility are different and it has not always adhered to conducting business through the merger of the three tenets of sustainability – economics, social equity/ethics and environment. Its aim was to improve business performance by giving something back and so much of CSR has been primarily associated with doing good deeds, and has tended to be activity based, self-contained and centred on single issues or one-off ventures which may or may not be within the spirit of sustainability but would tend not to provide long-term holistic solutions.

The purpose of 'old CSR' is probably best summarised by well-known CSR writers Philip Kotler and Nancy Lee who in answer to their own question – 'Why do good?' (i.e. why engage in CSR?) – give the follow answers:[23]

- increased sales and market share

- strengthened brand positioning

- enhanced corporate image and clout

- increased ability to attract, motivate and retain employees

- decreased operating costs

- increased appeal to investors and financial analysts.

Kotler and Lee go on to subdivide corporate social responsibility into six distinct social initiatives: cause promotions, cause-related marketing, corporate social marketing, corporate philanthropy, community volunteering and socially responsible business practices. CSR was primarily meant to do business good and if other stakeholders or the environment benefited as a result then that was a noble, worthy but often secondary objective. In many respects this kind of CSR practice might be termed 'old CSR' while 'new CSR' has moved closer and closer to sustainability over recent years. Critics of CSR will continue to highlight how it is tainted by its past misuse, particularly when used as a public relations tool, pointing to the meaningless CSR reports published year after year, often by companies that should never be termed responsible. For example, the tobacco company Philip Morris spent $108 million advertising its philanthropic charity donations (worth just $60 million) while obviously continuing to sell cigarettes.[24]

But it must be recognised that CSR is changing. Advocates of corporate social responsibility have begun to claim more ground in the sustainability debate and 'new CSR' is more frequently described and defined using the vocabulary of sustainability.[25] Corporate social responsibility has moved on and definitions begin to reflect this reconciliation. The World Business Council for Sustainable

Development has defined corporate social responsibility as 'business' commitment to contribute to sustainable economic development, working with employees, their families, the local community and society at large to improve their quality of life'.[26] From this, it would appear that *corporate sustainability* is already beginning to replace corporate social responsibility.

Researching sustainability: Review the literature

While the practice of CSR continues to make positive moves towards sustainability it is still heavily criticised. For example, the word *discretionary* in CSR vernacular is significant since it essentially makes CSR initiatives voluntary and therefore a company will undertake CSR activities when it makes sound business sense to do so but perhaps not when it only makes sense on social or environmental grounds.

In academic terms the relationship between CSR, sustainable development and sustainable marketing is worth further investigation. In Table 1.3 there is a selection of comments on corporate social responsibility from different observers together with a possible interpretation of each of them. As you read them you may notice a possible bias, do you think the person who chose the comments has a particular bias?

Review some of the literature on CSR and sustainability yourself. Complete Table 1.4 by investigating the concept of sustainability and collecting your own set of comments from different sources. What do you learn from each of the comments? How will you interpret them? Notice that the final comment on CSR appears to be in direct contrast to the first comment given on sustainability below. Can you find other contrasting comments to further distinguish CSR from sustainability? Write up your findings in no more than 250 words.

Table 1.3   Review the literature: CSR

Possible interpretation	Comments on CSR
Not everyone thinks that companies should engage in CSR activities	'. . . a fundamentally subversive doctrine . . . there is one and only one social responsibility of business . . . to increase its profits'[27]
Key terms lack clarity	'the use of terms such as *ethics* and *social responsibility* is at present rather casual'[28]
A PR-led reaction to poor business practice	'a business-led response to the growing public scepticism'[29]
Not as broad as sustainability with an element of corporate self-protection	'CSR as a business movement is specifically associated with ethical issues – doing what's right and fair and avoiding harm . . . as such CSR can be seen as a way of corporate self-regulation'[30]
CSR is compartmentalised, not a whole company activity	'a mistake companies often make is to think about green issues in a very corporate way assigning it to particular departments, such as CSR'[31]

Table 1.4   Review the literature: sustainability

Possible interpretation	Comments on sustainability
The nature of sustainability is highlighted together with the need for a holistic approach throughout the business	'sustainability is far more wide reaching and there must be inclusion at every level'[32]

Not sure where to start . . .? Go to the 'Getting started' section below and the online resources.

Getting started

1. Start by searching academic journals for both sustainability and CSR, perhaps through Emerald (www.emeraldinsight.com) or Sage (www.sagepublications.com).
2. Remember, placing key words in an advanced search under 'title' or 'abstract' will increase the relevance of the results.
3. Will you reveal a bias in your own opinions through your selection of comments and the comparison between CSR and sustainability?

Environmental marketing variants

The last decades of the 20th century saw a fragmentation of marketing thought on both the micro and macro levels. Some of this break-up simply reflects the incorporation of new technological capabilities used to make marketing more efficient, such as database marketing, while others pick up on social change such as the use of social media marketing. Behind these and similar innovations in marketing are specific marketing objectives such as re-segmenting the market, identifying and accessing new target markets, delivering more efficient communications, etc. and are examples of micromarketing, which form the individual marketing activities carried out by different organisations to achieve their own goals.

In contrast, the field of macromarketing has developed as a means of analysing and debating the impact of marketing on society in general. It is concerned with the wellbeing of society and what has been referred to as the spillover of costs and benefits of marketing and how marketing might resolve the difficulties of meeting the conflicting goals of society such as continued consumption versus preservation and conservation of resources.[33] It is clear that other aspects of the fragmentation of marketing thought have macromarketing connections. This stemmed from the inability of the original marketing concept to provide for long-term sustainable development and the gradual realisation of the serious environmental, social and economic consequences for society resulting from a

Table 1.5 Marketing responses to a changing business environment

Marketing approach	Exponents	Focus
Ecological[34]	Henion (1972) Fisk (1974) Henion & Kinnear (1976)	• Centred on environmental issues of non-renewables • Limited to major industries responsible for most environmental damage • Business tended to deal only with its obligations towards the environment
Environmental[35] Green[36]	Coddington (1992) Peattie (1995) Charter (1992) Peattie (1992) Ottman (1993)	• Similar approaches in 1980s and 1990s reached their height • Broader industry focus than ecological approach • Included design, product, packaging focus • Target market specific: green consumer
Societal[37]	Lazer (1969) Kotler & Levy (1969)	• 'Marketing must serve not only business but also the goals of society' (Lazer 1969, p.3) • Marketing to take into account the long-term interests of the consumer and society balancing short-term wants against long-term welfare
Social[38]	Kotler & Zaltman (1971) Wiebe (1972)	• To promote societal behavioural change • Aimed at individuals and groups for their benefit and the overall benefit of society • Tend to be government/NGO driven • Business collaborations
Ecopreneurship[39]	Varadarajan (1992) Isaak (1997) Menon & Menon (1997) Keogh & Polonsky (1998)	• Also referred to as enviropreneurship • Increasing interest through the 1990s • Described as 'one of the biggest business opportunities in the history of commerce'[40] • Small businesses led by entrepreneurs are viewed as change agents influenced by the Triple Bottom Line not a single issue

system built on continued growth and consumption facilitated by those same marketing systems.

Table 1.5 shows the main marketing approaches that developed in response to the changing business, ecological and social environment of the time. It identifies some of the original proponents of each and their main features in order to provide a starting point for more research. The table is not a deliberate attempt to draw a timeline or show a developmental link between approaches to finally result in sustainable marketing. Nevertheless, traces of the sustainable approach to marketing can be seen throughout.

The realisation of the physical limits to continued expansion gave birth to a number of environmental movements under titles such as ecological, environmental and green marketing. The environment was the starting point of all these approaches. In the case of ecological marketing of the 1970s it was the sole focus, a reaction against those major industries causing the depletion of natural, non-renewable resources while damaging the environment through their extraction and through pollution from processing and manufacture. Business was reactive rather than proactive to pressure and legislation at this time, although legislation tended to be weak with few significant sanctions for non-compliance. Typical solutions were *end-of-pipe* ones – that is, dealing with the pollution and dangerous by-products caused by manufacture at the end of the processes rather than designing them out through completely new processes to avoid the problems appearing in the first place.

Definitions of green marketing have tended to highlight environmental concerns more than social and economic issues and the phrase 'there is no economy unless there is a planet'[41] has often been used to demonstrate the importance of the natural environment above all else. Green marketing proponent Martin Charter defined green marketing in these terms: 'Greener marketing is a holistic and responsible management process that identifies, anticipates, satisfies and fulfils stakeholder requirements, for a reasonable reward, that does not adversely affect human or natural environmental well-being.'[42]

Proponents of such environmental and green approaches published frequently during the 1980s and 1990s describing a more encompassing environmental approach to marketing aimed at what proved to be an elusive target market – the green consumer – as we shall see in more detail later in the text. Notably, the environmental/green marketing of the 1980s and 1990s had moved towards proposing specific product solutions, some of which are now commonplace. Well-known sustainable household sector brand Ecover brought out its phosphate-free detergent as early as 1980. Despite the initial enthusiasm around green marketing in those two decades, it failed to become a mainstream approach for a number of reasons, primarily due to its inability to compete with the conventionally marketed brands and its narrow niche-type focus, as we will see in later chapters.

Societal and social variants

While the original marketing concept implies there is a two-way relationship between the consumer and the business, the societal marketing concept includes more stakeholders and proposes a broader relationship between the consumer, the business and society as a whole, promoting long-term consumer and public welfare without sacrificing the standard organisational goal of profitability. Thus, the societal concept takes into account both the needs and wants of the consumer and those of society, and views that the business should determine the needs, wants and interests of the consumer and cater for them in a way that maintains or improves both the consumer's and society's wellbeing. In contrast with the environmentally oriented approaches, the societal approach provided a much broader base for marketers to consider the implications of their actions as societal wellbeing could embrace many other issues beyond the ecological such as health, social equity and economic equity as well as general quality of life for all.

The aim of societal marketing to balance the needs of business against the desires of the consumer and the wider needs of society is not an easy task. Both business and consumers would appear to be caught by conflicting interests, which highlight one of the key dilemmas behind sustainable marketing practice.

For example, a mobile phone company would want to sell as many mobile phones as possible to be a profitable business, but in an already saturated market this is difficult. In order to continue to sell, the company brings out on a regular basis new models, styles and features to encourage consumers to purchase new phones or run the risk of being left with old-fashioned phones with out-of-date technology, even though they would still be in full working order for their principal purpose – communication. Likewise the consumer would be motivated to purchase more frequently, feeling secure that they have the latest, most advanced model.

However, society's needs are different. In order to conserve non-renewable natural resources the opposite should take place. Mobile phone companies should produce fewer variants which are more durable, but how could they reconcile this with objectives of growth and profit? Consumers should keep the same mobile phone for much longer, but many are motivated to purchase more frequently as they desire variety, style and more functionality. With freedom to choose what they want, consumers are more likely to select short-term, personal goals above long-term societal goals.

In common with societal marketing, social marketing has quality of life at its core. Social marketing is concerned with the wellbeing of individuals and society as a whole, and in that respect is often involved with macromarketing issues related to the effects of marketing on society. It is generally associated with public health campaigns and focuses on changing people's detrimental behaviour (smoking, alcohol abuse, dietary problems, etc.), substituting the undesirable behaviour with beneficial ones. As social marketing is designed to create beneficial behavioural change, its use to promote sustainable consumption habits could be significant and this will be dealt with in a later chapter.

Ecopreneurship

Ecopreneurship, enviropreneurship and enviropreneurial marketing are terms that have become more popular since the mid-1990s and mark the increasing interest of the entrepreneur to exploit sustainability as a business opportunity rather than a business threat. Enviropreneurial marketing combines environmental concerns and social performance with entrepreneurship into a long-term approach to business, creating revenue by providing exchanges that satisfy the organisation's economic objectives without compromising its social and environmental performance.

Enviropreneurial marketing is different from other earlier environmentally based marketing approaches, as it is usually not a reaction to legislation or public pressure. It tends to involve adopting an innovative or technology based solution to a business opportunity, bringing the three elements of the Triple Bottom Line together under an entrepreneurial orientation.[43]

Corporate social responsibility, societal and environmental approaches have all contributed to understanding aspects of sustainability and in particular have helped to 'improve the relationship between marketing and the natural environment'.[44] These approaches mark significant milestones in the development of marketing practice. However, as sustainability issues begin to take hold of all aspects of business it is evident that sustainable marketing will be different from any other variant of marketing to date and represents a paradigm shift in marketing practice.

Snapshot: Sustainability issues take hold

In computer terminology a snapshot is the state of a particular system at a specific point in time. A sustainability snapshot at a given point in time highlighted the following developments among consumers, businesses, marketing professionals and other interested parties.

Consumers . . . are already making their voice heard in no uncertain terms.

According to The Co-operative Bank: *The Ethical Consumerism Report* (2007).[45]

- The total UK ethical market is worth £32.3 billion, up 9 percent from the previous year.
- 96 percent of the population reported recycling in the previous 12 months.
- More than eight out of ten consumers shop to support their local shops.
- One-third of consumers will check a company's reputation.
- Over one-third of consumers feel guilty about unethical purchases.
- One out of four consumers campaigned on a social or environmental issue in 2007.

Boycotts by ethically motivated consumers cost brands £2.6 billion a year in 2006, ethically motivated boycotts increased in food and drink by 22 percent (£1,214 million), in clothing by 20 percent (£338 million).[46]

Businesses are reacting:

- Marks and Spencer launched its £200 million sustainability plan, known as Plan A in 2007 intending to go carbon neutral by 2012. Its slogan, 'Plan A because there is no plan B', underlines the importance assigned to the project.
- New job titles are appearing such as *sustainable development officer*, *sustainability manager*, *ethical trading manager, director of corporate and social responsibility* and *chief ethics officer.*
- Diageo, the world's leading premium drinks business, says that one of its ambitions in the UK is to change the drinking culture for the better. 'Promoting responsible attitudes to alcohol is pivotal to our business strategy – we promote the importance of responsible drinking because it's the right thing to do', says a spokesman. Most recently, Diageo has also run television advertising, created by ad agency Abbott Mead Vickers BBDO, showing how one very drunk person can have an effect on everyone around them on a night out.[47]

Marketing professionals are adopting a new way of doing things:

The Chartered Institute of Marketing (CIM), the professional body of marketers, has recognised the significance of ethics, social responsibility and sustainability issues in its Shape the Agenda paper (Issue 11, 2007) *The Triple Bottom Line,* and the CIM emphasises that marketers are best placed to make a difference. This is reinforced in its following Agenda paper, *Tomorrow's* ▶

Word (Issue 12, 2007). The Marketing Trends Survey (2006) found that 75 percent of marketers believed that sustainability practices will increasingly affect consumer purchase decisions.[48]

The rise of the specialist agency has started as business seeks to reposition itself in the sustainable environment.

Feel relaunches as an ethical marketing specialist

Feel, the agency that became part of the integrated agency Blac two years ago, is being relaunched as an ethical marketing specialist. Chris Arnold, the former Saatchi & Saatchi integrated creative director, who founded Feel, commented to *Campaign* magazine, 23 February 2007: 'The market is mature enough for a specialist agency delivering full service.'

Clownfish, led by CEO Diana Verde Nieto, specialises in producing campaigns focused on sustainability and social responsibility.

It was reported to *Campaign* magazine on 2 November 2007 that the charity sector direct marketing agency Cascaid and the ethical consumer marketing specialist Ideas Eurobrand have merged to create The Good Agency; with total billings of £13 million. The new agency will combine Cascaid's charity clients, including the Royal Society for the Protection of Birds (RSPB) and the National Society for the Prevention of Cruelty to Children (NSPCC), with Ideas, Eurobrand's mainly public and voluntary sector client list.

Organisations are warning of the consequences of apathy:

- The World Wildlife Fund estimates we need three earths to maintain current levels of consumption.[49]
- *Stern Review: The Economics of Climate Change* suggests global warming could reduce the world economy by 20 percent.[50] The original report from Stern estimated it would take 1 percent of global gross domestic product (GDP) to escape the more damaging effects of climate change, although this estimate rose to 2 percent in 2008.

Now write your own update for this snapshot. What is the current state of play for these organisations and issues? What new factors should be included in the snapshot to better reflect the contemporary sustainable business environment?

The foundations of sustainable marketing

Most commentators on sustainability point to the 1972 United Nations Conference in Sweden on the Human Environment as the starting point of international debate on sustainability, which was followed by the 1987 Brundtland Report, *Our Common Future* by the World Commission on Environment and Development, which inspired many of the later standard definitions of sustainability as can be seen below.

> . . . a new era of economic growth that is forceful and at the same time socially and environmentally sustainable; an economy is sustainable if it meets the needs of the present without compromising the ability of the future generations to meet their own needs.[51]

Noteworthy is the wording of the Brundtland Report. It indicated an attempt to resolve conflicting issues by balancing economic growth against concern and care for the natural environment, as well as calling for social justice and social equity, and proposing the equitable distribution and use of natural resources. Core to the broad vision of sustainability as outlined in *Our Common Future* is the premise that world sustainability can be achieved, in part, via sustainable business development which is based upon three key elements: social equity, economic sustainability and environmental sustainability. These three elements form the basis of the framework known as the *Triple Bottom Line*.

The phrase the *Triple Bottom Line*[52] was coined by John Elkington co-founder and chair of SustainAbility, a sustainable business consultancy. Elkington believed that the standard business paradigm was changing as a result of seven 'revolutions' which were rapidly altering the structures of business, leading business to a more sustainable future, as depicted in Table 1.6.

Table 1.6   The 7 revolutions to a sustainable future

Markets	Increased competition in more demanding, volatile markets making businesses more susceptible to the effects of economic crises, e.g. 2008–2009 banking crisis leading to the collapse of major entities in finance, insurance, travel and tourism
Values	Worldwide shift in human/societal values making businesses susceptible to values-based crises when society finds them wanting, e.g. public outcry regarding BP's handling of the oil spill in the Gulf of Mexico in 2010 leads to resignation of the CEO
Transparency	Increased transparency resulting from more open access to information, more authority of stakeholders to demand information, adoption of scrutiny and reporting systems, e.g. the Body Shop produces an annual Values Report to communicate its performance on its five core values as a responsible business
Life-cycle technology	Acceptability and appraisal of products at point of sale loses significance and the focus rests on the whole of the supply chain from acquisition of raw materials, manufacture, transport and storage through to disposal or recycling after consumption, e.g. in 2008 outdoor clothing specialist Patagonia launched its 'footprint chronicles' allowing consumers to trace its products from raw materials to finished item including final destination options such as landfill or back to Patagonia for recycling
Partnerships	Business partnerships will become more varied with campaigning groups entering relationships with business organisations (even with those once regarded as enemies), e.g. in May 2010 Nestlé announced it would work with the Forest Trust to review its palm oil supply chain to ensure it is not associated with illegal rainforest and peatland clearance
Time	Sustainability issues lengthen time considerations making planning for sustainable business a matter of years, decades, even generations, e.g. the first stage of Marks and Spencer's Plan A for sustainability was from 2007 to 2012, and the second stage from 2010 to 2015
Corporate governance	Evolving corporate governance to include the representation of all relevant stakeholders not just shareholders, keeping the corporate board focused on all aspects of the sustainable agenda, e.g. the 2008 stakeholder panel of the Body Shop consisted of representatives from the British Union for the Abolition of Vivisection (BUAV), Oxfam-UK, Traidcraft and World Wildlife Fund (WWF)

Source: Adapted from Elkington, 2004[53]

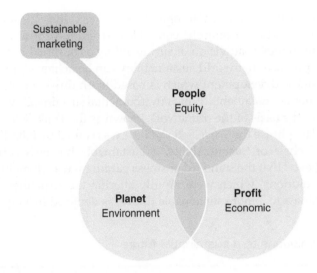

Figure 1.1   The Triple Bottom Line

The sustainable marketing paradigm sits where the three elements of the Triple Bottom Line converge and intersect, as can be seen in Figure 1.1. As a result, the sustainable marketing concept has broken free of previous narrow interpretations based solely on environmental concerns, as it correctly recognises that the success of business is intertwined with environmental, social/ ethical and economic performance.

The sustainable marketing paradigm is therefore 'a more holistic, integrative approach that puts equal emphasis on environmental, social equity and economic concerns in the development of marketing strategies'.[54] Split into environmental, social and economic sustainability, the Triple Bottom Line has also been referred to by the phrase *people, planet and profit*, and also called the *three Es* – equity, economic and environment. The framework provided by the Triple Bottom Line allows companies to assess their progress towards sustainability by measuring overall organisational success, including social and environmental performance, not only economic performance.

Apply it: Sharkah Chakra – The slow fashion Fairtrade specialist

Following is a brief extract from the website of the sustainable fashion brand Sharkah Chakrah:

The way Sharkah Chakra sees it . . .

Our philosophy is to make the world's best and only hand-made denim using a simple age-old concept of treating others as you wish to be treated. This ethical philosophy is at the heart of Sharkah Chakra. We aim to care for all the artisans involved in making our denims; the Fairtrade cotton farmers, the indigo farmers, the indigo dyeing craftsmen, the handloom weavers, the tailors and the laundry masters. Creating a circle where everybody benefits from the work that we do. Keeping things simple we wanted to share with you the principles that are interwoven into our denim.

1. Explain to what extent Sharkah Chakra follows the principles of the Triple Bottom Line. Use Table 1.7 to help you and find more sources of information on the brand to complete your analysis.

Table 1.7 Sustainability issues

Sustainability issue	Broad considerations
Ecological sustainability Planet	Renewable versus non-renewable energy sources, carbon and water footprints, responsible exploitation of natural resources, replenishment of natural resources, impact of man-made materials, pollution, long-term wellbeing of the natural environment
Social sustainability People	Social equity, community relationships and the wellbeing of individuals and the community (local/global), ethics, ethical treatment of all stakeholders including channel members and supply chains
Financial sustainability Profit	Long-term economic stability, sustainable and fair financial reward for all stakeholders and profit for business to continue to reinvest, longer-term ROI, full cost accounting

Getting started

1. Start at the Sharkah Chakra website – www.sharkahchakra.com
2. Notice mentions of Sharkah Chakra's jeans that appear in many fashion magazines. Check fashion magazines to see if you can find more features on this pioneering sustainable fashion brand.
3. Look for more information on the Triple Bottom Line – start with John Elkington, the person who first coined the phrase.

Defining the parameters of sustainable marketing

In their text *Natural Capitalism,* Paul Hawken, Amory Lovins and Hunter Lovins[55] make a compelling argument for change and herald the advent of the next industrial revolution – the sustainable revolution. In order to live in a more sustainable society, the practice of marketing will need to change and the assumptions of conventional marketing must be re-evaluated and altered accordingly. Sustainable marketing recognises that all human activity is dependent on the existence of the natural capital provided by the planet and acknowledges that long-term, sustainable economic viability only results from both environmental stability and societal equity. The sustainable marketing paradigm aims to address these challenges.

When defining sustainable marketing it is important to understand its all-encompassing nature from strategy to tactics and implementation, viewing the business as a whole from one single objective: to become as sustainable as possible, socially, environmentally and economically. Sustainable marketing can therefore be defined in the following terms.

> Sustainable marketing is a holistic approach whose aim is to ensure that marketing strategies and tactics are specifically designed to secure a socially equitable, environmentally friendly and economically fair and viable business for the benefit of current and future generations of customers, employees and society as a whole.

It is also important to note that sustainable marketing is much broader than conventional marketing and it also performs a role beyond the purely business-oriented one. Sustainable marketing acts as an agent of change within society. Society in general needs to re-evaluate its relationship with consumption and re-address consumption-driven lifestyles. Educating, persuading and convincing society of the need to adopt new habits such as recycling, shopping for seasonal local food products, reducing food waste, composting, collecting rainwater, reducing energy usage, generating alternative energy in the home, etc. are sustainability challenges that can be met by using sustainable marketing techniques adapted from social marketing in collaboration with government, local authorities, non-governmental organisations (NGOs) and business. Table 1.8 highlights some of the main implications of the paradigm shift from conventional to sustainable marketing practice, indicating some of the key changes at strategic and tactical level which will be commented on throughout the text.

Table 1.8 Comparison of conventional and sustainable marketing

Conventional		Sustainable
Strategic considerations		
Industrial capitalism neoclassical economic theory simply liquidates non-renewable resources to produce income and profit	Natural capitalism	Recognition of the interdependency between production of man-made capital and the maintenance and supply of natural capital (resources) from the planet.
Maximise shareholder value	Satisfy stakeholder needs	Planet and people are the most important stakeholders, not profit for the sake of shareholders

(continued)

Table 1.8   (*Continued*)

Conventional	Sustainable	
Strategic considerations		
Competitive strategy	Coopetitive strategy	Sustainability is addressed by both competing and cooperating in the marketplace and including non-business partners such as NGOs
Short- and medium-term vision	Long and longer term	Benefits of sustainable consumption on people and planet may take years to take effect and become apparent
Role of marketing		
Marketing drives consumption and encourages consumer attitudes and behaviour to continue to consume without considering the consequences	Marketing drives resource efficiency	Marketing to change consumer attitudes and behaviour towards sustainability and adopting sustainable consumption habits and practice
Marketing tactics are seen as complicit with the problems of overconsumption	Marketing is seen to be a significant part of the solution	
Product and production		
From non-compliance to compliance with legal restrictions	Beyond compliance	Moving beyond legal compliance presents business with new opportunities for product design and production techniques
Take – make – waste energy/resource intensive	Resource productivity	Energy and resource depletion and pollution reduced by the more effective use of natural and human resources
Reactive pollution and waste control through 'end-of-pipe' technology	Cyclical, cradle to cradle PLC Closed-loop processing	Proactive pollution and waste control with businesses responsible for whole product lifecycle (PLC) including pollutants, waste and recycling
Greening	Sustaining	
Supply chain efficiency	Supply chain sustainability	Social and economic equity in the supply chain and environmental control
Marketing communications		
Exaggeration in relation to product claims and benefits often accepted by consumers as normal practice	Exaggeration seen as greenwash	Increasingly marketing savvy public, cynical of company claims
Green positioning often just a gesture or an appeal to a niche target market	Repositioning of green as mainstream	Marketing communications will not only persuade, they will inform and educate into sustainable consumption habits and dissuade from unsustainable practice
Aim to persuade	Aim to educate	

Sustainable transformations

Sustainable marketing practice has the potential to transform businesses and the communities in which they operate. Companies that already practise sustainable marketing are keen to emphasise the benefits of the people, planet and profit approach. Craig Sams, the Founder of Green and Blacks, underlines the ecological, social and economic benefits provided to the cocoa suppliers of his organic chocolate brand, Britain's first fair trade product. In Belize, he highlights the economic benefits, stating that the growers incur fewer debts by following organic methods. He explains that the percentage of Maya children attending secondary school has increased from 10 percent to 70 percent and that money gained by the community, controlled by the women, is spent on health, education and good nutrition. He also points out the benefits of following organic farming methods, with the rivers recovering from excessive silt and pesticides, the return of migratory birds to increasing tree cover and the disappearance of skin disease from the use of pesticides. Sams foresees a future where all business must adopt sustainable practices to survive and those rejecting it will not be tolerated.

> Nowadays the net is closing on businesses that make their money by raping the environment and putting the burden of their waste onto society. *(Craig Sams, Founder of Green and Blacks)*[56]

Professional Practice: New communications focus for Kellogg

In 2003 Kellogg distributed 55 million toy inserts in its cereal packets aimed at the children's market. This was often combined with the use of cartoon character promotions and Kellogg also used licensed tie-ups with films such as *Shrek the Third* to appeal to the children's cereal market. With consumers becoming more sensitive towards the marketing of food to children and the use of key ingredients such as fat, salt and sugar and their health implications, there is increased pressure on Kellogg to change position. Children's cereals are the largest share of the breakfast cereal market and Kellogg has decided to abandon its use of kids' cartoon character promotions in order to position itself as more responsible when engaging with children.

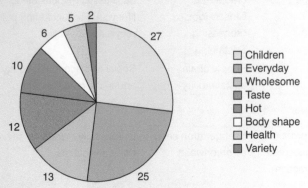

Figure 1.2   Market share for breakfast cereals

In March 2008, Kellogg's marketing operations and media controller, David Walker, said the firm would not return to either cartoon character promotions or the use of toy inserts.[57] This decision left Kellogg needing a change in strategy.

You work for a marketing agency. Your agency specialises in social responsibility and understands that Kellogg needs to reposition its children's cereals but *maintain sufficient appeal for both children and their parents*. You are to prepare a pitch to Kellogg presenting a new focus for its communications for the children's cereals market.

Getting started

1. Look for more information on the market sector (e.g. Mintel), the client (Kellogg's website) and identify products that fit each of the categories given in the market share analysis.
2. Look for information on advertising to children (Advertising Standards Authority).
3. Consider the competing conventional and sustainable values that may be applied to the children's cereal market: Fairtrade, organic, locally sourced, additive free, taste, quality, price.
4. See 'How to prepare a pitch' in the online resources.

Summary

The influence of the business environment on marketing has been a constant since the original marketing concept was established. The realisation that business has a responsibility to all stakeholders, not just shareholders, signals the beginning of the end for the marketing concept as it undergoes successive modifications and revisions in an attempt to ensure the inclusion of all stakeholders and cater for their welfare. These amendments to the original marketing concept can be seen in the societal and green marketing concepts although these failed to gain significant ground as they did not provide a holistic approach to the issue of sustainability. Corporate social responsibility can be easily confused with a sustainable approach when CSR campaigns appear to contain sustainable features, but in general CSR tended to focus on specific social issues with particular campaigns. CSR has often had stronger links to corporate image and brand building than to planned sustainable practice for all stakeholders, although there is evidence this is changing.

The Triple Bottom Line has become increasingly common in business parlance as organisations seek to organise, justify and measure their social, environmental and economic performance in keeping with the concept's sustainability principles based on people, planet and profit. Sustainability is recognised to affect every single person on the planet and becomes the driver for significant change. Sustainability involves anticipating, managing and evaluating all human activity in the business environment and beyond in order to maintain social, environmental and economic activity indefinitely, without detrimental effects on present or future generations.

Sustainable marketing is a holistic long-term view of marketing which seeks to facilitate sustainable business practice and represents a true paradigmatic shift in marketing. Simply facilitating profitable exchanges between interested parties is no longer enough. Sustainable marketing is conceived to ensure that profitable exchanges are based on social equity, environmental balance and renewal and long-term economic benefit and to take into account all the costs involved in setting up such exchanges. As a result, sustainable marketing requires full-scale changes if the goal of sustainability is to be achieved and the effects of sustainable practice can be seen in all aspects of the marketing effort.

Case study: Hans Merensky: ahead of the times

The Hans Merensky (HM) Group provides an example of how sustainability values and practice can permeate all aspects of a business. The group is structured as follows:

Hans Merensky Holdings: This is the holding company of the Hans Merensky Group, and is an enterprise based on sustainable natural resources. It is their vision to grow and add sustainable economic value through exceptional practice, applied research and continuous development into the respective value chains; and to be the benchmark in environmental management and social awareness.

Merensky: Merensky is South Africa's leading sawmilling forestry group, providing a comprehensive range of hardwood, softwood and panel products.

Westfalia Agri Business: This is the largest avocado grower in Southern Africa, with its brand name Westfalia recognized as a worldwide leader. It is also a major supplier of mangoes, various processed fruit products and grows litchis, citrus and macadamia nuts. Its nurseries and research facilities are important contributors to the production of high quality produce

Ahead of the times

Hans Merensky Holdings, situated in South Africa, takes its name from its visionary founder who died in 1952. Many years before his death, Hans Merensky had shown himself to be one of the most progressive agriculturists of the last century, setting up and developing a system of environmentally sustainable agriculture on his estate in South Africa, which would prove to be decades ahead of its time.

Passionate about sustainability, the company ensures that soil conservation, reclamation and revitalisation remain at the heart of its forestry and sub-tropical fruit operations. Its commercial timber operations have seen the development of a rapidly maturing hardwood through a genetically improved eucalyptus that has reduced the growth cycle from 200 to 25 years, thus reducing the use of unsustainable hardwood sources from Central Africa and Asia, which may take 75 years to cultivate for use in construction. All HM timber operations are run on a sustainable basis and have received Forestry Stewardship Council certification. Eucalyptus trees were originally introduced from Australia and, although they consume water, they have been planted away from rivers and are cultivated on a sustainable basis, maximising returns for each litre of controlled irrigation.

Its Westfalia brand for niche fruit products – avocados and mangoes – is internationally recognised and supplied, including directly to retailers such as Woolworth's in South Africa, Albert Heijn in the Netherlands, Kesko in Finland and Sainsbury and Waitrose in the UK. Westfalia's revenue from fruit comes from avocados – 60 percent – mangoes – 30 percent – and litchis – 10 percent. The focus of the sub-tropical fruit business for Westfalia has centred on three elements:

- The growing, packing and ripening of avocados and mangoes so they arrive at their destination 'ripe and ready'.

- The aim to become a contract supplier to retailers providing all year round supplies of avocados and mangoes, even when the growing season has ended in South Africa, by establishing partnerships with suppliers in South America, notably Chile and Brazil.

- Diversification of product away from a single reliance on fresh fruit to include dried mango and avocado purée as well as avocado oil, which is used as a healthy cooking oil and alternative to olive oil, and is also used in cosmetics.

Accredited sustainable agriculture

Sustainable practice in agricultural processes ensures the continued production of fruit without damage to the environment. Water is used sparingly through controlled irrigation methods, while compost is made from factory processing by-products and orchard waste to replace the nourishment taken from the soil. Westfalia farm is a Natural Heritage Site due to conservation of a large area of Afro-Montane forest containing endangered plant and animal species conserved for the future in a protected area where no development will take place. The company's overall environmentally sensible agricultural practices have been recognised and certified internationally.

Since receiving full organic certification by the world-renowned and most stringent certifier BCS Oko-Garantie of Germany, over a third of avocado and mango orchards have been converted to organic farming. Westfalia was the first farm in Africa to achieve the GLOBAL G.A.P. (European Retailers' Produce Working Group's Good Agricultural Practices) certification, which ensures the safe, sustainable, environmentally sound and socially responsible production of food.

It was also the world's first avocado farm to receive Tesco's Nature's Choice certification (Gold) imposed by the British retail chain on all its fresh produce suppliers worldwide and it was the first farm outside Britain to be awarded the LEAF Marque (Linking Environment and Farming), a key differentiator from its competitors

Other third-party accreditations include the global standard for food safety from the British Retail Consortium, Fairtrade, Hazards and Critical Control Points (HACCP) and International Organization for Standardization (ISO) 9001.

A sense of community

Support for emerging farmers including access to training and markets is just one way Westfalia helps the community. In fact, improving the lives of employees and the communities which surround the Merensky farms is just as important as the environmental aspects of the business. Projects aimed at enhancing quality of life are often joint affairs with the retailers they already supply

▶

with fruit: Waitrose and Albert Heijn Foundations, certifying organisations such as Fairtrade and the South African government.

The Community Development Department liaises with community stakeholders at municipal, provincial and national government levels, and oversees numerous development schemes:

- Day-Care Centres: State-registered pre-schools and crèches provide safe and reliable day care and pre-school education for Westfalia staff as well as people from the surrounding area at the different Westfalia estates.

- Adult Basic Education and Training: Westfalia's Adult Basic Education Training (ABET) conforms to the South African Department of Education standards and provides much-needed basic education and computer skills. Westfalia is assisting its South African partners to set up the scheme on their own farms.

- Community Gardens: In keeping with the practice of its founder, Westfalia has cleared an area of land in the Makgobo Village on Westfalia Estates which is being used to cultivate a variety of vegetables for home use and for sale to other members of the community, ensuring a varied and healthy diet for employees and the community.

- Wellness Centres: Initially these provided general health clinic services to staff and their families. Now this scheme includes preventative healthcare programmes with the goal to provide primary healthcare that is proactive rather than reactive. Services include: VCT (Voluntary Counselling and Testing) for HIV/AIDS and other major illnesses, HIV/AIDS awareness campaigns, Adherence counselling in preparation for antiretroviral (ARV) treatment, provision of ARVs for HIV/AIDS-infected staff, peer group educators, TB awareness and testing.

- Community Cultural Centre: The objective of the Community Cultural Centre is to introduce unemployed people to entrepreneurial skills. The centre produces tourist-oriented crafts for sale to local curio shops and stalls, and at time of writing provides jobs for 28 women. It also has an active sewing group, which contracts its services to local business.

Follow-up

1. Assess the threat posed by the 'eat local' movement to the fruit export business of Westfalia Agri Business. Will a simple food miles sticker prevent the successful growth of the company?

2. Visit the website (www.hansmerensky.co.za) and update your knowledge. How is the company dealing with its carbon footprint from the transport of its goods?

Dilemma part 2:   Behaving responsibly

As a marketer you will often have to deal with challenging situations and sustainable marketing seems to produce more than its fair share of dilemmas.

British American Tobacco (BAT) is a Premier Member of Business in the Community (BITC) and is described on BITC's website as the world's most international tobacco group with a responsible approach to doing business from crop to consumer. There is also much information on BAT's website (www.bat.com) under the *Operating Responsibly* section detailing the socially responsible and sustainable practices of the company. However, a visit to Chiquita's website (www.chiquita.com) (one of the largest sustainable producers of bananas) reveals similar language being used with the same kinds of criteria together with a large amount of information about all aspects of its sustainable business practice.

If both cigarettes and bananas can be portrayed as socially responsible and sustainable, how does the consumer know how to judge the different claims? Are they believable as a result? What about new organisations and businesses that want to portray themselves as socially responsible and sustainable, what can they do and say to be believed by the public?

Devise the strategy

The local independent shops in your area have decided to form a coalition in part to defend themselves against the larger branded retailers of the area, as more and more the local shops lose market share to well-known town centre stores, supermarkets and retail parks, and in part because they believe sustainability is such an important issue they want their customers to know what they are doing about it.

The coalition believes that their size, together with the fact they are local and close to the community will allow them to compete on sustainability in a way that the major retailers will not be able to match.

You have been asked by the new association of local retailers to help establish them as a sustainable coalition. In order to start this work you have decided to create a set of core values in order to communicate the sustainable philosophy of the coalition and upon which to base its future strategy.

Now . . . formulate the core values.

Getting started

1. Choose a name for the coalition and think of the different kinds of local businesses that would be involved – you might find it easier to base it on where you live.

2. Research associations, organisations and companies that have already established their own core values on sustainability

3. What aspects of sustainability will you choose to mention in the core values

4. Remember these local independent retailers want to compete in a believable, credible way on sustainability.

References

1. Borin, N. and Metcalf, L. (2010) 'Integrating Sustainability Into the Marketing Curriculum: Learning Activities that Facilitate Sustainable Marketing Practices', *Journal of Marketing Education* 20 (p. 2).

2. Ipsos MORI Reputation Centre (2007) *Sustainability Issues in the Retail Sector,* London: Ipsos MORI (p. 3).

3. Atkinson, R. (2007) *Actionable Consumer Insights: Turning Environmental Concerns into Competitive Advantage.* ESOMAR, Consumer Insights Conference, Milan May.

4. Berry, L.L. (1980) 'Services Marketing Is Different' *Business,* May–June: 24–29.

5. Chartered Institute of Marketing (2007) *Tomorrow's Word: Re-evaluating the Role of Marketing.* Shape the Agenda Paper Issue No. 12.

6. Dresner, S., McGeevor, K. and Tomei, J. (2007) *Public Understanding Synthesis Report: A Report to the Department for Environment, Food and Rural Affairs.* Policy Studies Institute. London: DEFRA.

7. Chartered Institute of Marketing (2007) *Tomorrow's Word: Re-evaluating the Role of Marketing.* Shape the Agenda Paper Issue No. 12. Maidenhead: UK (p. 2).

8. Chartered Institute of Marketing (2007) *Tomorrow's Word: Re-evaluating the Role of Marketing.* Shape the Agenda Paper Issue No. 12 (p. 14).

9. Kotler, P. (1967) *A Framework for Marketing Management,* Upper Saddle River, NJ: Prentice Hall.

10. Kotler, P., Armstrong, G., Wong, V. and Saunders, J. (2008) *Principles of Marketing,* 5th ed., Harlow: Prentice Hall (p. 17).

11. Belz, F. and Peattie, K. (2009) *Sustainability Marketing,* Chichester: John Wiley

12. Friedman, M. (1970) 'The Social Responsibility of Business is to Increase its Profits', *New York Times Magazine,* 13 September cited in Hartman, L. (2005) *Perspectives in Business Ethics,* 3rd ed., Boston, MA: McGraw-Hill, 280–285. You can read this article and other arguments for and against social responsibility in Hartman's text.

13. Maignan, I. and Ferrell, O. (2004) 'Corporate Social Responsibility and Marketing: An Integrative Framework', *Journal of the Academy of Marketing Science* 32(1), 3–19 (p. 4).

14. Werther, W. and Chandler, D. (2006) *Strategic Corporate Social Responsibility: Stakeholders in a Global Environment,* London: Sage.

15. Kotler, P. and Lee, N. (2005) *Corporate Social Responsibility. Doing the Most Good for Your Company and Your Cause,* Hoboken, NJ: John Wiley (p. 3)

16. World Business Council on Sustainable Development (2000) Corporate Social Responsibility: Making Good Business Sense, www.wbcsd.org (accessed 7 July 2010).

17. Blowfield, M. and Murray, A. (2008) *Corporate Responsibility: A Critical Introduction,* Oxford: Oxford University Press.

18. H.J. Berry: see its website, www.hjberry.co.uk and see also an interview with the owner, www.youtube.com/watch?v=lf5-4OIsSZE (accessed 7 July 2010).

19. Vogel, D. (2006) *The Market for Virtue: The Potential and Limits of Corporate Social Responsibility,* Washington, DC: Brookings Institution Press.

20. Newman, A. (2007) 'Unilever Shuns Stereotypes of Women (Unless Talking to Men)', *New York Times,* 15 October.

21. Business for Social Responsibility (BSR) (2008) *Eco-promising: Communicating the Environmental Credentials of Your Products and Services* BSR, www.bsr.org/reports/BSR_Eco-Promising_April_2008.pdf

22. See a selection of the Dove Campaign for Real Beauty adverts, www.dove.us/ #/features/videos/default.aspx[cp-documentid=7049560]/(accessed 16 February 2010). See also the Greenpeace criticism of the Dove campaign, www.greenpeace. org/international/campaigns/forests/asia-pacific/dove-palmoil-action/dove-onslaught-er-hd (accessed 16 February 2010).

23. Kotler, P. and Lee, N. (2005) *Corporate Social Responsibility. Doing the Most Good for Your Company and Your Cause*, Hoboken, NJ: Wiley (p. 3).

24. Stoll, M. (2002) The Ethics of Marketing Good Corporate Conduct. In Hartman, L. (Ed.) *Perspectives in Business Ethics*, 3rd ed., Boston, MA: McGraw-Hill.

25. Hawkins, D. (2006) *Corporate Social Responsibility: Balancing Tomorrow's Sustainability and Today's Profitability*, Basingstoke: Palgrave Macmillan.

26. World Business Council on Sustainable Development (2000) *Corporate Social Responsibility: Making Good Business Sense*, January, www.wbcsd.org (accessed 9 July 2010).

27. Friedman, M. (1970) 'The Social Responsibility of Business is to Increase its Profits', *New York Times Magazine*, 13 September, cited in Hartman, L. (2005) *Perspectives in Business Ethics*, 3rd ed., Boston, MA: McGraw-Hill (p. 285).

28. Crane, A. (2000) 'Marketing and the Natural Environment: What Role for Morality?', *Journal of Macromarketing* 20(2): 144–154.

29. Davis, C. and Moy, C. (2007) *The Dawn of the Ethical Brand*. Market Research Society Golden Jubilee Conference, 21–23 March, Brighton.

30. Strategic Direction (2008) 'Mainstreaming Corporate Responsibility and Sustainability: Creating an Advantage', *Strategic Direction* 24(3): 9–12 (p. 10).

31. Atkinson, R. (2007) *Actionable Consumer Insights: Turning Environmental Concerns into Competitive*. Consumer Insights Conference, Milan, ESOMAR, May

32. Hawkins, D. (2006) *Corporate Social Responsibility: Balancing Tomorrow's Sustainability and Today's Profitability*, Basingstoke: Palgrave Macmillan (p. 156).

33. Fisk, G. (1981) 'An Invitation to Participate in Affairs of the Journal of Macromarketing', *Journal of Macromarketing* 1(1): 3–6.

34. Fisk, G. (1974) *Marketing and the Ecological Crisis*, London: Harper and Row. Henion, K.E. (1972) 'The Effect of Ecologically Relevant Information on Detergent Sales', *Journal of Marketing Research* 9(1): 10–14. Henion, K.E. and Kinnear, T.C. (1976) *Ecological Marketing*. American Marketing Association First National Workshop on Ecological Marketing, AMA: Chicago, IL.

35. Coddington, W. (1992) *Environmental Marketing*, New York: McGraw-Hill. Peattie, K. (1995) *Environmental Marketing Management*, London: Pitman.

36. Charter, M. (1992) *Greener Marketing – A Responsible Approach to Business*, Sheffield: Greenleaf. Peattie, K. (1992) *Green Marketing* London: Pitman. Ottman, J.A. (1993) *Green Marketing: Challenges and Opportunities for the New Marketing Age*, Lincolnwood, IL: NTC.

37. Lazer, W. (1969) 'Marketing's Changing Social Relationships' *Journal of Marketing* 33: 3–9. Kotler, P. and Levy, S.J. (1969) 'Broadening the Concept of Marketing', *Journal of Marketing* 33: 10–15.

38. Kotler, P. and Zaltman, G. (1971) 'Social Marketing: An Approach to Planned Social Change', *Journal of Marketing* 35: 3–12. Wiebe, G. (1972) 'Merchandising Commodities and Citizenship on Television', *Public Opinion Quarterly* 15: 679–691.

39. Varadarajan, P.R. (1992) 'Marketing's Contribution to Strategy: The View From a Different Looking Glass', *Journal of the Academy of Marketing Science*, 20: 335–343. Isaak, R. (1997) 'Globalisation and Green Entrepreneurship', *Greener Management International* 2: 80–90. Menon, A. and Menon, A. (1997) 'Enviropreneurial Marketing Strategy: The Emergence of Corporate Environmentalism as Market Strategy', *Journal of Marketing* 61: 51–67. Keogh, P.D. and Polonsky, M.J. (1998) 'Environmental Commitment: A Basis for Environmental Entrepreneurship?', *Journal of Organizational Change Management* 11(1): 38–49.

40. Hart, S.L. and Milstein, M.B. (1999) 'Global Sustainability and the Creative Destruction of Industries', *Sloan Management Review* 41(1): 23–33 (p. 25).

41. Charter, M., Peattie, K., Ottman, J. and Polonsky, M. (2002) *Marketing and Sustainability*, Massachusetts: Centre for Business Relationships, Accountability, Sustainability and Society (BRASS), in association with the Centre for Sustainable Design, MIT (p. 10).

42. Charter, M. (1992) *Greener Marketing: A Greener Marketing Approach to Business*. Sheffield: Greenleaf Publishing.

43. Menon, A. and Menon, A. (1997) 'Enviropreneurial Marketing Strategy: The Emergence of Corporate Environmentalism as Market Strategy', *Journal of Marketing* 61: 51–67.

44. Van Dam, Y. and Apledoorn, P. (1996) 'Sustainable Marketing', *Journal of Macromarketing* 16: 45–56 (p. 45).

45. The Co-operative Bank (2007) *The Ethical Consumerism Report*, www.co-operativebank.co.uk/ethicalconsumerismreport (accessed January 2008).

46. Crane, A. (2000) 'Marketing and the Natural Environment: What Role for Morality?', *Journal of Macromarketing* 20(2): 144–154.

47. 'A Question of Ethics', *MediaGuardian*, 21 January 2008.

48. Marketing Trends Survey (2006) Winter, Ipsos MORI/CIM.

49. Kleanthous, A. and Peck, J. (2007) *Let Them Eat Cake: Satisfying the New Consumer Appetite for Responsible Brands*, World Wildlife Fund, www.wwf.org.uk/letthemeatcake March (accessed 2008).

50. *Stern Review: The Economics of Climate Change*, London: HM Treasury.

51. World Commission on Environment and Development (1987) Brundtland Report, *Our Common Future*, London: HM Treasury.

    According to Holmberg and Sandbrook (1992) there are more than 100 definitions of sustainable development – see Holmberg and Sandbrook (1992) *Sustainable Development: What is to be Done?*, in Holmberg J. (ed.) *Policies for a Small Planet*, London: Earthscan.

52. Elkington, J. (1994) 'Towards the Sustainable Corporation: Win-win-win Business Strategies for Sustainable Development', *California Management Review* 36(2): 90–100. See also Elkington, J. (1998) *Cannibals with Forks: The Triple Bottom Line of 21st Century Business*, Stony Creek, VA: New Society Publishers.

53. Elkington, J. (2004) 'Enter the Triple Bottom Line', in Henriques, A. and Richardson, J. (eds) *The Triple Bottom Line: Does it All Add Up?*, London: Earthscan (p. 3). Also available at: http://www.johnelkington.com/TBL-elkington-chapter.pdf

54. Bridges, C. and Wilhelm W. (2008) 'Going Beyond Green: The "Why" and "How" of Integrating Sustainability into the Marketing Curriculum', *Journal of Education Marketing* 30: 33–46 (p. 35).

55. Hawken, P., Lovins, A. and Lovins, H. (1999) *Natural Capitalism: Creating the Next Industrial Revolution*, London: Earthscan, www.natcap.org

56. Sams, C. (2008) *Start your Business*. Issue 23 (March), 60–65 (p. 63).

57. Charles, G. (2008) 'Kellogg Shelves Character Work', *Marketing,* 27 March, p. 1.

2 The backdrop to sustainability

Questioning growth is deemed the act of lunatics, idealists and revolutionaries. But question it we must[1]

Professor Tim Jackson Director ESRC Research group on Lifestyles, Values and Environment

Chapter objectives

After studying this chapter you should be able to:

1 Understand the relevance of how an economic system based on growth affects sustainability.

2 Understand the significance of the growing impact of business activity upon the natural environment.

3 Explore current developments in the marketing environment and their role in stimulating or impeding the progress of sustainability.

4 Understand alternative approaches to a sustainable economy.

Dilemma part 1:   Who decarbonises first – business?

Dealing with the carbon footprints of countries and businesses by regulating greenhouse gas emissions is one of the main pillars of action for governments around the world in their efforts to avoid the detrimental effects of climate change. Highlighted in the Kyoto Earth Summit of 1997, the debate around the issue of carbon dioxide emissions resulted in the development of a carbon emission trading scheme (ETS) aimed at reducing the amount of gas released in the atmosphere by all the signatory nations. Only weeks before the climate change summit in Copenhagen in December 2009, commentators were already suggesting that the Kyoto protocol for the reduction of carbon was flawed and that the carbon emissions trading scheme had failed to address the problem adequately. Critics pointed to a number of issues:

- The ETS can be perceived to legitimise the right to pollute through the purchase of permits.

- In the UK, politicians have avoided sending a clear message of urgency to the public and businesses by setting a target of 80 percent carbon reduction by 2050 (when they will be conveniently out of office and maybe not of this world). Politicians want loose carbon limits, scientists want tight ones.

- Too many carbon allowances have been allocated to industry for free.

- The over-allocation of carbon allowances has led to *hot air carbon credits* which do not result in any actual emissions cuts because they go unused but can be kept to be utilised in the future. This means some businesses have enough hot air credits to eliminate the need to cut their emissions until 2015.

- Free allowances have not been adjusted for the economic downturn of the recession, adding to the problem of over-allocation.

- The scheme has not yet succeeded in driving investment in low-carbon technology.

- The ETS price for a tonne of CO_2 in July 2009 was €14. To make it economically viable for electricity suppliers to switch from coal to less-polluting gas requires a price of €25 per tonne and carbon capture and storage technology needs a price of €50 a tonne to be worth investing in.

- In September 2009, United Nations inspectors suspended SGS UK (a carbon offset vetting company) after it was unable to prove that its staff had vetted carbon offsetting schemes adequately under the Clean Development Mechanism (CDM), which allows countries and companies to offset pollution by buying emissions credits from low-carbon schemes, often in the developing nations. A Norwegian company, DNV, was the single largest auditor of this type, until it too was suspended for irregularities in 2008. Both incidents have damaged the credibility of the ETS.

Discuss the following:

1. What prevents countries from reaching agreements on climate change?

2. To what extent did the Copenhagen climate change summit manage to deal with the criticisms of the carbon emissions trading scheme?

3. Did COP16 (the 16th Conference of the Parties under the United Nations Framework Convention on Climate Change) held in Cancún, Mexico from 29 November to 10 December 2010 make any significant progress beyond the Copenhagen talks?

The backdrop to sustainability

Continued economic growth is generally regarded as the means of achieving robust development together with the quality of life benefits for society associated with it. The pursuit of continued economic growth is taken as a given by developed and less developed nations but its compatibility with sustainability remains unresolved.

With the world still structured around the basic capitalist principles dominant since the Industrial Revolution and an economy that is based on carbon, it is difficult to imagine that any other different system could exist. The scale of sustainability is daunting and will require a collective endeavour on the part of society as a whole if we are to move towards a more sustainable way of living and it is most likely to go against the short-term vested interests of many of the stakeholders involved whether they are governments, businesses or consumers.

Tim Jackson's words that open this chapter underline the depth of feeling. As recession hits, companies fail and unemployment increases, and even countries such as Greece have seen themselves on the edge of collapse. The collective panic that ensues from the political and financial sectors, from business and society in general only serves to reinforce their belief that economic growth is the solution.

This chapter explores a series of issues that form a significant part of the background to sustainability, focusing on origins and causes of the current, unstable state of affairs and potential changes and solutions. First, the features and consequences of an economic system based on the pursuit of growth are commented on, in order to gain an understanding of the practices that have lead to a situation that is no longer sustainable. Second, the ecological footprints of human behaviour are also discussed and how government and business are already reacting to mitigate the environmental implications of these impacts. Finally, the role of technological innovation and different approaches towards sustainable development are highlighted to indicate how a more sustainable future may be attained.

Certainly, the business practice of the future will not be *business as usual*. It will entail breaking the habits of a lifetime and creating conditions to allow society to thrive and prosper within its means – economically, socially and environmentally.

The habits of a lifetime

As the saying goes – first we make our habits and then our habits make us – so just how do you break the habits of a lifetime? This is precisely the challenge for marketers aiming to change an economy based on production, growth and consumption, which continues regardless of the consequences. Working *towards* sustainability could be understood as working *against* how we usually do things and how things are usually done – working against what is referred to as the dominant social paradigm (DSP).

The dominant social paradigm

The dominant social paradigm (DSP) is the collection of norms, beliefs, values, and habits that form the most commonly held world view within a culture and has governed the way people do things in the developed world since the Industrial Revolution.[2] The DSP is therefore 'the way people perceive and interpret the functioning of the world around them' and is such a widespread view of the world that it is barely noticed or questioned.[3] This dominant social paradigm has assumed that continued economic growth via continued production and consumption would ensure progress for everyone involved and marketing has facilitated the embedding of this belief and its practice. It also assumed that natural resources were limitless and that science and technology would compensate for shortfalls through increased efficiency.[4]

The new sustainable marketing paradigm is at odds with this erroneous world view of the DSP. The sustainable paradigm is based on the reality of one planet living, whereas the DSP requires more than two planets-worth of resources just to continue at its present rate. As well-known sustainable advocators Paul Hawken, Amory Lovins and Hunter Lovins highlighted, marketing was originally designed to be efficient but not sufficient, aggressively competitive but not fair and certainly not intended to achieve sustainability, as marketing under the DSP does not contemplate that there is a limit to growth.[5] The World Wildlife Fund, in its recent publication *One Planet Business*, points out that a significant change is required to move society away from opposing sustainable objectives to actually supporting them and they state:

> The defining challenge of the 21st century will be to transform the system governing markets so that they work for, rather than against, sustainability.[6]

The usual suspects maintain the old habits

It is worth noting that a paradigm is not necessarily dominant because it is held by the majority but because it is held by dominant groups who use it to legitimise the prevailing institutions and actions that support their mutual interests. Essentially the dominant groups of stakeholders in the DSP are governments, political parties, businesses and financial institutions following their objectives of continued economic growth and the accumulation of capital. If the current system that governs world markets is to be transformed, the dominant group of stakeholders will have to abandon the very paradigm which has maintained its position of influence until now and it is daunting to think that the ones who are to lead the way to sustainability are the very same ones who are responsible for maintaining the present unsustainable situation.

This has led to some confusion regarding how to proceed, since to continue to grow under the present system is incompatible with becoming sustainable. However, old habits seem to be maintained even though sustainability is being professed as the main goal of developed countries. In the UK, government rhetoric finds it hard to avoid the same key words of the DSP related to economic growth. For example, in the UK government's 1999 sustainable development strategy, high and stable economic growth was regarded as a prerequisite for sustainable development and in the 2005 sustainable development strategy it stated growth and prosperity 'should not be in conflict with sustainability'.[7]

Recession and sustainability

The world economic recession that started in 2008 with the collapse of numerous financial institutions across the world has caused governments to send out more messages that conflict with their *consume less and be sustainable* intentions. In fact, in order to bring the world out of recession, consumers have been asked and encouraged to consume more – as is the case in Ireland.[8] It seems that economic recession has distracted government, businesses and the general public from dealing with sustainability. For example, in the 2008 US presidential campaign, the economy was cited as the number one concern of Americans while the environment remained outside the top five concerns.[9] The lowering of taxes in EU countries such as value added tax (VAT), the introduction of government-sponsored scrapage deals for trading in older cars to purchase a new one and the lowering of interest rates follow the maxim of the established DSP that consumption is good and more consumption is better.[10] Jonathon Porritt, Chairman of the Sustainable Development Commission, lamented the unprecedented unity of the major economic powers in restoring the economic system of the world during the 2008–2009 recession in comparison with the lack of agreement and initiatives on sustainability.[11] Again this shows the continued political interest in maintaining the DSP and unfortunately brings to mind the much quoted phrase attributed to Albert Einstein about the impossibility of solving problems by using the same thinking that had created them in the first place.

Recent market research carried out in 2010 indicates that sustainability is at risk of dropping off the corporate agenda, as businesses pursue strategies to gain short-term profit to try and ease themselves out of the recession. The report, *Harnessing Change: Preparing for Business in the Next Decade,* was carried out for mobile phone company O_2 and surveyed 500 senior executives from companies with turnovers between £5–50 million. According to the survey, while 46 percent of business leaders planned to prioritise sustainability over the following two years, another 36 percent had decided to abandon investing in sustainability, at least for the short term.[12]

Inequality and consumption

It has been argued that inequality in society is also responsible for driving unsustainable consumption and that the pursuit of economic growth has become a substitute for the lack of equality of income.[13] As long as governments can promise economic growth to those who are worse off, those less wealthy people can still conserve the hope to improve their lot. Therefore the economic gap between different socio-economic segments of the population is only made tolerable with the expectation of progress through growth for those who are less fortunate.

As a result, people take part in continued consumption in order to improve on the position they feel they have already gained. They continue to purchase goods and services because they believe they have to defend the status they have already achieved in comparison with others and avoid the feeling of inequality. For many, maintaining this position gained through consumption can only be done by consuming more and better versions of products over time or they will feel left behind, out of fashion or out of date in comparison with everyone else. Such consumption is further motivated by the visible consumption of richer people who add to the feelings of dissatisfaction of the not so well off.

The stark reality of the situation is that economic growth has not solved the problems of inequality and poverty in the world. Inequality still exists and is higher than it was 20 years ago in the nations of the Organisation for Economic Co-operation and Development (OECD), the rich are richer, the middle class stagnated and the poor are poorer, with two billion people still having to live on less than $2 a day. In fact, for continued growth to take place, inequality and poverty must remain.

For sustainability to take hold we must be prepared to break with our old habits and adopt a new paradigm, and business will never be *as usual* again. The next section looks at the environmental impact of the DSP, now more often referred to as our footprints, and the initial reactions of governments to deal with one of the key impacts – carbon.

Business cannot be *as usual*

The way society deals with the natural environment, the extent to which it is cared for and protected or used and exploited, depends largely on society's moral perception of its relationship with the natural environment. There are two competing ways of understanding the extension of the moral, ethical perspective to nature – ecocentrism and anthropocentrism.

Ecocentrism represents the belief that the ecosystem has an intrinsic value and this reason alone is sufficient for protecting it. This ethical view of nature was first debated by Aldo Leopold, an American professor and environmentalist in the 1940s, and articulated in his seminal work, *A Sand Country Almanac*, in 1949.[14] At that time, Leopold pointed out that humanity's relationship with the land was economic but that the ethical consideration of the natural environment was an ecological necessity. The ecocentric view therefore sees humans as another member of the natural community; nature is not subordinate to humans and should be respected and protected from harm.

In contrast, anthropocentrism considers humans to be the most important life form on the planet, and that nature is only important to the extent that it affects human life or can be useful to humans. Anthropocentrism therefore encompasses both altruistic and egoistic values and represents the belief that the environment could be protected from degradation or preserved to avoid harm to humans or to benefit them.[15] Anthropocentric approaches are mainly concerned with the preservation of nature as a resource and, from such a viewpoint, support for the natural environment is conditional, depending on the level of compromise required that may affect living standards, convenience or even cost of product.

Our footprints on the planet are a reflection of our ecocentric and anthropocentric values and indicate that the time to change is overdue. Before you continue with the chapter and the rest of the text it would be a good idea if you assessed your own ecological values. Take the ecological values questionnaire provided in Table 2.1.[16] Record your answers on the following website:

Table 2.1 Questionnaire to measure pro-environmental tendencies[17]

Listed below are statements about the relationship between humans and the environment. Indicate the degree to which you agree with each item	Strongly disagree	Mildly disagree	Neutral	Mildly agree	Strongly agree
We are approaching the limit of the number of people the earth can support.	☐ 1	☐ 2	☐ 3	☐ 4	☐ 5
Humans have the right to modify the natural environment to suit their needs.	☐ 1	☐ 2	☐ 3	☐ 4	☐ 5
When humans interfere with nature, it often produces disastrous consequences.	☐ 1	☐ 2	☐ 3	☐ 4	☐ 5
Human ingenuity will ensure that we do not make the earth unlivable.	☐ 1	☐ 2	☐ 3	☐ 4	☐ 5
Humans are severely abusing the earth.	☐ 1	☐ 2	☐ 3	☐ 4	☐ 5
The earth has plenty of natural resources if we just learn how to develop them.	☐ 1	☐ 2	☐ 3	☐ 4	☐ 5
Plants and animals have as much right as humans to exist.	☐ 1	☐ 2	☐ 3	☐ 4	☐ 5
The balance of nature is strong enough to cope with the impacts of modern industrial nations.	☐ 1	☐ 2	☐ 3	☐ 4	☐ 5
Despite our special abilities, humans are still subject to the laws of nature.	☐ 1	☐ 2	☐ 3	☐ 4	☐ 5
The so-called 'ecological crisis' facing humankind has been greatly exaggerated.	☐ 1	☐ 2	☐ 3	☐ 4	☐ 5
The Earth is like a spaceship with very limited room and resources.	☐ 1	☐ 2	☐ 3	☐ 4	☐ 5
Humans were meant to rule over the rest of nature.	☐ 1	☐ 2	☐ 3	☐ 4	☐ 5
The balance of nature is very delicate and easily upset.	☐ 1	☐ 2	☐ 3	☐ 4	☐ 5
Humans will eventually learn enough about how nature works to be able to control it.	☐ 1	☐ 2	☐ 3	☐ 4	☐ 5
If things continue on their present course, we will soon experience a major environmental catastrophe.	☐ 1	☐ 2	☐ 3	☐ 4	☐ 5

Source: Dunlap *et al.*, 2000

www.prenhall.com/divisions/hss/app/social/addchap9.html, in order to see whether your attitudes are more or less pro-environmental than the average. You might wish to retake the test upon completing the text to see if your values have changed.

Realising the impact of our footprints

Footprints can be found on the cover of this textbook and it is the impact of our footprints on the planet that drive much of the sustainability agenda. The carbon footprint mentioned in the dilemma of this chapter is only one of the footprints referred to by advocates of sustainability. The broader, more holistic ecological footprint is also an important measure of human impact and the water footprint is yet another.

The ecological footprint

The ecological footprint is a means of accounting for humanity's competing demands on the planet by comparing human demand against the regenerative capacity of the planet. To achieve this, the calculation of the ecological footprint is made up from all the types of areas required to provide the renewable resources people use in their daily lives, as shown in Figure 2.1. Carbon is the only waste product currently included in the footprint.

In determining whether total human demand for renewable resources and the absorption of carbon dioxide can be maintained, the ecological footprint is compared with the regenerative capacity or biocapacity of the planet. Biocapacity is the total regenerative capacity available to serve the demand represented by the ecological footprint. Both the ecological footprint (which represents demand for resources) and biocapacity (which represents the availability of resources) are expressed in units called global hectares (gha), with 1gha representing the productive capacity of 1ha of land at world average

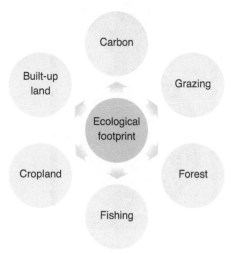

Figure 2.1 The ecological footprint

productivity. Since people consume resources from all over the world, the ecological footprint of consumption combines these areas regardless of where they are located on the planet.

Ecological overshoot

Although concern for humanity's footprints – carbon, water or ecological – may seem to be a more recent phenomenon, it was as early as the 1970s when humanity as a whole passed the point at which the annual ecological footprint became greater than the planet's annual biocapacity. This is known as *ecological overshoot*: the situation that arises when the total human population began consuming renewable resources faster than ecosystems could regenerate them and releasing more carbon dioxide than the planet's ecosystems could absorb.

If no remedial action is taken the point of ecological overshoot will arrive a little earlier each year. Just like going into overdraft when you have no more money left in your bank account at the end of the month, the only difference being that it is much more difficult to pay back the debt to the planet's ecosystems. In 2010 overshoot day was reached on 21 August 2010 (see Figure 2.2) according to the Global Footprint Network (an independent think tank based in the US, Belgium and Switzerland, founded in 2003 to work on tools for advancing sustainability). In 2007 the overshoot was already measured at 50 percent with the ecological footprint at 2.7gha per person against planet Earth's biocapacity of 1.8gha per person.

Figure 2.2   The point of ecological overshoot for 2010
Source: The Global Footprint Network

The water footprint

At this point it is worth mentioning the water footprint. While much publicity is duly given to our carbon footprint, our water footprint is equally significant and governments and businesses will be acknowledging its increased importance and impact in the future. It is recognised that demand for water, our water footprint, will continue to rise around the world and it will become progressively more challenging to meet this demand without actually damaging the very sources of water we need and use.[17] By 2025, it is estimated that about two-thirds of the world's population, over five billion people, will live in areas facing moderate to severe water crises.

Water footprinting has also allowed for the appreciation of the amount of virtual water embedded in commodities, services and products. The virtual water content of a product is the volume of freshwater used to produce the product, measured at the place where the product was actually produced. It refers to the sum of the water use in the various steps of the production chain. The adjective *virtual* refers to the fact that most of the water used to produce a product is not contained in the product. The real-water content of products is generally negligible if compared with the virtual water content.

The App

Source: Raureif GmBH

The water footprint of a cup of black coffee is about 140 litres, a 300g beefsteak about 4,500 litres and a 100g apple 70 litres. As these goods are traded between countries, so a country's water footprint is increased. An average household in the UK uses around 150 litres per person per day, but when coupled with the UK's consumption of products from other countries it turns out that each person in the UK can consume up to 4,645 litres of the world's water every day. As with the carbon footprint of countries, the difference between producing country and receiving country reveals significant data. A recent study established that 62 percent of the UK's water footprint was actually virtual water embedded in agricultural commodities and products imported from other countries, while UK domestic water resources only accounted for the remaining 38 percent.[18]

For those who are keen to reduce the impact of their water footprint by modifying their consumption patterns, iPhone has produced an app to allow consumers to access information on the virtual water footprint of products and the ability to compare products to guide their purchase decisions (shown in the photo on the previous page). Making people pay for their footprints rather than just informing them about the potential size of their impact is another means of encouraging sustainable behaviour from businesses and consumers. What is new is that such impacts have not previously been regarded as a cost by many conventionally run businesses.

Snapshot: From footprints to paw prints

Time to Eat the Dog? is a controversial book by Robert and Brenda Vale.[19] They argue that owning a pet can be just as damaging to the environment and as much a drain on natural resources as driving a 4 × 4 car. Their calculations are based on the land needed to produce the food that pets eat. This ecological footprint, a tool that measures our natural resource consumption and our global environmental impact, represents the total quantity of land and sea area required to produce the food, fibre and minerals we consume, absorb the waste we produce (including CO_2 emissions) and provide the space for our infrastructure. The ecological footprint is usually shown in global hectares and is the sum of all those areas needed for consumption wherever they are on the planet. The Vales argue that meat- and cereal-eating animals add to the already high ecological footprint of the average person in the developed world, increasing the number of hectares of land needed to support each individual (and his dog).

For example, a medium-sized dog will have an annual ecological footprint of 0.84 hectares, that is around twice the 0.41 hectares required by a 4 × 4 driving 10,000 kilometres a year, including the energy to build the car, while the eco-footprint of a cat, some 0.15 hectares, equates to that of a Volkswagen Golf.

Such comparisons are more shocking when they are made with human beings. In 2004, the average citizen of Vietnam had an ecological footprint of 0.76 hectares and an Ethiopian 0.67 hectares. It seems there may easily come a time when owners have to justify their choice of pet and even consider how to counteract its footprint on the resources of the planet.

According to David Mackay, physicist at the University of Cambridge and energy adviser to the UK government: 'If a lifestyle choice uses more than 1 percent of your energy footprint, then it is worthwhile reflecting on that choice and seeing what you can do about it. Pets definitely deserve attention . . . the energy footprint of a cat is about 2 percent of the average British person's energy footprint.'[20]

The cumulative environmental impact of pets sounds worse. The estimated cat population for the top ten cat-owning countries require over 400,000 square kilometres of land to feed them, according to the Vales' research – the equivalent of one-and-a-half times the area of New Zealand. The top ten dog-owning countries require another five New Zealands.

Pet pollution is another problem. Cat excrement is particularly toxic and a parasite found in its faeces is responsible for marine animals dying of brain disease after their excrement is flushed down toilets by their owners, contaminating rivers and estuaries.

If you still want to keep a pet you could reduce its paw print by feeding it scraps from your own food rather than commercially produced pet food and, rather than a resource burden, keeping pets as a source of meat for human consumption could make a significant contribution to developing a sustainable lifestyle. For example, two rabbits could provide 36 offspring a year, amounting to some 72 kilos of meat.

However, for some people eating their pets may be a step too far. They are companions and entertainers, as well as antidotes to loneliness and stress. So when choosing a pet that you do not intend to eat, keep in mind that two hamsters would be consuming resources equivalent to running a plasma television, while a goldfish, the most sustainable of pets, uses just 0.00034 hectares or two mobile phones.

Externalising versus internalising costs

Despite the deep-seated belief that economic growth is an indisputable necessity, continued and sustainable growth hardly seems feasible for developed and developing nations, given world population increases and limited natural resources. Perhaps what has been misunderstood is the nature of the different types of capital needed for growth and the contribution they each make. Conventional definitions of capital tend to focus on accumulated wealth in the form of investments, property and equipment, when in reality an economy can only exist and grow with the presence of four types of capital.[21]

human	– labour, knowledge, intelligence, culture
financial	– cash, investments, monetary instruments
manufactured	– including infrastructure, machines, tools, factories
natural	– resources, living systems, ecosystem services

Business practice under the dominant social paradigm has failed to acknowledge the importance of human and natural capital, hence the problems of social equity and environmental degradation. Indeed, it has been common practice to ignore the social and environmental costs throughout the whole of the product lifecycle from raw materials to production, product consumption and recycling, reuse or disposal. They have often just been excluded from the total costs of business and have similarly been excluded from the price paid by consumers.

Thus, in order to maximise profit and short-term gain, the act of depletion of non-renewable natural resources has not been regarded as a cost for the present or future generations and does not figure in company accounts. Only the acts of extraction and exploitation of natural resources are registered as costs, but not the reduction of those resources or the damage incurred by the environment and society. Equally, the detrimental effects on populations from poor working conditions, low remuneration and poor living conditions in areas where natural resources are extracted or where product manufacture takes place, resulting in pollution, loss of human and wildlife habitats, and loss of community, culture and livelihood, are not figured into costs. Effectively the social and environmental costs incurred are externalised by the producer, leaving members of society as a whole to take responsibility for paying the price of mitigating the negative effects they have caused.

Sustainable producers are obliged to consider all their costs and internalise them. This process results in the producers incurring the social and environmental costs of their own business activities, which will likely be added to the price charged to consumers. In environmental terms this is often referred to as the polluter pays principle. Whether by obligation or choice, the internalisation of social and environmental costs will result in higher prices for the consumer. Paying to improve the social and economic conditions of employees and local communities, particularly across extensive supply chains, can prove effective in improving their quality of life, but it is not clear that paying to compensate for pollution will actually provide a solution to environmental issues.

Polluter pays

While environmental pollution is considered an economic externality and its consequences are shared by society as a whole, the polluter reaps the economic benefit of such actions and therefore has no incentive to stop polluting. The polluter pays principle addresses this market failure by ensuring that polluters internalise the costs of environmental damage, often through fines, diverting the profits gained from polluting to environmental charities to repair the damage or by the levy of green taxes such as landfill tax.

In the case of car manufacturing in the EU, both manufacturer and consumer pay to pollute. Government car tax levied on the owner of the car varies according to the size and level of carbon emissions of the engine. In this way governments hope to divert consumer demand towards less polluting cars, which will in turn stimulate manufacturers to produce them. In the UK, the government initiated a second tax on vehicles according to the carbon emissions in addition to road tax. This measure came into effect from April 2010 on all new vehicles as a one-off *showroom tax*, with the highest polluting cars having an extra £1,000 tax added to their price. At the same time, the EU Commission has also set standards for manufacturers with all vehicle CO_2 emissions to be no more than 130 g/km by 2012. Those manufacturers that fail to do so will be facing gradually rising fines for every gram over the target. There will be no showroom tax levied on cars emitting up to 130 g/km.

Making the polluter pay has given way to the trading of carbon emissions, making carbon international legal tender.

Carbon – the new global currency

The implication of imposing a sustainability-led economy to help achieve a manageable balance between the elements of the Triple Bottom Line is that it requires the countries of the world to follow policies which are seen to be fair and equitable in relation to the use of natural resources. For example, in dealing with carbon dioxide emissions a contraction and convergence economy model, sometimes referred to as cap and share or cap and trade, is already being implemented. Contraction and convergence is a carbon cap and trade policy designed to stabilise and then gradually reduce carbon dioxide emissions. In order to implement this policy, a global carbon budget and carbon allocation mechanism is being established, fixing a carbon entitlement to each region, country, or business.

Carbon allowances systems and carbon offsetting are now the chosen means for controlling carbon emissions and encouraging their reduction through market mechanisms, as companies will be motivated to reduce their emissions to save money. The basis of carbon emissions trading came as a result of the 1997 Kyoto Earth Summit and, although the schemes did not come into force until 2008, the EU started the largest and most comprehensive ETS in 2005, involving some 12,000 installations across Europe with a combined trading volume of 1.2 billion tonnes of carbon dioxide, concentrated mainly in energy-generating industries and other intensive producers of carbon dioxide such as the construction industry. While ambitious, the EU's ETS has been heavily criticised for giving away 90 percent of its emissions permits to industry for nothing, thereby disincentivising carbon reduction. This has been compounded by initial over-allocation of permits and the downturn in production due to the recession, allowing companies to hold on to unused permits to cover future emissions. Some critics believe the current system allows rich countries to buy themselves out of making necessary savings and cuts in emissions. Globally, the carbon trading market was worth €92 billion (£79 billion) in 2008, trading five billion tonnes.

Different countries are using and adapting the ETS for their own purposes and contexts. For example, from October 2009 the UK's Department of Energy and Climate Change initiated its new Carbon Reduction Commitment scheme which required any company consuming more than 6,000 MWh of electricity per year (equivalent to the UK's largest 5,000 companies) to measure its emissions and buy equivalent carbon allowances in order to offset them. Each allowance certificate (also referred to as a permit or unit) allows the company to emit 1 tonne of carbon dioxide. By achieving efficiencies in their business operations perhaps by reducing their carbon footprint in the manufacturing process or in the transport of goods, companies can buy fewer carbon allowances and therefore save money. Companies face penalties when they do not acquire enough certificates to balance out the CO_2 they have emitted.

With the introduction of this scheme it is hoped that reducing carbon emissions becomes the cheaper option, in comparison with buying allowances and facing fines, and that companies will become more willing to deal with their carbon footprint. As the total number of allowances available will shrink, over time companies will be gradually forced to act. In addition to the emissions certificates allocated by the state, companies can also make use of other flexible mechanisms. If they invest in emissions reduction projects in other countries, for example, they receive additional emissions allowances, which can also be traded, when they are not needed. Furthermore, any allowances not finally used by a company can be sold at a profit; that is to say, traded in the carbon market, nationally or internationally, to those companies that require them.

Figure 2.3 shows a similar emissions trading scheme which has run in New Zealand from the beginning of 2008. The New Zealand scheme covers emissions of the following six greenhouse gases: carbon dioxide, methane, nitrous oxide, hydro-fluorocarbons, per-fluorocarbons and sulphur hexafluoride, all covered by the Kyoto Earth Summit. The scheme introduces a price on all greenhouse gas emissions to provide an incentive for companies to reduce those emissions and plant forests to absorb carbon dioxide. Participants in the scheme can choose how to comply with their obligations, even buying and selling carbon credits outside New Zealand, enabling them to employ the least-cost method to compensate for or reduce their emissions.

EU companies also have the option to offset their emissions by buying credits from outside the EU, usually from hydroelectric or other schemes in China and India. As much as 900 million tonnes of carbon emissions could be available up

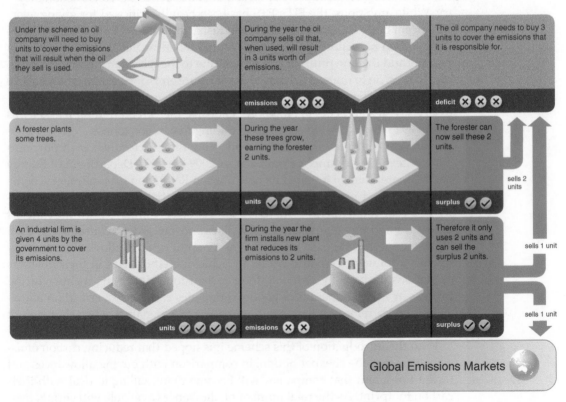

New Zealand's Emissions Trading Scheme (ETS)
The ETS is based on units, which must be obtained to cover emissions. These units can be bought and sold.

Figure 2.3 The New Zealand Emissions Trading Scheme[22]

Source: New Zealand Ministry for the Environment

to 2012 from sources outside the EU, and can be banked by companies for use or resale up to 2020.

It is a safe assumption that the general public expects and supports restrictions on industry to control carbon dioxide emissions but such support is likely to diminish when it is applied to individuals' consumption of carbon.

Carbon – the new household currency

A system of individual, personal carbon quotas shared equally to all inhabitants of the planet was proposed as early as 2006 in Britain by David Miliband, the then Secretary of State for the Environment. This would effectively turn carbon into a standardised global currency for individuals as well as businesses. Imagine having a carbon debit card with which you accessed your home energy needs, travel requirements and foreign holidays, in fact for the purchase of any carbon emitting goods or services. It would certainly be a means of controlling and modifying consumer behaviour. Those using less than their allocation could sell surplus carbon back to the central carbon bank, while others could buy more to supplement their ration.

In theory this scheme would encourage individuals to control and reduce their personal carbon footprint in the same way as businesses already had to adopt. It is hoped such contraction and convergence would allow for the production of carbon dioxide to be reduced across the world at a controlled pace and permit the balancing of consumption between nations, until it is eventually shared out equally. With an estimated planetary carrying capacity of 12 billion tonnes of carbon divided among the current global population, the resulting target for personal carbon allowance amounts to 2 tonnes per person per year.

The significant challenge of reaching such a target can be seen when comparing the average carbon consumption for developed and developing countries. The US produces 24 tonnes of carbon per person per year. The EU averages 12 tonnes, the UK 4.25 tonnes, China 6 tonnes and India 1.7 tonnes per person per year. Clearly great inequality exists and it is not certain that citizens from developed nations will be prepared to make the necessary lifestyle sacrifices to reduce their personal carbon footprint, and thereby the footprint of their country.

For the moment, the more proactive control of carbon consumption of the general public is confined to taxes on purchase of certain goods and services, and initiatives designed to demotivate polluting activities such as congestion charges on city-centre traffic circulation in some cities. These programmes are coupled with an increasing number of government communication campaigns to encourage voluntary reductions from the population. Currently, the UK government Act on CO_2 campaign seeks to instil new habits and persuade members of the public to insulate their homes, turn off unused lights, replace old light bulbs with eco-friendly ones, turn off electrical equipment rather than leave it on stand-by and even reduce weekly car usage by driving 5 miles less a week.

Just as businesses attempt to offset their production of carbon dioxide, individual consumers have tried to compensate for their own carbon emissions by ensuring that an equivalent amount is saved or absorbed elsewhere. In particular, consumers have been encouraged to pay a plus on their product or service to be invested in renewable energy technology schemes such as solar or wind power or storing carbon in soils and biomass by planting trees or sponsoring the changing of land-use practices. However, companies that offer this practice to individual consumers are already starting to question its use and effectiveness.

Snapshot: Offsetting is irresponsible

Responsibletravel.com, the Brighton-based travel agent that specialises in offering responsible holidays, was the first travel agent to offer its customers a carbon offsetting programme, as early as 2002. The travel company was also one of the first to stop giving its customers the opportunity to offset the emissions of travelling in 2009. While major manufacturing industries and energy suppliers are being obliged to reduce carbon footprints and purchase offsets for their excess emissions it seems that other businesses are already signalling the beginning of the end of offsetting.

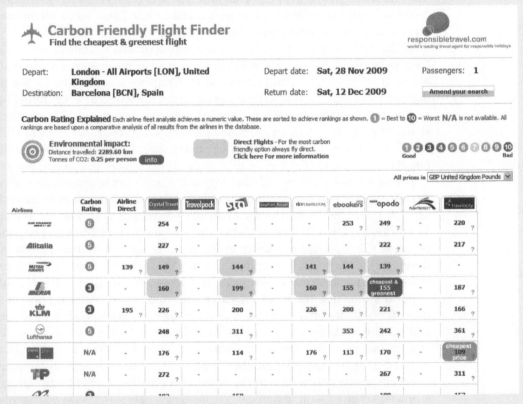

Source: Reprinted with the kind permission of Responsible Travel, www.responsibletravel.com

In press releases and information on its website, Responsibletravel.com has explained its reasons for rejecting the use of offsetting. Responsibletravel.com now believes that travelling less or only travelling responsibly is the best way to reduce carbon emissions and thinks that other travel companies have been using offsetting as a means of justifying or masking growth, with a resulting increase in emissions. One long-haul return flight can produce more carbon dioxide per passenger than the average UK motorist in a single year, and the travel company reiterates that offsetting will not solve this problem and that carbon reduction is the only solution.

In an effort to encourage carbon reduction, Responsibletravel.com offers travellers a flight search system which compares not only prices, but also the carbon emissions of different airlines for requested routes (see screenshot). The company has therefore established carbon performance as an additional product attribute for consumers to consider prior to purchase, allowing for a better informed choice.

Conventional attributes for flight purchases such as price and availability now compete with carbon footprint, and consumers can compare both price and carbon by using responsibletravel.com's carbon-friendly flight finder. This new flight search facility has been created in partnership with Global Travel Market and the Carbon Consultancy – with Responsibletravel.com donating 50 percent of income from the flight search to TravelPledge, which has committed to funding a project supporting local communities adapting to the impacts of global warming. In this way, it is thought that consumer demand will start to be diverted to the most carbon-efficient airlines, encouraging others to disclose their exact fuel consumption and to pollute less.

Despite suggesting that people should fly less, Responsibletravel.com recognises that people will still want to travel and that tourism in many developing countries when it is organised in a responsible manner can bring many social and economic benefits to those communities. For those who decide to take a holiday with Responsibletravel.com there is plenty of advice on the carbon caution page of its site such as the slogan *'when you fly make it count'* including recommendations such as always choosing a direct flight (lower footprint for fewer stops and changes) and flying economy (more seats on the plane means a lower carbon footprint per person).

It remains to be seen whether by its actions Responsibletravel.com loses business, because it actually manages to persuade people to fly less. Alternatively the company may end up gaining market share. Because of its strong and unique stance on carbon, it may attract more consumers who, when they do want to travel, want to do so as responsibly as possible. Of course the company goes beyond carbon reduction and consumers can choose them in the hope that they can contribute to the livelihoods of locals, support local economic development and aid in the conservation of the world's cultural and natural heritage.[23]

Apply it: Carbon transparency

By abandoning offsetting and adopting what could be termed a carbon transparency strategy, Responsibletravel.com is changing the rules of the marketplace affecting its competitors, consumers, airlines, etc. Offsetting has been portrayed as less virtuous and ineffective and consumers are being encouraged to consume less and/or only responsibly using carbon performance as one means of judging competing products.

1. Find other examples of companies that have decided to adopt a policy of carbon transparency and compete on carbon performance.
2. Suggest sectors or businesses that would benefit from adopting a similar strategy.

New habits for old

The international community is clear on the main areas where sustainable behaviour goals need to be achieved with the general public:

- energy usage
- water usage
- natural non-renewable resources usage
- natural renewable resources usage
- travel behaviour
- food consumption
- waste recycling
- waste disposal.

These broad areas are being translated into more specific goals for behaviour change by the EU, national governments, NGOs, charities and individual businesses and part of the marketer's remit is to communicate these goals to all stakeholders and persuade them to adopt the relevant behaviours. Such initiatives to promote new sustainable habits and behaviours are directed at both producers and consumers of products and services.

Faced with the growing obligation to change consumption patterns and general behaviour, consumers are left with four options involving varying degrees of compromise or sacrifice, ranging from ceasing the behaviour completely, reducing the behaviour, modifying the behaviour or adopting a new one as a replacement.

For example, when it comes to individuals' travel and food consumption, the desired behavioural goals for sustainability vary from the easily achievable to the more problematic, as can be seen in Table 2.2. Restricting people's ability to travel freely or stopping them from obtaining imported foodstuffs or modifying their customary diet are changes that are likely to be met with strong resistance as consumers will feel such transformations in lifestyle require the sacrifice of long-held personal freedoms.

Table 2.2 Consumer behaviour goals for travel and food

Travel	
Reduce/stop	• Avoid using the car for short trips of less than 5 kilometres • Avoid domestic short-haul flights • Avoid intra-EU flights
Modify/adopt	• Use low-carbon means of transport • Use public transport • Share means of transport (e.g. car sharing) • Drive only fuel-efficient vehicles

(continued)

Table 2.2   (*Continued*)

Food	
Reduce/stop	• Eat less meat
	• Waste less edible food
	• Eat less
	• Eat less/no imported food
Modify/adopt	• Buy local, regional and national food
	• Buy seasonal food
	• Buy certified food (e.g. organic, freedom food, sustainable fish)
	• Buy loose fruit and vegetables to avoid packaging
	• Eat healthily
	• Adopt a lower-impact diet (e.g. reduced carbon footprint, natural environment-friendly)
	• Cook collectively with friends/neighbours
	• Cook less and eat more raw food
	• Compost food leftovers in garden
	• Grow your own food
	• Rear your own animals

Apply it: Identifying behaviour goals

Water usage		Examples/marketing activities
Reduce/stop	•	
Modify/adopt	•	

Energy usage		Examples/marketing activities
Reduce/stop	•	
Modify/adopt	•	

1. Draw up your own tables for two more of the main areas where sustainability goals need to be achieved: energy usage and water usage.

2. Identify the consumer behaviour goals for sustainability for each area.

3. Give examples of any business initiatives where these goals have already been interpreted as business opportunities.

4. Give examples of government/local government initiatives and the marketing activities that are already in place to promote these goals.

5. Can you find evidence to indicate how successful any of these current initiatives are?

The contribution of technology

Political agreements, legislative control, voluntary change to consumption patterns, consumer attitude and lifestyle change are only part of the sustainability solution within a volatile, rapidly changing business environment. Science and technology developments are also expected to play their part in response to environmental damage, fossil fuel shortages and other problems related to the consumption of non-renewable natural resources. Alternative energy sources, alternative materials, water conservation, waste reuse and recycling have been the focus of many technological developments. Solar power, wind power, micro-generation, hybrid cars, light-emitting diodes, biofuel, algae fuel, carbon capture systems are just some of the technology-driven solutions designed to reduce our addiction to fossil fuel and increase future energy supplies without adding to the carbon footprint.

However, while such advances are important, Professor Kevin Anderson, Director of the Tyndall Centre for Climate Change Research, believes that low-carbon technology alone is not enough.[24] Despite the climate change summits and initiatives, current UK lifestyles now have 18 percent higher emissions than they did in 1990 and those emissions added to the atmosphere since Kyoto will remain there for another century.[25] This means that the world population (particularly of the developed economies) can no longer afford to wait for the effect of new low-carbon technologies and it is therefore imperative for them to adopt low-carbon lifestyles during the transition to new technologies and make these lifestyles the future norm.

Unfortunately, on many occasions, technology can prove to be a double-edged sword and what it gives in carbon reduction on one side it takes away on the other. Household energy-saving technology in particular is susceptible to this problem. More fuel-efficient cars, better designed appliances and more insulated homes save on carbon emissions and save consumers money as well. However, these carbon savings tend to get swallowed up by the increase in our living standards as a result of having more money to spend. Often referred to as the rebound effect, it tends to provoke an increase in consumption as a side-effect of the introduction of a more eco-efficient technology. Consumers may even choose to use appliances more often just because they are labelled as eco-friendly. For example, the use of energy-efficient light bulbs with potential energy savings of 75 percent may actually generate only 45 percent of energy savings since consumers tend to use them more.[26]

Snapshot: Technology . . . waste not want not

On average the user of a flush toilet can get through 15,000 litres of water in a year but only actually produces about 50 litres of faeces and 500 litres of urine. In contrast, some 700 million people across 50 countries suffer health problems from eating food irrigated with untreated sewage. If sterilised, nitrogen-rich human urine is used for agriculture instead of artificial fertiliser that consumes 1 percent of the world's energy supply; this would result in a saving of 180 million tonnes of carbon emissions a year. The Stockholm Environmental Institute has reported on a scheme in the Chinese Dongsheng District to build an eco town for 3,000 people.[27] This is the largest urban project of its kind in China and so far a urine collection system has been installed in 800 apartments, collecting and treating it onsite so it can be reused as agricultural fertiliser with benefits some ten times more than the investment cost.

Animal manure, normally seen as just a natural fertiliser, can be treated to become a source of methane gas for fuel as well. Biogas results from the decomposition of organic matter such as manure without oxygen, so-called anaerobic fermentation, when mixed with grain. Penkun in Germany is now the site of the world's largest biogas plant, converting 84,000 tonnes of manure into fuel, providing electricity and heat for the town's 50,000 inhabitants, and even the fermented by-product from the biogas production can be used as high-quality fertiliser.[28]

Green slime may not seem to amount to very much but algae can grow at a frenetic rate while ingesting more than two times its weight in carbon dioxide from the atmosphere and produce 100 times more biofuel per hectare than corn, sugar or soy. Its cultivation could replace the entire world's supply of diesel using only a small amount of land in comparison with other alternative crops and it does not compete with the food supply as corn or maize do. Once the oil has been extracted the remaining by-product is a non-toxic, high protein animal feed. From 2010 the US company PetroAlgae (www.petroalgae.com) will open a 2,000 hectare algae biodiesel plant in China. If all power stations turned to this source of biodiesel global CO_2 emissions would drop by about 9 billion tonnes.[29]

With just a cup of water and a small amount of detergent, Xeros, the world's first virtually waterless washing machine gets clothes clean and dry using 90 percent less water and 40 percent less energy than a conventional machine. The machine uses small nylon beads that pull stains off garments and lock them into the nylon's molecular structure and they can be used hundreds of times. The UK-based start-up company has reached an agreement with US commercial cleaner GreenEarth Cleaning to field test the machines in 2010 before considering fully launching them in both the industrial and household markets.[30] The savings in the household market alone could amount to 28 million tonnes of carbon emissions.

Professional practice: For a more sustainable business

In order to help raise the profile of your company, your marketing director has asked you to prepare a practitioner article to be placed in an appropriate industry publication. The general aim of the article is to keep marketing professionals informed about the current state of your business sector and any developments that might be expected in the future.

You have decided to take a current issue stemming from a single aspect of the macro-environment (political, economic, socio-cultural or technological) and relate that issue to its relevant implications for sustainable marketing practice within the context of your business sector.

▶

Having already read numerous articles on marketing for sustainability, which were a little depressing and pessimistic, your marketing director has requested that your article should be more upbeat and optimistic about the future. Your article should identify changes and trends on the horizon and suggest how the professional marketer might be preparing strategies to embrace these challenges and opportunities.

Getting started

1. Choose an appropriate sector to contextualise your answer.
2. Carry out a PEST analysis for your chosen sector.
3. Review recent articles in professional publications of your chosen sector, as well as professional publications aimed at marketers, in order to identify emerging trends related to sustainability.
4. Choose the focus of your article based on your research and write it in an informative and positive style.

Approaches to sustainable development

Will the way we do business ever be sustainable or has the concept of sustainable development been flawed in its design since it was first proposed? For some commentators, even the definition of sustainable development contained in the Brundtland Report echoes anthropocentric attitudes towards natural resources by placing them as subordinate to the human needs of current and future generations.[31]

Arran Stibbe, Chair of the Education for Sustainability Group for the Environmental Association for Universities and Colleges (EAUC), presents *development* as an already tarnished concept, associated with developed nations squandering riches in the name of economic growth and progress to the detriment of other under-developed nations. In the 1970s the term *equitable development* was used; it was followed by the term *sustainable development* in the 1980s, which appears to combine both the damage (economic growth) and the remedy (sustainability).[32] Global recession has both dulled and sharpened the debate on how to achieve economic growth, which is simultaneously socially responsible, economically equitable and environmentally sustainable depending on the perspective of each of the (self-) interested parties involved. Yet one common denominator unites the disparate stakeholders in the sustainability debate – the imperative to build a low-carbon economy. Unfortunately, there has often been little clarity and agreement on the most appropriate route to take to achieve such a goal.

Routes to sustainability

Bill Hopwood of the Sustainable Cities Research Institute classifies approaches towards sustainable development into three separate orientations (status quo, reform and transformation) according to the extent of their orientation towards the environment and issues of social equality.[33]

Status quo oriented

This view corresponds closely with the dominant social paradigm, with business and government recognising the need for change but without this being fundamental for society. A lack of knowledge and appropriate mechanisms and ineffective technology are seen to be the barriers to sustainability, but less attention is paid to socio-economic issues. Business, the marketplace and technological advances are seen as the main drivers towards sustainability, and economic growth is seen as indispensable for the achievement of sustainability. Consumer power, with consumers informed and motivated to be sustainable, will stimulate business change and be accompanied by little or no legislation and regulations from government which rely on business to adopt a managerial, incremental top-down approach towards sustainable practice.

Reform oriented

This view holds that sustainability challenges can be met by government intervention in business through controlling taxes and subsidies as well as promoting more research and development. Technological development is seen as an opportunity to do business and be sustainable at the same time, combined with the internalisation of environmental costs which were previously regarded as external.

Transformation oriented

This view holds that the dominant social paradigm is the root cause of the socio-economic and environmental problems facing humanity and that only a more radical approach will be sufficient to solve those problems. Socio-economic issues and the environment are seen to be interconnected and there is a strong commitment to social equity including access to livelihood, good health, resources and economic and political decision making.

Many transformation-style campaigns closely link environmental, social, economic and anti-globalisation movements and present a significant challenge to status quo and reformist views. Such movements have been seen to start with indigenous peoples claiming back control of their lives and establishing stable and fair livelihoods by mixing social equity, economic sustainability, the defence of culture and environmental protection. Transformation orientations point to significant changes in dealing with the economy and population growth.

Towards a steady-state economy

The recent global financial crisis indicates that the pursuit of continuous growth is not the panacea for all our ills. Some would say that the crisis demonstrated that economic growth had become uneconomic. Proponents of an alternative more sustainable economic system advocate turning to a steady-state economy by varying the function and roles of the four types of capital. In a steady-state economy there would be a stable population and stable stocks of goods, which would be much more durable in order to be serviced and maintained over the long term rather than just used and discarded. The maintenance of longer-lasting goods would reduce the need to produce new ones, diverting labour to services rather than manufacture and as a result production would be kept at the lowest possible levels conserving both raw materials and energy.[34] Reducing the burden of continuous growth via continuous production and consumption would allow natural capital to do what it does best, provide the planet with free, renewable life-support systems and services such as water, oxygen, agricultural produce and hospitable habitats. The steady-state economy concept raises many questions not only about the nature of economic activity but also about one other significant factor for sustainability – population control.

Offsetting the population

While there is much attention being paid to offsetting greenhouse gasses, the issue of population growth remains pending. The world population increases by almost 1.5 million every week and, according to the United Nations (UN), it is forecast to grow from around 6.8 billion in 2009 to over 9 billion in 2050. Estimates for a more sustainable global population vary, but all point out that the maximum capacity for the planet has already been surpassed and the populace would need to shrink to 5.1 billion.[35]

Just as continued economic growth and use of natural resources is not sustainable, neither is continued population growth. Population is a taboo topic for most people, many governments do not want to tackle the question of regulating population growth but the problem remains that future sustainability will depend on controlling the growth of the global population to planet sustainable levels.

Population and environmental impact are inextricably intertwined and, without any population control, all of the other measures being used or suggested to move towards sustainability will not be enough to compensate for population growth. Jonathon Porritt, Chairman of the Sustainable Development Commission and patron of the Optimum Population Trust (OPT), has campaigned for population control for some time, but describes the issue as toxic for even the pro-sustainability groups as religion, culture, human rights and immigration policy get in the way of debating and agreeing a solution.[36]

Porritt suggests that two measures combined together would reduce the UK population over the coming years from a predicted 77 million in 2050 to around 55 million (6 million fewer than 2009 levels), easing the pressure on natural resources, space, housing and transport.[37]

- Net zero immigration – preventing that more people enter the country than leave each year.

- Stop at two – persuade the 26 percent of women in the UK who are expected to have more than two children to stop at two.

The Optimum Population Trust has set up PopOffsets, a unique way to tackle population growth and carbon emissions.[38] Subscribers to PopOffsets are given the opportunity to offset their carbon footprint by funding family planning initiatives in developing countries. For example, PopOffset is assisting a family planning association in Madagascar, which has one of the world's fastest growing populations, with an average fertility rate of over five births per woman and nearly half of the its population currently under fifteen years of age.

Researching sustainability: Searching for specific information

Investigate further the concept of the steady-state economy. Search for articles to increase your depth of knowledge on the subject to find answers for the following questions:

1. To what extent would it allow for sustainable business to take place?
2. What would be the role for marketing in such an economy?
3. What barriers exist to establishing the steady-state economy?

Summary

There is widespread recognition of the need to embrace sustainability. However, the underlying factors that dominate the world economy with its dual addiction to growth fuelled by increasing consumption has been actively encouraged by the marketing function for decades and this continues to work against the establishment of a system of sustainable development. Inequality prompts consumption, the poor aspire to be richer and developing nations aspire to the wealth and lifestyle of the developed nations, creating a circle of consumption and desire to grow that is difficult to break. Even the recent global recession has not been taken as an opportunity to reduce consumption. Governments around the world have reacted by encouraging consumer confidence and spending to re-establish the characteristic growth associated with the dominant social paradigm.

Continued consumption reduces natural non-renewable resources and contributes to the deterioration of the natural environment and humanity's ecological, carbon and water footprints are leaving their mark.

Yet there are also clear signs of change, changing attitudes and changing practice. The process of weaning nations, industries and consumers off carbon has already begun and a new vocabulary of carbon trading and quotas is rapidly becoming commonplace. Even the individual rationing of carbon to the general public has been proposed. Also, more muted, low-carbon lifestyles are being suggested as alternatives, made possible by substitute technologies to provide energy and resource-saving solutions in order to maintain a course towards sustainable development without sacrificing quality of life. Breaking long-established habits and doing things differently should soon become the new norm for business and for consumers.

Case study: Muji – less is more

There are many advocates of sustainability who herald the opportunity to embrace a sustainable lifestyle by returning to the *good life* or the *simple life*. Following the idea that *less is more* first associated with the architect and furniture designer Ludwig Mies van der Rohe, the Japanese company Muji has turned simplicity into a core brand value by developing new uncomplicated, plain products at reasonable prices, making the best use of raw materials while considering environmental issues. Having initially started selling 40 products in a store in Japan in 1983, Muji is now an international company selling some 8,000 products in 98 stores outside Japan, spanning 16 countries. Their simple designs aim to complement people's desires to follow more minimalist, less complicated, more sustainable lifestyles. In the opinion of Masao Kiuchi, the age of consumption as a virtue is coming to an end and, rather than live to consume, people are becoming more concerned with consuming to live simply and happily.

Restraint in design, restraint in lifestyle

By careful choice of raw materials, Muji pursues the deliberate avoidance of bleaching or dyeing of materials in order to use and highlight their natural colours. Objects are not complicated by unnecessary functionality or over-decoration in keeping with Muji's policy of conserving resources, as well as reducing waste and pollution from manufacture or recycling. Muji remains faithful to its philosophy that having objects that do enough, is good enough.

Equally, packaging is not meant to decorate the product to make it seem more than it is but be purely practical in order to be in keeping with the natural colours. Plain, uniform containers allow for bulk packaging and reduce wastage, and the products can appear on store shelves and speak for themselves.

Restraint in design is matched by Muji's brand discretion; packaging and labelling are understated to project a no-logo or no-brand image implied in the name. The full Japanese version of the company name is *Mujirushi Ryohin*, which literally means *no-label quality goods*. The calculated rejection of strong logo-based marketing is fundamental to the company image and its products are consistently positioned as everyday and basic products.

Ikko Tanaka, Muji's chief advisor, explains the philosophy of 'basic' in these terms:

> You may feel embarrassed if the person sitting next to you on the train is wearing the same clothes as you. If they are jeans, however, you wouldn't be worried, because jeans are what we could describe as 'basic' clothing. All Muji products are such 'basic' products.[39]

Reuse, recycle, refill, rescue

Muji promotes the recycling and reuse of its products, reflected in the *mu* of its brand name, which represents infiniteness in Japanese. Since its lines are plain and not driven by fashion, unsold products can be stored for resale at any time. The provision of products in this way encourages people to make a lifestyle choice based more on self-restraint and moderation. The ability to recycle goods is also important and the use of noxious substances in manufacture is not allowed. When Muji discovered that the covers of appointment books that they had released for sale in February 2009 had used vinyl chloride, these items were recalled and recycled.

Strength in simplicity

Muji turns its minimalist strategy, product design and style into a strength. Rather than appearing bland and dull, many Muji products allow for mass customisation by the consumer, turning a standardised product into something personal and unique.

For example, the handle of the plain white Muji umbrella allows for a strap or charm to be added to serve for easy identification but also for the owner to personalise the object. Similarly, the Muji bag offers customers an opportunity to literally stamp their personality on their purchase. Customers are invited to make use of a set of stamps and an ink pad while they are in store to print something on their bag. As a result a typically featureless Muji object becomes a fashionable, one-of-a-kind bag, unique to the individual carrying it. Muji has also produced a t-shirt with a rubber square on the chest for customers to design their own logo or message.

Beyond the product concept

Muji, and its parent company Ryohin Keikaku Company Ltd, extend its sustainable practices beyond the core product concept. A five-point plan outlines its coexistence with Earth in environmental and societal terms and its business partners were asked to adhere to the same principles. Consumers can also contribute with suggestions. For example, Muji began to stock Fairtrade products in response to requests from customers, starting with coffee in 2006.

Muji operates three campsites and manages 231 hectares of forest for use by the local community, including children's summer camps which are run by staff volunteers recruited from within the company.[40]

Follow up

1. How do others talk about Muji? Is the brand portrayed favourably or negatively? Look for articles, reviews and features on the brand in lifestyle magazines and on the internet and visit the fan club on Facebook.

2. An alternative is needed for conspicuous consumption, which allows people to demonstrate their adherence to more sustainable values than only the ostentation of affluence or status just for the sake of it. To what extent can the Muji concept fill this gap and drive a frugal, minimalist and functional style to become more mainstream?

Dilemma part 2:   Who decarbonises first – the consumer?

Our inability to reduce our dependence on fossil fuels has made a significant contribution to our current economic and environmental difficulties. There is no alternative but to build a low-carbon economy based on the general population adopting a low-carbon lifestyle.

But how far will the general public go to reduce their carbon footprint? Will people cut back on flying, use their cars less and public transport more, avoid purchasing power showers, bath with

▶

a friend and eat meat only once a month? Whatever the sacrifices there will be complaints and resistance, but one way to avoid opposition to low-carbon living is to give people the means to decide which carbon-consumption products and activities they maintain or do without.

Rationing carbon would be one means of allowing consumers to decide how they want to carbon manage their lifestyles. As it is generally acknowledged that some 40 percent of a developed country's carbon emissions come from the consumption of individuals and the households where they live, the carbon consumption of the general population will have to be regulated in some way and the use of a carbon credit card is only one suggestion.

> It [carbon credit card] could be more empowering than many forms of regulation because instead of banning particular products, services or activities, or taxing them heavily, a personal carbon allowance enables citizens to make trade-offs.

> It is also empowering because many citizens want to be able to do their bit for the environment, but there is currently no measurable way of guiding their decisions.[41]

Devise the strategy

- As an advisor to the Department of Energy and Climate Change you have been charged with devising the strategy for low-carbon living. As a part of that work you have decided to investigate the incentives and barriers that may exist to the use of the carbon credit card.

- Make a list of possible incentives and barriers. Based on your list, what marketing actions could be developed to reduce resistance and encourage acceptance of the carbon credit card?

References

1. Jackson, T. (2009) *Prosperity Without Growth: Economics for a Finite Planet.* Britain in 2010, Economic and Social Research Council (p. 24).

2. Pirages, D.C. and Ehrlich, P.R. (1974) *Ark II: Social Response to Environmental Imperatives,* San Francisco, CA: Freeman.

3. Milbrath, L. (1989) *Envisioning a Sustainable Society,* Albany, NY: State University of New York Press (p. 116).

4. Dunlap, R. and Van Liere, K. (1978) 'The New Environmental Paradigm – a Proposed Measuring Instrument and Preliminary Results', *Journal of Environmental Education* 9: 10–19.

5. Hawken, P., Lovins, A. and Lovins, H. (1999) *Natural Capitalism: Creating the Next Industrial Revolution,* Earthscan, London, www.natcap.org

6. Greenfield, O., Narberhaus, M., Salazar, C., Elkington, J., Beloe, S. and Fennell, S. (2007) *One Planet Business: Creating Value Within Planetary Limits,* Godalming: World Wildlife Fund.

7. HM Government *Securing the Future: Delivering UK Sustainable Development Strategy,* www.defra.gov.uk/sustainable/government (p. 3).

8. McConnell, D. (2009) 'We Need to be Encouraged to Spend our way out of Recession', *The Independent,* 5 April, www.independent.ie/opinion/analysis/we-need-to-be-encouraged-to-spend-our-way-out-of-recession-1698842.html

9. Chiarelli, N. (2008) *Shades of Green Environment, Ethics & Causes in a Downturn,* GfK Roper Consulting Presentation at Organic Exchange, Porto, October.

10. Kilbourne, W., McDonagh, P. and Prothero, A. (1997) 'Sustainable Consumption and the Quality of Life: a Macromarketing Challenge to the Dominant Social Paradigm', *Journal of Macromarketing* 17(4): 4–24.

11. Sustainable Development Commission (SDC) (2009) *Breakthroughs for the Twenty-first Century,* Foreword by Jonathan Porritt, London: SDC.

12. The Future Laboratory (2010) *Harnessing Change: Preparing for Business in the Next Decade,* Report for O$_2$.

13. Wilkinson, R. and Pickett, K. (2009) *The Spirit Level: Why More Equal Societies Almost Always do Better,* London: Allen Lane.

14. Leopold, A. (1949) *A Sand Country Almanac: With Essays on Conservation from Round River,* New York: Oxford University Press.

15. Kortenkamp, K. and Moore, C. (2001) 'Ecocentrism and Anthropocentrism: Moral Reasoning about Ecological Commons Dilemmas', *Journal of Environmental Psychology* 21: 1–12.

16. Dunlap, R.E., Van Liere, K.D., Mertig, A.G. and Jones, R.E. (2000) 'Measuring Endorsement of the New Ecological Paradigm: A revised NEP scale', *Journal of Social Issues* 56: 425–442.

17. Gleick, P., Cooley, H., Cohen, M., Morikawa, M., Morrison, J. and Palaniappan, M. (2009) *The World's Water 2008–2009: The Biennial Report on Freshwater Resources,* Washington, DC: Island Press.

18. Chapagain, A.K. and Orr, S. (2008) *UK Water Footprint: The Impact of the UK's Food and Fibre Consumption on Global Water Resources,* Godalming: WWF-UK.

19. Vale, B. and Vale, R. (2009) *Time to Eat the Dog? The Real Guide to Sustainable Living,* London: Thames and Hudson.

20. Ravilious, K. (2009) 'How Green is Your Pet?', *New Scientist* 2731, 23 October.

21. Hawken, P., Lovins, A. and Lovins, L. (1999) *Natural Capitalism: Creating the Next Industrial Revolution*, London: Earthscan, www.natcap.org (p. 4).

22. New Zealand Government (2008) *Carbon Emissions Trading Scheme,* www.climatechange.govt.nz/emissions-trading-scheme/ets-diagram

23. Starmer-Smith, C. (2009) *Green Tour Operator Abandons Carbon Offsetting,* Responsibletravel.com, www.responsibletravel.com; Responsible travel.com (2009) *Carbon Caution and Advice – Flying and the Responsible Traveller,* www.responsibletravel.com/Copy/Copy101331.htm; Responsible travel.com (2009) Responsible travel.com becomes the first travel agent to offer a carbon comparison flight search, Media release, 1 December, www.responsibletravel.com/Copy/Copy101492.htm; *The Telegraph* 6 October 2009; *The Economist* (2009) 'No More Carbon Offsetting, 15 October, www.economist.com/blogs/gulliver/2009/10/no_more_carbon_offsetting.

24. Anderson, K. (2009) 'The 10:10 Campaign Offers more than Emissions Reductions', *The Guardian,* 3 September

25. Kappeler, M. (2009) 'Professor Kevin Anderson: Point of No Return', *The Independent,* 21 September.

26. United Nations Environment Programme (UNEP) (2005) *Talk the Walk: Advancing Sustainable Lifestyles through Marketing and Communications,* UNEP, www.unglobalcompact.org/docs/news_events/8.1/ttw_fin.pdf

27. Stockholm Environmental Institute (2009) www.sei-international.org/index.php/news-and-media/1204-its-time-for-ecological-sanitation-sei-experts-say

28. See www.german-renewableenergy.com/Renewables/Navigation/Englisch/Biomasse/case-studies,did=210910.html

29. PetroAlgae (2009) www.petroalgae.com/docs/the-future-of-biofuels-now.pdf

30. Murphy, I. (2009) *GreenEarth Launches New 'Polymer' Wash Process,* American Dry Cleaner, www.americandrycleaner.com/article.cfm?articleID=17928

31. Lee, K. (2000) 'Global Sustainable Development: its Intellectual and Historical Roots', in Lee, K. Holland, A. and McNeill D. (eds) *Global Sustainable Development in the 21st century,* Edinburgh: Edinburgh University Press, 31–47.

32. Stibbe, A. (2009) Keynote address at the conference *The Language of Sustainability: Shouting but not Being Heard,* 27 April, the Institution for Environmental Sciences, London.

33. Hopwood, B., Mellor, M. and O'Brien, G. (2005) 'Sustainable Development: Mapping Different Approaches', *Sustainable Development* 13: 38–52.

34. Daly, H. (1991) *Steady-state Economics,* 2nd ed., Washington, DC: Island Press.

35. The Optimum Population Trust (2010) www.optimumpopulation.org

36. Leake, J. and Montague, B. (2009) 'UK Population must Fall to 30m, Says Porritt', *The Sunday Times,* 22 March.

37. Porritt, J. (2009) *A Sustainable Population,* posted by Jonathon Porritt on 4 March, www.jonathonporritt.com/pages/2009/03/a_sustainable_population.html

38. PopOffsets (2010) www.popoffsets.com.

39. Tanaka, I. (2000) *Ryohin Keikaku Co. Ltd. 2000 Corporate Data,* http://ryohin-keikaku.jp/eng/corporate/pdf/2000_e.pdf.

40. *Fair Trade News* (2006) *MUJI (Ryohin Keikaku Company Ltd) Will Jump into Fairtrade Market,* 6 October, www.fairtrade-net.org/e/modules/news1/article.php?storyid=9; *Environment and Planning* 39: 555–569; Muji, www.muji.com; Muji (2010) *Environmental Activities,* http://ryohin-keikaku.jp/eng/csr/; Ryohin Keikaku Company Limited (2000) *Corporate Data,* http://ryohin-keikaku.jp/eng/corporate/pdf/2000_e.pdf; Ryohin Keikaku Company Limited (2009) *Corporate Data,* http://ryohin-keikaku.jp/eng/corporate/pdf/2009_e.pdf.

41. Allianz AG (2006) *Knowledge Kit: Climate and Emissions Trading,* Allianz AG, http://knowledge.allianz.com/nopi_downloads/downloads/emissions_trading.pdf

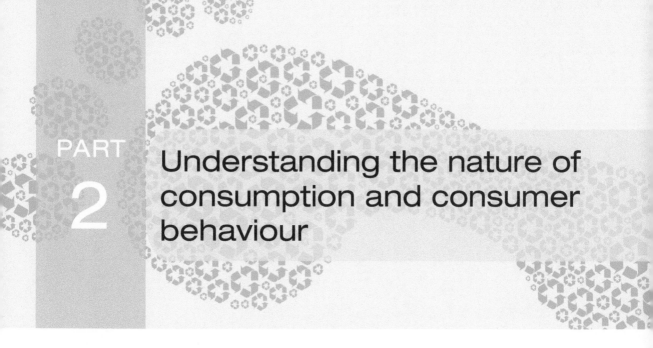

Understanding the nature of consumption and consumer behaviour

3 Understanding attitudes towards consumption and sustainability

> Sustainability, as a societal goal, includes all producers and consumers, willing or not, and requires a change in virtually everyone's behaviour.[1]
>
> *Ynte Van dam and Paul Apledoorn*

Chapter objectives

After studying this chapter you should be able to:

1 Understand the nature of consumption in relation to sustainability.

2 Identify and evaluate the different forms of consumption behaviour and their impact on sustainability.

3 Explore the underlying attitudes of consumers towards sustainable consumption.

4 Examine the reasons behind the contradictions in attitudes and behaviour of consumers considering sustainable purchases.

Dilemma part 1:   Is there a sustainability crunch?

Who said recession was a bad thing – employers, employees, the unemployed, the government . . . bankers? There seems to be universal consensus that the recession which has resulted from the credit crunch is a bad thing but there does not seem to be the same amount of agreement regarding its effect on sustainable consumption patterns. The assumption that many sustainable products are more expensive than their non-sustainable equivalents, and are therefore cut from the shopping list, is a common one, but others argue a different case. Nevertheless, just as the sustainability agenda was beginning to gain ground the public's attention has been sidetracked by a failing world economy.

Discuss the following:

1. To what extent has the global economic crisis resulting from the credit crunch favourably or adversely affected sustainable consumer behaviour and sustainable consumption? Who are the winners and losers?

Understanding attitudes towards consumption and sustainability

We need to know more about the attitudes that lie behind the act of consumption itself and how these attitudes may be affected by the need to become more sustainable. We have had a long relationship with consumption, it is complex and deep-rooted in the behaviour of society but this relationship needs to be understood if marketers are to be able to guide consumers to a more sustainable lifestyle.

For a long time researchers were stuck on only one type of sustainable consumer – the green consumer. But the new challenge facing marketers is not how to access the sustainable green niche. The already sustainably motivated consumer is not the only one marketers should be seeking, as this would continue the mistakes of the green marketers of the 1980s and 1990s, and result in the same disappointment that followed the failure of the green revolution.[2] The green marketer had sought only to target the green consumer as a sub-segment of the total consumer base via the use of product substitution, offering a limited selection of green alternatives for products such as toilet paper, household cleaners, etc. Therefore marketers had envisioned the green consumer as a specialist niche with particular motivations that made them stand out from the rest, by appearing to behave differently. Yet, despite this initial niche attractiveness, it did not result in a mass green consumer movement and the small but committed ethical segment stagnated, while the mainstream markets were largely unaffected by things green and ethical.[3]

The new challenge for marketers is to target everyone. The sustainable consumer, which marketers should be seeking, is no longer a niche market; the new sustainable consumer has no specific profile, belongs to no particular socio-economic grouping and portrays no single characteristic psychographic profile because, by necessity, the market for sustainability is the whole market and therefore the consumer for sustainability . . . is everyone.

Nevertheless, there exists a number of difficulties for the marketer, not least the fact that the consumer's relationship with the concept of sustainability is fraught with misunderstandings and misperceptions. Also, sustainability currently competes with non-sustainable, conventional attitudes, values and practice, and many consumers do not want to be sustainable at all. Such contradictory attitudes towards sustainability have led to equally contradictory behaviour from the consumer and even the act of consumption itself is at odds with sustainability.

In this chapter the nature of sustainable consumption is explored including the reasons behind consumers' ambivalent and sometimes contradictory attitudes and behaviour when considering sustainable purchases.

First, the act of consumption itself is examined; the motivations behind consumption affect our ability to become more sustainable and may be used to work for or against the installation of sustainable consumption habits. Second, attitudes towards sustainability are mixed and understanding the reasons for favourable and unfavourable feelings is essential if marketers are to encourage the adoption of sustainable consumer behaviour. Four key factors emerge as influencers of sustainable behaviour: reciprocity, solidarity, credibility and sacrifice. Finally a closer study of attitudes reveals a changing mindset among consumers, as sustainable attributes and benefits compete more effectively with conventional ones and consumers begin to reassess their decision-making criteria and behaviour as their willingness to change habits increases.

The nature of consumption

According to the Oslo Symposium on Sustainable Consumption, sustainable consumption is 'the use of goods and services that respond to basic needs and bring a better quality of life, while minimizing the use of natural resources, toxic materials and emissions of waste and pollutants over the life cycle, so as not to jeopardize the needs of future generations'.[4] In order to encourage more sustainable forms of consumption it is necessary to understand the nature of consumption and the motivations that exist behind it, particularly if the marketer is going to fully explain the different levels of willingness and reluctance of the consumer to engage in sustainable consumption.

Consumption can be classified under different categories such as: rational, habitual, socio-psychological, hedonistic, self-identity, symbolic and communication-based.[5] These aspects of consumption and how they might relate to sustainable consumption are now discussed in more detail.

Rational consumption

In rational consumption it is assumed that the sustainably motivated consumer makes purchases as a result of going through a logical decision-making process based on reason, having evaluated the product against both conventional and sustainable criteria. It is presumed, therefore, that the importance and significance of sustainable credentials will influence the purchase decision-making process and that sustainable consumption results from people being well-informed.

This is an appealing type of consumption for the sustainable marketer as it suggests that consumer behaviour can always be influenced by marketing efforts that are grounded in logic and provide complete information for the cognitive evaluation of the product choices available. However, it is doubtful that the actions of individual rational consumers, influenced by rational and scientific data, will be enough to establish sustainable consumption as the norm.[6] Indeed, while the profile of 'the rational, welfare-maximising, perfectly informed *homo economicus*'[7] provides a convenient explanation of consumer behaviour, it is, in fact, an over-simplification of a much more complex situation. It has also been argued that rational behaviour would not necessarily result in sustainable consumption – in fact quite the opposite – as rational decision makers would be more inclined to favour their own short-term personal interest over other considerations such as long-term societal sustainability.

Habitual consumption

The rational, constant and consistent evaluation of products before purchase does not explain the majority of consumer behaviour. Routines and habits account for many purchase decisions – it is illogical to think consumers would deliberate every purchase, particularly for more mundane products. We buy the brands we normally buy: they are old friends we see every time we go to the stores and we even instinctively know where they are placed – the aisle, the section, the shelf height. Stores often rearrange sections of their floor space in order to break the habits of their consumers, forcing them to view new products they would not normally pay any attention to as they seek out their routine purchases.

The general disinterest that results from habitual consumption is responsible for consumers not bothering to adopt more sustainable routines such as buying more local food produce or reducing meat consumption.[8] The slogan of the supermarket chain Sainsbury's, *Try Something New Today*, is a clear attempt to break consumer habit and inertia. It is not only the difficulty of establishing different, regular sustainable shopping routines facing the marketer. The prospect of single, one-off sustainable changes can also fall victim to inertia. For example, changing banks in order to use an ethical financial services provider or installing a new, more efficient water heater may seem to require more effort than they are tangibly worth to the consumer.

The Elaboration Likelihood model suggests that for habitual types of purchase the ability, motivation and opportunity of the consumer to gather and process information is low and therefore consumers rely on simple cues to make their decisions.[9] This process is referred to as heuristic evaluation – when brand attitudes are inferred from a single brand attribute because consumers

Table 3.1 Heuristic cues for sustainability

	Cue	Heuristic
Packaging	Green colours on packaging	If it uses green colours it is more environmentally friendly
Message	The use of the prefix eco	If it says eco it is more environmentally friendly
Endorsement	Jamie Oliver – famous TV chef	If Jamie endorses it, it must be healthy

are unwilling for whatever reasons to compare all brands available to them on all relevant attributes. Sustainable businesses seeking to turn their products into routine purchases are making use of heuristic cues to attract the habitual, pro-sustainability consumer, as can be seen in Table 3.1.

Sociological consumption

Shopping is seen to fulfil specific social and cultural needs. From this perspective consumption is embedded in the socio-cultural fabric of society with a particular role to play in the lives of individual consumers and in consumer groups. Sociological consumption implies that people engage in consumption for the sake of consumption as a means of social engagement with family, friends and peers, which is a phenomenon likely to work against long-term sustainability, if our goal is to consume less. It would therefore take a huge cultural change to move society as a whole towards more sustainable consumption, although this is not ruled out by those who feel marketing can make a positive contribution to such a change by making consumers 'feel culturally aligned and connected' to the issues of sustainability.[10] Establishing sustainable consumption as the new social norm would be the desirable result of such a cultural change.

Hedonistic consumption

Pleasure is sometimes derived from the very act of shopping itself. The use of goods and services or merely their possession is how some consumers derive satisfaction and personal gratification. If consumers are addicted to consumption because of the enjoyment they derive from the act of shopping itself and the accumulation of material possessions, it is clear that this facet of consumption also works against sustainable principles.

Self-identity consumption

'I shop therefore I am' – a phrase used in the artwork of artist Barbara Kruger in 1987 and repeated more recently by Selfridges department store in one of its sales campaigns clearly suggests that consumption is a significant part of our behaviour for establishing and reaffirming our identity. The problem of trying to link sustainability to self-identity in order to encourage sustainable consumption habits results from the perceived depositioning of sustainable behaviour as something less aspirational than conventional consumption. While conventional consumption is viewed as 'a sacred process to be celebrated, a cornerstone in the construction of identity', the sustainable practice of the disposal of waste is perceived to be something 'far more secular and mundane'.[11] What is required is access to more aspirational role models based on positive associations with sustainable lifestyles to provide more desirable self-identities.

Consumption as communication

With clear links to building self-identity, consumption can be used as a means of communication with others. For example, the purchase of particular items of fashion by teenagers may be made to establish social relationships and gain access, or demonstrate allegiance to particular social groups. Self-identity, personal taste, status and personality may all be expressed and communicated to others through a demonstration of consumption. The symbolic value of goods is therefore significant. Goods are a significant representation of personal and cultural meaning and the importance they represent for the consumer cannot be underestimated. The communication of sustainable behaviour through consumption can already be seen in the high street. The number of recyclable jute shopping bags being used instead of plastic bags is on the increase and a signal to others to do the same. The value of such highly visible sustainable behaviour in favourably influencing the behaviour of others is important. For example, attention has been drawn to the visual influence of kerbside recycling containers in establishing recycling norms of behaviour for the community, as individuals feel the need to conform to the values and practice of their recycling neighbours.[12]

The circle of consumption

With a world economy based on continuous economic growth, consumption and its enjoyment have become a way of life, an accepted part of our culture, and as such we consume whenever we can to fulfil deep-seated psychological needs to obtain pleasure and happiness. Although many material goods are only practical tools that make life easier, as signs of social identity they perform more important psychological functions such as establishing social standing, sex-role identification or socio-economic status. Alternatively, material goods may represent a person's unique qualities and attitudes, and form a record of personal history, events and memories attached to family, friends and significant others. The purchase of goods can also comfort us in times of depression or simply lift our mood when faced with the monotony of routine life or personal misfortune.[13]

However, it is clear that consumption alone does not permanently satisfy many of these psychological needs, so we continue to consume. This situation has been described by French sociologist and philosopher Jean Baudrillard as the point where consumption 'has grasped the whole of life' and that all activity has been condensed into 'the simple activity of perpetual shopping'.[14]

This repetitive, cyclical nature of consumption is evidenced in the pursuit of hedonistic and self-identity benefits, particularly when viewed from the perspective of self-discrepancy theory. Expounded by E. Tory Higgins, professor of psychology and management at Columbia University, USA, self-discrepancy theory proposes that the self can be understood to be composed of three separate domains: the *actual* self, the *ideal* self and the *ought* self.[15] These different perceptions of self could be the result of either of two different standpoints: the person's own personal standpoint or the standpoint of some significant other person such as a family member, partner, friend, etc. It is the interaction between the three selves that reveals a noteworthy relationship between the self and consumption:

- Actual self – the way you are at the present point in time.

- Ideal self – the way you aspire to be.

- Ought self – the way you think you really should be.

The ideal self serves as a motivator or stimulus to pursue and attain a perfect state. While we feel there is a significant discrepancy between the actual and ideal self we will try to reduce or bridge that perceived gap. The ought self has a regulatory function and serves as a reminder of how we ought to be, thus avoiding any excessive reactions when trying to bridge the gap between actual and ideal states. The ought self reminds us of our duties, responsibilities and may help to reduce and alleviate any negative feelings regarding the discrepancy between actual and ideal self.

With regard to the consumption of material goods motivated by bridging the gap between actual and ideal, consumption takes place in order to minimise the perceived gap. However, for many consumers the purchases made to reach this idealised state do not tend to provide any long-lasting satisfaction. Rather, once obtained they lose their idealistic meaning and the real self then continues to aspire to an unobtainable ideal through more consumption.[16] But while consumption does not provide for long-term happiness, it does provide pleasure, even though the pleasure obtained may be ephemeral. Once the material goods have been purchased the pleasure derived from them decreases and so the process of consumption begins again in order to seek more pleasure.

The pursuit of pleasure in itself should not necessarily be criticised, since it is only when this goal is pursued through *continued consumption* that it becomes an obstacle to sustainability. The fact that such pleasures do not produce long-term happiness and a reduction or cessation of consumption is the issue that concerns much of the recent literature on this topic.[17]

In order to achieve change in this type of behaviour, the circle of consumption in pursuit of an idealised happiness needs to be broken. This may mean substituting old ideals for more sustainable ones or enhancing the guiding, compensatory influence of the ought self. An understanding of the role of self and its influence on behaviour has already been used to understand detrimental health-related addictions such as eating disorders and anorexia and may still shed some light on how to deal with an addiction to consumption. As mentioned later in the text, this implies a shift in culture and values from *having more* to *being more* accompanied by the portrayal of more inspiring, aspirational role models, products and services which are sustainable.

This implies this cannot be a one-sided change in consumption patterns on the part of the consumer alone. Businesses have exploited the gap between actual and ideal self in order to motivate consumers to continue purchasing and it is clear that they will now have to change their underlying principles too.

In pursuing growth, businesses have followed a strategy based on the production and consumption of novelty.[18] Consumers have been taught and trained for decades to feel dissatisfied with what they have and effectively have been encouraged and trained to consume more and more frequently. The choice of goods and products available to consumers is ever larger, thus stimulating more consumption. Those same products have shorter and shorter life spans, either as a result of technological advances, changes in style or fashion, or due to their built-in obsolescence through design, materials used or manufacture. In essence, consumers continue to purchase in order to renew their self-identity because they are under pressure to keep up with the pace of change of material goods. If consumers choose not to renew their possession-driven identity regularly they will become isolated from their peers and out-of-date, their identity will be lost. Consumers are actively encouraged to buy a new IPod because they have a new range of colours and a more rounded shape and to buy a new mobile phone to avoid the embarrassment of having to reveal their 'old' one in front of friends. In the sales, posters ominously warn customers not to delay their purchases because *'when it's gone, it's gone'*.

Nowhere is this more apparent than in the fast-fashion sector. The advent of fast fashion was provoked by the ability of producers to shorten lead times between the appearance of a garment on the catwalk and its availability in the high street store. Fuelled by media attention and celebrity worship, this has resulted in encouraging a more intense consumption of fashion. With the shortening of lead times has come the shortening of the lifecycle of fashion, also made possible by the deliberate reduction of quality of the garments. This has increased the frequency of purchase still further and has made fashion appear disposable in the mind of the consumer.

Snapshot: The infectious nature of consumption

It was the 18th-century philosopher Denis Diderot who commented on the infectious and addictive nature of consumption, which became known as the Diderot effect. Diderot's essay, entitled 'Regrets on parting with my old dressing gown',[19] describes how he swapped an old gown for a new one, but when comparing the new garment with his other possessions he realised that they looked in poorer condition and so he started to make a series of purchases to compensate for this, changing old possessions for new ones, ending up dissatisfied and in debt.

Conspicuous consumption was first referred to by economist and sociologist Thorstein Veblen in his 1899 publication entitled *The Theory of the Leisure Class*.[20] Veblen used the term to describe the behaviour of the *nouveau riche*, a new class of rich of the late 19th century; a product of the wealth gained from increasing industrialisation. Their behaviour was characterised by the ostentation of wealth: a desire to demonstrate affluence and social power through the continued purchase of goods and services. The conspicuous use of leisure time and engagement with leisure pursuits are also examples of conspicuous consumption.

In modern society, consumption to distinguish oneself from others continues to be apparent and satisfying these essentially non-material needs of hedonism and status by material means have become the norm. Yet conspicuous consumption is no longer the exclusive reserve of the very rich and it is practised at different levels of socio-economic class through the purchase of goods and services more for their symbolic value of status in front of others than for their utility. Even poorer groups may engage in conspicuous consumption in order to avoid being perceived by others to be poor.

Affluenza – the disease

Affluenza – a combination of the words affluence and influenza – describes an addiction to consumption, fuelled by an unsustainable dependence on economic growth and a desire to attain happiness and self-fulfilment through consumption which can never be achieved.

Critics of the affluenza phenomenon portray its nature in strong terms, describing it as a painful, contagious epidemic that can be socially transmitted from one person to another and results in over-consumption, debt, stress and unhappiness from constantly attempting to consume and accumulate more.[21, 22] Affluenza causes people to place a high value on money, possessions, physical appearance, social status and fame to such an extent that people can no longer distinguish between what they really need and what they want just for the sake of having it.

The Affluenza Exhibition (see photos) is part of an on-going project to discuss, debate and tackle the issues caused by the consumer addiction to consumption.[23]

Source: The Affluenza Exhibition 2009, created and organised by Hege Sæbjørnsen (www.hegesaebjornsen.com) Art direction: Iskra Tsaneva, Design; Chris Clarke

The extent of the problem of affluenza is borne out by a number of studies. Indicators of the relationship between dissatisfaction and increased consumption are evidenced by happiness index studies. Comparisons between happiness indicators and rising gross domestic product (GDP) levels in developed countries in Europe as well as the US and Japan, show that the increasing wealth of nations has not led to an increase in happiness in the population.[24]

Apply it: Advertising and consumption

1. When designing their marketing communications marketers may choose to create messages which appeal to different types of consumption. Such appeals may be hedonistic in nature, particularly when linked to seasonal celebrations and special events. Make a collection of print advertisements that focus on each of the different types of consumption and record them to complete Table 3.2.

   What about more sustainable consumption. Can you find examples of each type of consumption with a sustainable twist?

   Table 3.2   Examples of consumption types in advertising

Consumption type	Example
Rational	
Habitual	
Sociological	
Hedonistic	
Self-identity	
Communication	

Source: Corbis: Borris Roessler/dpa

When attitudes do not match behaviour

When dealing with the female, grey or the family market, marketers do not seem to agonise as much as when they are faced with the market for sustainability. Perhaps their problems stem from the difficulties they experience when trying to define and effectively understand the sustainable market which appears to be both elusive and contradictory. The regular reporting of favourable attitudes towards sustainability issues has not delivered large-scale demand for

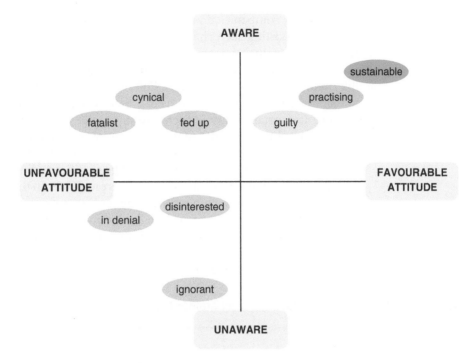

Figure 3.1 Attitudes to sustainability

sustainable products and services from the consumer, and has not resulted in a movement towards a mass market for sustainability. So what is impeding the transfer of the acceptance of sustainability into sustainable behaviour?

Favourable and unfavourable attitudes

Many consumers simply feel that their personal actions, being too small and insignificant, will have no real impact on sustainability issues. Other consumers reveal more complex reasons for their behaviour.

Figure 3.1 compares awareness of sustainability issues against attitudes towards sustainability and shows that the unfavourable attitudes towards sustainability outnumber the favourable attitudes. Inertia, apathy and inactivity result from different levels of awareness and understanding of the issues, as well as varying levels of motivation. Motivation to engage with sustainability is different in comparison with more conventional purchase processes based on a standard exchange of money for benefits, due to four key issues: *reciprocity, solidarity, credibility* and *sacrifice.*

For many potential sustainable consumers there exists the need for reciprocity between consumer and the other parties involved, resulting from the perceived sacrifice or inconvenient changes to lifestyle that may be encountered by the consumer of sustainable products and services. Therefore, the potential consumer is more likely to purchase sustainably if such behaviour is duplicated by the other stakeholders involved; that is, *as long as* other consumers do the same, *as long as* the company demonstrates it is also acting sustainably, *as long as* competing companies do the same, *as long as* the government is seen to be actively supporting such changes and so on. This requirement for reciprocity, for mutual sustainable behaviour between parties, also results from the need of potential consumers to see that they are not acting alone in exchange for invisible, intangible rewards for society. Potential consumers for sustainability need to feel mutual solidarity, as, with this, their actions gain credibility and their sacrifice for sustainability is therefore not made in vain. Sacrifice may seem a strong word but even the mere exchange of money for goods in a conventional purchase situation involves 'sacrifice to acquire something we desire'.[25] Sustainable sacrifices, however small, will be significant, since they are not necessarily an addition to the bundle of benefits on offer with the product and may involve an increase in price, a reduction in performance, a decrease in image or status, a change in behaviour or even less frequent consumption.

The characteristics of each of the consumer unfavourable attitude types are described in Table 3.3 but they only partially explain the phenomenon of non-engagement with sustainability.

Table 3.3   Unfavourable attitudes to sustainability

Unfavourable attitudes	Characteristics
Ignorant	The ignorant lack sufficient knowledge of the issues and often belong to lower socio-economic groups D and E
Fatalist	The fatalists see no point in doing anything because they feel it is either too late to influence anything or they feel it will not affect their lives long enough before they die. The fatalists may include the elderly
In denial	Those in denial are not convinced by the evidence provided, particularly when contrasting views are expressed regarding sustainable issues, such as by Channel 4's programme 'The Great Global Warming Swindle', which claimed that climate change was not due to human activity. The programme was even cited by Defra as a research limitation in its report on sustainable energy consumption in the home, stating that for some respondents the documentary legitimised their reluctance to change and allowed them to avoid taking any responsibility for climate problems[26]
Cynical	The cynical struggle to link their personal activities to sustainable concerns and are sceptical that their contribution will make a difference. They may mistrust companies and think companies use sustainability as an opportunity to position themselves more favourably against the competition or merely to charge higher prices
Disinterested	The disinterested are just not interested, and feel it has nothing to do with them just as some of the participants in the Channel 4 programme 'Dumped', which had people living off a landfill site and scavenging in the rubbish for items to improve their quality of life during their stay (see 'Snapshot: Dumped'). Governed by self-interest, they are more selfish and often feel too busy to care; they are fickle and may be easily distracted by other issues they feel are more pressing and relevant to them, such as the recession and the credit crunch, for example
Fed-up	The fed-up view sustainability as a fad that will eventually go away after having heard too much about it in the media and from companies

Table 3.4 Favourable attitudes to sustainability

Favourable attitudes	Characteristics
Guilty	The guilty are aware of sustainability issues and engage in sustainable consumption from time to time but will not do this consistently. They may consume sustainably for some specific matters with an obvious gain, such as saving money by reducing energy consumption. Drifting in and out of sustainable practice and ignoring those issues that require too much sacrifice, they feel guilty, but not guilty enough to become more sustainable
Practising	The practising have more knowledge and understanding than the previous group, and consume sustainably when they can. They know they have more to learn and are open to more ways to adopt a sustainable lifestyle, recognising that they could improve their performance
Sustainable	The sustainable are those who have embraced sustainability completely and enthusiastically. They are likely to be aware of all three sustainability concerns – environmental, social and economic – and feel they are doing as much as they can to be sustainable

Table 3.4 shows a range of more favourable attitudes towards sustainability that exist among the general public.

A conflict of interests

The contradictions between pro-sustainable attitudes and non-sustainable behaviour have never been more efficiently expressed than by the 30:3 ratio – when it was found that while 30 percent of people expressed concern for sustainability issues only 3 percent actually modified aspects of their consumption behaviour.[27] These contradictions come from the natural antagonism between recognising collective responsibilities for sustainability, the need for change to provide collective solutions and the individuals' desire to protect their own self-interest. Thus, public concern in general terms for economic, social and environmental sustainability may be increasing but, at the same time, on an individual basis each single consumer demonstrates an aversion to specific remedies that require behavioural change on their part, especially those that entail personal impacts, effects and consequences for their lifestyle.[28]

Individuals therefore appear to protect what they regard as their personal rights and freedoms to consume in the way they want and the feeling of entitlement to enjoy choice and variety without interference from government or other stakeholders is strong enough to prevent the widespread adoption of sustainable behaviours. Essentially dependent on the level of compromise the individual wishes to engage in, the consumer weighs up the possible favourable outcomes of sustainable behaviour and trades them off against the sacrifices required as a result.

Snapshot: Dumped

When the 11 contestants of the UK's Channel 4's programme 'Dumped', shown in 2007, were told they would participate in an ecological challenge for a share of £20,000, most of them assumed they were going abroad, certainly not thinking for one moment they would end up on a local rubbish tip.

Source: Pearson Education Ltd

However, both contestants and audience showed some reluctance to embrace the challenge. The final episode of the programme was watched by just 1.9 million people an 8 percent share, while BBC1's 'Traffic Cops' gained a 25 percent share with 5.5 million viewers.

One contestant left after just three days, saying the exercise had taught him nothing. This participant owned four cars, went regularly on long-haul flights and spent £50 a week on socks and underwear rather than washing them. He said he would not change his lifestyle, apart from donating his old underwear to the Third World and flew to Las Vegas for a holiday. Channel 4 head Julian Bellamy did not suggest it was the programme concept itself or its ecological theme that led to reduced viewing figures, but the lack of human narrative and that it was too similar to other reality TV shows.

Table 3.5 Competing product attributes

Sustainable	Conventional
Ethical	Price
Socially responsible	Brand
Eco-performance/friendly	Availability
Cost-effectiveness	Superior performance
Recyclable/recycled	Quality
Pollution-free	Convenience of use
Healthy	Image
Safe/harmless	Style
Functional	Design
Long lasting/durable/reusable	Disposable

Trade-offs and self-interest

Table 3.5 shows that there are both sustainable and conventional (although not necessarily both) attributes competing for salience when consumers are contemplating a purchase. The attributes and associated benefits of conventional products – cost, convenience and quality – compete for importance with sustainable benefits in the mind of the consumer. While acknowledged as key obstacles from the perspective of the consumer, issues regarding cost, convenience and quality have also been described as 'prevalent myths' in the public consciousness in studies on sustainable behaviour.[29]

It matters little whether the perception of particular sustainable products is myth or reality, it is the opinion of the consumer that counts. Early versions of some green products such as lighting and cleaning products performed badly and that perception has stayed with consumers. Many sustainable products have been priced higher than their conventional counterparts, in some cases reflecting the internalising of traditionally external socio-environmental costs and in others to establish and benefit from a premium priced niche market.[30] Whatever the case, once perceived as expensive alternatives, sustainable products will find it difficult to become mainstream.

Convenience attributes also remain a sticking point for many sustainable products and actions. Too much marketing on the sustainable benefits for humanity and not enough on persuading people to accept the sacrifice and inconvenience involved will slow or prevent the voluntary acceptance of many products – getting parents to give up disposable nappies for washable, reusable ones being a good example. For the consumer, a process of trade-off occurs while judging products on the two competing sets of attributes – sustainable attributes against conventional ones. Each consumer will develop his/her own personal hierarchy of needs and motivations to be matched to a selection of pertinent attributes. Many mainstream consumers will be more influenced by concerns related to conventional attributes such as price and brand if they have issues of familiarity, trust and reliability with regard to their purchases.

Other consumers may be swayed by sustainable attributes without having any clear convictions towards sustainability. In this way the sustainable behaviour of some has been described as a 'by-product' of particular lifestyle choices focused more on health, safety and nutrition.[31] Recent research points to the way in which sustainability is naturally occurring among older generations, particularly in times of recession. These generations, who were brought up to live frugally and not waste resources of any kind whether energy, food or water, value thrift and economy even though they are not convinced by contemporary arguments regarding sustainability.[32]

However, it would appear that for many consumers the extent to which they engage with sustainability, or not, is dictated by the influence of their own self-interest. Therefore, contradictions naturally arise from the intervention of self-interest generated by the clash between sustainable sacrifice and non-sustainable self-interest. In research conducted among teenagers in 2008 by the National Centre for Research Methods, it was found that while most respondents thought they should be engaging in more sustainable behaviour, only a minority of teenagers were talking to their families about doing so. The most common reason for such inaction was a reluctance to change lifestyle patterns.[33]

Contradictions and lack of trust

Cynicism and mistrust also play a role in the failure to change behaviour. The combination of a strong feeling of individual personal rights with a healthy mistrust of both business and government makes for a significant barrier to engagement with sustainability. It is sufficient for people to feel that they are being forced into doing something for them to rebel against it, for the simple reason that they feel very strongly that they have the right to continue as they are.

Mistrust of business is difficult to counteract, particularly due to the worldwide discrediting of the banking system since 2008. Typically, marketing communications aimed at regaining consumer trust are often not believed, particularly when those communications highlight contradictory actions. For example, while Lloyds TSB was running its *most trusted* bank campaign in the UK at the beginning of 2009, the media was commenting on the bank's record $350 million fine from the US government for illegal financial dealing. Public scepticism of the sustainable credentials of business seems to continue at the same pace as businesses attempt to communicate with their consumers on environmental claims. The Advertising Standards Authority has registered record numbers of complaints in recent years regarding misleading green claims[34] and the term 'greenwash' – to over-claim or give misleading green credentials – has already entered the marketer's and the public's vocabulary.

Despite mistrust, the public still look to both business and government for information, guidance and sustainable solutions, although both of these parties have much progress to make before they succeed in convincing consumers. Fiscal intervention in the form of green taxes is hardly likely to be popular with the general population and such proposals by government in the UK have been branded as *stealth taxes* by the opposition. This has made it more difficult for government to change consumer behaviour through raising taxes, although reducing tax on more sustainable options such as cars that pollute less can be perceived positively and acted upon by the public. Nevertheless, the role of government in moving towards sustainability will be fraught with difficulty. In the UK alone more than one-third of the electorate thinks that neither of the two main parties can be trusted to deal with the issue of climate change effectively.[35]

Both obstacles to change and agents of change, the lack of public trust in businesses and governments will remain for as long as they fail to provide consistency, honesty and sincerity between message and actions. For example, the UK government's Act on CO_2 campaign runs alongside its support for the expansion of airports, with the consequent increase in air traffic pollution. At the same time Northern Ireland's environment minister actually tried to ban the Act on CO_2 television campaign in 2009, branding it as 'insidious propaganda' and 'patent nonsense', leaving the public perplexed and political parties and pro-environmental groups calling for his resignation.[36]

It is clear that positive attitudes towards sustainability are fraught with contradictions and consumers can appear to be ambivalent in their opinions and practice. Certainly the marketer must recognise that the pro-sustainable attitudes and behaviour of the general public are quite fragile, easily influenced and swayed by any number of factors, and that they need to be nurtured if sustainable consumption is going to enter the mainstream.

The risk of sustainability

From the consumers' perspective many of their purchases involve risk. The risk may be financial 'Is it worth the money and can I afford it?' or the risk may be related to performance 'Will this product give me the same results as the previous one I bought?' If consumers have perceived different types of risk related to their purchase up till now, then the added consideration of sustainability issues can only increase their awareness of risk. Research into risk has revealed six types which may affect the consumer and the purchase decision-making process[37, 38, 39] which are presented in Table 3.6 and applied to the context of sustainable purchase.

The type and level of perceived risk will vary from consumer to consumer depending on a series of conditions such as level of experience of the purchaser, the amount of research required prior to purchase or the amount of time available to make the decision. However, what is clear is that the perception of

Table 3.6   Perceived risks of sustainable purchase

Type of perceived risk	Perception of risk from sustainability issues
Financial	Will the extra cost incurred from purchasing sustainable products represent value for money or save me money over time? Will others benefit from me paying a higher price? e.g. Fairtrade products, loft insulation products
Performance	Will the sustainable product still provide the same quality and benefits as the non-sustainable alternative? e.g. environmentally friendly household cleaning products
Physical	Will the sustainable alternative be just as safe for me to use as the non-sustainable alternative? e.g. the mercury level in a compact fluorescent lamp
Social	Will those people who are important to me be impressed by my purchasing sustainable products? e.g. solar panels
Ego	Will I feel better about myself by making sustainable purchases? e.g. ethically produced clothing
Time	Will I find the sustainable option convenient? Will it take me more time than I expect to use it or to receive the benefits? e.g. recycling household rubbish, composting vegetable leftovers for use in the garden

risk will not necessarily diminish after purchase in the context of sustainability. It is precisely because many sustainably motivated purchases depend on credence or because certain benefits take a considerable amount of time to become apparent (such as a reduction in energy bills over a year after insulation) that the perceived level of risk may last long after purchase and extend cognitive dissonance and the post-purchase evaluation period considerably.

The challenge for the marketer will be to guide the consumer through the whole of the purchase decision-making process alleviating at each stage the different types of perceived risk by providing the right information and support at each of the crucial times and maintaining contact with the consumer deep into the post-purchase period.

Apply it: Reducing risk

1. Find examples of how marketers are managing the six different types of risks to prospective consumers in order to dispel their potential misgiving about making sustainable purchases.

Researching sustainability: Focus group

Marketing focus groups have become so popular in marketing research that it is difficult to proceed with marketing actions without the benefit of their insights.[40] For the UK Association of Qualitative Market Research Practitioners, they are the most commonly employed research technique in market research and therefore all prospective marketers should be acquainted with their use.[41] Because they allow for in-depth discussion between participants, focus groups are ideally suited for problems that involve clarification of perspective, the revealing of attitudes and the explanation of behaviours.

Carry out the focus group as suggested below, ideally with a group of people who are not involved with this subject as their opinions will not have been influenced by studying this material.

Task

In order to gain an insight into opinions and attitudes towards sustainability set up and carry out a focus group activity so a group of four to six people can discuss their attitudes and behaviour towards the subject.

Discussion should focus on the following three question areas, as shown in Figure 3.2:

1. What do you consider are the main global issues affecting sustainability?

2. What do you consider are your main local issues affecting sustainability?

3. What actions do you take towards becoming more sustainable?

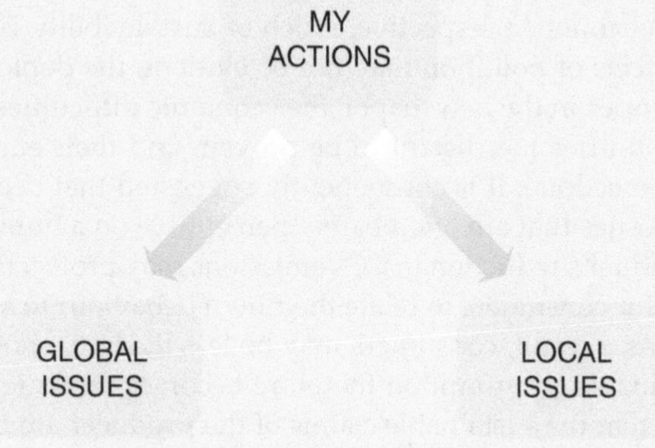

MY
ACTIONS

GLOBAL
ISSUES

LOCAL
ISSUES

Figure 3.2   Global versus local sustainability issues

Getting started

Visit the website that accompanies this book to get more ideas on how to organise your focus group. Record and summarise your results so they can be discussed in class using the questions below to guide you.

1. What do you learn about the participants' general attitudes towards sustainability?
2. What is revealed when participants compare global and local issues?
3. To what extent do the participants' actions reveal their understanding of sustainability?
4. Do participants see that global and local issues and their actions are all linked?
5. What are the implications of your findings for professionals involved in sustainable marketing?

A citizen's act of faith

Another significant facet of sustainable behaviour is that sustainable purchases tend to exhibit the qualities of credence goods.[42] Credence is a term typically applied to services. The intangible nature of services means that consumers have little evidence available to them upon which to make judgements about product quality, either prior to or even after purchase. In the case of dental services, for example, the consumer must trust the dentist regarding the need for the suggested treatment as well as how it should be administered. In the same way sustainable purchases are essentially based on credence because generally those things that make the product *sustainable* (recycled material, recyclable components, equitable treatment of supply chain members, etc.) are essentially hidden from consumers' view or at least very difficult to evaluate. In fact, from the consumers' perspective, much of sustainability is based on the invisible – the effects of pollution may not be evident, the depletion of natural resources just stories in the newspaper, the economic difficulties of suppliers in developing countries too distant to be proven, and their employees' working conditions anecdotal. It is consequently suggested that because sustainability deals with issues that are often barely perceptible on a human scale (such as how an individual's reduction in CO_2 emissions may protect the polar ice caps) it is difficult for consumers to relate their own behaviour to any tangible positive benefits. As a result, consumers may be less likely to choose a sustainable route.[43] Sustainable consumption therefore becomes an issue of trust, followed in the belief that the sustainable claims of the producer are truthful and accurate and the purchase itself beneficial for all stakeholders.

Thus sustainable consumption is transformed into an act of faith by consumers, no longer labelled as such, but referred to as *citizens* to mark their contribution to society through sustainable behaviour.[44] Current consumer behaviour is neither completely sustainable nor completely unsustainable; rather it is a mixture of behaviours resulting from different levels of acceptance, understanding and conviction regarding sustainability. A comparison of *old* and possible *new*,

Table 3.7 Consumer versus citizen attitudes, behaviours and contradictions

Old non-sustainable consumer	Emerging sustainable citizen
No/little inclination towards sustainability	Tendency to exaggerate sustainable orientation Engages less with sustainability despite many declarations in favour
Influenced by one-off CSR activity	Desirous of a genuine long-term commitment to sustainability
Influenced by marketing communications and CSR-driven public relations (PR)	Suspicious of CSR claims and sustainable credentials Unable to judge sustainable claims
Expected to make rational decisions based mainly on price, quality, value for money or emotional decisions based on brand, image, etc.	Expected to make rational decisions based mainly on ethics, social responsibility, environmental claims Sustainable goods have perceived loss of quality, status and image
Wants to make own independent decisions	Expects to make retailer-guided choices Perceived loss of autonomy of decision making and practice resulting from legislation
Received few sustainable messages	Receives many sustainable messages
Buys non-credence goods	Buys credence goods
Needs no specialist knowledge beyond the product itself	Needs specialist knowledge beyond the product, ability to understand CO_2 measurements, evaluate social responsibility claims
Believes a single action can make a difference	No longer believes a single action can make a difference
Wants best price	Often unwilling to pay a higher (although ethical) price
Driven by self-interest	Driven by societal interest, giving things up, sacrifice, lifestyle changes Self-interest still gets in the way particularly for economic reasons

emerging behaviours reveals the extent of change that is implied, as the transition from consumer to citizen starts to impact on society. But the comparison also reveals the numerous contradictions and misperceptions that remain, as can be seen in Table 3.7.

Professional practice: Report back

The head of marketing research at Tesco has asked you to prepare a short report on the current trends in green and ethical household expenditure, with a particular emphasis on how the recent economic downturn may have affected trends. You have come across the information in Table 3.8, which you have decided to use to help organise your ideas – write the report in 600 words.

▶

Table 3.8   The greening of the UK household expenditure

	2006	2002	Now? In your country?
Green mortgages	£16	£1	
Insulation	£10	£9	
Renewable energy	£6	£0	
Energy efficiency	£132	£44	
Sustainable household products	£81	£65	
Food and drink	£190	£109	

Source: Adapted from the Co-operative Bank[45]

Not sure where to start . . . ? Go to the 'Getting started' section following.

Getting started

1. The Cooperative Bank Ethical Consumerism Reports are excellent resources, as are Mintel reports.

Summary

There are numerous motivations behind consumption and the marketer needs to understand all of the possible guises in order to steer consumption towards sustainability. While sustainable consumption seems to be a contradiction in terms, once the nature of consumption is understood it is possible to re-educate, guide and steer the consumer to behave more sustainably.

In order to be able to modify consumer behaviour in this way it is essential that the attitudes and perceptions of consumers with regard to sustainability are understood. From the consumers' perspective sustainability is often difficult to understand and associated with factors that demotivate its adoption such as sacrifice, inconvenience, higher prices and poorer quality.

Such misperceptions have resulted in a lack of trust on the part of the consumer. The decision-making process has become more complex and entails greater perceived risk as sustainable attributes and benefits compete with conventional ones in the mind of the consumer while they weigh up and trade off opposing product features.

The emerging sustainable citizens exhibit different characteristics to conventional consumers as they gradually learn more about sustainability. With increasing experience their consumption behaviour changes as they begin to adopt more sustainable habits, although contradictions in their behaviour continue to make their conversion to sustainability incomplete and a wholesale adoption of sustainable consumer behaviour will not be straightforward.

Case study: 360 Vodka

As the name suggests, 360 Vodka strives to be sustainable from whatever angle you look at it all 360 degrees. The brand describes itself as the first eco-friendly premium vodka, a vodka with

a 'green state of mind' and its producer, the Earth Friendly Distilling Company, is driven by its own eco-awareness and the desire to behave responsibly. Its sustainable philosophy permeates all aspects of the business and is captured in its *Blend in with nature* campaign.

Eco-product and eco-production

- Made from locally grown grain to cut down carbon in the supply chain.
- State-of-the-art distilling equipment reduces the use of fuel in the distilling process by 21 percent in comparison with standard methods and by 200 percent in comparison with traditional pot distilling.
- The distillery captures the CO_2 it produces, has reduced its sulphur dioxide emissions by 99.7 percent and its dust particle emissions by 50 percent.

Recycled and recycling

- Industry-leading 85 percent recycled glass bottle.
- Close the loop – this campaign encourages consumers to return the characteristic retro swing top of the bottle in a pre-paid envelope attached to every bottle. Not only can the company save on resources by reusing the bottle tops on future products but it also donates $1 for each one received to environmental causes (as is a proportion of each bottle sold).

Source: McCormick Distilling

▶

- All marketing materials are printed on 100 percent recycled paper, the billboards are made from biodegradable vinyl and the website is powered by renewable energy.
- Additionally, an on-site recycling cooperative with a drop-off centre was set up to support employees' home recycling efforts.
- Every effort is made to make sure that paper and printing used by 360 Vodka is ecologically friendly and the company uses an eco-paper specialist, New Leaf Paper, to maintain its sustainable credentials in this aspect of its business.

Attention to detail

- Downloadable mini-guides are available to consumers to learn more about the sustainable credentials of the brand and discover how they might adapt to more sustainable, low-carbon living.
- The boxes used to ship bottles are 100 percent recycled cardboard. Double-walled and sturdy with convenient handles, they are designed to be the right size to store typical office file folders, but could be used for any type of storage or transport of items. The 360 Vodka bottle itself, with its particular swing-top seal, could be used for storing other products, or be purely decorative or just recycled.
- FOREST 360 is a project to plant indigenous trees on 40 acres of the land around the distillery in conjunction with the Earth Friendly Distilling Company's business partners.

From billboard to bag

- In a more unusual initiative, 360 Vodka converted its special eco-friendly vinyl billboards into a variety of limited edition haute couture bags, handbags and related accessories at the end of the *Blend in with nature* campaign, using billboards that had appeared in Times Square, New York. All of the accessories would biodegrade when thrown away at the end of their usefulness. This came about after sponsoring the *Best Green Handbag* award at Independent Handbag Designer Awards in 2008 in conjunction with the eco-friendly handbag designer Ecoist. Ecoist specialises in upcycling – the repurposing of a material into a product of higher quality – and is well known for its range of one-of-a-kind, limited collection handbags made from sweet wrappers, food packages and labels. In this way, waste that was destined to go to landfill would be given a new lease of life as a completely different product.

Follow up

1. What can you find out about the 360 Vodka brand now? How well is it performing and does it remain faithful to its sustainable philosophy?
2. Profile the New Leaf Paper Company and the Ecoist. Analyse their sustainable business activities and decide which business provides the most beneficial sustainable impacts.

Dilemma part 2:   Is there a sustainability crunch?

But is there really a sustainability crunch?

When the crunch bites who gets bitten?

The extent to which the fragile, ambivalent attitude towards sustainability has been exposed by the credit crunch has produced contrasting viewpoints. Observers have noticed behavioural change, particularly in everyday shopping habits such as food shopping, which is an area consumers are likely to see as an opportunity to reduce expenditure. More food shoppers are clearly seeking promotional deals and coupon redemption is on the increase, while more sustainable options, such as organic, are falling as consumers turn to either cheaper alternative ethical food sources or even non-sustainable foodstuff.

Conventional research tends to point to the fact that as consumers' anxiety over their personal economy increases there will be a significant reduction in their spending, particularly on non-essential goods. Consumers are less likely to make major purchases such as furniture or electrical equipment/household goods and are even less likely to give to charity. The demise of furniture providers MFI and Land of Leather bear witness to the effects of the bite, with consumers shunning all non-essential spend. As consumer attention is diverted to a single product attribute – price – consumers engage in more research, using price comparison websites in increasing numbers in order to get better deals for utility bills and financial services such as insurance. This will be combined with a trading down effect. Trading down refers to consumers spending less by choosing to purchase from cheaper retailers, swapping to cheaper branded products or turning to retailers' own brands or their basic, value ranges. In the latter part of 2008, as established players started to see trading down as a threat to their own business, they reacted by combating on price. For example, Tesco started its own 'discounter' campaign in order to prevent bleeding customers to lower-priced competition such as Aldi and Lidl. On the other hand, Marks and Spencer has seen the trading down phenomenon as an opportunity, starting its *Dine in for £10* campaign to encourage people to pamper themselves more economically by choosing to trade down from eating out.

A sustainable recession

The bite of the credit crunch clearly affects both businesses and consumers, and economic growth diminishes. However, logic dictates that if continuous growth is not sustainable then recession must produce the opposite effect. If the result of the credit crunch is that we buy less and therefore consume less, then recession must be a good thing for sustainability, particularly environmental sustainability. It means we are using up fewer natural resources, polluting less and also sending less to landfill as a result.

Recent research into behavioural change highlights consumers' decisions to replace goods only if they are completely worn out and not before, to recycle goods by buying and selling more on websites such as eBay, to cook from scratch rather than use convenience food, to buy cheaper, local seasonal produce rather than more expensive imports, to stop shopping

▶

for the fun of it, to cut back on energy consumption and to car share or cut back on travel. Yes, it can be argued that all of these actions are motivated to reduce expenditure during the credit crunch, but at the same time these actions are resulting in more sustainable consumer behaviour.

Winners . . .

Sustainable *saving* has become an attractive proposition in a time of recession rather than unsustainable *spending*. The fact that sustainability appears to have won by accident is neither here nor there. Those organisations that can demonstrate a saving benefit will be the winners because they will have the opportunity to position themselves on the side of the consumer. Exclusively sustainable attributes such as durability and functionality (often disregarded by mainstream consumers) will now be able to cross the divide to become conventionally accept-able product attributes to the general public, for at least as long as the recession lasts and hope-fully beyond that point.

. . . and losers

The organic food and drink market is worth some £1.6 billion but almost half of all organic shoppers are predicted to reduce or stop buying organic produce during 2009. After five con-secutive years of growth by some 16 percent per year until 2008, the organic market is falling victim to the credit crunch and the trade-down effect. In addition to the economic crisis, organic faces other difficulties. As more players enter the sustainable market they compete against each other as well as against non-sustainable options, allowing consumers two options: trade down to non-sustainable or trade down to cheaper sustainable options.

Organic effectively competes with a number of alternative ethical choices including welfare, fair trade and locally sourced foods, most of which have the benefit of being cheaper. Recent research suggests that local sourcing is now the most sought after ethical food type with pur-chase intention among consumers belonging to that segment at 33 percent in comparison with fair trade at 26 percent and organic at 21 percent.[46, 47]

The increase in the number of farmers' markets coupled with retailers' increased emphasis on local sourcing of food products and the labelling of air freighted goods highlighting food miles have all contributed to the growing interest in locally sourced foods. In December 2008 the organic situation became more confused when the Soil Association together with other organic certification bodies requested an organic 'holiday' from just some of the stricter organic rules, such as the use of organic feed for animals, which is twice the price of normal feed.[48] This holi-day would allow farmers to get through the difficult economic period but would mean they would lose their organic label during the holiday period.

Devise the strategy

1. How would you protect the organic market from further decline? Devise a five-point strategic recovery plan for the organic food market in the light of the challenges it faces.

Getting started

1. Consider the four competing ethical food types: organic, welfare, fair trade and locally sourced. Compare and contrast their conventional and sustainable attributes, as in Table 3.5, to understand how they compete with each other – the four ethical food types are not all sustainable in the same way.

2. Investigate the typical strategies and tactics used to combat the threat of substitutes, particularly competition based on price. Look for articles on marketing during a recession.

3. Look for more information on the market sector (e.g. Mintel) and case studies in the professional marketing publications.

References

1. Van Dam, Y. and Apledoorn, P. (1996) 'Sustainable Marketing', *Journal of Macromarketing* 16: 45–56 (p. 52).

2. Peattie, K. and Crane, A. (2005) 'Green Marketing: Legend, Myth, Farce or Prophesy?', *Qualitative Market Research: An International Journal* 8(4): 357–370.

3. Gordon, W. (2002) *Brand Green: Mainstream or Forever Niche?*, London: Green Alliance.

4. Oslo Symposium on Sustainable Consumption, cited in Reisch, L. (1998) *Sustainable Consumption: Three Questions About a Fuzzy Concept*, CEC Working Paper No. 9, Copenhagen Business School (p. 9).

5. Schaefer, A. and Crane, A. (2005) 'Addressing Sustainability and Consumption', *Journal of Macromarketing* 25(1): 76–92. See also Jackson, T. (2005) *Motivating Sustainable Consumption: A Review of Evidence on Consumer Behaviour and Behavioural Change*, Guildford: Sustainable Development Research Network.

6. Van Dam, Y. and Apledoorn, P. (1996) 'Sustainable Marketing', *Journal of Macromarketing* 16: 45–56.

7. Green Alliance (2004) *Getting to Grips with Consumption*, www.green-alliance.org.uk

8. Owen, L., Seaman, H. and Prince, S. (2007) *Public Understanding of Sustainable Consumption of Food: A Report to the Department for Environment, Food and Rural Affairs*, Opinion Leader, London: Defra.

9. De Pelsmacker, P., Guens, M. and Van Den Begh, J. (2007) *Marketing Communications: A European Perspective*, 3rd ed., Harlow: Pearson.

10. Dolan, P. (2002) 'The Sustainability of Sustainable Consumption', *Journal of Macromarketing* 22(2): 170–181 (p. 179).

11. Coverly, E., McDonagh, P., O'Malley, L. and Patterson, M. (2008) 'Hidden Mountain: the Social Avoidance of Waste, *Journal of Macromarketing* 28(3): 289–303 (p. 289).

12. McKenzie-Mohr, D., Nemiroff, L.S., Beers, L. and Desmorais, S. (1995) 'Determinants of Responsible Environmental Behaviour', *Journal of Social Issues* 51(4): 139–156.

13. Dittmar, H. (2004) 'Are you what you have?', *The Psychologist* 17(4): 206–211.

14. Baudrillard, J. (2001) 'Consumer Society', in Poster, M. (Ed.) *Jean Baudrillard: Selected Writings*, 2nd ed., Palo Alto, CA: Stanford University Press, 36–38.

15. Higgins, E.T. (1987) 'Self-discrepancy: a Theory Relating Self and Affect', *Psychological Review* 94: 319–340.

16. McCracken, G. (1990) *Culture and Consumption*, Bloomington, IN: Indiana University Press.

17. Evans, D. and Jackson, T. (2008) *Sustainable Consumption: Perspectives From Social and Cultural Theory*, RESOLVE Working Paper 05–08.

18. Jackson, T. (2009) *Prosperity Without Growth? The Transition to a Sustainable Economy*, London: Sustainable Development Commission.

19. Diderot, D. (1875) Oeuvres complètes de Dederot, Paris: Gorgier. See also McCracken, G. (1990) *Culture and Consumption*, Indianapolis, IN: Indiana University Press.

20. Veblen, T. (1899, 1994) *The Theory of the Leisure Class*, Mineola, NY: Dover Publications.

21. James, O. (2007) *Affluenza*, London: Vermilion.

22. De Graff, J., Wann, D. and Naylor, T. (2005) *Affluenza: The All Consuming Epidemic*, London: Berrett-Koehler.

23. See www.theaffluenzaexhibition.org

24. Layard, R. (2003) *Happiness: Has Social Science a Clue?*, Lionel Robbins Memorial Lectures, delivered on 3–5 March, London School of Economics.

25. Monroe, K.B. (1990) *Pricing: Making Profitable Decisions*, 3rd ed., New York: McGraw-Hill (p. 5).

26. Brook Lyndhurst (2007) *Public Understanding of Sustainable Energy Consumption in the Home*, London: Brook Lyndhurst Ltd.

27. Gordon, W. (2002) *Brand Green: Mainstream or Forever Niche?* London: Green Alliance.

28. Ipsos MORI Reputation Centre (2007) *Sustainability Issues in the Retail Sector*, www.ipsos-mori.com

29. Dresner, S., McGeevor, K. and Tomei, J. (2007) *Public Understanding Synthesis Report: A Report to the Department for Environment, Food and Rural Affairs*, London: Policy Studies Institute, Defra (p. 8).

30. Peattie, K., and Crane, A. (2005) 'Green Marketing: Legend, Myth, Farce or Prophesy?', *Qualitative Market Research: An International Journal* 8(4): 357–370.

31. Evans, D. and Jackson, T. (2007) *Towards a Sociology of Sustainable Lifestyles*, RESOLVE Working Paper 03–07 (p. 14).

32. Evans, D. and Abrahamse, W. (2008) *Beyond Rhetoric: The Possibilities of and for Sustainable Lifestyles*, RESOLVE Working Paper 06–08.

33. National Centre for Research Methods (2008) 'Young People Worry about Climate Change but Resist Lifestyle Change', in Economic and Social Research Council (ESRC), *Britain in 2009*, Swendon: ESRC (p. 19).

34. Singh. S. (2008) 'In the eyes of the watchdog', *Marketing Week*, 1 May: 22–23.

35. Downing, P. and Ballantyne, J. (2007) *Social Marketing and Climate Change: Turning Point or Tipping Point?*, Ipsos MORI Social Research Institute, www.ipsos-mori.com

36. BBC News (2009) *Quit Call over Blocked Green Ad*, 9 February, http://news.bbc.co.uk/1/hi/northern_ireland/7878399.stm

37. Settle, R. and Alreck, P. (1989) 'Reducing Buyers' Sense of Risk', *Marketing Communications* (January): 34–40.

38. Stone, R. and Gronhaug, K. (1993) 'Perceived Risk: Further Considerations for the Marketing Discipline', *European Journal of Marketing* 27(3): 39–50.

39. Murray, K.B. (1991) 'A Test of Services Marketing Theory: Consumer Information Acquisition Activities.', *Journal of Marketing* 55: 10–25.

40. Burns, A. and Bush, R. (2003) *Marketing Research*, 4th ed., Upper Saddle River, NJ: Prentice Hall.

41. Bryman A. and Bell, E. (2003) *Business Research Methods*, New York: Oxford University Press.

42. Fearne, A. (2008) *In Pursuit of Sustainable Consumption: Insights From Supermarket Loyalty Data*, RESOLVE Research Seminar, Surrey University, 31 March.

43. Van Dam, Y. and Apledoorn, P. (1996) 'Sustainable Marketing', *Journal of Macromarketing* 16: 45–56.

44. Downing, P. and Ballantyne, J. (2007) *Social Marketing and Climate Change: Turning Point or Tipping Point?*, Ipsos MORI Social Research Institute, www.ipsos-mori.com

45. The Co-operative Bank (2007) *The Ethical Consumerism Report*, January www.co-operativebank.co.uk/ethicalconsumerismreport.

46. Scott-Thomas, C. (2008) 'Organic Sales Set to Slip Says Mintel', 25 November, www.foodanddrinkeurope.com/Consumer-Trends/Organic-sales-set-to-slip-says-Mintel

47. Hills, S. (2008) *Organic No Longer Seen as Recession Proof*, 12 November, www.foodnavigator-usa.com/Financial-Industry/Organic-no-longer-seen-as recession-proof

48. *The Daily Telegraph* (2008) 'Organic Farmers Are Asking for Standards to be Temporarily Relaxed After They Suffered a Severe Drop in Sales', 22 December.

4 The evolution of sustainable segmentation

Timberland's boot from recycled material is a huge success because it's a cool product, not because it's a green product. It's cool and it's green. . . . But if it had been a bad product, it wouldn't have sold.[1]

Georges Kern, CEO of the International Watch Company

Chapter objectives

After studying this chapter you should be able to:

1   Appreciate the relationship between human needs and consumer attitudes and behaviour towards sustainability.

2   Understand how to identify different segments of the population by their willingness and ability to adopt sustainable practice.

3   Understand the similarities and differences between frameworks for segmenting the population by their attitudes to sustainability and their behaviour.

4   Explore the conflicts and ambiguity that exist in the mind of consumers with regard to sustainable behaviour.

Dilemma part 1:   Back to nature?

Is going back to nature, particularly using animals, a part of the solution to producing sustainable clothes and adapting to sustainable living? Some would argue that it is impossible to expand the rearing of animals only for their skins, despite it appearing to be a natural resource that replenishes itself.

In the UK the addiction to leather continues, with some £4 billion of leather fashion imports arriving each year. The pro-leather segment of the fashion industry suggests that leather is a natural sustainable material, a by-product of the meat industry that is too good and too useful to throw away. However, evidence suggests that the by-product argument is losing ground, as global production of raw cattle hides is growing at a faster rate than the production of cattle meat.

Leather is also notoriously noxious in its different stages of production. The tanning process uses chromium, acids, salts and fungicides, which all pollute the environment. In fact the whole process produces many contaminates such as ammonia and hydrogen sulphide which find their way into the air, earth and groundwater supplies. Taking into account the large amount of water used to make leather and the energy used, leather appears to be far from natural, or environmentally friendly.

Typically, such highly polluting production methods are no longer legal in the Economic Union (EU) and the US and most leather production now takes place in developing countries where standards and controls are difficult to impose and control.

There have been some efforts to clean up the leather industry, using less toxic chemicals in the tanning process and incorporating vegetable dyes. The German–Chinese company ISA Tan, one of the largest producers of leather in the world, has opened a more environmentally friendly leather tanning operation in Vietnam in 2009, costing $12.1 million. The facility is able to produce 2 million square metres of leather a year, supplying companies including Timberland, New Balance and Hush Puppies. The company's overall process for making its Low Impact to the Environment leather (LITE leather for short) uses 30 percent less energy and 50 percent less water, and emits 35 percent less carbon dioxide than industry standards derived from the British Leather Technology Centre. In a similar facility in Guangzhou, People's Republic of China, ISA Tan uses solar panels to heat water and has fitted windmills to pump water, as well as planting bamboo to help treat and filter wastewater.

Vegan brands such as Beyond Skin attempt to cater for the eco-friendly, animal-loving purchasers of shoes by offering an alternative to leather. The drawback is that many vegan synthetic leathers are actually made from petrochemicals such as polyurethane (PU) or polyvinyl chloride (PVC) and are therefore consuming non-renewable resources in the same way as conventional tanning does. Vegan shoe producers and organisations such as Peta (People for the Ethical Treatment of Animals) suggest that PU leaves less of an environmental burden than leather processing, but Greenpeace highlights PU's petrochemical origins and the fact that its creation results in dioxins.

Investigate the following:

1. Fashion marketers can play a key role in promoting sustainable solutions for clothing, and making ethical fashion appeal to the mainstream consumer – ensuring it is desirable, functional and stylish.

    What is the current composition of the leather market? Try subdividing the leather market for shoes and clothes in different ways. For example: leather, eco-leather, fake leather, recycled leather. How big are the alternative leather markets such as vegan leather? Identify and profile the vegan leather consumer. What future do these leather market segments have, given the need to become more sustainable?

The evolution of sustainable segmentation

The use of segmentation to understand consumers' behaviour towards sustainability has evolved considerably over time. Conventional segmentation aims to make marketing more efficient by subdividing the market into potential target markets chiefly on the basis of their attractiveness for ease of access, economic growth and profit, and then choosing the best segments to receive appropriate, tailored marketing activity. Less profitable, unattractive segments would be ignored and logic would dictate that there would be groups of the population of no interest at all to the marketer because they would never be purchasers of the products or services on offer for whatever reason (no match to needs and wants, not enough disposable income, etc.). Efforts would be made to profile the most attractive target markets in order to understand them better using a set of standard variables such as demographics, geographics and psychographics.

Attempts to apply a standard segmentation process to the green consumer of the 1980s and 1990s focused on treating such consumers as a discrete niche target market but resulted in contradictory results in terms of trying to establish a definitive and consistent consumer profile. Inconclusive studies profiled the green consumer as male or female, old or young and educated or uneducated[2] and often concentrated on only those consumers of environmental products rather than a broader view of sustainability to include social and ethical issues.

With standard marketing research directed towards the aims of increasing consumption and maintaining economic growth, segmentation research for sustainability will have to compensate for the lack of specific information that exists, particularly on behaviour. Conventional behaviour-based segmentation systems such as MOSAIC or Acorn cannot properly account for the motivations behind the behaviour they describe, while previous sustainable research tends to be based on attitudes to issues without revealing or explaining actual behaviour. Indeed, while early sustainability surveys highlighted increasing positive attitudes towards sustainability issues, they were unable to clarify why these attitudes did not translate into sustainable behaviour to the same degree.

This chapter explains how marketers may choose to divide and subdivide the population into target segments according to their acceptance and practice of sustainable behaviours. First, an understanding of how people may be grouped by their basic human needs and motivations provides insights into how they may relate to sustainability. Second, the chapter explains how marketers' understanding of sustainable behaviour has evolved and improved over time, resulting in a more sophisticated portrayal of the potential target segments for sustainability and their willingness and ability to participate in sustainable practices. Finally, the differences and contradictions in behaviour that are still apparent despite more sophisticated segmentation tools are explained, and the different levels of engagement between advocate and opponents are highlighted, indicating the areas where marketers will need to concentrate their efforts to encourage the dissemination of good practice and the participation of more excluded groups.

The evolution of human needs

One influential approach to understanding human motivations was put forward by psychologist Abraham Maslow.[3] After studying the behaviour of monkeys, he found that they looked for water before creating a shelter and created the shelter before looking for a mate. His development of a hierarchy of needs was his attempt to explain human personal growth towards attainment and self-actualisation. By proposing a hierarchical progression it is suggested that people must reach a certain level before being able to move on to the next, from physiological needs at the bottom (the most important for human survival) to self-actualisation needs (the least important for human survival) at the top.

Although Maslow's Hierarchy of Needs should not be taken too literally or understood too rigidly, as it is still culture and context bound, it does remind marketers that people will have different needs at different times and will attach different priorities to these needs, whether or not they progress up the ladder in the same way as others.

Table 4.1 shows how international marketing agency Young and Rubicam (Y&R) has used Maslow's work to develop a system of segmentation for the general public based on adherence to a particular core motivation. The framework identifies seven different segments – reformer, explorer, succeeder, aspirer, mainstream, struggler and resigned – each driven by its own core need.

When applying the framework to the context of sustainability, a number of considerations become apparent. Meeting physiological needs such as food and drinking water have been largely taken for granted, at least in the developed world, just as the safety need for shelter. As food supplies have become more abundant and reliable, the emphasis on physiological needs has given way to the higher psychological needs, at the same time more consumerist consumption has taken hold of society.

In contrast, in the UK during the Second World War the whole nation had to *Dig for Victory* using as much of the land available to provide food for the civilian population and supply the war effort. On the physiological level the population was fighting to survive. Over 50 years later the general public in the UK no longer fight for survival through having to cultivate as much food as they can themselves; at most they secure their food supply by fighting for a good parking space in their local supermarket.

However, sustainability issues are changing how the hierarchy of needs should be interpreted. Needs at either end of the hierarchy seem to be under threat as the hierarchy is reinterpreted through the sustainability agenda. Environmental sustainability highlights the threats to people's physiological needs as food and fresh water supplies have come under increasing pressure due to climate change, soil degradation and population increases. Equally, environmental sustainability draws attention to people's safety needs for shelter as rising sea-levels due to the melting of the polar ice caps jeopardise the living space of low-lying coastal communities around the world. In the UK, recent flooding in many parts of the country has placed an emphasis on safety needs which had previously been taken for granted.

Table 4.1 Young and Rubicam's basic motivations within Maslow's Hierarchy of Needs

From Maslow's Hierarchy	Y&R's cross-cultural consumer characterisation	
	Consumer type	Core need and characteristics of each segment
Self-actualisation needs	Reformer	Enlightenment The most anti-materialistic, perceived as intellectual, socially aware, value their own judgement and pride themselves on tolerance, they seek the authentic and the harmonious, are often at the leading edge of society
Need to know/ understand	Explorer	Discovery Young at heart, often the first to try new ideas, seek new challenges and frontiers, responding to brands offering new sensations and indulgence
Esteem needs: • Self-esteem	Succeeder	Control Self-confident, organised, goal oriented, supportive of the status quo, seek reward, prestige, believe they deserve the best
• From others	Aspirer	Status Materialistic, acquisitive people, driven by others' perceptions of them rather than by their own values, they respond to image, appearance, persona, charisma, fashion
Belongingness/ love needs	Mainstream	Security Largest group, follow daily routines responding to established brands, family brands and value for money
Safety needs	Struggler	Escape Live for the present, often perceived as victims, losers, disorganised, goalless with few resources beyond physical skills
Physiological needs	Resigned	Survival Older, with constant unchanging values, respectful of institutions, traditional and nostalgic, seek the familiar, safety and economy

Source: Adapted from Young and Rubicam[4]

Moving up the hierarchy, a different situation has developed. Higher-level psychological needs are more associated with unsustainable materialistic consumption, which provides only temporary satisfaction. For example, esteem needs seem to be incompatible with sustainability as they tend to be satisfied by more consumerist consumption activities such as purchasing associated with the fabrication of self-identity and communication with others.

It would appear that Maslow's Hierarchy of Needs is still relevant for understanding the market, as once it is applied in the context of sustainability it becomes apparent that both marketers and consumers will have to readdress the importance of the core needs at each stage of the hierarchy and how these core needs may be satisfied via alternative sustainable means.

Apply it: Motivation and bags

1. What evidence can you find that marketers are using their understanding of human needs and motivations in order to market sustainability issues and products?
2. Use the seven consumer-types framework of Young and Rubicam to explore how marketers can meet the core needs of the reformer, explorer, succeeder, aspirer and mainstream segments without compromising on sustainable practice.

Getting started

The Snapshot, 'Conspicuous bags', shows how marketers may meet the esteem and status needs of the aspirer segment while using a sustainability context.

Esteem needs:		
From others	Aspirer	Status
		Materialistic, acquisitive people, driven by others' perceptions of them rather than by their own values, they respond to image, appearance, persona, charisma, fashion

According to Young and Rubicam's framework, the aspirer is materialistic and seeks to enhance his/her own esteem and status in front of others through conspicuous consumption relying on image, appearance and fashion to send appropriate messages to other people.

Logically this type of consumption is not normally associated with sustainability as it tends to encourage consumption for the sake of it. Stopping people from aspiring to have status in front of others would be an impossible task for marketers but perhaps people could be persuaded to aspire to status through a more sustainable conspicuous consumption as suggested by this Snapshot.

Snapshot: Conspicuous bags

For example, in April 2007 Sainsbury's supermarket sold some 20,000 designer shopping bags at £5 each within an hour of opening its stores.[5] The bag was conceived by the fashion accessories designer Anya Hindmarch and bore the now famous slogan *'I'm NOT A Plastic bag'*. The reusable cotton bags were part of a campaign with the *We Are What We Do* movement to help cut the number of plastic carriers used in the UK. The campaign was supported by an array of celebrities such as the international models Twiggy and Erin O'Connor and the likes of actresses Keira Knightley and Jessica Biel. The bag was automatically made a must-have fashion accessory when it was used as a goodie-bag for guests at the 2007 Vanity Fair Oscar Night party. Restricting purchase to just one bag per customer and only having 30 bags available in each store created queues of people outside Sainsbury stores hours before opening. Literally an overnight, highly conspicuous symbol of ethical intent, the bag reached £200 for resale on eBay. Ownership of the bag clearly sent out a status message of sustainability for those lucky enough to obtain one.

UK charity Bottletop funds projects which aim to have a positive impact on young people worldwide, paying particular attention to sexual and reproductive health education. In order to raise the funds necessary, Bottletop has turned to the music and fashion industry for inspiration. In collaboration with luxury fashion brand Mulberry, Bottletop used recycled waste – just bottletops – to create a must-have fashion bag and a selection of matching accessories generating sales in excess of £250,000 and over £500,000 in publicity from public relations activities. More recently, while working with the brand Fenchurch, Bottletop has created the Bottletop Fenchurch Bag, made from recycled ring pulls from drinks cans and manufactured in Brazil by a female-based cooperative which benefits the local community. The cooperative is supplied with the ring pulls by the local community and it pays people £3 per kilo for the metal they bring in. Again this is a sustainability inspired organisation that produces products aimed at catering for the esteem and status needs of the aspirer, with endorsements from Bill Clinton, Kofi Annan, Justin Timberlake, Annie Lennox, Peaches Geldolf and Natalie Imbruglia.[6]

Understanding segmentation for sustainability

More recently, specific sustainable activities and the level or extent of their incidence have become the common denominator of research in different segmentation studies. Since the main drive behind much of sustainable marketing is to achieve behavioural change, the most logical way to segment the market is along behavioural lines, as well as the degree to which people are willing to change, taking into account four key aspects:

● The extent to which consumers already behave sustainably.

● Whether such behaviour can continue and be extended into other aspects of lifestyle.

● The reason why sustainable behaviour is adopted or rejected.

● How distinct groups can be identified and targeted via their behaviour.

Table 4.2   Basic segmentation of sustainable behaviour

Segments		Commitment level
Committed	Engaged	High
Mainstream	Aspirational	Medium
Occasional	Basic engagement	Low
Non-environmentalist[7]	Disengaged[8]	None

Table 4.3   Roper Starch Worldwide USA segmentation[9]

True Blue Greens	11%	Major green purchasers and recyclers
Greenback Greens	5%	Will buy green, will not make lifestyle changes
Sprouts	33%	Concerned but unwilling to spend more
Grousers	18%	The environment is somebody else's problem
Basic Browns	31%	Disinterested

Source: Roper Starch Worldwide, 2000

Most early models of segmentation have been more dominated by environmental concerns than trying to understand the social and economic sensitivities of the general public for sustainability. These models divided the public into four basic groupings according to their level of commitment to sustainable practice, but this tended to state the obvious rather than provide clear insight into understanding sustainable behaviour.

This four-way division resulted in the sustainable categories of high, medium, low and non-engagement, as shown in Table 4.2, but this provided a simplistic framework of understanding which could be used to describe and categorise anyone's level of engagement with anything from sustainable practice to watching football. More sophisticated analyses resulted in three much referred to consumer segmentations, specifically those from Roper Starch, Lifestyles of Health and Sustainability (LOHAS) and MORI. Now out of date, they went further to try to profile the segments (which were given more colourful epithets) and highlight their differences, as can be seen in the Roper Starch segmentation in Table 4.3.

Towards a better understanding – Roper Green Gauge 2008

Recent research in the US and the UK reveals more detailed profiles of consumer behaviour, identifying six and seven distinct segments respectively, documenting knowledge, attitudes, perceived barriers and behaviour within the context of sustainability, which are summarised in Tables 4.4 and 4.5.

Table 4.4   Roper Green Gauge Survey 2008 (US)[10]

---

1. Genuine Greens 17%

Environmental activists or just strong advocates, they do not perceive barriers to sustainable behaviour and are most likely to be willing to cooperate with initiatives

2. Not Me Greens 21%

Strong pro-environmental attitudes, but not behaviour because they feel the problems are too much for them and only engage in easy behaviours such as recycling

3. Go-With-the-Flow Greens 16%

Moderate attitudes following easy behaviours such as recycling, less concerned about environmental problems such as global warming

4. Dream Greens 13%

Limited green behaviour, although more than average, their biggest barriers to behaviour are lack of knowledge/resources, could improve if given the chance

5. Business First Greens 21%

Less than average concern and behaviour than total population, believe business/industry will take action and cite barriers preventing their own initiative

6. Mean Greens 11%

Claim to be knowledgeable but cynical and apprehensive about environmentalism, and can be hostile to initiatives

---

Source: Chiarelli, 2008

How the population may be segmented for sustainability will clearly vary from country to country. Roper Starch Worldwide also monitors global attitudes towards sustainability. On average, 43 percent of global consumers know a lot or a fair amount about climate change and global warming. This figure compares with just 42 percent and 49 percent in the US and UK respectively, showing that they have average levels of knowledge despite the many campaigns. The countries that appear to be the most knowledgeable about climate change are Thailand (79 percent) and South Korea (72 percent) with France placed third as the highest EU country with 68 percent. Similarly, populations have different levels of confidence about their own ability to contribute to environmental sustainability. In Thailand 63 percent of the population think that their actions can have an influence, while in China it is 13 percent and in Russia just 5 percent.[11]

However, knowledge and awareness about the subject of climate change do not appear to be the same as conviction and belief in climate change. Current research from both the UK and US suggests that belief in the validity of climate change and its causes has diminished over time. In the space of only three years, the percentage of Americans who believe that world temperatures are rising dropped by 20 percent to only 57 percent in 2009.[12] In the UK the percentage of people who feel that the threat of climate change has been exaggerated doubled in the space of five years up to 2009 to 29 percent.[13]

Table 4.5   Defra pro-environmental behaviours 2008 (UK)[14]

1. Positive Greens 18%

Most motivated towards environmentally-friendly behaviour, least likely to be influenced by generic barriers, prepared to spend more, buy local, ethical and fairtrade products, heavy recycler, saver of energy and water in the home, likely to feel guilty, 75 percent of group would like to do more

2. Waste Watchers 12%

Driven more to avoid waste than reduce their own impacts, 75 percent are content with their level of engagement focused on home energy/water, fuel-efficient car and purchasing ethical, local/national products, least likely after group 7 to feel guilty

3. Concerned Consumers 14%

Broad pro-environmental attitudes although less conviction, and strongly reject that future growth is limited/on-coming environmental crisis, two-thirds would like to do more, they have green attitudes towards travel, but have average car usage and take more flights than any other segment

4. Sideline Supporters 14%

Despite weak pro-environmental attitudes, actual behaviour is less than all groups except 6 and 7 due to general inaction, lack of knowledge and proactive attitude, less action taken in the home and, although acknowledge barriers and the need to do more, this is not translated into behaviour

5. Cautious Participants 14%

Their worldview is close to the average for the population, they recognise the issues but are pessimistic, pro-environmental behaviour focus on home, water, energy but cite more barriers to act including lifestyle, self-identity and habit, likely to feel guilty, 50 percent of group report doing little or nothing, 75 percent of group would like to do more, but feel other individuals/countries can cancel out their own behaviour

6. Stalled Starters 10%

Lowest socio-economic profile, lowest education level, lowest level of knowledge of issues, with confused views thinking climate change has been exaggerated and is too far in the future, most say have no impact and environmental behaviour is a low priority, most likely to see green as embarrassing or an alternative lifestyle, despite doing little most say they are happy with contribution and do not want to do more

7. Honestly Disengaged 18%

Show complete lack of interest and concern, a large proportion more than any other group express no opinion on issues either for or against and of all groups, they have the highest level saying they are happy with what they are doing, and they do not want to do more to help the environment even though more than half already do little or nothing, the least likely of all groups to feel guilty, they make no excuses for their behaviour and do not want information about how to do more

In part, these figures also reflect the level of significance given to the environment by the governments of the individual countries. In a survey of different countries' economic stimulus packages for 2009 including the percentage of the aid that would go to environmental initiatives conducted by the HSBC Bank,[15] it was found that the US had set aside 12 percent of available funds for environmental projects and the UK only 15 percent in comparison with 79 percent in South Korea.

Researching sustainability: Presenting quantitative data

Geographic segmentation is a standard means of dividing the marketplace, and information given in this chapter has already highlighted the existence of national differences in attitudes towards sustainability, particularly in relation to climate change.

Spain and climate change

Attitudes: Spain is the one of the most concerned countries of the EU about the issue of climate change. In research carried out by Havas Media[16] some 43 percent of Spanish respondents described themselves as very focused on the issue of climate change in comparison with only 17 percent in the UK and 15 percent in Germany. In contrast only 11 percent of Spanish respondents were deemed eco-apathetic compared with 34 percent in the UK and US, and 32 percent in Germany. The eco-apathetic, while recognising the concept, do not tend to feel responsible either for its causes or for contributing a solution to the problem.

Reactions to climate change: The majority of Spanish respondents (75 percent) agree that tackling the issue of climate change will require lifestyle changes that will affect them and their families, although only 52 percent believe they can make a positive contribution to solving the problem. If sustainable goods maintained their level of quality and price, Spanish respondents would be more likely to buy them (56 percent) and 38 percent would be willing to pay more for such goods.

Responsibilities: 56 percent of Spanish respondents would be more likely to buy environmentally friendly goods in the next 12 months if they were at the same price and standard as their usual brands. Companies are seen to be providers of solutions to climate change, with 73 percent of the Spanish population prepared to buy from them if they are trying to reduce their contribution to global warming. On the other hand, only 10 percent of Spanish respondents agree that their government is making a significant effort to combat climate change.

1. Carry out research on any three countries, collecting data to compare and contrast their attitudes and reactions to climate change and how they ascribe responsibility for solutions to climate change. Present your findings in the form of graphs and tables in order to highlight the key points and emphasise the similarities and differences between the countries.

Towards a better understanding – Defra pro-environmental behaviours 2008

The Defra pro-environmental behaviours segmentation exercise is an example of more detailed and sophisticated understanding of population attitude and behaviour towards sustainability. While it is context specific to the UK, many other countries will find similar situations exist in their general populations.

As can be seen in Figure 4.1, further insights can be gained when each segment together with the desired sustainable behaviour changes are plotted onto a matrix. In Figure 4.1 four of the seven Defra segments are plotted against

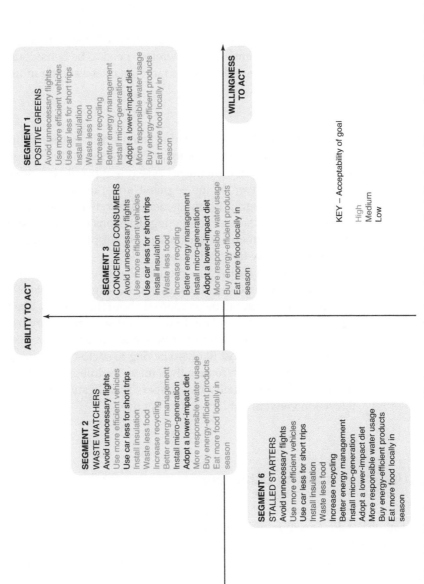

Figure 4.1 Desired behaviours of some Defra segments plotted against their ability and willingness to act

Source: Adapted from Defra[17]

ability and willingness to act as these are the sources of the main obstacles to behavioural change. As the figure demonstrates, each segment occupies a different position on the matrix according to these two criteria. The result is that, even within a segment such as segment 3: concerned consumers, the level of engagement with sustainable behaviour will not be consistent across all possible desired actions. The level of acceptability of each goal within each of the segments provides valuable insights into attitudes towards potential behaviours. In the light of this research it could be concluded that campaigns for change aimed at particular segments would therefore need to be behaviour specific and focus on those actions regarded by the target market as being more problematic.

Building profiles

Having identified differentiated segments, it is necessary to build profiles for each of the segments in order to fully understand the background and circumstances of the segment members. A segment profile is essentially a description of a typical member of the segment and may include demographic, socio-economic, psychographic and general lifestyle information. Such data will aid the sustainable marketer in making decisions on how best to access members of each of the segments to encourage the adoption of sustainable consumption habits and modify their behaviour.

For example, DEFRA has profiled Positive Greens as those who have the most pro-environmental attitudes and the highest levels of knowledge of sustainability. They tend to be passionate about their views, like to work independently and are the most likely to do volunteer work. They feel they do as much as they can to reduce their environmental impact but feel that there is scope to improve. They are most likely to belong to socio-economic groups A and B; the group is slightly more female than male, middle-aged, has the highest average income and reads quality newspapers and lifestyle magazines. They are light television viewers but heavy internet users.[18]

Apply it: Segmenting by behaviour

1. By using the Defra Omnibus questionnaire you could assess the environmental attitudes of your class and segment the group according to the Defra segmentation criteria. Visit the Defra website (www.defra.gov.uk/evidence/statistics/environment/pubatt/download/omnibus-question.pdf) to download the questionnaire. You might consider using an Excel® spreadsheet or SPSS software to record and analyse the results.

2. Visit the Defra website (www.defra.gov.uk) to investigate the profiles of the other segments. Across each of the seven Defra segments one behaviour *Adopt a low impact diet* has a low level of acceptance. Why do you think this one behaviour trait would be common to each of the segments?

Inconclusive consumer perceptions

Other studies have confirmed a lack of agreement and consistency in the way that people regard different sustainable behaviours. Segmenting according to willingness and ability to behave sustainably is clearly an advantage but an analysis of specific behaviours can reveal that motives for not participating in particular behaviours can be quite different. This situation can make it difficult for marketers to draw conclusions and design actions for specific segments because in order to be successful they will need to neutralise different demotivations for each desired behaviour within each target segment.

Table 4.6 shows results from a study by academic researchers, Seonaidh McDonald and Caroline Oates, in which they found an almost equal split between respondents regarding the extent to which they felt ethical banking would make a difference to sustainability and whether it was easy to engage in.

Other activities that exhibited similarly unstable perceptions included: buying organic food or clothes; boycotting companies with poor human rights records or environmental concerns; composting; using hankies rather than tissues; and reading on-screen rather than printing out. The fact that many actions have no stable perception profile at all causes difficulties for marketers whose task it is to promote these behaviours.

In fact, only five out of 40 behaviours (those related to energy use and recycling) which were tested in the McDonald and Oates study scored consistently in the same quadrant of the matrix – the high difference/low effort quadrant – with most people more likely to put activities that they actually did themselves in that quadrant than in any of the other three. For many respondents of the study, actions that were perceived to make a lot of difference and require little effort were ones they already engaged in, implying that getting people to start a new action or behaviour from scratch is the main challenge.

Given the misperceptions and resistance that exist to complete conversion to sustainability and the fact that the sustainable habits that have already been assimilated tend to be placed automatically in the most favourable quadrant of the matrix, the marketer should adapt strategies to match the situation. Persuading people to trial new behaviours as an intermediary step to conversion with an emphasis on how easy the actions are may be more effective than going for all-out overnight conversion. Linking the trial to immediate tangible results for the participants would also aid conversion.

Table 4.6 Consumer perceptions of changing to ethical banking

	Not much effort (%)	A lot of effort (%)
A lot of difference	23	28
Not much difference	23	26

Source: Adapted from McDonald and Oates, 2006[19]

A hierarchy of concerns

By segmenting the population along sustainable behavioural lines it becomes apparent that there exists among the general public a hierarchy of concerns regarding sustainability. Different sustainability issues move up and down a Top Ten list, just like songs on a radio station playlist. They gain ground as they become a hot topic, perhaps through media exposure, celebrity endorsement or becoming a key point in a political party agenda; other issues lose ground as the public's attentions are directed elsewhere.

The 2007 Green and Ethical Consumers Mintel Report for the UK segmented the population into five distinct groups by concentrating more on attitudes than specific behaviours in contrast with the Defra study, resulting in the segment profiles in Table 4.7.

The profile of the segments is based on their attitudes to 12 issues, which are shown in Figure 4.2, detailing the level of personal concern each segment feels for each separate issue. In this hierarchy of concerns, environmental issues dominate the top five, which most likely reflects the amount of attention given to these issues in the media at the time. The survey also reveals that the more emotive the social issue the more likely it is to score higher than less controversial issues, almost regardless of which segment respondents belong to. For example, the more sensitive issue of child labour scores higher than other social equity issues such as the general exploitation of workers. Excessive company profits languish in mid-table and reflect public opinion in the UK before the banking crisis. It is likely that opinions on economic sustainability and business

Table 4.7 Mintel 2007 Segment Typology[20]

Keen to be green 24%	Very conscious of a number of wide-ranging issues, they try their best to take green and ethical issues into account even if this is inconvenient for them and they may feel guilty when they feel they are not doing enough.
Confused but willing 23%	Open to learn more about green and ethical issues as they admit they do not know enough to be able to take action. They are less cynical than the non-sympathetic groups, and are more likely to adopt sustainable practice to enhance their image with others.
Too busy to care 20%	An apathetic disinterested group claiming to be too occupied to be concerned by sustainability, with only 19 percent of this segment taking into account only one issue of sustainable practice.
Green overload 17%	Most likely to say that they are fed up of hearing about sustainability; they are cynical and feel that they cannot be sure any actions would really make a difference.
Greener-than-thou 16%	Feels they are already sustainable enough and that they do as much as possible without feeling guilty that they could do more.

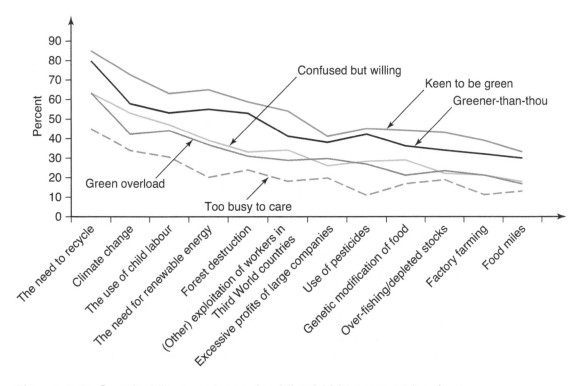

Figure 4.2 Sustainability concerns using Mintel 2007 segment typology

Source: Adapted from *Green and Ethical Consumers*[21]

ethics would now appear much higher on this list. How do these priorities now compare with later studies from Mintel or other sources?

Simplicity versus materialism

Despite the alignment of the population into specific segments for sustainability, their membership is often fluid and changeable, dependent on the particular aspect of sustainable behaviour and its circumstances. Often belonging to one segment or another, or appearing to change between groups at times, will be a reflection of people's lifestyle choices divided between sustainable simplicity and mainstream materialism.

Consumers and citizens – divided ethics

Sustainable marketing departs from conventional marketing in numerous aspects, something which can be clearly seen in the process of segmentation and targeting. Sustainable marketing is different because it aims to change everyone's lifestyle, not only the lifestyles of those segments that will be most amenable to change. Therefore, in segmenting the entire population for sustainability, willingness to adopt sustainable habits becomes a fundamental factor in making the subdivisions, as can be seen in the surveys of Defra and Roper. Such divisions then require different marketing interventions according to whether segments are willing, reluctant, resistant or even hostile to change.

While segmentation by sustainable attitudes and behaviour has resulted in identifiable, distinct groupings that are easier to target, inconsistencies in consumer behaviour have not been completely removed from within these groups. Closer examination of consumer profiles reveals discrepancies between consumer willingness and consumer behaviour, resulting in the appearance of contradictory behaviours within segments. In many cases different behaviours among members of the same segment appear to be incompatible, such as reducing the carbon footprint of the home while driving a 4×4 car. Some research has explained this by suggesting that ethical behaviour is not practised equally and that individuals negotiate their own set of consumer ethics according to the contexts in which they find themselves, placing ethical boundaries on their own behaviour but choosing to cross them when personally convenient.[22]

This type of contradictory behaviour dilutes the establishment of social norms and therefore impedes the wholesale adoption of sustainable behaviour by the general public. The appearance of behaviour which is at odds with the sustainable norm has been attributed to the battle that takes place between the public's consumer and citizen personas encompassed in 'their perceptions about their rights and responsibilities, and their aspirations and values'.[23] The two battling personas represent the two conflicting views of consumption – consumerist consumption versus sustainable consumption[24] – and it is an ever-present conflict. As citizens, the public want to avert the socio-economic and environmental crises by behaving more sustainably but as consumers the public want to drive cars, take flights and buy products which they quickly get tired of only to replace them with more. Depending on each aspect of sustainability the general public will experience competing mindsets and be either more motivated, or tempted, to act as sustainable citizen of the world or unsustainable self-interested consumer.

This vision allows for another means of segmenting the market as much driven by the nature and characteristics of each sustainable behaviour choice itself as by developing a deeper understanding of the motivations behind each consumer segment torn between consumer and citizen behaviour choices, as can be seen in the matrix shown in Figure 4.3.

The matrix shows the different options available to stakeholders for the management of individuals' car usage based on the consumer–citizen divide in attitudes towards sustainability and individuals' desired behaviour. Each context of sustainable behaviour (car usage, air travel, recycling, energy usage, etc.) presents government, business and general public with four possible scenarios, first depending on the level of motivation to behave as a mainstream consumer or a sustainable citizen, and second on how much engagement with

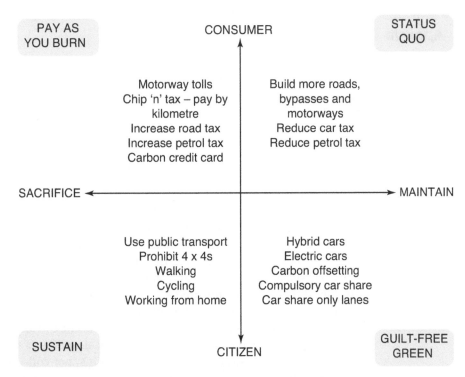

Figure 4.3   Consumer–citizen behaviour matrix for car usage

sustainability there will be and the degree to which desirable or undesirable behaviours will be preserved or changed.

The matrix shows the four possible behaviours different segments would be willing to follow with regard to using their cars for personal transport. It equally demonstrates the possible strategies each interested party may support. For example, the government may choose to impose restrictions, or pro-environmental groups may lobby for change.

The right side of the matrix is labelled *maintain*, which marks the desire of some to continue to use the car without restrictions from government or anyone else. The *guilt-free green* citizens would like to continue to have the use of cars but be more sustainable, therefore they would be motivated by cleaner technologies such as hybrid and electric cars to allow them to do so. *Status quo* consumers do not want to accept restrictions in car usage, which they regard as a right, and would therefore require infrastructures to be increased in order to continue unimpeded.

The left side of the matrix is labelled *sacrifice* and signals that some will have to give up something in order to continue to use the car or even give it up altogether. Some will *pay as they burn* and incur financial disincentives or restrictions on car usage. The *sustain* quadrant shows the most radical option for the highly motivated sustainable citizen wishing to avoid the impacts of car usage as much as possible.

Apply it: **The behaviour matrix**

1. Devise your own consumer–citizen behaviour matrix for long-haul flights–holidays. Can you vary the labelling of the four quadrants accordingly and apply the matrix to the context of food consumption?

Voluntary simplifiers – convinced by simplicity

Voluntary simplicity is a belief system and a practice of an alternative culture to conspicuous consumerism. The term voluntary simplifier refers to someone who chooses, out of free will, 'to limit expenditures on consumer goods and services, and to cultivate non-materialistic sources of satisfaction and meaning'.[25] This kind of consumer is therefore one who has chosen to lead a more extreme sustainable lifestyle and as such is a segment worthy of study, providing lifestyle examples for others to imitate and helping marketers to understand better how to convert the public to particular behaviours. Giving up the material for the non-material is not a new phenomenon and is often associated with religious movements, but the voluntary simplifier is someone who limits his/her impact on society through reducing his/her consumption for reasons of ethical and environmental concern and solidarity with his/her community.

Resulting primarily from the works of American author and sustainability activist Duane Elgin, the lifestyle of a voluntary simplifier is based on five values.[26]

● *Material simplicity:* consuming fewer but not necessarily cheaper products and services, using products which are more resource efficient and of reduced impact on society, more durable and not mass produced.

● *Human scale:* living and working in smaller, simpler settings which are decentralised so individuals can see the results of their work.

● *Self-determination:* meeting needs while reducing reliance on large commercial organisations such as supermarkets, multinational corporations, financial organisations and public organisations. Increasing the personal control of individuals is important and being driven by personal values rather than the opinion of others or the media, including aspects of self-sufficiency such as home food production, mending and even doing without at times.

● *Ecological awareness:* protecting the environment by reducing consumption of natural non-renewable resources and reducing waste and pollution. It also includes aspects of social responsibility and equality, caring for others and increased community involvement.

● *Personal growth:* the pursuit of self-realisation, gaining satisfaction through the development of personal practical, creative or intellectual abilities, accumulating new experiences instead of consumption (sharing links with alternative hedonism).

Voluntary simplicity places personal, non-material satisfaction above consumerist consumption but does not require its advocates to have less of everything.[27] The sustainability to be gained from voluntary simplicity implies less material consumption but not less non-material consumption. The non-material consumption allows for personal growth and is essentially an investment in self, which is all-important for self-esteem and self-realisation as it provides the pleasure and happiness previously gained through the continuous accumulation and consumption of material wealth. Voluntary simplicity has another inherent quality in that it need not be initiated by a negative reaction to or rejection of consumerist consumerism and materialism but can equally be a positive reaction seeking quality of life and a sense of wellbeing.

Snapshot: Keeping business close

Harveys is the oldest brewery in Sussex, dating back to 1790. It is an extremely successful brewery, having gained a host of awards for its products, some 57 accolades since 1952, not counting other smaller prizes for its business activities.[28] Yet if you have never heard of the brewery, it should come as no surprise.

Most of Harveys' business is located within 60 miles of its brewery and 80 percent of its beer is consumed no more than 30 miles from where it is located.

Harveys pursues a strategy of local sustainability and has decided to segment its market geographically rather than behaviourally to remain sustainable. The brewery believes that large companies cannot be truly sustainable; their very size prevents them from being sustainable and their claims can only amount to greenwash. For Harveys, small is not only beautiful; it is sustainable because remaining local allows it to cut the beer miles in its distribution network and organise the recycling of both its casks and bottles, which are cost-effectively (and environmental-effectively) returned for reuse. As a result, waste packaging is virtually non-existent at Harveys.

Harveys goes further. Locally grown hops and barley, and gravity extracted spring water form the main ingredients of its brews. No effluent goes to local rivers and all agricultural by-products are returned to the locality – spent hops for mulch fertiliser and spent grains for cattle feed. No waste is sent to landfill. Support for the local community also extends to the local complementary currency of the area, even creating a special edition beer Quids In, to celebrate the launch of the Lewes pound. Miles Jenner, the head brewer, describes the relationship between brewery and the local community as symbiotic; they both need each other and they both support each other.[29]

Professional practice: Gaining currency with the locals

The coalition of local shops you advised in Chapter 1 has gone from strength to strength, so much so that a variety of other local businesses are now interested in joining. They are not all from the retail trade: some are local suppliers such as a builder's merchant, an office supplies company, two public houses and three restaurants among others.

▶

You have been approached by the coalition again, this time to propose more ways of strengthening its position against competition from the major players of the region, and provide more substantial sustainable benefits to the local economy and the community.

You have researched the concept of complementary currencies and how their use can aid the progress of sustainable development, and can now produce a short report outlining the benefits of the system as well as the criticisms and possible pitfalls. After creating a balanced argument, what will be your final recommendation – to adopt a complementary currency or not?

Getting started

1. Visit the following website: www.smallisbeautiful.org
2. Find out what Totnes and Lewes in the UK have in common with Berkshire, Massachusetts, US.

Summary

Rather than only aiming at a subsection of the total population, marketing interventions for sustainability should aim to target as much of the general population as possible because it will require behavioural changes from everyone to obtain the largest number of sustainable benefits. Since changing behaviour is the key to consumer-led sustainability, efforts to understand the marketplace have concentrated on dividing and subdividing the total market according to their willingness and ability to behave sustainably, and the extent to which they already engage in or accept different aspects of sustainable practice.

Over recent years, marketers' understanding of consumers' attitudes and behaviour with regard to sustainability has grown, leading to greater insights into the make-up of each of the possible segments and reaching a better understanding of the variety of influences that exist within each segment, which vary in intensity and significance.

Despite having more sophisticated and accurate groupings of people, inconsistencies in behaviour are still apparent as consumers struggle between the two distinct consumption and lifestyle choices of sustainable citizen and unsustainable consumer. An understanding of more radical sustainable lifestyle choices such as voluntary simplifiers may provide answers to persuade less motivated groupings to move towards becoming more sustainable in the future by using them as role models and examples of good lifestyle practice.

Case study: Time to think outside the bottle

Mineralwaters, a non-profit consumer organisation that offers comprehensive information on the bottled water market, estimates that there are around 3,300 different brands available across some 130 countries. While still an almost £1.86 billion business in the UK alone, the bottled water industry has come under increasing pressure in more recent years and sales have begun to decline as environmental issues have gained more ground among the general public and as recession has taken a hold on the world economy.

Bottled water – a product which consumes a precious natural resource, creates tonnes of rubbish and consumes large amounts of energy – became almost an overnight success in many developed countries. The consumption of bottled water rapidly became a symbol of status and fashion, fuelled by heavy branding and the emergence of a diet, health and fitness oriented urban consumer niche and, as a result, sales rose quickly. By 2004, global consumption of bottled water had reached 154 billion litres – up nearly 60 percent on 1999 – and the value of the sector continued to rise until 2007.

Increasing pressure and condemnation

Perhaps what is surprising is that the negative effects of the bottled water industry coupled with some rather dubious production methods and marketing activities did not influence a downturn in the market sooner than they did. Criticisms of the water industry have multiplied during the last decade. In part, economic reasons during a recession are beginning to make more sense to the consumer. A litre of bottled water sold for about £1 costs about 500 times more than filling an empty bottle with water straight from the tap. Other arguments point to sound ethical and sustainable reasons why the bottled water market has run into difficulty:

- Many see water as a human right and not a commodity to be bought and sold for profit and they think investment in access to public water systems should be the priority.

- Bottled water has been positioned as safe and healthy, based on the perceived purity of spring water and by depositioning public water supplies, portraying them as contaminated and unreliable, scaring the public into using bottled sources.

- Despite the previous tactic, in reality many companies sell bottled water sourced from standard tap water supplies, some 40 percent of bottled water in Canada and the US is actually tap sourced.

- Bottled water companies are responsible for the depletion and exhaustion of underground freshwater reserves.

- Bottled water has a high carbon footprint, as water is transported from source and distributed to retailers and customers. The use of plastic bottles and packaging adds to the carbon footprint.

- Water tends to be sold in single-serving plastic bottles made of polyethylene terephthalate (PET), the most commonly used plastic, and millions of barrels of crude oil go into making it. PET is difficult to recycle and is hard to turn scrap PET into new bottles, meaning more crude oil is always necessary.

▶

- Many plastic bottles end up in landfill and can take up to 1,000 years to fully biodegrade, incinerating them would release toxic by-products such as chlorine. In the US it was reported that up to 40 percent of bottles returned for recycling were exported for that purpose to countries as far away as China. Only about a third of some 13 billion plastic bottles of all types sold in the UK in 2008 were recycled.

The backlash

2007 marked a turning point in the bottled water sector, as sales began to drop for the first time. The backlash was principally led by civil authorities who felt forced to defend the quality of their tap water supplies from the comparative advertising campaigns of bottled water companies. In order to do this counter-arguments focused on the ethical and environmental credentials of bottled water.

Numerous American cities banned the purchase of bottled water by government departments, even water coolers, such as the cases in New York, San Francisco and Salt Lake City. In the UK in 2008, London's Westminster Council banned bottled water and coolers from its installations, replacing them with cooled tap water dispensers instead. Meanwhile, in London's *Evening Standard*'s *Water on Tap* campaign, restaurants, bars and nightclubs have been encouraged to offer customers free tap water instead of bottled water and Thames Water Authority proposed allowing commuters at rail and bus stations to fill their own water containers for free or a nominal charge to maintain the upkeep of machines in order to wean them off buying bottled water.

Bottled water companies have also been pressured into acknowledging the source of their product, something they have been reluctant to do when the source has been the municipal tap supply. Both Coca-Cola's Dasani water brand and Pepsi's Aquafina brand have been criticised for selling filtered municipal tap water and now include the words *Public Water Source* on their labelling. However, the phrase *Public Water Source* may not be immediately recognised by consumers and it might not make it clear to consumers that the water is actually from a standard tap. Some brands place this information underneath the bottle top, although some may more cynically think that it is the last place a consumer would look for product information. In contrast, when the source of bottled water is a natural spring, such information tends to take pride of place on the label.

Bottled water strikes back

In September 2008 Britain's largest water bottlers formed the National Hydration Council (NHC). Although it sounds more like an official government body, the NHC is actually formed by Danone Waters, Nestlé Waters and Highland Spring, and incorporates well-known brands such as Evian, Vittel, Buxton and Volvic to defend the sector against growing criticism and restore market growth. Its stated objectives include the research and promotion of the environmental, health and sustainable benefits of naturally sourced bottled water and assistance in helping consumers make informed choices about bottled water.

The NHC's first campaign launched in April 2009 was aimed at promoting the health benefits of drinking bottled water and was a sign that the sector had decided to move away from attacking its traditional competitor – tap water – to concentrate on three selected benefits of staying hydrated: keeping teeth and gums clean and healthy, maintaining a sharp mind, improving physical performance during exercise and anti-obesity.

Positioning bottled water as a healthier alternative to sugary soft drinks presents the sector with an easier target and allows it to maintain its long-standing health message without prolonging the fruitless debate it has had with tap water

Certainly, in comparison with other drinks, bottled water can claim a better environmental performance. A litre of bottled water creates about a third of the greenhouse gases of those associated with a bottle of fizzy drink and just an eighth of those from fruit juice. But when compared with tap water, bottled water loses out and produces nearly 400 times more carbon dioxide per litre.

Not all brands have chosen to avoid painting tap water as the enemy. Hildon (not a member of NHC) is an upmarket bottled water, not distributed via supermarkets but associated with status venues and events such as the Savoy Hotel and the Royal Opera House. Under pressure from the threat of major venues wanting to demonstrate their sustainable credentials to the public by removing bottled water from their facilities, Hildon took out a 20-page trade magazine advertisement attacking tap water and placed the document on its website, under the title *A Statement from Hildon Natural Mineral Water*, in May 2009.

The message from the trade magazine asked if tap water was really safe, stating that impurities existed in it, though this was described as scare-mongering by the Drinking Water Inspectorate. This was a stark contrast from other Hildon campaigns such as their 'The King and I' campaign which featured a bottle of their water as a companion to fine wine.

Some brands have attempted to divert attention from the environmental aspects of their product by establishing relationships with water charities in the developing world. For example, Volvic launched its *1 for 10* campaign, generating 10 litres of drinking water for people in Africa for the sale of every 1-litre bottle in partnership with the water-well building organisation World Vision. Ethical brands have also entered the market, including One Water, Thirsty Planet and Fairbourne Springs – the Co-operative's own brand with profits from sales going directly to water projects around the world.

Diversify or die

While plain bottled water accounts for 90 percent of the current market, there is already evidence that companies are diversifying in order to avoid a stronger downturn in the future by entering the enhanced water market, which is worth £450 million in the UK. One notable entrant to this market has been Glacéau, the vitamin water from Coca-Cola. Its marketing communications have included a Facebook page sponsoring the film 'New Moon', released in 2009 as the second part of the highly popular cult work *The Twilight Saga*.[30]

Follow up

1. Visit the Hildon website, www.hildon.com, and evaluate the company's sustainability credentials.

2. Conduct brief analyses of the plain and enhanced water markets. Where do their futures lie?

Dilemma part 2:   Nature makes a comeback

Whereas the term organic has been quickly applied to the clothing sector with organic cotton, there has been little movement towards applying animal welfare criteria to clothing. In the UK, the RSPCA suggests that clothing manufacturers should ensure that the leather and other animal skins they purchase are by-products of the meat industry and are not from endangered species, and are cruelty free. The RSPCA also has a no fur policy. In its entry guidelines for its 2009 Good Business Awards, the RSPCA asked entrants to explain their policies on merino wool, cashmere, angora and feathers.

The New Zealand Merino Company Limited has established Zque and can now offer the world's first traceable supply chain for Merino wool. Zque's ethical wool accreditation programme ensures environmental, social and economic sustainability, animal welfare (non-mulesed sheep) and traceability back to the source.

In a move that is bound to cause controversy, the Fur Council of Canada has viewed the sustainability movement as an opportunity to reposition and revitalise its fur industry. Its campaign *Fur for an Eco-Conscious World* states that fur is a renewable resource, durable, reusable and recyclable, biodegradable and energy and resource efficient (see photo).

Devise the strategy

A mainstream, high street fashion retailer is considering introducing a section to its store dedicated to fur and other animal-sourced materials on the basis of their renewable, sustainable qualities.

As an independent marketing consultant you have been asked to present a feasibility study to help the retailer decide whether it can establish a sustainable fashion section to its stores. It intends to brand the section as *Nature's Bounty* and include a number of natural, sustainable lines in fur, leather, merino wool, angora, peace silk and cashmere.

Source: The Advertising Archives

Research the market potential as well as the issues of sustainability and ethics behind the proposal and, using the evidence you have gathered, make a recommendation to the retailer on whether to proceed or not. Are the arguments of sustainability strong and credible enough to ensure sufficient demand from a viable target market? Would you recommend carrying just some but not all of the lines? Do ethical concerns regarding fur differ from those of the other materials? If so, why, and is there justification for these differences?

References

1. Kern, G. (CEO of the International Watch Company) cited in Hopkins, M. (2009) 'What the "Green" Consumer Wants', *MIT Sloan Management Review* 50(4): 89.

2. McDonald, S. and Oates, C. (2006) 'Sustainability: Consumer Perceptions and Marketing Strategies', *Business Strategy and the Environment* 15: 157–170.

3. Maslow, A. (1970) *Motivation and Personality*, 2nd ed., New York: Harper and Row.

4. Young and Rubicam (2002) *There are Seven Kinds of People in the World*, www.4Cs .yr.com

5. Osborne, H. (2007) 'Sainsbury's Shoppers Snap Up Designer Bags', *The Guardian,* 25 April.

6. Goodman, M. (2009) 'Peaches Geldof Gets Ringpull Handbag From Brazil Recycling Project', *The Sunday Times*, 6 September.

7. Barr, S., Gilg, A. and Shaw, G. (2006) *Promoting Sustainable Lifestyles: A Social Marketing Approach*, Final Summary Report for Defra, University of Exeter.

8. Downing, P. and Ballantyne, J. (2007) *Tipping Point or Turning Point? Social Marketing and Climate Change*, Ipsos MORI, www.ipsos-mori.com.

9. Roper Starch Worldwide (2000) Roper Green Gauge Survey, www.gifkamerica .com/about_us/index.en.html

10. Chiarelli, N. (2008) *Shades of Green Environment, Ethics & Causes in a Downturn*, GfK Roper Consulting Presentation at Organic Exchange, Porto, October.

11. Chiarelli, N. (2008) *Shades of Green Environment, Ethics & Causes in a Downturn*, GfK Roper Consulting Presentation at Organic Exchange, Porto, October.

12. Pew Research Center (2009) *Fewer Americans See Solid Evidence of Global Warming*, 22 October, http://people-press.org/report/556/global-warming

13. Derbyshire, D. (2009) 'US Belief in Climate Change is Cooling Fast', *The Daily Mail,* 24 October.

14. Defra (2008) *A Framework for Pro-environmental Behaviours*, London: Defra.

15. Davis, T. (2009) 'How Green do we want us to be, Ask Business Leaders', *The Sunday Times*, 6 September.

16. Havas Media (2008) *Climate Change Research Spain Factsheet*, 14 May, www .havasmedia.com

17. Defra (2008) *A Framework for Pro-environmental Behaviours*, London: Defra.

18. Muckle, R. [Social Researcher for Defra] (2009) *Segmenting for Greener Living*, Presentation given at The Green Agenda: Are we engaging the customer?, Conference at Kingston University, 22 April.

19. McDonald, S. and Oates, C. (2006) 'Sustainability: Consumer Perceptions and Marketing Strategies', *Business Strategy and the Environment* 15: 157–170.

20. Mintel (2007) *Green and Ethical Consumers UK*, January, London: Mintel International Group.

21. Mintel (2007) *Green and Ethical Consumers UK*, January, Mintel International Group.

22. Bedford, T. (2007) *Ethical Consumerism: Everyday Negotiations in the Construction of an Ethical Self*, RESOLVE Seminar, 15 February.

23. Downing, P. and Ballantyne, J. (2007) *Tipping Point or Turning Point? Social Marketing and Climate Change*, Ipsos MORI, www.ipsos-mori.com (p. 42).

24. Jackson, T. (2005) *Motivating Sustainable Consumption: a Review of Evidence on Consumer Behaviour and Behavioural Change*, Guildford: Sustainable Development Research Network.

25. Etzioni, A. (1998) 'Voluntary Simplicity: Characterization, Select Psychological Implications and Societal Consequences', *Journal of Economic Psychology* 19: 619–43 (p. 620).

26. Elgin, D. (1981) *Voluntary Simplicity: Toward a Way of Life that is Outwardly Simple, Inwardly Rich*, New York: William Morrow; Elgin, D. and Mitchell, A. (1977) 'Voluntary Simplicity', *The Co-Evolution Quarterly* 3 (Summer): 4–19; Elgin, D. and Mitchell, A. (1977) Voluntary Simplicity: Lifestyle of the Future?, *The Futurist* 11: 200–261.

27. McDonald, S., Oates, C., Young, C. and Hwang, K. (2006) 'Toward Sustainable Consumption: Researching Voluntary Simplifiers', *Psychology & Marketing* 23(6): 515–54.

28. Harveys (2010) *Awards received by Harveys Since 1952*, www.harveys.org.uk/awards.php.

29. Ellis, H. (2009) 'Companies That Get a Buzz Out of Caring and Sharing', *The Times*, 30 July.

30. Bainbridge, J. (2009) 'Making a Smaller Splash', *Marketing*, 2 December, 32–33; De Coverly, E. et al. (2008) 'Hidden Mountain: the Social Avoidance of Waste', *Journal of Macromarketing* 28: 289–303; Fortson, D. (2009) 'Bottle vs tap grudge match hots up', *The Sunday Times*, 7 June; Mineralwaters (2009) www.mineralwaters.org; National Hydration Council (2009) www.naturalhydrationcouncil.org.uk; Prigg, M. (2008) 'Free Tap Water at all London Bus and Rail Stations', *The Evening Standard* 10 June; Thomas, J. (2009) 'Bottled-water Alliance Rolls Out First Campaign', *Marketing*, 22 April, p. 3. National Hydration Council campaign www.yououghttodrinkmorewater.co.uk/Be-Naturally-Better/default.html

PART 3

Marketing as an agent of change

5 Motivating behavioural change

We need to be better at painting a compelling, inspiring picture of a sustainable future[1]

Alan Knight, Sustainable Development Commissioner

Chapter objectives

After studying this chapter you should be able to:

1   Understand the importance of behavioural change for sustainability.

2   Explain the social and psychological motivators behind pro-sustainable behaviour.

3   Understand the use of appealing to altruistic, environmental and egoistic values to promote behavioural change.

4   Explore the use of social marketing for planning for and implementing behavioural change in consumers towards a more sustainable lifestyle.

Dilemma part 1:   The bottom line

The choice between acting to protect the environment or not has often been defined as a social dilemma, because pro-environmental behaviour may require the individual to restrain egoistic tendencies for the benefit of others. The dilemma centres on the decision to act in one's own individual self-interest for immediate gain or act in the interest of the group or collective and entail the consequences of the short-term sacrifices. Although deciding in favour of the collective can be seen as the morally and ethically right choice to make, this does not always result in the sustainable choice being made. The possible solution to this social dilemma may lie in the reinterpretation of collective interest, so it directly equates to the individual's own self-interest. Collective and individual interest could become one and the same. It would therefore need to be demonstrable that decisions made against the interest of the collective would result in everyone suffering the negative consequences of those actions and that the individual, reluctant to engage with sustainable practice, would be better off by cooperating from the start.

The disposable nappy is the epitome of the convenience product; use once and throw away. Yet the word *disposable* gives the wrong impression – it implies that it is simple and safe to throw away after a single use but it is not. The disposable nappy is most definitely difficult to dispose of. Following are some nappy facts:

- Figures vary, but an average baby will use about 6,000 nappies until it is potty trained, reaching about 1 tonne in weight.

- 8 million nappies are thrown away per day in the UK, some 3 billion a year, with 90 percent ending up in landfill sites, meaning tonnes of untreated sewage per year. Normally raw sewage cannot be disposed of in this way.

- 20 billion nappies are thrown away each year in the EU and 27.4 billion disposable nappies are used each year in the US (accounting for more than 3.4 million tons of waste dumped into landfills in the US).

- Birmingham, the UK's second city, accumulates about 22,000 tonnes of waste on disposable nappies, costing the City Council over £750,000 in disposal.

- Nappies contribute biodegradable waste to landfill sites and by 2020 the EU Landfill Directive requires the UK to reduce biodegradable municipal waste sent to landfill by over two-thirds compared with today's levels.

- A large part of disposable nappies is made from synthetic materials which do not biodegrade and are a waste of natural resources.[2]

Discuss the following:

1. An estimated 90 percent of parents use disposable nappies for one main reason: convenience. How can the marketer neutralise the convenience barrier that prevents parents from adopting *real nappies* – the washable, reusable, more sustainable alternative – to the disposable nappy?

Motivating behavioural change

In order to devise successful strategies for change it is necessary to acknowledge the obstacles to change that exist and understand that the consumer may be both willing and yet resistant to change at the same time. Stimulating concern for the principal issues related to sustainability among the general population is something that can be achieved, but, at the same time, such concern is not likely to be automatically translated into a change in behaviour. Because pro-sustainable intention does not consistently result in pro-sustainable behaviour, it is the role of the marketer to understand the reasons why this is so and devise the strategies needed to turn intention into behaviour. Not surprisingly, investigation into consumer behaviour seems to attract the lion's share of attention in the academic literature and government-commissioned research into sustainability.

An analysis of the reasons why people do not embrace all aspects of sustainable behaviour reveals a number of significant obstacles. For example, Defra's study of pro-environmental behaviours highlights potential barriers to behavioural change, ranging from misperceptions of sustainable products, or lack of trust or knowledge, down to just plain disinterest and indifference.[3]

For many people, it seems unfeasible to become as sustainable as possible because full sustainability lies just beyond their own personal limits. This barrier, when encountered by consumers, is not necessarily related to individual, specific actions such as recycling glass or buying fairtrade, but to the possibility of adopting a completely sustainable lifestyle as a result of accumulating a number of sustainable practices. There are many actions that can be taken which, when combined, would result in a more fully sustainable lifestyle. However, if these actions are placed on a continuum indicating the amount of effort and sacrifice required for each one, it is clear that most people reach a limit regarding the amount of sacrifice or compromise they are willing to accept. By highlighting only a selection of actions, it can be seen in Figure 5.1 that the more far-reaching the action to improve sustainability the less likely the public will be willing to adopt the behaviour, if it requires a significant lifestyle sacrifice that they are not prepared to make. Different groups of people will reach their lifestyle sacrifice barrier, beyond which they will not voluntarily pass, at a different point on the continuum. These thresholds, which limit the adoption of sustainable consumer behaviour, in part are dependent on the strength of consumers' adherence to the more conventional product attributes of convenience, price and availability, and in part are dependent on personal considerations such as individual levels of motivation and willingness, ability to take action, personality, life stage, socio-economic group, etc.

The challenges beyond the threshold

One threshold or barrier that attracts much attention is car usage, particularly short local trips and the commute to and from the place of work. As can be

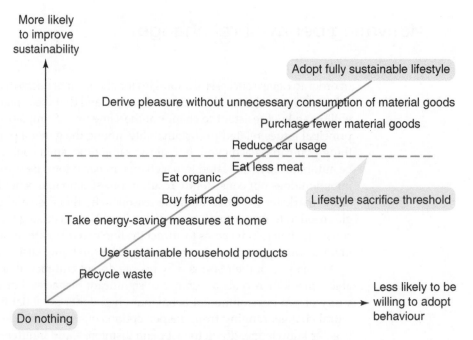

Figure 5.1 Plotting the lifestyle sacrifice threshold

seen in Figure 5.1, reducing car usage appears just above the lifestyle barrier in recognition of how difficult people may find this particular lifestyle change due to their negative predisposition, established habits, lack of opportunity or cost factors.

A study into willingness to reduce car usage in Sweden revealed that the two different underlying attitudes towards the environment – ecocentrism and anthropocentrism – were partly responsible for pro- or anti-environmental behaviour related to driving.[4] An ecocentric individual would tend to want to protect the environment even if it meant some sacrifice to his/her quality of life. On the other hand, an anthropocentric individual might only provide conditional support and be less likely to protect the environment if such actions compromised other values such as quality of life.[5] Reduction of car usage on environmental grounds was therefore found to be partly dependent on these opposing attitudes towards the environment. In most studies, reducing usage or giving up the car meets with significant levels of resistance.[6]

Reducing the purchase of material goods and deriving pleasure without unnecessary purchases also remains a difficult but not impossible barrier to overcome in the pursuit of sustainability. There are already those who write about the poverty of affluence and propose an alternative form of hedonism not based on consumerist consumption but on the dignity of citizenship.[7]

Whether voluntary, compulsory or both, change towards sustainability is most definitely on the business agenda and marketers can learn how to stimulate change in this direction through a more thorough understanding of consumer attitudes and behaviour towards sustainability.

This chapter focuses on how to achieve change in consumer behaviour in order to move consumers closer to a sustainable lifestyle with particular emphasis on making sustainable behaviour standard, everyday behaviour. It is recognised that inspiring voluntary change is likely to be much more successful than compulsory change, and this chapter details two means of achieving voluntary behavioural change. First, from the perspective of marketing psychology there is an examination of norms of behaviour, how they function and how they might be used to encourage the adoption of more sustainable habits of consumption. Second, there is an exploration of social marketing theory and how social marketing frameworks appear to have much in common with the issues and challenges facing marketers who want to encourage sustainable consumer behaviour. To this end it is suggested how social marketing frameworks may be adapted for that purpose.

Changing norms of behaviour

Campaigns directed towards the public aimed at changing their behaviour (anti-smoking, drink-driving, healthy eating) tend to be either information-based or exhortation-based. However, while both of these methods tend to be the most used, they are likely to be the least effective in promoting a change of behaviour. They seek to persuade people to behave differently by either rationally informing them of the consequences of their actions or emotionally pleading with them to change their ways though often without much success.[8]

Despite the great quantity of information available to the public, this does not necessarily lead to increased awareness, and nor does increased awareness lead to action. Information provision, whether through whole campaigns led by the government, specific advertisements from NGOs, individual initiatives of companies, point-of-sale displays or product labelling, must be supported by and blended with other approaches taking the long-term view of permanent change rather than only achieving a short-term temporary effect.

Equally, emotion-led appeals have their limitations. Emotional exhortation based on the extent of the global problems faced by humanity tend to create a sense of paralysis in people rather than action, as they feel there is little individuals can do to alleviate global problems.

This section does not intend to be an exhaustive account of consumer behaviour theory but elements of the models chosen, when viewed together, point to how governments and businesses may apply such understanding to their own circumstances in order to establish sustainable behaviour as the norm. Three areas of consumer behaviour with links to motivating pro-sustainable behaviour now follow and they fall into the following categories:

● copying others

● thinking of others

● thinking of ourselves.

Do as others do

There has been much interest in reducing non-sustainable behaviour by establishing sustainable behaviour as the new norm, by depicting it as normal conventional behaviour and leaving behind the legacy of the fringe, marginal and sometimes comic perceptions of the earlier green movement.[9] This goal has led to growing interest in the conceptual models available to explain the social and psychological influences on consumer behaviour and the contribution that can be made to sustainable practice by applying theories devised to explain how we learn from and copy the behaviour of others – in effect, it seems we often 'do as others do'.

Numerous scholars have commented on the natural tendency to copy the behaviour of others. For example, social psychologist Robert Cialdini in his 'A focus theory of normative conduct' proposes that such behaviour is guided by two types of social norms – descriptive and injunctive.[10]

Descriptive norm

The descriptive norm refers to *what is done, what most people do* and, while it does not always exert a moral or ethical influence, it can have a powerful effect on people's behaviour as people tend to want to behave in a socially appropriate manner and follow the rest rather than stand out awkwardly for being different. Significantly there is a tendency for people to underestimate the frequency, commonness and effectiveness of the descriptive norm, which can increase the likelihood of people adopting the norms of their peers as a standard against which they compare their own behaviours, resulting in them imitating what they see as the acceptable norm.

It is also suggested that people choose to follow the descriptive norm, as it is often regarded as an easier, more practical and convenient course of action, a shortcut which requires less mental deliberation and reflection. In this way descriptive norms serve as examples of behaviour which people may choose to copy, particularly when they are highly visible, such as the use of roadside recycling containers for paper, glass and plastic. However, the peer social pressure exerted by the descriptive norm can sometimes have less effect when the desired behaviours occur out of the visual sight of others, such as the installation of a water butt at the back of the house.[11] Nevertheless, the importance of visible norms of behaviour should not be undervalued, as they are habit forming and may lead from isolated sustainable behaviours to more interconnected sustainable behaviours – often described as 'sticky behaviours' – as it has been suggested that the adoption of one sustainable behaviour can act as a catalyst leading to the adoption of others over time.[12]

Injunctive norm

The injunctive norm refers to *what ought to be done* and therefore is a reflection of the moral codes of society and the social group. Injunctive norms can either motivate or restrict people's behaviour, as they can result in social rewards or punishments for people if they do not behave in certain ways. Injunctive norms may take the form of social disapproval and result in exclusion from the group or may take the form of legal restrictions and sanctions such as fines or confiscation.

Both types of norms are likely to apply to any given situation and may or may not be adhered to according to their salience within a particular context. For example, neighbours may follow the descriptive norm of putting their recycle boxes on the pavement each week but may not stick to the rules of the injunctive norm and disguise soil in their garden rubbish container when only vegetation is allowed, therefore running the risk of a fine.

The invisible influence of descriptive social norms

People are not very good at understanding why they behave as they do and this issue is particularly apparent in the use of social norms. In an experiment studying whether passers-by would give money to a street musician, research accomplices would give the musician money in full view of approaching normal individuals. It was observed that those who saw another person give a donation were eight times more likely to contribute than those who did not see anyone giving change.[13] However, when those who donated were asked why they had given money they answered it was because they liked the song, they felt sorry for the musician or because they just had spare change. They did not recognise that they had copied the people in front of them and that the similar actions of others had acted as the causal antecedents of their own behaviour and the influence of the social norm was not apparent to them.

It seems people tend to find a convenient and plausible explanation for their behaviour. Explanations may naively point to an unrelated cause or be the result of erroneous introspection after the event. Whatever the case, it appears a given behaviour is not always linked to its true cause and people are either reluctant or just unable to recognise the contribution of following the example of others. What is clear is that marketers need to identify and use the true causes of behavioural change, not the imagined ones from the perspective of the consumer, because if marketers do not use the correct motivating factor they will be wasting their efforts.

Marketing with social norms

Much of sustainable marketing has logically focused on changing behaviour by appealing to one, some or all of three basic values: altruistic, egoistic or biospheric, as shown in Table 5.1. However, since an extensive behavioural change has not been achieved in the general population, it indicates that only particular segments are influenced by these means, leaving marketers requiring different strategies to extend behavioural change to other groups. Evidence demonstrates that marketing with social norms can provide another and perhaps more efficient way of changing behaviour towards sustainability.

Changing habits is a key challenge for sustainable marketers.[14] Since habit is responsible for the occurrence of much non-sustainable behaviour in numerous facets of lifestyle and consumption, the opportunity to establish new habits

Table 5.1   The influence values on behaviour

ALTRUISTIC VALUES →	Humanity
	People in the community
In the best interest of others	Future generations
	Children
EGOISTIC VALUES →	Me
	My future
In my own best interest	My lifestyle
	My health
	My prosperity
BIOSPHERIC VALUES →	Marine life
	Animals
In the best interest of the planet	Plants/trees
	Air/water

to advance sustainability is of great importance. With social norm marketing the focus of the appeal is not so much on sustainability itself, as on habit, specifically the habits of others, encouraging people to adopt through imitation the habits of others and follow a more sustainable lifestyle as a result.

In a recent study it can be seen that the social norm can outperform the conventional sustainability appeals in achieving behavioural change.[15] When asked to rate the following motivations for energy conservation, participants in the study gave these reasons in the following order of importance:

1. Protecting the environment – biospheric.

2. Beneficial to society – altruistic.

3. Saving money – egoistic.

4. Others are doing the same – descriptive norm.

It can be seen that the top three motivations reflected the basic values already referred to in Table 5.1. Participants were clearly able to recite the standard reasons which they had doubtless been exposed to for some time through many different channels before the experiment took place. However, in practice, what was occurring was the opposite. Participants were provided with information that indicated that the majority of people in the area were already regularly conserving energy. Results of further experiments showed that it was this information regarding the descriptive norm that had the strongest effect on participants' energy consumption behaviour. Participants started to conserve energy because they felt that everyone else was doing the same. It was this perceived behaviour of their peers that was unconsciously directing their energy conservation behaviour and the study concluded that following the norm was potentially more effective in changing behaviour than standard, conventional appeals. Thus, while respondents were giving in reply what they thought should motivate energy conservation, the real reason behind their actions was invisible to them – the descriptive norm.

While there is no doubt regarding the success of the above experiment and its potential for driving behavioural change, two more issues regarding the use of the descriptive norm need to be highlighted.

First, the success of such interventions may depend on participants not being contaminated by becoming aware of how normative information was being provided to them and used to create a behavioural change. Certainly it would be vital to make sure that such normative information was honest and factual in order to avoid outright rejection, or negative or biased behaviour.

Second, one study draws attention to three different effects of the use of normative information for behavioural change: constructive, destructive and reconstructive.[16] These three facets resulted from participants being informed of average consumption rates of energy for the local community as part of the information communicated in the descriptive norm.

- Constructive effect – participants who saw their own level of energy consumption as being above the average of the descriptive normative information reduced their consumption, demonstrating the powerful influence of the desire to copy social norms.

- Destructive effect – participants who saw they were already consuming below the neighbourhood average increased their consumption as they felt it was acceptable to match the norm.

- Reconstructive effect – in order to neutralise the destructive effect, descriptive normative information was combined with an injunctive message of social approval stating that other people approved of low-consumption behaviour. This message stopped those people with below average consumption from increasing their consumption, showing injunctive norms could be used in tandem with descriptive norms to maintain the positive effects of the descriptive norm.

Recent research into the use of social norms for sustainable behavioural change has further highlighted the strength and value of its influence. It was found that other conditioning factors could play a part in the establishment of pro-environmental behaviour.[17]

1. People needed to feel they belonged to an active pro-environmental social group in order to feel that their own behaviour was acceptable and valuable.

2. Shared meanings of being a good person by following the group pro-environmental norm were important.

3. For those not belonging to a social group adopting a pro-environmental norm had little social value.

4. Strong personal norms or the desire to maintain status and self-identity could impede the influence of group behaviour and the adoption of pro-environmental norms.

Plainly, social norms can be used to encourage sustainable behaviour patterns although such interventions will require careful planning to avoid negative effects and complete failures.[18] The use of social norms will be commented on again in relation to the use of marketing communications in Chapter 8.

Apply it: Using social norms

Household food waste has quickly become a significant issue for sustainability for a number of reasons:

- High quantities of edible food sent to landfill increase greenhouse gas emissions.
- Restrictions on food waste being sent to landfill are becoming tighter.
- Current food production will not be able to match forecasted world population increases.
- Climate change and loss of agricultural land are reducing food production quotas.

Governments are so concerned they are beginning to produce food security assessments in order to plan for the maintenance of future, more sustainable food supplies for their countries, particularly with the aim of becoming more self-sufficient.[19]

1. How can an understanding of social norms be used by marketers to persuade the general population to reduce their edible food waste? Discuss possible approaches in small groups and choose the most feasible to present to other groups.

Soap operas and social learning theory

World renowned psychologist Albert Bandura also highlights the influence and effectiveness of learning by observing and then imitating the behaviour of others in his highly influential *Social Learning Theory*, sometimes referred to as social cognitive theory.[20] Bandura's theory suggests people learn both by their own direct experience and significantly by example, through observing the behaviour of others, who may be any noteworthy stakeholder – peers, parents, neighbours, media personalities, celebrities.

Building on this theory, Bandura has used entertainment-education in order to promote social change through the use of radio and television serial dramas or soap operas. The protagonists of the dramas provided three different types of role models whose interactions and storylines would combine to highlight the personal and social effects of different lifestyles for the audience. *Positive* models would show the benefits of the change in lifestyle, *negative* models would demonstrate the detrimental effects of rejecting change and *transitional* models would demonstrate the paths to follow, including how to deal with setbacks and impediments. Bandura emphasised the need to use *vicarious motivators*; that is, incentives showing the explicit effects of lifestyle change, for example the joy, happiness and pleasure that can be derived upon adopting a more beneficial behaviour pattern. Equally the disincentives, the negative, harmful consequences of unfavourable practice and their costs would also be portrayed through the negative models, as learning would not only be achieved through imitation but also by active avoidance of the negative consequences depicted by the anti-role models.[21]

This approach has been particularly effective with sustainability issues of social equity in countries ranging from the Sudan, Tanzania, Kenya, Mexico, India and Brazil, dealing with many social concerns including sexual health, birth control, gender inequality and adult literacy, using hundreds of episodes over several years to allow viewers to form strong emotional bonds with role models who evolve and modify their behaviour in a believable way over a realistic timeframe. In Mexico, a campaign designed to promote a national adult literacy programme by encouraging people who could already read to organise self-study groups to teach others, enrolled 90,000 people on the programme in one year. It was discovered that there were three barriers preventing people from engaging in the scheme: some believed you could only learn to read at a young age; some felt they lacked the ability to learn; and others felt an educated person would not want to devote time to helping them read. During the year when the reading campaign was supported by a television drama in which a popular star played the role of a literate person, persuading diverse characters to overcome these perceived barriers and showing them how to overcome natural setbacks in the process, 1 million people enrolled on the literacy programme.[22]

Snapshot: The chef and social learning

Research has indentified the influence of celebrity television chefs over the greener segments of the population for changing to more sustainable and healthier food consumption habits.[23] One such chef, celebrity TV chef Jamie Oliver, sees encouraging people to cook healthy, balanced meals from fresh, local ingredients as a means of improving the quality of people's lives. His TV programmes are shown in 40 countries worldwide and not without controversy, as he tries to get people to change their eating habits.

Jamie Oliver's *Ministry of Food* (2008) was a four-part series aired from 30 September to 21 October 2008 on Channel 4 in the UK. Based in Rotherham in South Yorkshire, Jamie Oliver

▶

aimed to get the town's inhabitants to learn how to cook food from fresh ingredients and estab-lish healthy eating as part of their daily lifestyle. An integral part of the project was the *Pass It On* campaign. Jamie Oliver taught local townspeople recipes and asked them to pass this knowledge on to family and friends who would in turn do the same, to create a chain. People could record their success at creating chains by registering them on the *Ministry of Food* website (www.jamieoliver.com/jamies-ministry-of-food) and the programme also gained a following on the social networking site Facebook.

Thinking of others

The interpretation of some forms of sustainable behaviour as altruism has stimulated investigation into models of altruistic behaviour to help explain the functioning of some sustainably motivated actions, in particular pro-environmental behaviour. Figure 5.2 shows the model of altruistic behaviour as proposed by social psychologist Shalom Schwartz, which describes the process through which social and personal norms combine to influence altruistic behaviour.[24, 25] The model starts with the social norms regarding moral behaviour which most people generally hold and also coincide with the values and attitudes of their significant others in their lives who would expect them to act in the morally proper way.

Personal norms are derived from the social norms and are more significant because they are linked to an individual's self-concept; therefore breaking a personal norm might prompt feelings of guilt, while following one may instil a sense of pride and satisfaction.

However, as depicted by the model, altruistic behaviour is dependent on two other elements: awareness of consequences and ascription of responsibility. Thus, for the personal norm to be acted upon and for behaviour to occur, the person must be aware of the consequences of his/her actions (or inaction) and feel individually responsible for the issue itself. The individual must also believe that his/her contribution will at least alleviate or even remedy the situation. Hence an altruistic decision is one in which the individual is aware that the wellbeing of others depends on his/her actions, and feels responsible for those actions and the consequences.

There have been numerous studies applying the model of altruistic behaviour to various aspects of pro- and anti-environmental behaviour such as the burning of garden rubbish, energy use and recycling.[26] The success of each of those cases depends wholly on the ascription of responsibility *to self* for the undesirable consequences *to others*, that is, the belief that one's own actions have contributed to or could alleviate those consequences.

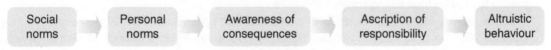

Figure 5.2   Schwartz's model of altruistic behaviour

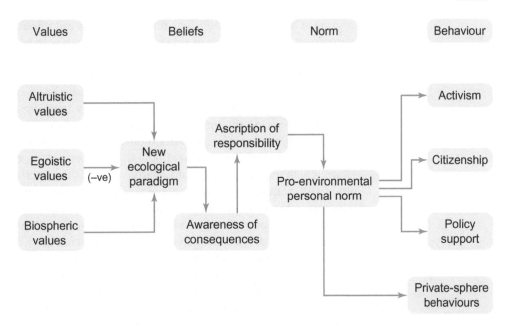

Figure 5.3 Stern's value-belief-norm model

Source: Adapted from Stern, 1999

Stimulating behavioural change therefore could depend on the use and encouragement of altruistic behaviour in others, but the tendency of people to put themselves first before others could impede the wholesale use of altruism as a means of stimulating change . . . unless thinking of ourselves and thinking of others becomes one and the same thing.

Thinking of ourselves

The value-belief-norm model[27] can be regarded as a breakthrough in understanding how pro-environmental beliefs can result in pro-environmental behaviour. While inspired by Schwartz's model, the value-belief-norm model (Figure 5.3) differentiates itself by acknowledging that pro-sustainable behaviour will not result exclusively from altruistic values. The model proposes that pro-environmental norm-based actions stem from three factors:

● acceptance of particular personal values

● beliefs that things important to those values are under threat

● beliefs that actions initiated by the individual can help alleviate the threat and restore the values.

Not all influences on the New Ecological Paradigm proposed by the model are positive and the model recognises that egoistic values can have a negative effect on potential pro-environmental behaviour in the form of general resistance or active opposition. Yet the model can go further since the incorporation of egoistic values allows for the explanation of behaviour towards the environment in general, not just sustainably motivated behaviour.

Recognition and appreciation that not everyone is automatically in favour of sustainable action is important if behavioural change is to be achieved. For example, people may not bother to recycle plastic containers for egoistic reasons because it is not convenient to go to the one recycling depot available for such activity. National fishing fleets will egoistically resist restrictive fishing quotas in order to protect their jobs, paradoxically ignoring the dwindling fish stocks that provide the employment in the first place. The model therefore better reflects the complexity of decision-making situations and allows for the understanding of different stakeholders' perspectives on environmental behaviour, which may be positive or negative towards the environment.

Going further than Schwartz's general awareness of consequences, the model incorporates beliefs about adverse consequences. Noticeably, it is threats to personal values not pure altruism (although altruistic values may contribute) that account for driving the pro-environmental behaviour. This is coupled together with the belief about being responsible for causing the threat or having the ability to carry out personal actions that can neutralise these threats. Thus, the pro-environmental personal norm is a personal moral obligation to act. The model also distinguished degrees of pro-environmental behaviour dependent on the strength and influence of the personal norm ranging from environmental activism (taking part in demonstrations), environmental citizenship (membership of a pressure group), policy support (voting in favour of green legislation) and private-sphere behaviours such as recycling of waste, or the composting garden waste.

A framework for change

The interest in using marketing techniques to change behaviour is not recent. The possibility was first raised in the 1950s when the question 'Why can't you sell brotherhood and rational thinking like you sell soap?'[28] was posed after a study of four social campaigns revealed that the more they had in common with commercial business the more successful they were. Since then social campaigners and marketers have worked together to achieve behavioural change, using a branch of marketing that has become known as social marketing, since the early 1970s.[29]

Social marketing

Social marketing is better known for its use in public health campaigns (anti-smoking, drink-driving, drug abuse, sexual health, etc.) and social marketers believe they have an ethical duty to try to change behaviours that impose large costs on others or society as a whole. As can been seen in the standard definition of social marketing, its focus on achieving behavioural change makes it ideally suited for the marketing of sustainability and encouraging sustainable behaviour.

According to Alan Andreasen, social marketing researcher, 'Social marketing is the application of commercial marketing technologies to the analysis, planning, execution and evaluation of programs designed to influence the voluntary behavior of target audiences in order to improve their personal welfare and that of society.'[30]

Terrance Albrecht, co-editor of *Social Marketing Quarterly*, collected together definitions of social marketing in 1996 to mark the 25th anniversary of its first definition.[31] Notable from those definitions is the degree of overlap between the aims of social marketing and the context of sustainable marketing. Social marketing aims to:

- benefit individuals and society as a whole
- reduce barriers to change
- act for the greater good, act ethically
- promote changes that are inherently good.

In standard business operations, marketing activity stimulates transactions through promoting exchange opportunities, the standard exchange between consumer and organisation being the consumer's money given in exchange for products or services, which provide the consumer with a series of benefits. In a standard social marketing context, such as an anti-smoking campaign, the concept of cost and the nature of the exchange is significantly different; the consumer *gives* a voluntary change in behaviour (gives up cigarettes) in exchange for better health, which benefits the individual (longer life, better quality of life) and society as a whole (reduced health service costs, healthier population/workforce).

When the cost of the new desired behaviour to the consumer (in terms of effort, sacrifice, convenience, time, etc.) is compared with the potential benefits to be gained, it can be seen in Table 5.2 that they can be classified as either tangible personal benefits or intangible societal benefits. Naturally it can be easier to generate demand for low-cost behavioural change benefits that are more personally relevant but significantly more difficult to personalise, justify and obtain intangible high-cost societal benefits. Of course, numerous sustainable actions might bring both personal and societal benefits, although the judgement of the consumers is likely to focus on their own personal benefits.

Table 5.2 Cost versus benefits of social marketing

	Benefits	
	Tangible personal	Intangible societal
Low cost	Breast cancer screening	Recycling household waste
High cost	Giving up smoking	Reducing private car usage

Source: Adapted from Rangan *et al*, 1996.[32]

Social marketing aims to access people's legitimate self-interest (not selfishness) and use it to motivate change. In some respects targeting consumer self-interest is also the key to successful sustainable marketing, while making every effort to avoid consumer selfishness which is liable to favour unsustainable behaviour.

Promoting sustainable behaviour through social marketing

The parallels between social and sustainable marketing contexts are immediately apparent. Both contexts are concerned with the replacement of undesirable behaviours with desirable ones, and consumer targets of social and sustainable marketing can be either individuals or collectives. Both contexts can involve some sort of sacrifice as the consumer gives up the perceived benefits of the undesirable behaviour in exchange for other personal benefits. If enough individuals adopt the new behaviour the accumulative effect is then eventually felt by society.

Table 5.3 shows how consumers contemplate four components involved in adopting a sustainable behavioural change:

- the undesirable behaviour itself

- sacrifices and costs associated with change

- the options for replacement behaviour

- the benefits of the new behaviour.

Table 5.3 The social marketing process applied to sustainability e.g. reduction of car usage for short journeys

	Four components of sustainable behavioural change		
Undesirable behaviour	Sacrifice/costs/ barriers	Possible replacement behaviours	Benefits
Using a car for local journeys under 5km	Speed	Public transport	**Societal:**
	Convenience	Walking	Less noise/air pollution
	Laziness	Cycling	CO_2 reduction
			Saving of natural resources
			Quality of life
			Individual:
			Exercise
			Better health
			Money savings

The consumers' adoption or rejection of new behaviour will be the result of how they evaluate and react to each of the four components. For the process to result in successful outcomes the substitute services and products must provide benefits that outweigh the costs of not changing.[33] This may be difficult to achieve where consumer habits are very entrenched and where convenience is the principal personal sacrifice required of the consumer.

Reducing individuals' car journeys on short trips is one of the current campaigns in the UK's Act on CO_2 programme but even individual benefits such as saving money may not be enough to change this particular behaviour.

Understanding the consequences for the individual for each of the components of behavioural change is vital.[34] This should include anticipating the need for supporting mechanisms and infrastructure in order to facilitate, motivate and maintain a permanent change to the desired behaviour. Table 5.4 indicates the necessary considerations for each of the components of behavioural change required to encourage a reduction in car usage for short journeys. Each of these components needs to be planned for if the marketing intervention to change behaviour is to succeed.

Table 5.4 Marketing considerations for the components of behavioural change, e.g. reduction of car usage for short journeys

Components	Considerations
Undesirable behaviour	How strong a habit is the undesirable behaviour?
	How widespread is the behaviour?
	Is the behaviour linked to personal freedoms?
	How is the total market for this behaviour segmented?
	Which segments would be easiest to target first?
Sacrifice/costs/ barriers	The barriers to behaviour replacement may be:
	• practical – inconvenient public transport timetables, no alternative transport available, unreliability of service
	• psychological – image problems such as dirty vandalised buses, perceived personal safety issues for walking
	• self-interest – no motivation to change, convenience, travel time, cost, laziness
Replacement behaviour	The organisation and infrastructure for replacement behaviours must already be in place *before* the intervention starts.
	For example, more local buses and routes, affordable/competitive fares, cycle lanes, improvement of public footpaths.
	Linkage with other stakeholders may be required or beneficial. Such as:
	• discount on cycle purchases on launch of scheme
	• police patrol presence

(continued)

Table 5.4 (*Continued*)

Components	Considerations
Benefits	Success may depend more on how much the benefits are valued and made personally relevant than on how society as a whole may benefit.
	Emphasis on personal benefits should take precedence when appropriate for the values of the target audience.
	Opportunities to increase the bundle of benefits should be taken potentially through linkage to other stakeholders: e.g. incentives to use local shops for those customers who adopt the scheme.

Apply it: Meat-free Monday, Tuesday, Wednesday . . .

The excessive production and consumption of meat has been a concern for many years. Global demand for meat has multiplied at the same rate as affluence has grown in the developed and developing nations, and has been made possible by the proliferation of large-scale, intensive animal rearing operations.

The second half of the 20th century saw the world production of meat increase fivefold. The figures sound startling. For example, as the production of poultry has increased there are more than twice as many chickens on the planet as there are people to eat them.[35] More meat production will contribute to more hunger, not less, as a third of the world's cereal crops and over 90 percent of soya goes to feed animals rather than people.[36] The UN's Food and Agriculture Organisation has estimated that meat consumption will double by 2050 and that meat production already accounts for nearly a fifth of global greenhouse gas emissions through production of animal feeds and the production of methane (a global warming gas more potent than carbon dioxide).[37] Dr Rajendra Pachauri, chair of the United Nations Intergovernmental Panel on Climate Change, called for people to gradually reduce their meat consumption, starting by one meat-free day a week and increasing the rate to achieve a national reduction of meat consumption of 60 percent by 2020.

1. Using the framework provided by Tables 5.2, 5.3 and 5.4 as a starting point for your analysis, outline the most significant marketing considerations which you would need to take into account if the general public had to be persuaded to reduce their consumption of meat to just twice a week.

Willing and unwilling participants

There are more similarities between social and sustainable marketing worth noting. It is important to remember that the consumer is an active participant in the process of change making the means of involving them in the process of change itself more significant than if they were just passive recipients of change. Management of sustainable lifestyle change is therefore a delicate operation requiring a deep understanding of the target participants and their personal circumstances and motivations that are liable to accelerate or inhibit change.

Table 5.5 Tailoring interventions to different consumer starting points

Level of consumer involvement			
Unaware/not considering	Attempting not succeeding	Contemplating but not acting	Actively resisting/ entrenched

Social marketing interventions

Inform
- Educate
- Communicate
- Advise

⟵———————————————————————⟶

Control
- Require
- Enforce
- Legislate

Source: Adapted from National Social Marketing Centre, 2007[38]

Although social marketers promote voluntary change and would prefer voluntary change, the use of some type of enforcement or regulations to stimulate change is not ruled out. The National Social Marketing Centre anticipates that a mixture of incentives, rewards, disincentives and restrictions will be necessary in the design of social marketing interventions to take into account the different levels of consumer engagement for any specific behavioural issue.[39] Table 5.5 shows that consumers may have different starting points for each potential new behaviour and require different types of interventions to persuade them to change designed to either change behaviour by informing them or controlling them or to apply a mixture of these types of actions.

While a one-off change such as a single visit to a recycling centre with rubbish should not be discouraged, as it may lead to permanent change, social marketing success tends to deal only with absolutes. In other words, the benefits of social marketing will only be achieved if the replacement behaviour is adopted completely *and* maintained – you cannot just drink-drive a little or partly give up drugs. Similarly, numerous sustainable behaviours would also be regarded as absolutes.

Professional practice: 10:10

The year 2050 seems a long way off and a reduction of 80 percent in carbon emissions planned for that date seems like an enormous target to achieve. Establishing targets is a necessary task but they need to be set in a way that encourages people to act rather than perceive them to be out of reach.

10:10 is a non-profit organisation whose mission is to unite every sector of British society behind one simple, realistic target to achieve a 10 percent cut in the UK's carbon emissions in 2010. The team behind the film *The Age of Stupid* started the campaign, which is now supported by a host of organisations and individuals who can make a public declaration of their support via their websites.

October 2010 saw the release of the short film *No Pressure* written by the British top comedy screenwriter Richard Curtis. The film was designed to gain maximum impact and awareness

▶

of the 10:10 campaign and included a number of well-known people such as footballers Peter Crouch and David Ginola, the actress Gillian Anderson and musical group Radiohead. However, the sight of children and adults exploding in the film created a strong public outcry and it was withdrawn from the 10:10 website, although it can still be seen on YouTube.

Research the 10:10 campaigns. Carry out a SWOT (strengths, weaknesses, opportunities and threats) analysis based on the evidence you can find and prepare a series of practical recommendations for the 10:10 organisation aimed to strengthen and expand the campaign and effectively set a new target marking the evolution of 10:10 to 15:15. What actions do you think are necessary to neutralise the negative effects of the 'No Pressure' campaign? Is there no such thing as bad publicity for such an organisation?

Getting started

1. Look at the 10:10 website.
2. Find independent reviews and commentaries of its campaigns (www.1010global.org).
3. View the *No Pressure* film
4. How does an understanding of social marketing assist you in enhancing the campaign in order to reset the target to 15:15?

Researching sustainability: Methodology concerns

In order to predict whether a person intends to behave sustainably marketers can carry out research to investigate the beliefs they hold about particular sustainable motivations and measure the extent to which that person will be willing to act upon them. One well-known psychological model of behaviour change, which has been widely used by social psychologists to explain how perceptions influence actions, is Icek Ajzen's Theory of Planned Behaviour.[40] The model has also been frequently employed to understand consumer behaviour by marketers including sustainable and ethical purchases.[41]

According to Ajzen human behaviour is directed by three kinds of considerations: behavioural beliefs, normative beliefs and control beliefs (as shown in Figure 5.4) and it is a combination of these beliefs that will lead to intention and behaviour on the part of the subject:

Behavioural beliefs:	beliefs about the likely outcomes of the behaviour and evaluations of these outcomes
Normative beliefs:	beliefs about the expectations of others and motivations to comply with these expectations
Control beliefs:	beliefs about the presence of factors that may facilitate or impede performance of the behaviour and the perceived power of these factors

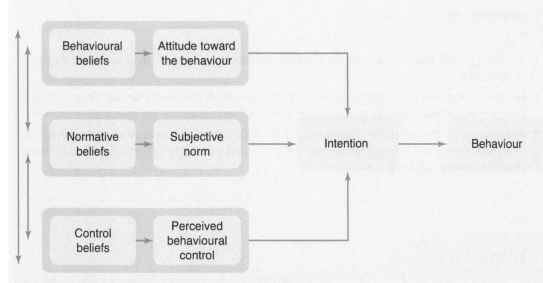

Figure 5.4 Ajzen's Theory of Planned Behaviour[42]

Source: Ajzen, 2006

As can be seen in Figure 5.4, behavioural beliefs produce a favourable or unfavourable *attitude toward the behaviour*. Normative beliefs result in perceived social pressure to conform known also as the *subjective norm*. Control beliefs give rise to *perceived behavioural control,* the extent to which the person feels in command of the situation.

As a general rule, the more favourable the attitude and subjective norm, and the greater the perceived control, the stronger should be the person's intention to perform the behaviour in question. When these factors are favourable people are expected to carry out their intentions when such an opportunity arises, therefore intention is assumed to precede actual behaviour.

Task

A major supermarket chain is reconsidering its policy on the local sourcing of food and the issue of food miles for imported products. The chain wants to assess the opinions and motivations of its consumers when deciding whether to buy local produce or produce with heavy food miles. It is particularly interested in the opinions of its customers for and against such a decision with regard to availability of out-of-season produce and price.

As a marketing consultant you have been asked to plan and carry out the research concentrating on fruit and vegetables and you have decided to use Ajzen's Theory of Planned Behaviour as part of your research methodology.

1. Devise a brief pilot questionnaire with just a few trial questions on each of the three belief types that feed into intention and on to behaviour: behavioural beliefs, normative beliefs and control beliefs. Consider how you might want to record the responses and analyse results, what would be the best means of doing so?

Getting started

1. Try visiting Icek Ajzen's website (www.people.umass.edu/aizen) for help on questionnaire construction.
2. Search for academic articles that have already used Ajzen's Theory of Planned Behaviour as a part of their methodology. What can you learn from them to use for this exercise?
3. Anticipate from the consumers' perspective the kinds of attitudes, influences and motivations that may be relevant to purchasing *local* fresh fruit and vegetables. How will you build these ideas into the questions?

Summary

The ability to change consumer behaviour has always been of vital importance to the marketer. In order to become sustainable the general habits and behaviours of consumers have to change. This will require a significant effort from marketing professionals and other stakeholders but also from the consumers themselves, who are likely to be reluctant to change their behaviour if it entails sacrifice or a notable modification to their lifestyle.

An appreciation of consumer psychology can help the marketer to modify behaviour over time, using an understanding of social norms. This may be particularly effective as the changes in behaviour and lifestyle are likely to be regarded as voluntary changes by consumers in keeping with their altruistic, egoistic and biospheric values. Such changes can be achieved by designing interventions to make sustainable behaviour the new norm, through instilling and then appealing to descriptive and injunctive norms in particular target markets for specific, desirable sustainable behaviours.

The contribution of social marketing expertise, which was designed initially to achieve behavioural changes in aspects of health and anti-social behaviour, also shows great potential to be adaptable to the sustainability context.

Case study: The carrot, the stick and the plastic bag

It has been estimated that Britain's high street stores alone give out around 13 billion single-use plastic carrier bags per year. The world uses more than 1.2 trillion of them a year, an average of about 300 bags for every adult and on average each plastic bag is used for only 12–20 minutes before being discarded. With some 80 percent of marine rubbish coming off the land and nearly 90 percent of that plastic, it may come as no surprise that you can find plastic bags everywhere, even beyond the Arctic Circle and around 100 million tonnes of plastic 'soup' are thought to be floating in the ocean between Hawaii and Japan.

As with many sustainability issues, short-term convenience results in long-term impacts for the planet. Although carrier bags represent less than 1 percent of household waste, they have become an iconic image of a throwaway society. Their consistent contribution to visible litter, coupled with their destructive nature, has made them a significant target of governments, NGOs and retailers, who have used a mixture of incentives and disincentives to persuade the general public to abandon their addiction to the throw-away plastic bag.

The first plastic-bag-free town in Europe

On 1 May 2007, the modest town of Modbury in Devon became the first town in Europe to stop using plastic bags. Rebecca Hosking, a wildlife filmmaker, who had worked for the BBC natural history unit on productions such as David Attenborough's *Life of Mammals* was born and raised in the area, and was so distraught by how plastic was destroying marine life around the planet that she decided to act locally on her return to the UK from filming in Hawaii. Motivated to take action, she managed to persuade all the 1,500 residences and traders of her home town of Modbury to stop using plastic bags in favour of more sustainable long-lasting alternatives. In this case Hosking's ability to persuade the town's retailers to adopt such a radical change was aided by her local knowledge, the trust she inspired, her circle of friends and acquaintances in the town (particularly among the retailers and traders) and her knowledge of the plastic-induced pollution she had witnessed, which she could communicate to others. Listed by the *Guardian* newspaper as one of the 50 people who could save the planet in the 21st century, her campaign added impetus to the anti-plastic-bag movement. Hosking has since said she had the advantage of doing this at home and hoped others would follow her lead in their own localities. Later, at the height of her campaign, she refused to front campaigns for two supermarkets after they had offered her large sums of money to become their public face for the environment.

The polluter pays

To date, government- and retailer-led attempts to curb the use of plastic bags have been composed of a mixture of voluntary initiatives and legislation-driven restrictions and, while both strategies have had a positive effect, there remains the risk that both strategies will eventually be rejected by the general public as they slip back into habits of convenience on the one hand or withdraw political support on the other. Making consumers pay for their bags, paying for the right to pollute, has shown signs of being successful in some instances.

In 2002 the Irish government introduced what became known as the Plas-Tax, a levy of €0.15 on single-use plastic bags in an effort to reduce the consumption of 1.2 billion bags per year. An information campaign was run before the introduction of the tax to encourage consumer engagement and the country experienced a 90 percent drop in bag consumption in its first year, while raising €10 million for an environmental protection fund. Retailers also benefited, saving €50 million a year by not having to supply the single-use bags.

In the UK, Marks and Spencer also introduced its own bag tax of 5p per bag in its supermarkets in 2008. Between May and August of that year, Marks and Spencer reduced the number of bags used by

▶

100 million in comparison with the same period in 2007, representing a reduction of 80 percent. Profits from the sale of bags went to Groundwork, a charity which helps create new parks and play areas.

Government reduction plans

In the UK, the British Retail Consortium in conjunction with leading retailers are working with the UK government to reduce the number of single-use and other carrier bags given away each year. Two voluntary agreements set targets for 2008 and 2009.

Reduction for 2008 25 percent

To reduce the environmental impact of all carrier bags by 25 percent by the end of 2008, based on a 2006 baseline to include single-use bags, bags for life and other reusable bags. The final results for 2008, reported in February 2009, showed that participants had achieved a 26 percent reduction in the total number of carrier bags used and a 40 percent reduction in the environmental impact, measured by the reduction in the use of virgin materials.

Reduction for 2009 50 percent agreement

To reduce the number of carrier bags given out by 50 percent by end of May 2009, based on a 2006 baseline. Results announced in July 2009 show a 48 percent reduction against the established target. The project will continue with another review in the summer of 2010. Overall the figures from the Waste and Resources Action Programme (WRAP) indicate that 870 million single-use plastic bags were handed out in the UK in May 2006, in comparison with 450 million for May 2009 – a 48 percent reduction.

Supermarket initiatives

Supermarkets have used a series of initiatives to encourage customers to use fewer plastic bags. Discount supermarkets Aldi, Lidl and Netto all charge for their bags. The larger supermarket chains have adopted different approaches, focusing on a more efficient use of resources in the manufacture of plastic bags as well as encouraging behavioural change in their customers, mainly through reward, education and communication rather than punishment, (as can be seen in Table 5.6).

Sainsbury's – *remind, reward, remove*

Sainsbury's campaign for plastic bag reduction was based on a three-part strategy – *remind, reward, remove* – and the supermarket has demonstrated its effectiveness through its Nectar points reward scheme. The supermarket began rewarding consumers with Nectar points for each bag reused at the checkout in June 2008, averaging 2.9 million points per month. A year later the average had increased to 4 million points per month. The *reward* part of the strategy with the use of Nectar points came as a result of customer surveys in which 75 percent of respondents stated they expected to be rewarded for reusing bags.

Remove referred to removing plastic bags from sight at checkouts so customers could be focused on the need to change habits as they would have to request bags for each shopping trip if they had not brought their own, effectively reminding them of the new habit they needed to adopt.

Table 5.6 Plastic bag initiatives at supermarkets

Customer focus	Actions
Removing free bags from sight at tills	Removing bags sends a message to customers that they need to solve their own problems. Even though still available on request, customers are forced to reflect on their behaviour and staff can engage them on the topic. Customers use fewer bags when they have to request them from the cashier.
Staff training	Staff trained to engage and inform customers about bag for life, recycling in-store and to encourage reduction of single-use bags.
Staff incentives	Stores rewarded for the highest and most improved bag reductions.
Customer incentives	Bag for life, jute bags, free or reduced cost on bag for life, reward points for bringing own bags (Nectar points, Tesco Green Clubcard points).
Communications	e.g. ASDA slogan 2008 'Saving the Planet One Bag at a Time!' Posters throughout stores, car park banners, in-store announcements, store magazine features. Staff bulletin boards, staff TV, table talkers.
Resource efficiency	**Actions**
Increased collection in-store	More collection points for old bags set up in store for recycling.
Increased recycled material in bags	Increased amount of recycled material in new bags to reduce the amount of virgin material required for production.
Lighter bags	Reduced weight of bags to reduce consumption of raw materials.

Remind was found to be a significant element of the strategy because one of the principal barriers to behavioural change was the forgetfulness of customers. Half of Sainsbury's customers surveyed either forgot to bring bags back into store for reuse or forgot to take them out of the car boot. The type of shopping trip also played a part in this, depending on whether the visit was a planned medium/large shopping trip or an improvised top-up visit. In response, on its 'Make the Difference Day' on 19 April 2008, Sainsbury's gave all its customers a free fridge magnet and car sticker to remind them to take their old bags with them when they went shopping. This was supported by car park posters and in-store radio, point of sale and checkout reminders.

In order to instil the new habit and reinforce the *remind* element of the strategy, Sainsbury's changed its checkout processes in March 2008, retraining 100,000 checkout staff to ask customers if they had brought bags for reuse, remind them to bring them on future visits and purchase a bag for life and tell them about the Nectar reward points as well as the bag recycling facilities in-store.

To complement this strategy, Sainsbury's also increased the recycled content in its orange carrier bags to 50 percent from the previous 33 percent and reduced the virgin plastic content from 57 percent to 40 percent.

▶

Bag suppliers unite

The recent debate over the introduction of an Irish-style plastic bag tax in Wales has resulted in a strengthening of the opposition to such measures. The plans have been called a stealth tax by opposing political forces, who felt that the money raised by the tax would not be used to benefit the public. Suppliers of plastic bags have also felt threatened. The Carrier Bag Consortium is a group of major UK carrier bag suppliers who have joined together to fight the possibility of a carrier bag tax being imposed in the UK. From their perspective, a carrier bag tax would result in job losses in their sector and bring no real benefits for the environment. The consortium has made a series of documents available on its website (www.carrierbagtax.com) to support its claims regarding the failure of plastic bag taxes, criticising heavily the Irish and Welsh initiatives and what its members regard as an unfair targeting of their products.

In July 2009 the Welsh Assembly revealed plans to introduce such a tax with a proposal of imposing a charge of 15p per bag. Subsequent debate on the issue has seen the proposed charge reduced to 7p and 5p on single-use bags and the start of the initiative has been delayed until October 2011. The British Retail Consortium has branded the levy as disappointing, stating that such a tax would impact on lower income households the most and highlighting that in a time of recession Wales would be the first country in the UK to impose extra charges on shoppers.[43]

Follow up

1. Why don't supermarkets just stop providing single-use bags completely? Would a supermarket that decided to do this be able to compete with others that chose to continue offering bags? What would it take for supermarkets and consumers to totally abandon the use of the single-use plastic bag?

2. The bag debate has not spilt over into clothes retailers; what actions have they taken on this issue?

3. There are both voluntary and compulsory initiatives being employed to cut single-use plastic bag consumption, which kinds of initiative are more successful and are likely to be more successful in the future?

4. Analyse the claims of the Carrier Bag Consortium. Are they valid? To what extent will they have an effect on voluntary initiatives?

Dilemma part 2:   The bottom line

Cumbria County Council spends some £600,000 of taxpayers' money a year on dealing with tonnes of disposable nappies thrown away with household rubbish for landfill. In response to the problem, Resource Cumbria, the county's waste partnership, organises nappuccino events. A nappuccino is not another variation on a frothy coffee. A nappuccino is a real nappy coffee morning where parents can chat about real nappies, see real nappies, receive a presentation and demonstration, and examine the variety of products available in a friendly relaxed atmosphere.

Devise the strategy

You are the sustainable development officer for your district council and have been asked to devise a strategy to reduce the number of disposable nappies that go to landfill in the county.

Apply the knowledge gained about social marketing to define the problem using Tables 5.2, 5.3 and 5.4 to organise your assessment of the situation. When devising your strategy consider the need to encourage as much voluntary change as possible. To what extent do you think you will need to use control measures in order to achieve broad, long-lasting change among parents (if so, which ones and how might they be implemented)?

Getting started

1. Collect information from real nappy support groups, real nappy companies, waste disposal organisations and local councils, etc. in order to start to devise a way forward and apply your knowledge gained from the chapter.
2. Expand your knowledge of social marketing techniques.

References

1. Knight, A. (Sustainable Development Officer) (2009) *Sustainable Lives,* London: Sustainable Development Commission (p. 2).
2. Cumbria County Council, www.resourcecumbria.org; Women's Environmental Network, www.wen.org.uk; London Community Recycling Network – Real Nappies for London, www.realnappiesforlondon.org.uk; Paul, P. (2008) 'Diapers go Green', *Time Magazine,* 10 January; The Clean Green Nappy Machine, www.cleangreennappy.co.uk; The Real Nappy Information Service, www.goreal.org.uk; Little Lamb, www.littlelamb.co.uk; Birmingham City Council Municipal Waste Management Strategy 2006 to 2026.
3. Defra (2008) *A Framework for Pro-environmental Behaviours,* London: Defra.
4. Nordlunda, A. and Garvilla, J. (2003) 'Effects of Values, Problem Awareness, and Personal Norm on Willingness to Reduce Personal Car Use', *Journal of Environmental Psychology* 23: 339–347.
5. Thompson, S. and Barton, M. (1994) 'Ecocentric and Anthropocentric Attitudes toward the Environment', *Journal of Environmental Psychology* 14: 149–157.
6. NESTA (2008) *Selling Sustainability Seven Lessons From Advertising and Marketing to Sell Low-carbon Living,* London: National Endowment for Science, Technology and the Arts.

7. Soper, K. (2007) 'Re-thinking the "Good Life": the Citizenship Dimension of Consumer Disaffection with Consumerism', *Journal of Consumer Culture* 7(2): 205–229.

8. McKenzie-Mohr, D. (2000) 'Promoting Sustainable Behavior: an Introduction to Community-based Social Marketing', *Journal of Social Issues* 56(3): 543–554.

9. Rettie, R. and Barnham, C. (2009) *Making Green 'Normal'*, Presentation given at The Green Agenda: Are we engaging the customer? Conference at Kingston University, 22 April.

10. Cialdini, R. Kallgren, C. and Reno, R. (1991) 'A Focus Theory of Normative Conduct: a Theoretical Refinement and Re-evaluation of the Role of Norms in Human Behaviour', *Advances in Experimental Social Psychology* 24: 201–234.

11. Davies, J., Foxall, R. and Pallister, J. (2002) 'Beyond the Intention–Behaviour Mythology: an Integrated Model of Recycling', *Marketing Theory* (2): 29–113.

12. Downing, P. and Ballantyne, J. (2007) *Tipping Point or Turning Point? Social Marketing and Climate Change*, Ipsos MORI, www.ipsos-mori.com (p. 5).

13. Griskevicius, V., Cialdini, R. and Goldstein, N. (2008) 'Social Norms: an Underestimated and Underemployed Lever for Managing Climate Change', *International Journal of Sustainability Communication* 3: 5–13.

14. Jackson, T. (2005) *Motivating Sustainable Consumption: A Review of Evidence on Consumer Behaviour and Behavioural Change*, Guildford: Sustainable Development Research Network.

15. Nolan, J., Schultz, P., Cialdini, R., Goldstein, N. and Griskevicius, V. (2008) 'Normative Social Influence is Underdetected', *Personality and Social Psychology Bulletin* 34(7): 913–923.

16. Schultz, P.W., Nolan, J.M., Cialdini, R.B., Goldstein, N. and Griskevicius, V. (2007) 'The Constructive, Destructive, and Reconstructive Power of Social Norms', *Psychological Science* 18(5): 429–434.

17. Bedford, T., Collingwood, P., Darnton, A., Evans, D., Gatersleben, B., Abrahamse, W. and Jackson, T. (2010) *Motivations for Pro-environmental Behaviour: A Report to the Department for Environment, Food and Rural Affairs*, London: RESOLVE Defra.

18. For example: Clapp, J.D., Lange, J.E., Russell, C., Shillington, A. and Voas, R. (2003) 'A Failed Norms Social Marketing Campaign', *Journal of Studies on Alcohol* 64: 409–414; Granfield, R. (2005) 'Alcohol Use in College: Limitations on the Transformation of Social Norms', *Addiction Research and Theory* 13: 281–292; Perkins, H.W., Haines, M.P. and Rice, R. (2005) 'Misperceiving the College Drinking Norm and Related Problems: a Nationwide Study of Exposure to Prevention Information, Perceived Norms and Student Alcohol Misuse', *Journal of Studies on Alcohol* 66: 470–478.

19. Murray, J. (2009) *Government Orders 'Radical Rethink' of UK Food Policy*, BusinessGreen, 10 August, www.businessgreen.com/business-green/news/2247574/government-orders-radical.

20. Bandura, A. (1977) *Social Learning Theory*, Englewood Cliffs, NJ: Prentice Hall.

21. Bandura, A. (2009) 'Social Cognitive Theory goes Global', *The Psychologist* 22(6): 504–506.

22. Bandura, A. (2009) 'Social Cognitive Theory goes Global', *The Psychologist* 22(6): 504–506.

23. Bedford, T., Collingwood, P., Darnton, A., Evans, D., Gatersleben, B., Abrahamse, W. and Jackson, T. (2010) *Motivations for Pro-environmental Behaviour: A Report to the Department for Environment, Food and Rural Affairs,* London: RESOLVE Defra.

24. Schwartz, S. (1970) 'Elicitation of Moral Obligation and Self-sacrificing Behaviour: an Experimental Study of Volunteering to be a Bone Marrow Donor', *Journal of Personality and Social Psychology* 15: 283–293.

25. Schwartz, S. (1977) 'Normative Influences on Altruism', *Advances Experimental Social Psychology* 10: 221–279.

26. Davies, J., Foxall, G. and Pallister, J. (2002) 'Beyond the Intention–Behaviour Mythology: an Integrated Model of Recycling', *Marketing Theory* 2: 29–113.

27. Stern, P., Dietz, T., Abel, T., Gragnano, G.A., and Kalof, L. (1999) 'A Value-Belief-Norm Theory of Support for Social Movements: the Case of Environmentalism', *Human Ecology Review* 6(2): 81–97; see also, Stern, P., Dietz, T. and Kalof, L. (1993) 'Value Orientations, Gender and Environmental Concern', *Environment and Behaviour* 25(5): 322–348.

28. Wiebe, G. D. (1951/1952) 'Merchandising Commodities and Citizenship in Television', *Public Opinion Quarterly* 15(4): 679–691.

29. Kotler, P. and Zaltman, G. (1971) 'Social Marketing: an Approach to Planned Social Change', *Journal of Marketing* 35: 3–12. See this seminal article for what is regarded as the first definition and explanation of the term social marketing.

30. Andreasen, A. (1995) *Marketing Social Change: Changing Behavior to Promote Health, Social Development, and the Environment,* San Francisco, CA: Jossey-Bass (p. 7).

31. Albrecht, T. (1996) 'Defining Social Marketing 25 Years Later', *Social Marketing Quarterly* Special Issue: 21–23.

32. Rangan, V.K., Karim, S. and Sandberg, S.K. (1996) 'Do Better at Doing Good', *Harvard Business Review* 74(3): 42–54.

33. French, J. (2009) in National Social Marketing Centre (NSMC) *Effectively Engaging People: Interviews with Social Marketing Experts,* NSMC, www.snh.org.uk/pdfs/sgp/A328465.pdf (p. 24).

34. Potter, I. (2009) in National Social Marketing Centre (NSMC) *Effectively Engaging People: Interviews with Social Marketing Experts,* NSMC, www.snh.org.uk/pdfs/sgp/A328465.pdf (p. 6).

35. Compassion in World Farming Trust (2004) *Reducing Meat Consumption: The Case for Urgent Reform,* Petersfield: Compassion in World Farming Trust.

36. Support Meat Free Monday (2010) *Reducing Meat Consumption Won't Save the Planet . . . Says Report Funded by Livestock Industry,* 25 March, www.supportmfm .org/news/reducing-meat-consumption-wont-save-the-planet-says-report-funded-by-livestock-industry.cfm

37. Jowit, J. (2008) 'UN Says Eat Less Meat to Curb Global Warming', *The Observer,* 7 September.

38. National Social Marketing Centre (2007) *Big Pocket Guide – Social Marketing,* 2nd ed., NSMC, www.snh.org.uk/pdfs/sgp/A328465.pdf

39. National Social Marketing Centre (2006) *Starting from: 'where the Customer is at'* available at www.nsmcentre.org.uk/component/remository/func-startdown/33/ accessed 7 December 2009.

40. Ajzen, I. (1991) 'The Theory of Planned Behaviour', *Organizational Behaviour and Human Decision Processes*, 50: 179–211.

41. See, for example: Chen, C. and Zimitat, C. (2006) 'Understanding Taiwanese Students' Decision-making Factors regarding Australian International Higher Education', *International Journal of Educational Management* 20(2): 91–100; Grunert, K. and Ramus, K. (2005) 'Consumers' Willingness to Buy Food through the Internet: a Review of the Literature, and a Model for Future Research', *British Food Journal* 107(6): 381–403; Kalafatis, S., Pollard, M. East, R. and Tsogas, M. (1999) 'Green Marketing and Ajzen's Theory of Planned Behaviour: a Cross-market Examination', *Journal of Consumer Marketing* 16(5): 441–460; King, T. and Dennis, C. (2006) 'Unethical Consumers: Deshopping Behaviour using the Qualitative Analysis of the Theory of Planned Behaviour and Accompanied (De)shopping', *Qualitative Market Research* 9(3): 282–296; Povey, R., Conner, M., Sparks, P., James, R. and Shepherd, R. (2000) 'Application of the Theory of Planned Behaviour to Two Dietary Behaviours: Roles of Perceived Control and Self-efficacy', *British Journal of Health Psychology* 5(1): 121–139; Scholderer, J. and Grunert, K. (2001) 'Does Generic Advertising Work? A Systematic Evaluation of the Danish Campaign for Fresh Fish', *Aquaculture Economics and Management* 5(2): 253–272; Tarkiainen, A. and Sundqvist, S. (2005) 'Subjective Norms, Attitudes and Intentions of Finnish Consumers in Buying Organic Food', *British Food Journal* 107(11): 808–822.

42. Ajzen, I. (2006) *Constructing a TpB Questionnaire: Conceptual and Methodological Considerations*, www.people.umass.edu/aizen/pdf/tpb.measurement.pdf

43. Carpenter, L. (2008) 'The Bag Lady: Rebecca Hosking', *Observer Food Monthly*, 27 January; De Coverly, E., O' Malley, L. and Patterson, M. (2008) 'Hidden Mountain: the Social Avoidance of Waste', *Journal of Macromarketing* 28: 289–303; Lambert, C. (2009) 'Plastic is a Rubbish Idea', *The Times*, 10 July, Martin, A. (2008) 'M&S Celebrates an 80pc Cutback in Plastic Bags', *Daily Mail*, 26 August; Vidal, J. (2009) 'Plastic Bag Revolt Halves Nationwide Use to 450m', *The Guardian*, 17 July; Waste and Resources Action Programme (WRAP) (2006) *Choose to Reuse*, WRAP April; Waste and Resources Action Programme (WRAP) (2009) *Reducing Carrier Bag Use*, WRAP July; Sustainable Wales (2010) *Welsh Assembly Government Plans for Single Use Bags Levy*, 10 September, www.sustainablewales.org/blog/?p=307; Carrier Bag Consortium, www.carrierbagtax.com.

6 Reconciling product sustainability

People do not eat sustainability, or drive it.
They eat food and drive cars and product
performance has to be the primary focus of
marketing, even for sustainable products.[1]

Sustainable Consumption Roundtable – Looking back, looking forward

Chapter objectives

After studying this chapter you should be able to:

1 Understand the role of product design in achieving sustainability.

2 Consider the sustainability issues in each of the stages of the product lifecycle.

3 Assess the product packaging lifecycle and its impact on sustainability.

4 Review consumer attitudes and behaviour towards product and package recycling.

Dilemma part 1:   The slow rise of ethical fashion

Primark, which is owned by Associated British Foods, began trading in 1969 in Dublin under the name Penneys, basing its business on low costs and fast turnover of goods. It entered the UK market in 1973 as Primark, adding 18 stores over the next ten years. Primark followed a strategy of acquisition to continue with its expansion. In 1995 there was significant development of the UK business following the acquisition of the BHS One-Up discount chain, mostly in the Greater London area, which were all of a significant size. The next major acquisitions were 11 stores from the Co-Op and 11 from C&A when they left the UK market.

Originally, Primark tended to locate its stores in cheaper, out-of-town sites in areas of low income, in order to reduce costs and gain proximity to its principal low-income markets. However, consumer attitudes towards cheap clothing have changed over time and what drives a large section of the market is the desire to consume fashionable garments more frequently at a lower price rather than consider buying more expensive clothes for their quality and durability. This change has also been fuelled, in part, by the increase in media coverage of the world of fashion and the rise of celebrity culture. The fashion industry has also seized the opportunity by the shortening of lead times between appearance of a fashion garment on the catwalk and its availability in the high street store, combined with reducing costs particularly in the supply chain, resulting in a more intense consumption of fashion known as *fast fashion*.

Primark has experienced rapid growth and seen a major strategic change, transforming itself from a pile-it-high and sell-it-cheap discount retailer to a mid-market brand of increasing status among a broader target market, as fast fashion has become a mainstream movement.

Primark's pursuit of growth appears to be relentless. In 2006, it increased its number of outlets by 22 percent and its total selling space by 40 percent. By June 2009, the retailer traded from 190 stores, across more than half a million square metres of trading space and continued to search for prime site locations in town centres, retail parks and shopping centres. Expansion has also occurred outside Ireland and the UK.

Number of stores trading at 3 December 2009

Ireland – 38
Spain – 14
UK – 138
The Netherlands – 1
Portugal – 2
Germany – 2
Belgium – 1

To support its expansion and shift in target market, Primark has carried out a number of actions to take its discounted clothes to a broader audience, including:

● improved store layouts that are more attractive and shopper friendly
● fast product design (a copy of the £3,000 Gucci bomber jacket selling for just £12 sold out in all 160 stores in 2007, the Primark jacket was made of faux leather in contrast with the Gucci version)
● purchase of the latest fashion goods at competitive prices from suppliers all over the world

- economies of scale as volumes and frequency of supplies increase
- an organisational culture that places a much greater emphasis on good customer service
- employment of high-quality staff with a range of retailing skills and experience
- publicity featuring celebrities wearing Primark clothing. Primark has even been featured in fashion magazine *Vogue*.

With its transformation nearing completion, Primark no longer targets exclusively the low-income customer, and Primark indicates that its primary target market is *young, fashion conscious under 35s* who want fashionable clothing at competitive prices.

Obtaining and staffing prime location sites has become crucial for Primark as it continues to seek growth in sales and increased market share. Primark builds links with local colleges, JobCentres and community groups to aid recruitment, gives new employees a three-week induction and training programme designed to communicate its organisational culture and build team spirit. The organisational culture attempts to maximise sales per employee by creating dynamic employees who can thrive in a fast-moving fashion industry and who enjoy putting the customer first.

Despite the recession Primark has continued to defy the retail gloom with 18 percent growth recorded in the first half of 2009. Primark stated the figures reflected an increase in selling space and excellent like-for-like sales growth, which rose by 5 percent. Its performance has had an effect on other players in the clothing retail market, who now find themselves as direct competitors for customers after Primark's shift in focus. Clothing sales at supermarkets Asda and Tesco have found themselves put under pressure by the rise of Primark and other specialist value chains such as TK Maxx and Peacocks, which have also done well. Meanwhile Marks and Spencer has lost market share to the value chains and the supermarkets.

Allegations of abusive work practices have frequently hit the fast fashion sector. Primark was accused of using factories in India where children worked long hours in poor conditions by the BBC documentary programme *Panorama* in mid-2008, while Tesco was accused by the lobby group War on Want for using a factory in Bangalore where workers were paid half the minimum wage and forced to work overtime.

Primark's reaction to allegations at that time also came in for criticism. Rather than send a spokesperson to the BBC programme to defend the brand, Primark opted to launch a website (www.ethicalprimark.co.uk) to promote its ethical credentials, make public its membership of the Ethical Trading Initiative and display its code of conduct. Primark went on to state that its suppliers had subcontracted to others, who had broken its code of conduct, and it had decided to stop using the suppliers. Its decision to cease business with those suppliers also created an adverse effect in the media, as it was claimed that it would have been more responsible to agree to work more closely with suppliers to encourage them to improve their work practices.

A year later and the Primark supplier controversy had not disappeared. Sir Stuart Rose, Executive Chairman of Marks and Spencer, criticised Primark at a shareholders meeting and stated he would not sell a t-shirt for £2 in the UK.

You cannot sell a t-shirt in the UK for £2 and pay the designer and pay for the raw materials and pay the manufacturer and pay the rents and pay the rates and pay the carriage and pay the insurance and pay the freight – and pay a fair living wage to the person who made it. *(Sir Stuart Rose Executive Chairman of Marks and Spencer)*[2]

▶

At the time Primark and Marks and Spencer had almost identical white t-shirts retailing at £1.50 and £5 respectively. However, Primark counterattacked and muddied the waters of the argument by confirming that M&S and Primark shared some suppliers and accusing them of hypocrisy.

Discuss the following:

1. Can fashion be both fast and ethical in the way it is produced and brought to market?

Reconciling product sustainability

The way in which products are designed and produced determines to a large extent how much energy, water and natural resources we use, and how much we waste. The design and planning of products have therefore become central to achieving sustainability, as depicted in Figure 6.1. It is not only that consumers need to behave more sustainably; they also have to have sustainable product choices made available to them.

The opening words of the chapter from the Sustainable Consumption Roundtable underline that even sustainable products will be judged on their performance but that is not to undervalue sustainability credentials at all. Far from it, products have to perform as sustainably as possible to ensure their success and their longevity in the marketplace, and sustainability performance will be high on the agendas of both businesses and consumers.

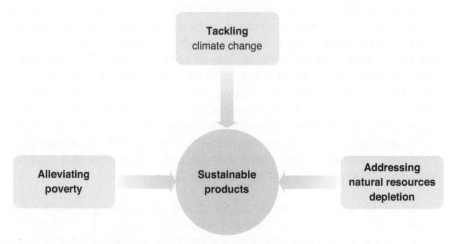

Figure 6.1 The three goals of sustainable products

Source: Adapted from Sustainable Development Commission, 2007, p. 4[3]

A new vocabulary is taking over product design, product usage and product lifecycle. The prefix 're-' is quickly becoming as significant for sustainability as the prefix 'eco-', as businesses adopt a new sustainable product-speak of re-pair, re-fine, re-think and re-design. This chapter explores the factors underlying the sustainability of tangible products. First, design issues are explored from a number of viewpoints. Unsustainable product features are gradually being designed out and this design process needs to take into account the whole of the product lifecycle from raw material extraction to end-of-life options. Consideration is also given to the use of legislation to ensure that products are produced and managed more sustainably and issues of recycling and reuse are also examined. Second, product packaging is considered. It is also important that the packaging of a product be just as sustainable as the product itself. Once just a means of physical protection for distribution and sale or communication and branding, packaging now has to adhere to the same sustainability criteria as the product itself.

Designing the sustainable product

Resource and energy efficiency is key to sustainable product design. It is calculated that we will need to achieve between factor 4 and factor 10 levels of resource and energy reduction in order to become sustainable.[4] Reconciling the design and manufacture of products within the demands of sustainability, product performance and consumer appeal will be a complex process requiring collaborative action from government, business and other stakeholders. Different initiatives are already being employed by each of the stakeholders involved in order to achieve the production of more sustainable products. Strategies such as choice editing, design techniques devised to recycle and reuse product material resources and minimise their impact on the environment such as cradle-to-cradle design and biomimicry, and control of packaging are all being used to contribute to sustainable product design.

Choice-editing

One means of directing consumers towards sustainable products is by denying them access to less sustainable alternatives. By cutting out unnecessarily damaging products consumers can focus on selecting from sustainable options. This process of reducing the number and type of products that consumers have available to them is known as choice-editing. Choice-editing frequently happens in business according to a wide range of criteria, although sustainability has only recently become more of a deciding factor for editing. Choice-editing for sustainability is about shifting the field of choice for mainstream consumers rather than for those groups of consumers who are already motivated to follow more sustainable lifestyles. Choice-editing does not only have the effect of focusing consumers on more sustainable alternatives but also stimulates manufacturers to design better products as demand is shifted towards greater sustainability.

Choice-editing is seen by consumers as increasingly desirable as they consider that business and government must bear part of the responsibility for driving sustainability. In this way mainstream consumers are released from the onerous duty of decision making which they feel should be made higher up the chain of supply anyway, even politically through legislation, and they can view it as simplifying previously complex purchase decisions, particularly when there are many competing options.[5] Thus, such pre-selecting of the particular range of products and services available to consumers can be carried out by manufacturers, retailers or by government.

In Japan, editing follows a top-runner approach, which is used to drive more sustainable product design. Manufacturers of household energy products are required to match the highest standards equivalent to the most efficient model within each category. Therefore any improvements by manufacturers will always extend best practice even further as they compete to improve rather than by lowering standards and cutting costs and quality. The setting of these minimum best standards is supported by legislation to fine manufacturers and importers who do not comply.

Energy-efficient fridges and freezers

The adoption of more efficient fridges and freezers by the general public has emerged from a combination of actions including legislation and manufacturers' and retailers' actions.[6] This process began in 1995 with mandatory EU labelling showing energy ratings from A to G but while labelling was informative for the consumer it was not enough on its own to drive consumption towards higher levels of efficiency. Despite the introduction of the system, A-rated purchases remained at less than 3 percent market share until the EU removed all appliances rated below C in 1999. It was apparent that the early announcement of legislation setting minimum standards started a virtuous cycle of rapid innovation and further choice-editing by retailers and manufacturers. Market share of A-rated appliances rose from 10 percent to 70 percent in 2001, thanks to price incentives from energy suppliers under the Energy Efficiency Commitment, while a voluntary agreement from manufacturers removed all C-rated appliances from the market in 2004 in response to both retailer and consumer demand. As a consumer, no change in behaviour was required; purchases were still made according to the same conventional criteria such as price, appearance and brand, only from an edited-down selection of products. Now the challenge to stimulate demand for A+ and A++ rated appliances to further increase energy efficiency in the home may require more choice-editing, particularly because the rebound effect (with people buying second fridges) is already cancelling out the energy savings being gained.

B&Q

DIY retailer B&Q's decision to phase out non-sustainable wood from all its stores helped establish the market for the Forest Stewardship Council (FSC) sustainable certification. The FSC was launched in 1993 as a forest certification and wood product labelling scheme. The total global market for FSC certified products has reached around $5 billion, with the UK accounting for approximately a third of the demand. The decision of B&Q to edit-out unsustainable wood sources in favour of FSC certified stock required no sacrifice from consumers in price or quality, but allowed the retailer to take up a sustainable stance and communicate this to customers.

B&Q was the first business to sign up with BioRegional to become an official *One Planet Living* business.[7] BioRegional is an entrepreneurial charity which initiates and delivers practical solutions for more sustainable living. The group works in partnership with organisations around the world, providing consultancy and education services and informing policy.

B&Q's initial actions to become a *One Planet Living* business included choice-editing of more products combined with other initiatives:

- Phase out patio heaters: even the smallest 4.5kW table-top patio heater emits as much CO_2 in two hours as the average individual electricity consumption for a whole day and B&Q was the largest seller of patio heaters in the UK. B&Q agreed to not restock patio heaters from the end of the 2008 season.

- FSC certified wood in B&Q kitchens: B&Q, also the UK's largest seller of kitchens, decided that all the wood elements of its kitchens would be FSC certified.

- Free growing kits and seeds: B&Q teamed up with Year of Food and Farming to send free growing kits and seeds to 5,000 schools throughout the UK.

The DIY retailer B&Q seems to have taken the lead on the competition through reinterpreting its business. Its actions in collaboration with the Forest Stewardship Council and Bioregional have allowed it to shift the emphasis of its business from plain home and garden improvement to sustainable living. By identifying the areas of its business that can contribute to low-carbon living and advance sustainable lifestyles it is creating a differentiated position in the DIY sector in contrast with its competitors.

Snapshot: Editing the light bulb

The gradual phasing out of conventional light bulbs, agreed across the EU, started in January 2009 with the 100 watt bulb the first to disappear from the market. The EU approved a ban which will see all traditional light bulbs phased out by 2012. The British government took the decision to implement the ban ahead of the EU schedule and the turn of the 60 watt bulb came in 2010. Some would say this instance of choice-editing was not before time, as the conventional bulb wastes 95 percent of its electricity on heat and has been around for over 100 years.

In contrast, the latest highly efficient, light-emitting diodes or LEDs will be able to last for up to 100,000 hours; effectively a bulb for life but this will be just one of a number of sustainable lighting options such as compact fluorescent lamps (CFLs) and their alternatives.

▶

When the *Sun* newspaper gave away two free energy-saving light bulbs in January 2008 it sold 3,908,000 copies, some 400,000 copies more than usual for that day of the week. This would seem to suggest that the public were motivated to save energy and their money, swapping the inefficient incandescent light bulb for a more sustainable alternative – the CFL. Not to be outdone, in the same month the *Daily Mail* offered two free energy-saving light bulbs to its readers.

However, on 7 January 2009, under the headline 'Revolt! Robbed of their right to buy traditional light bulbs, millions are clearing shelves of last supplies', the *Daily Mail* offered its readers completely the opposite opportunity to the previous year – 25,000 free incandescent light bulbs – despite the fact they are obviously far from being environmentally friendly.

For apparent journalistic reasons, the choice-editing of light bulbs came under fire from the newspaper as an example of a loss of consumer choice and a loss of control due to government and particularly EU legislation. The *Mail* went on to report panic buying from the public, with stores running out of stock of the 'condemned' 100 watt bulb. This was coupled with emotive language referring to the rights of the individual to choose, 'the end of light as we know it' and 'beloved bulb will disappear for good'. But the newspaper article also made use of the criticism of the technology itself and the fact that there is an increasing and perhaps confusing number of sustainable alternatives becoming available in the marketplace. The UK's reaction was not unique. Later, in 2009, German, Austrian and Hungarian consumers were all reported to be stockpiling incandescent light bulbs ahead of their own ban planned for September.

The readers of the *Daily Mail* would certainly be confused as to whether to support sustainability through product choice-editing or not, because the *Mail on Sunday* gave them two free compact fluorescent lamps just 17 days after they had been campaigning against the change.

In contrast with the British government's stance, in New Zealand the Labour government scrapped its plans to phase out incandescent light bulbs in 2008, despite calculating the measure could save $NZ500 million by 2020, because during the election campaign the opposition National party was using the issue as an example of Labour's *nanny state* mentality.[8]

Researching sustainability: Evaluating potential for change

Choice-editing has the potential to transform markets and enable mainstream consumers to make more sustainable choices. Find two other examples of product choice-editing and account for the level of success each initiative has had to date. Take into account the following factors:

1. The use of national government intervention including legislation.

2. The use of supranational legislation from EU.

3. The use of price incentives.

4. Manufacturers' initiatives.

5. Retailers' initiatives.

6. Consumers' reactions.

What future market opportunities are there for business by applying a choice-editing strategy? Are there plans for other product categories to be edited?

Cradle-to-cradle: the closed loop economy

The phrase *end-of-pipe* has epitomised the way businesses have chosen to deal with the consequences of their products and their manufacture, concerned only with mitigating the impacts of the by-products of their production and of the final disposal of the product at the end of its lifecycle. Regarded as an external cost for too long, it is no longer a cost that society is prepared to take on. Products will need to become more durable, more reusable, more recoverable, and more recyclable but instances of genuine, purposeful redesign of products with these criteria in mind are not yet commonplace.

Our general conceited attitude and behaviour towards our use of natural resources has resulted in following a cradle-to-grave strategy in product design since the beginning of the Industrial Revolution. In fact, efficient product design can help mitigate up to 80 percent of a product's environmental impact. Why would we set up a system which mined and cut down valuable natural resources, many irreplaceable, to produce products that would eventually end up in landfill, literally burying any value those used resources might retain?

While it is too late to go back now, it is not too late to adhere to the principles of sustainability and adopt cradle-to-cradle strategies in product design. Cradle-to-cradle product design was proposed by chemist Michael Braungart and architect William McDonough.[9] Finding inspiration in nature and its ability to only produce safe, recyclable, reusable waste, Braungart and McDonough propose that products should be designed from the start so that, after their useful lives, they will provide material for future generations of products, or biodegrade naturally and safely to restore the soil. Essentially, the product or its component materials travel full circle to become another product or fuel for the natural environment.[10] Also referred to as the closed-loop economy, in order to be more sustainable products need to be designed to give the most back at the end of their usefulness and the phrase end-of-lifecycle should become a thing of the past.

In order to be considered a cradle-to-cradle designed product it should be:

- Cyclical – materials used in the product should go full circle and either go back to source and benefit nature without causing contaminating by-products or be recuperated for use in a similar or different product. Surplus waste material should be reduced, landfill disposal should be avoided.

- Raw materials efficiency – avoidance of scarce materials or those likely to become scarce in the future, avoidance of materials that have an unacceptable ecological footprint, whether in extraction, production, use or disposal.

- Energy efficiency – in manufacture, in use and in disposal; such products should consume safe, renewable energy.

- Water efficiency throughout the whole product lifecycle, including reuse or recycling.

- Non-pollutant – in manufacture, recycling, reuse or back to nature, cradle-to-cradle products and by-products should not contaminate air, water or land.

Waste Electrical and Electronic Equipment Directive

The Waste Electrical and Electronic Equipment Directive (WEEE Directive) became European law in 2003 and was introduced into UK law in 2007. The WEEE Directive aims to reduce the amount of electrical and electronic equipment being produced and encourage everyone to reuse, recycle and recover it. The directive also aims to improve the environmental performance of businesses that manufacture, supply, use, recycle and recover electrical and electronic equipment.

The responsibility for the disposal of waste electrical and electronic equipment falls on the manufacturers and requires the establishment of an infrastructure for collecting WEEE, allowing private households to return their waste goods free of charge. Collection and disposal of WEEE should be done in a responsible environmentally friendly manner and allow for ecological disposal, reuse or repair.

The WEEE Directive covers all aspects of production and supply along the product lifecycle, affecting all those businesses that:

- manufacture or import electrical or electronic equipment

- distribute electrical or electronic equipment

- generate any electrical or electronic waste

- collect electrical or electronic waste from final consumers for treatment or disposal

- operate a waste treatment facility

- export electrical or electronic waste.

Table 6.1 shows there are a series of end-of-life options available to the producers of tangible products, either to reuse or repair goods at the end of their lifecycle

Table 6.1   End-of-life options

Re-use	
Direct reuse	Placed back into sale – returned goods with no faults
Repurposing	Use of a product for another application, either wholly or partly
Repair	
Refurbishment	Restoration of major components to working order, not 'as new' quality, although a limited guarantee is often provided
Reconditioning	As refurbishment, although with less emphasis on cosmetic appearance
Remanufacture	A series of manufacturing steps acting on an end-of-use part or whole product in order to return it to like-new or better state and performance, with warranty
Recycling	The series of activities by which discarded materials are collected, sorted, processed, and used as raw materials in the production of new products

Sony followed a cradle-to-cradle strategy with its Playstation 2 (PS2) games consoles. When consumers returned faulty consoles under 30 days old Sony provided them with a brand new console, provided they returned the faulty machine. Instead of being scrapped and thrown away, these machines were then remanufactured to the same quality standard as new machines. Those machines that were beyond repair were dismantled for reuse of parts and the recycling of the remaining materials. The scheme allowed for the sale of an extra 50,000 units without the need for the production of brand new units from scratch to meet that demand and it also allowed for the recycling of 36,000 kilos of plastic from plastic PS2 covers and 14,000 kilos of electronic waste from unusable circuit boards.[11]

One means of developing products to be more efficient and environmentally friendly has been proposed by visionary, nature-inspired scientist Janine Benyus, who explains that products which aim to be inoffensive to nature should learn from and imitate nature.[12]

Biomimicry

The term biomimicry is made up from two Greek words *bios,* meaning life, and *mimesis*, meaning imitation. Therefore, biomimicry, as detailed in the work of Benyus, seeks to imitate nature in such a way that it allows for innovative product design by taking the best ideas from nature without causing harm, just as natural systems, plants and animals live and adapt to environments for millions of years without causing the reduction of non-renewable resources, waste or pollution.

Biomimicry is a new science that studies nature's models and then emulates these forms, processes, systems and strategies to solve human problems – sustainably.[13] In order to utilise biomimicry, industry must avoid standard unsustainable *heat, beat and treat* industrial processes, taking vast amounts of raw materials, heating them, beating them, treating them with chemicals, and placing them under enormous amounts of pressure to produce relatively small amounts of finished product in comparison with the waste created, the often toxic by-products, and the vast amount of energy used in the process.[14]

To avoid this, biomimicry is centred on nature through three types of applications: *model, measure and mentor.*[15]

Model – Nature provides problem-solving models to be copied and adapted for a variety of applications. For example, from studying the natural ability of mussels to stick to rocks underwater, Columbia Forest Products developed a super strong, toxin-free, waterproof glue, removing the need for toxic formaldehyde to be used to waterproof its wood products. The same glue has been used to glue broken tendons together in the human body.

One of the more well-known examples of the application of biomimicry is that of the glue-free adhesive tape inspired by the feet of the gecko lizard. The gecko holds onto surfaces by using the millions of tiny bristles on its feet which carry positive and negative charges known as Van der Waals forces. Van der Waals force is one of the weakest attractive forces known to man, but when used through the millions of bristles of the gecko it creates one of the strongest adhesive powers available. The gecko tape does not lose its adhesive qualities under water or in space. While the applications of the tape are limitless, the true benefits derive from its praiseworthy sustainable credentials. It is not toxic, does not contaminate and can therefore be used safely in multiple applications. The bond also completely separates at an angle of 30°, allowing for simple disassembly of components for reuse elsewhere or for recycling.

Measure – If nature has created long-lasting solutions over millions of years, then new materials and new products should measure themselves against the same criteria and look to use the same processes. For example, super-strong Kevlar® is used in bulletproof jackets and is made in a heated, pressurised vat of concentrated sulphuric acid. In comparison, spider silk is tougher than Kevlar® and is made by spiders on a diet of insects, without a heavy industrial process. The spider web is also totally biodegradable and can be eaten by its maker to build a new one.

Mentor – Teacher, guide and mentor are the roles designated for nature under biomimicry rather than viewing nature as something to be controlled and exploited without having to account for any actions taken and damage caused to eco-systems. According to Benyus, biomimicry allows for 'the conscious emulation of life's genius'.[16] For example, the Namib Desert beetle is able to collect tiny droplets of water from morning fog on its wing cases, as different parts of its body attract and repel moisture to channel it to its body. In this way the beetle can survive in the Namib Desert that receives only 10 millimetres of rain a year. Scientists at the Massachusetts Institute of Technology have created a material that mimics this action, which could be used for water harvesting or as a self-decontaminating surface that could channel and collect harmful substances, among other applications.[17] By learning how crabs auto-repair their shells, researchers at the University of Southern Mississippi have developed a self-repairing paint. When it is scratched it responds to ultraviolet light by forming chemical chains that bond with other materials in the paint, eventually smoothing over the scratch and repairing the damage.

Imitating the skin of sharks has helped researchers to improve the performance of ships. The artificial shark scales have the effect of increasing speed through water by reducing drag and therefore reducing the amount of fuel needed to make the journey. The scales better resist the build-up of contaminants on the hulls of boats, reducing the need for toxic chemicals to be used to clean them and at a constant speed of 4–5 knots the hull becomes self-cleaning. This synthetic shark-inspired skin made a significant impact at the 2008 Beijing Olympics with Speedo's Fastskin FSII swimsuits helping swimmers to break numerous world records.[18]

Even imitating potentially fatal scorpion venom has provided scientists with the prospect of producing a super-strength painkiller which mimics the way the toxic venom affects the nervous system at the molecular level. The new painkillers will have no side effects and will not be addictive like morphine.[19]

Apply it: Finisterre – achieving sustainable goals

1. Investigate the Finisterre brand and evaluate to what extent its performance in product design contributes towards achieving the three goals of sustainability as shown in Figure 6.1 earlier in this chapter.

Getting started

Finisterre, based in Cornwall, is a specialist provider of clothing and accessories for surfers and those who pursue an outdoor life. A small company, it is dedicated to making the best garments, technically superior but with a minimal environmental impact, pioneering work with universities and suppliers of recycled and recyclable fabrics, following sustainable design philosophies and transparent ethical practice. The company has won numerous awards on the back of its sustainability credentials.

Finisterre jackets and base layers are ideal for those who love the outside life, surfing, hiking, skiing and climbing. High-performance wool from sustainably raised merino sheep are a key ingredient for these products, but Finisterre also incorporates biomimicry into the design of its clothing linings.

The Napa lining mimics the structure of otter fur. It has multiple layers that work to keep heat close to the body while filtering away moisture created by the wearer. In this way Finisterre avoids the use of artificial, energy- and resource-intensive membranes, which are usually laminated to the outer fabric preventing their recycling. Recycled polyester is also used in Finisterre jackets and can easily be recycled.

Through the cradle-to-cradle lens

The environmental impacts of manufactured goods can only be reduced if their design takes into account sustainability throughout the whole product lifecycle, minimising impacts at every stage even, and especially, at end-of-life. This requires consideration of the implications of materials selection, materials sourcing, product design, manufacturing processes and part fixing methods employed, as well as product energy efficiency and non-renewable consumables used.

Just as important are the strategies to deal with the post-consumer stage, specifically providing opportunities for remanufacture, use of design for easy dismantling and allowing for the reuse of parts or the recovery of materials used. Design should always aim to minimise lifecycle impacts at the end-of-life stage as well as the intermediary stages. Avoiding landfill through design for recycling or at least providing for innocuous degradability is also a key design issue.

Figure 6.2 shows the considerations to be taken into account at each of the stages of product design. All product materials and components are viewed

1.
- **Product need**
- Can the consumer need be satisfied with a more sustainable product?

2.
- **Raw materials**
- Are raw materials limited or restricted by legislation?

3.
- **Material extraction**
- Does location and extraction of raw materialise minimise impacts?

4.
- **Manufacture**
- Is manufacture resource efficient and of low impact on supply chain?

5.
- **People**
- Does product improve the wellbeing of people in the supply chain?

6.
- **Packaging**
- Is the minimum amount of environmentally friendly packaging used?

7.
- **Transport**
- Energy efficent or can supply chain and sourcing be brought closer?

8.
- **Information**
- Is product marketed with appropriate information?

9.
- **Energy in use**
- Are energy-using products more energy efficient?

10.
- **In use**
- Is product safe and environmentally friendly in normal use?

11.
- **Disposal**
- Is product designed for easy reuse, recycling or safe, friendly disposal?

12.
- **Disclosure**
- Is complete, transparent, verified product information provided?

Figure 6.2 Product design checklist

Source: Adapted from Sustainable Development Commission, p. 9[20]

through the cradle-to-cradle lens, minimising impact while maximising opportunities for reuse and recycling at each of the stages including post-consumer use.

The product design and development phase cannot be underestimated as it can account for more than 80 percent of the economic cost connected with the product as well as 80 percent of the product's environmental and social impacts throughout the whole of the product lifecycle.[21]

Apply it: Sustainable product design

1. Using the product design checklist in Figure 6.2, analyse the sustainable credentials of three different products. Choose companies that already make their sustainability credentials public, visit their websites and review their company reports. How do their claims match to the product design checklist? Are all the different points covered?

Packaging the sustainable product

One aspect of the tangible product which is growing in significance is the packaging in which it is contained. Each year 10.5 million tonnes of packaging is used in the UK and, while on average some 60 percent of this is recycled, less than half of the 4.7 million tonnes used for consumer goods is recycled.[22] The high visibility of packaging to the final consumer combined with calls for the reduction of waste and more recycling has resulted in growing consumer concern about how they should deal with packaging. Even the terminology related to packaging disposal has left consumers confused, as terms such as degradable, biodegradable, recyclable, compostable and home compostable all compete for the attention of the consumer.

Packaging lifecycle management

Packaging specification is based on many factors, including the technical properties of the material, fitness for purpose, sourcing, functionality, manufacturing capability and cost. If packaging is poorly specified the resulting damaged products or wasted food would probably have far more of an environmental impact than that of the packaging itself. While an increasing amount of the packaging is recycled, a high proportion is not.

The difficulty of designing and managing packaging sustainably results from the constant changes of roles and functions that packaging must perform as it goes through the different stages of the lifecycle. Figure 6.3 shows a conventional packaging lifecycle for the retail sector from the initial specification setting and design stage through to the alternatives that lie beyond the disposal stage. Resolving the sometimes conflicting demands of the varied stakeholders

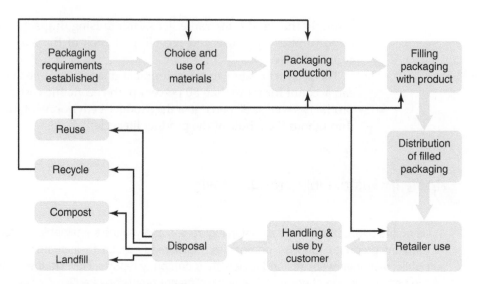

Figure 6.3 The packaging lifecycle
Source: Adapted from WRAP, 2009[23]

is a significant challenge; such as protecting the product for transport, grouping and loading the product for transport, stacking and displaying the product in-store, consumer viewing and handling in-store and consumer transport home. In addition, food product packaging would involve hygiene and health issues, safe storage in transit, at store and at home.

Apply it: Packaging cycle analysis

1. Choose any two examples of fast-moving consumer goods (FMCG) and analyse their packaging lifecycles. Collect examples of their packaging and evaluate the composition information and recycling instructions provided. Use Table 6.2 to help. Draw up your own lifecycle for your examples in order to identify the key stages of the cycle and where environmental impacts are made and where and how they can be avoided or reduced.

More than just a package

Beyond the practical, functional attributes of packaging, an equally important role it has is less tangible. Packaging serves as a means of communication about the brand, it identifies and differentiates the brand and can become a focus of attention at point of sale, a means of sales promotion or simply an iconic symbol of the brand. Consumer perceptions of value, quality and performance can also be influenced by the use of packaging.

Table 6.2 Sustainability information on packaging

Sustainability issue	Example information on packaging
Specific ingredients	Dolphin-friendly tuna, GM free, free-range eggs
Social equity	Fairtrade labelling
Environmental issues	Shade-grown coffee, sustainable fish stocks
Healthy diet	Salt, fat, sugar, fibre content, Five-a-Day
Production methods	Carbon footprint, water footprint
Product materials	FSC certified wood, organic cotton
Packaging materials	Recyclability, post-consumer waste content
Disposal information	Recyclable, home compostable

Also, in terms of communication the packaging has to make space for an increasing amount of information, not just what is expected as standard product data but also for an increasing range of sustainability issues, as can be seen in Table 6.2.

A framework for packaging best practice

Based on the waste hierarchy (see Table 6.5 on page 180), packaging can be designed through a framework in order to maximise its efficiency while minimising its impact on manufacturer, retailer, consumer and environment following an eliminate, reduce, reuse, recycle sequence.[24] All elements of the packaging framework can be largely influenced at the design and specification stage – by determining which materials are used, how much packaging is used and how easy it is to reuse or recycle.

Table 6.3 highlights the main considerations for each of the four options. Eliminating unnecessary packaging should always be the first option as this will make the most savings for the company, reduce resource consumption and the production of waste. Where packaging is essential, reducing weight and density will have numerous cost, resource and transport benefits.

Packaging designed for reuse will also provide the same kinds of benefits as the previous options in closed-loop systems between consumers and suppliers. Companies may also have the possibility of gaining consumer loyalty through the reuse of packaging by providing accessible, easy to use refill packs. There is already increasing use of reusable packaging for business-to-business markets, while in business-to-consumer markets some companies are trying to change consumer habits by persuading them to buy refills to top up their original container in a great variety of products and product categories from fabric conditioner to coffee.

Table 6.3   Sustainable packaging options

1. Eliminate	• Is all packaging used necessary?
	• Is there an unnecessary inner layer of packaging?
	• Is product damage likely to increase by eliminating a layer?
	• Can increased strength of materials used allow for elimination of other layers of packaging?
	• Can retail staff handling and transport be modified to compensate for eliminated packaging?
	• Can packaging contribute to eliminating post-consumer product waste through:
	  • Resealable/recloseable packaging
	  • Portion packaging
	  • Packaging to extend shelf life
	  • Improved on-pack consumer communication

2. Reduce	• Is weight reduction a viable option? • Can product volume be reduced, e.g. concentrated liquid detergents? • Is 'Best in Class' packaging – lowest weight packaging for a specific product range – being used? • Can packaging be reduced from the consumer's perspective – less to dispose of? • Is packaging being used to give the consumer a false impression of size or amount of product? • Can additional information be printed on the inside of packaging to allow for pack size reductions? • Can additional information be printed on point-of-sale displays to allow for pack size reductions?
3. Reuse	• Can packaging be reused as part of a closed-loop system to reuse packaging for exactly the same purpose – by the retailer, supplier? • Can packaging be reused – by the consumer? As a container for refills of the same product as part of a refill strategy from the producer? As a general storage container – biscuit tins, glass jars, tupperware? • Can packaging be part of the product? As storage for the product itself or a protector when not in use.
4. Recycle	• Can a single material be used for ease of recycling? • If different materials used can they be easily separated for recycling? • Are clear or white plastics used? Easier to recycle and more valuable. • Are package windows to view goods made of recyclable material? • Is package window material necessary? • Are plastic and foil coatings on paper and card minimised? • Are on-pack recycling instructions clear and understandable?

Rather than regard packaging as disposable waste which may or may not be recyclable, the waste management business TerraCycle encourages people to reconsider waste as value.[25] TerraCycle specialises in upcycling, the use of non-recyclable materials, particularly packaging for other purposes, making

Source: TerraCycle: Christopher Crane

affordable, eco-friendly products such as bags, purses and even shower curtains from virtually anything – drinks pouches, yoghourt packets, sweet wrappers, etc. TerraCycle works with its partners to find innovative uses for all of their waste streams and arranges collection programmes to collect waste from businesses and organisations (many free of charge) and then finds commercial solutions for the collected waste either through recycling or upcycling.

As for the final option of recycling, it is often inevitable that packaging which prevents waste (of product) subsequently becomes waste itself. The burden of dealing with waste then falls on the purchaser and this is where the packaging industry still has issues to address.

Understanding public perceptions

Although the packaging industry is making progress with regard to the sustainability of its packaging products, the perception of the general public towards the industry has worsened. In an Ipsos MORI survey carried out for the Industry Council for Packaging and the Environment (INCPEN), views on over-packaging and the environmental problems that packaging causes had hardened, with 79 percent of respondents believing products were over-packaged and 82 percent believing packaging was a major environmental problem.[26] Both of these results from the end of 2008 had increased by more than 10 percent in comparison with their 1997 survey. Also, when asked to choose just three phrases they associated with packaging, respondents' negative opinions dominated.

Table 6.4   Public perceptions of packaging

Uses too much material	46%
Protects the product	35%
Is difficult to dispose of	35%
Is bad for the environment	34%
Keeps product safe and hygienic	30%

Source: Adapted from Ipsos MORI, 2008[27]

Most respondents tended to be more concerned about packaging once they had got their purchases home, reflecting their problems of recycling or disposing of material. However, negative perceptions do not match consumer behaviour towards packaging. Some 70 percent of consumers did not recognise the Recycle Now logo.[28] In another survey it was revealed that only 10 percent of respondents always look for recycling information on the pack labelling, while 55 percent never looked for such information.[29]

Consumer perceptions of over-packaging tend to be focused on specific products, not aimed in general at all products. Above all other products, consumers believe that Easter eggs are over-packaged.[30] Nestlé is aware of such attitudes and has introduced Easter eggs with less packaging.

Nestlé UK & Ireland continues to lead the way in reducing the weight of Easter packaging and increase the quantity of recyclable materials. Since 2006, the weight of packaging for Nestlé small and medium eggs has reduced by

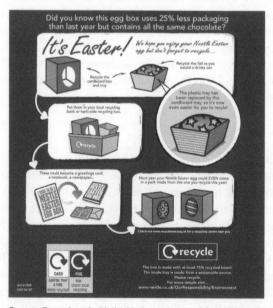

Source: Reproduced with the kind permission of Société des Produits Nestlé S.A.

30–50 percent and plastic inserts have now been removed from 90 percent of all Easter eggs. Packs feature the WRAP approved 'Recycle Now' logo and show consumers the recycled content of the packs. The 2010 Smarties and KitKat Easter eggs packaging was printed with a guide to encourage children to recycle the packaging in a simple attractive way.

Nestlé continue to improve their performance year on year:

● In 2009, Nestlé Confectionery UK became the first major confectionery company in the country to replace non-recyclable plastic with recyclable cardboard packaging in 20 million Easter eggs, 80 percent of the 25 million it produced that year.

● Packaging for small and medium-sized eggs was reduced by 30 percent in 2009, helping to save over 700 tonnes of materials. The 30 percent reduction exceeded the WRAP industry agreement to reduce medium egg carton weight by 25 percent.

● In 2010, cardboard trays were introduced to many of its large Easter eggs, replacing plastic inserts and reduced the packaging used in large eggs by 50 percent.

● For 2011 Nestlé Confectionery UK reduced the amount of packaging materials used for medium Easter eggs by a further 100 tonnes and aims to remove plastic inserts from all its Easter eggs by 2012.

Professional practice: Packaging and luxury goods

Many luxury items rely on packaging to communicate their lavish, extravagant qualities to the public. In many cases, perfume for example, packaging is an essential part of the product and

it would not appear to be the same without it. Even simpler products use packaging to indicate more upmarket credentials. Magnum Temptation (see photo on left) was an attempt to establish a luxury category within the hand-held ice cream sector, presenting the product in its own individual box. However, on its launch marketing professionals deemed the decision as excessive and ill-timed, given the focus on the need to use less packaging and to recycle.[31]

Choose any luxury sector and produce a presentation on its use of packaging, indicating the extent to which sustainability is affecting its use. What recommendations can be made for the sector for its future use of packaging?

Source: The Advertising Archives

Snapshot: Compulsory composting

With difficult targets for the reduction of biodegradable waste to be sent to landfill set by the EU, the pressure on individuals to contribute by composting their food rubbish at home is increasing. Calls for making the composting of food waste compulsory continue to come from the UK government, with Michael Jack, Chairman of the Environment, Food and Rural Affairs Committee, describing home composting as a key opportunity to reduce waste otherwise destined for landfill.[32]

Precedents are already being set for such action in other parts of the world. San Francisco has become the first US city to introduce a compulsory composting law as part of its plan to completely stop sending rubbish to landfills and incinerators by 2020.[33] The city currently diverts 72 percent of its waste from landfills via recycling, but hopes that the new programme will allow it to divert 90 percent. Fines of $100 for individuals and $500 for companies will be levied for those who fail to comply.

Landfill does not provide a suitable solution for organic waste. When fresh organic matter is sent to landfill it soon becomes buried and the lack of oxygen results in a process of anaerobic decomposition which produces the greenhouse gases carbon dioxide and methane. In contrast, composting is an all-round win-win activity. Carbon dioxide and methane can be avoided by the correct home composting of organic material: adding equal amounts of 'brown' (cardboard, shredded paper, newspaper) to a compost bin in layers or mixing it in with 'greens' (vegetable peelings, grass clippings). This encourages aerobic decomposition, allowing oxygen to access the material, which produces very little greenhouse gas as well as a free fertiliser for the garden after about nine months.

The potential for home composting in the UK is significant, some 19 million homes have gardens and already 6.5 million of them use home compost bins.

Summary

For a product to be regarded as wholly sustainable it should contribute to the achievement of the sustainability agenda embodied in the three principles of the Triple Bottom Line. The process of delivering such a product involves resolving complex, multiple differences. Balancing the different demands between using renewable or non-renewable resources, enhancing speed of production versus encouraging responsible consumption of more durable goods, design and production techniques versus reuse and recycling considerations, requires a holistic approach taking into account all the possible impacts throughout the product lifecycle.

Product design consequently encompasses much more than the technical specifications of the product itself and from a materials and resources perspective must follow a cradle-to-cradle strategy at the same time as catering for the human and economic impacts related to the product at each stage of the lifecycle. Even considerations of product packaging have to reconcile conflicting objectives; its functionality and design often clash with packaging's role in marketing communications and product positioning, not to mention its recyclability and sustainability.

The responsibility for managing and improving product sustainability falls on a variety of players, not only businesses. Consumer demand and consumer habits play their part, as does government in its decisions to restrict access to products or delete their availability altogether. In many cases the truly sustainable product remains elusive or is the reserve of niche operators on the fringes of mainstream consumer markets.

Case study: Recycling (mis)behaviours

Encouraging people to recycle their rubbish is a vital part of becoming more sustainable. The more effective use of resources provides a number of major benefits:

- Less depletion of natural resources at the beginning of the value chain.
- Less destruction of the environment from resource extraction.
- Less pollution at the end of the value chain.
- More employment in resource recovery services and recycling industries.
- Lower costs for business.
- Lower costs for society.

At times there seems to have been little logic in how governments have chosen to deal with waste disposal. Rather than reduce consumption (the principal cause of waste in the first place), efforts have centred on the control and reduction of waste with a bias towards the responsibilities of the individual in how he/she disposes of waste despite the more pressing problems caused by industrial waste. There are examples of waste control campaigns directed at the individual in many countries, such as Keep Britain Tidy (which dates back to 1955) and the US equivalent Keep America Beautiful. These campaigns have carried general long-running messages concerned purely with just throwing rubbish away, while others have been short run, instigated for very specific reasons or events such as the Barcelona *Més net que mai* campaign (Barcelona, Cleaner than ever) which coincided with the run-up to the 1992 Barcelona Olympics.

However, waste management has historically been dominated by a cradle-to-grave vision. For example, as recently as 2000, 90 percent of household waste was sent to landfill in England, despite calls from the waste industry itself to manage waste according to the waste hierarchy, as shown in Table 6.5, which places final disposal in landfill only as a last resort.

As a result of the lax policy on the disposal of household waste, unconcerned consumers were absolved of the sin of creating waste just by placing it in their bin and forgetting about it. Out of sight, out of mind, this was guilt-free consumption accompanied by the social avoidance of the waste it left behind.

Now the situation has changed. The 1999 EU directive on landfill usage imposes a gradual reduction on tonnes of waste to be disposed of in that way in the member states, forcing administrations to rethink their strategies. The pressure to recycle more and more waste is now being

▶

Table 6.5 The waste hierarchy

Least impact

↑ Minimisation
Reuse
Recycle
Recover energy
Disposal in landfill

passed on to the individual. Once again waste is the individuals' responsibility just as it was in the original anti-litter campaigns, but, having been taught for decades to just throw everything away and forget about it, everyone now has to learn how to recycle.

While the millions of tonnes of recycled materials for the year 2008 in the UK appear to be very encouraging, the reality is that enough is not yet done. In 2008 60 percent of household waste still went to landfill in England and only 21 percent of London's rubbish is recycled when 60 percent could be. The barriers to good recycling behaviour are multiple.

Loss of faith

The public have lost faith and therefore do less than they could. Like lots of other sustainable behaviours, recycling rubbish relies on faith as the public has to blindly believe that their efforts to select, sort, wash and categorise their rubbish ready for collection or to take to the recycling centre themselves is not a wasted effort. There have been incidences where rubbish has just been stock-piled to rot rather than be recycled. Due to falling demand and falling prices for recyclable material in 2009, many companies have found themselves in difficulty. One company in the UK, Greencycle, went out of business in 2009 with debts of over £2 million and a stockpile of 100,000 tonnes of waste paper. Toxic waste from the UK, including syringes, condoms and nappies, has been found as far away as Brazil. Italian multinationals were found to have dumped radioactive and other hazardous waste in Somalia. Although the European Waste Electrical and Electronic Equipment directive bans the export of any electrical item unless it is working, this is not being enforced as it should and unscrupulous organisations ship the goods as 'second-hand' in order to escape the restrictions. Long-distance dumping of such waste from developed countries continues to be an issue, with countries such as Nigeria receiving some 100,000 computers a month. Most are unusable and end up as e-waste dumped in tips or landfill, which are then scavenged by locals who risk their health searching for the small but valuable amounts of aluminium, cadmium, copper and other minerals

All about the money

The sale price of plastic bottles for recycling in 2002 was around £10 per tonne; by mid-2008 it had risen to £230, in part due to the rising cost of oil, making plastic recycling more viable and profitable. *Green gold, cash in the bin* – these are expressions being used to describe the profitable aspects of recycling but this has left the public wondering who profits and how would they and their community benefit from the money being made from their own waste. Scepticism regarding the profit made from recycling acts as a barrier to continued positive behaviour and has added to the difficulties of the sector, with people equating recycling their rubbish to giving away money.

Paper mountains dent confidence

The global recession has also influenced public opinion, making them doubt further the benefits of recycling. As the prices for recyclables have dropped due to a general fall in demand, recycling companies have found it difficult if not impossible to sell on their recyclate. Paper recycling is a fragile market. It cannot be stored for more than three months because it rots and attracts vermin, thus making it worthless. In the UK, 8.6 million tonnes of paper and cardboard are saved each year for recycling but the country only has the capacity to pulp half of that amount. The remainder was usually exported to China but with the collapse of the Chinese recycling market during the recent recession the paper has stayed in the country. The condemnation of the system in the press, with pictures of thousands of tonnes of paper rotting and going to waste because it could not be sold on, has dented the UK public's opinion of the value of recycling.

Convenience counts

Studies on recycling behaviour have often found that even when people took their rubbish to specific recycling areas they were just too lazy to place each of their items in the appropriate containers classified for glass, metal paper, etc. Kerbside collection of recyclate from households by local authorities often requires the public to sort out their rubbish into different categories using different containers, but the inconvenience involved has led to reduced public participation in such recycling schemes.

Recycling companies recommend co-mingled collections, where all dry recyclables are placed in one container for collection and are sorted and separated by machines at the recycling plant. Local authorities that have switched to this method have seen an average increase in recycling rates of 20 percent.

(Dis-)incentives

There was a more nostalgic time when the British public needed neither incentives nor disincentives to recycle and reuse products and packaging. The British doorstep milk delivery system worked reliably without a deposit system; empty bottles were simply left on the doorstep for collection and reuse. In 1974, 94 percent of milk was supplied by doorstep delivery but now it is below 11 percent with its market eroded by price competition from supermarkets and lifestyle changes.

The options for other products to have refillable containers which need to be taken back to store are limited. Refillable drinks containers have to be strong enough to withstand repeated journeys, cleaning and fillings, they are heavier and take up more space than single-trip containers and therefore usually use more resources and energy.

▶

And the public do not seem to connect with the idea of take back to store and reuse, even when there is a deposit on the container or a discount on future purchases. The Body Shop discontinued its offer of a 10 percent price reduction if customers returned containers to the shop for refilling, in 2002, because only 1 percent of them used the service.

In the US, 11 out of 50 states have mandatory deposits on non-refillable containers to encourage less littering and more recycling. However, the deposit schemes are expensive to run and have achieved higher recycling rates because they tend to divert some recyclable containers from kerbside collection schemes and community collection points into a parallel system and thus make them more expensive to operate.

Feedback or just a thank you?

The public are not thanked for recycling, either in word or deed. In fact, recycling is now being interpreted as more of an obligation and an imposition, particularly from the perspective of the collection of household rubbish which is fast becoming subject to rules, regulations and restrictions. Yet tracking what public waste goes on to become might be a better way to motivate recycling. People need to see what they have achieved, receive feedback on their performance and do not necessarily require a financial reward all the time, although some schemes are reinvestigating the possibility of rewarding through kerbside collection schemes.

A scheme to be piloted in 2010 in several London boroughs covering 100,000 homes will see microchips installed in household wheelie bins. This will allow for the monitoring of bins, which will be scanned and weighed upon collection. A reward scheme based on the amount of recyclable waste collected in the form of vouchers worth up to £150 a year and redeemable at local shops will be used to encourage public engagement. Fines and loss of entitlement to rewards will be imposed on those who abuse the system.

Bristol City Council aims to be one of the first in the UK to offer householders a cash reward for reducing the amount of black bin waste that would be normally sent to landfill. The proposed pilot scheme would be run with the residents of some 2,300 properties who could choose to participate on a voluntary basis. Chipped black bins will be weighed at every collection and the performance of the households will be monitored according to the number of people in the household. Those that manage to reduce their per capita landfill waste will be rewarded in the pilot scheme, but those who fail to do so will not be fined.

The borough of Windsor and Maidenhead launched its recycle reward scheme in June 2010, targeting some 60,000 households. During a pilot scheme, of the eligible households 70 percent activated their reward accounts in order to receive their Recyclebank Points and 5 million points were earned for discounts and offers at over 100 shops, leisure centres, businesses, attractions and cafés/restaurants worth up to £135 per household per year. Many participants in the pilot scheme gave their points to charities and schools.

The scheme has been made simpler by having just one bin for all recyclate, meaning residents no longer have to separate different types of recyclables into different containers and during the trial residents increased their recycling by 35 percent.

However, the use of microchips in bins to monitor and manage such schemes, affectionately known as 'chip and bin', has received criticism from detractors who claim that local councils will effectively be spying on them and only want to establish a polluter-pays scheme, fining and taxing those who produce more than average amounts of household waste. By the beginning of 2010 it was estimated that some 2.5 million bins with microchips had been distributed by different local councils.[34]

Follow up

1. Evaluate any local kerbside collection scheme for its communication with the general public and its use of incentives/disincentives.

2. Certain cities in numerous countries now have a target of zero waste to be sent to landfill in the near future. How might retailers help in achieving this target? What examples can you find of retailer action?

Dilemma part 2:   The slow rise of ethical fashion

Sexiness, luxury, fashion, corporate social responsibility and ethics can work in harmony.   (*Peter Ingwersen* – founder of the ethical clothing label Noir)[35]

According to British retail expert Mary Portas, Primark and the value sector in general are responsible for destroying good taste and wiping out independent clothing retailing. Portas is of the opinion that the aggressive actions of the value chains such as Primark are endangering the independent quality retailer and that consumers will eventually lose the heart and soul of independent fashion shopping. Trade figures seem to bear out her declarations. Independent clothing retailers saw their market share fall 0.6 percent to 7 percent over the 12 weeks to 21 June in 2009, whereas clothing multiples, including the value sector, saw market shares rise 1.6 percent to 27 percent over the same period.

Although some analysts predicted that issues to do with business ethics and sustainability would lose ground as a result of the recession as consumers became more price sensitive, this has not always been the case.

The UK government has also attacked the trend for cheap throwaway fashion encouraged by the value chains because of the increase in waste it has created. Textiles are now the fastest growing type of household waste. Every year consumers in the UK buy 2 million tonnes of clothes, of which 1.2 million tonnes end up in landfill while just 300,000 tonnes are reused or recycled while the rest gathers dust in the homes of the consumers. A recent government investigation found the proportion of textile waste dumped at one council site had risen from 7 percent to 30 percent in a year due to what is now referred to as the *Primark effect*.

In contrast, ethical fashion remains on the fringes of the mainstream fashion markets but there are indications that it is gaining ground. Fair trade and organic cotton is slowly increasing. Oxfam and Marks and Spencer now collaborate over the reuse or recycling of clothes donated by M&S consumers. Ethical clothing brands such as People Tree, Sharkah Chakra and From Somewhere are appearing more frequently in the gaze of the public. For example, People Tree's recent collaboration with the film star Emma Watson brought a rapid increase in sales for the

▶

company. The 2009 London Fashion Week, one of the major shows on the international fashion calendar, opened with the launch of Estethica – a showcase of ethical designer fashion – which has also gained government backing and was used by the Department of the Environment, Food and Rural Affairs for its own launch of its Sustainable Clothing Action Plan. The 37 designers in the Estethica showcase have to adhere to at least one of three principles – organic, fair trade or recycled.

There is some indication that mainstream players might begin to engage with the ethical, sustainable movement in fashion. In collaboration with ethical clothing pioneers From Somewhere, Tesco has created a range of recycled clothing made from the store's end-of-line stock for their Florence & Fred label. Tesco's plan is to initiate a cradle-to-cradle system to *upcycle* waste within its own supply chain while still keeping its fashion credentials. The collection stays true to From Somewhere's signature look of body contour shapes and bright colours; a limited range of items will be available exclusively online through Tesco's website and should appeal to the teenage and 20-something market.

This end-of-line Tesco stock, which would otherwise end up in landfill, is being produced in one of the most environmentally friendly factories in the world. Not all ethical clothes companies have been as fortunate as From Somewhere, and Ascension (formerly Adili) was forced to suspend shares and was subsequently sold to an investor for a token £1.

Other ethical clothing retailers find it difficult to increase sales and break into more mainstream markets. Equa is a women's wear boutique based in Islington, London, the first to offer ethical fashion on the high street, founded in 2005. Committed to improving sustainability in the fashion industry, at Equa there are organic cotton collections, clothing made from other sustainable fabrics such as bamboo and soya, shoes that have been made using reconstituted leather dyed using environmentally friendly dyes and vegan accessories.[36]

Devise the strategy

1. Equa is a long way from becoming the ethical fashion retail equivalent of the Body Shop. To what extent is there sufficient gap in the market and opportunity to establish a sustainable fashion clothing retail chain to compete as a mainstream fashion provider? What are the barriers preventing the mainstreaming of ethical fashion for companies such as Equa? What strategy would a company like Equa need to follow to develop into a successful chain?

References

1. Sustainable Consumption Roundtable (2006) *Looking Back, Looking Forward. Lessons in Choice Editing for Sustainability*, London: Sustainable Development Commission.

2. Leroux, M. (2009) 'M&S accused of Hypocrisy After Rose Attack on Cut-price Fashion', *The Times*, 10 July.

3. Sustainable Development Commission (SDC) (2007) *You Are What You Sell*, London: SDC (p. 4).

4. Charter, M. and Chick, A. (1997) 'Editorial', *The Journal of Sustainable Product Design* 1: 5–6.

5. Sustainable Consumption Roundtable (2006) *Looking Back, Looking Forward. Lessons in Choice Editing for Sustainability*, London: Sustainable Development Commission.

6. Green Alliance (2006) *Achieving a Step-change in Environmental Behaviours.* A report from three Green Alliance workshops held with civil society organisations in October and November.

7. Grover, S. (2008) 'B&Q Becomes One Planet Living Business, and Stops Selling Patio Heaters in the Process', *Business and Politics,* 24 January, www.treehugger.com/files/2008/01/bg-bioregional_one_planet_living_business.php

8. Brook, S. and Jha, A. (2009) 'How the Mail made Readers Incandescent', *The Guardian,* 12 January, www.guardian.co.uk/media/2009/jan/12/dailymail-lightbulbs-giveaway; Derbyshire, D. (2009) 'Revolt! Robbed of Their Right to Buy Traditional Light Bulbs, Millions are Clearing Shelves of Last Supplies', *The Daily Mail,* 7 January, www.dailymail.co.uk/news/article-1107290/Revolt-Robbed-right-buy-traditional-light-bulbs-millions-clearing-shelves-supplies.html; Defra (2008) *Products and Appliances: Energy Saving Light Bulbs,* www.defra.gov.uk/environment/climatechange/uk/household/products/cfl.htm; Booker, C. (2009) 'Dimwits! Those Bright Sparks Over in Brussels Have Decided to Stop You Buying Old-fashioned Light Bulbs', *The Daily Mail,* 7 January www.dailymail.co.uk/debate/article-1107403/CHRISTOPHER-BOOKER-Dimwits-Those-bright-sparks-Brussels-decided-stop-buying-old-fashioned-light-bulbs.html; Schäfer, D. (2009) 'Germans Fail to See the Light on Bulbs', *Financial Times,* 21 August; Gibson, E. (2009) 'Public Favours Light Bulb Ban', *The New Zealand Herald,* 4 May, www.nzherald.co.nz/politics/news/article.cfm?c_id=280&objectid=10570220

9. Braungart, M. and McDonough, W. (2009) *Cradle to Cradle: Remaking the Way We Make Things,* London: Vintage.

10. McDonough Braungart Design Chemistry Consultancy (MBDC) (2009) *Design is the First Signal of Human Intention,* MBDC Consultancy Brochure, www.mbdc.com

11. King, A., Mayers, K. and Barter, N. (2010) *Closed-loop Servicing of Sony Playstation,* Centre for Remanufacturing and Reuse, www.remanufacturing.org.uk/pdf/story/1p390.pdf

12. Benyus, J. (2002) *Biomimicry,* New York: Harper Collins.

13. Biomimicry Guild (2009) *The Biomimicry Guild Product and Service Reference Guide 2009,* www.biomimicryguild.com/guild_product_service_reference_09.pdf

14. Bernstein, A. (2006) 'Janine Benyus: The Thought Leader Interview', *Strategy+Business,* 28 August.

15. The Biomimicry Institute (2009) www.biomimicryinstitute.org/about-us/what-is-biomimicry.html

16. Bernstein, A. (2006) 'Janine Benyus: The Thought Leader Interview', *Strategy+Business,* 28 August.

17. Trafton, A. (2006) 'Beetle Spawns New Material', *MIT News* 14 June, http://web.mit.edu/newsoffice/2006/beetles-0614.html

18. Natural History Museum (2008) *Olympic Swimsuit Mimics Shark, Skin,* www.nhm.ac.uk/about-us/news/2008/august/olympic-swimsuit-mimics-shark-skin18219.html

19. *The Medical News* (2010) 'Research Suggests Scorpion Venom Could be an Alternative to Morphine Painkiller', 17 February, www.news-medical.net/news/20100217/Research-suggests-scorpion-venom-could-be-an-alternative-to-morphine-painkiller.aspx

20. Sustainable Development Commission (SDC) (2007) *You Are What You Sell*, London: SDC.

21. Charter, M. and Tischner, U. (2001) *Sustainable Solutions: Developing Products and Services for the Future*, Sheffield: Greenleaf Publishing.

22. Packaging Resources Action Group (PRAG) (2009) *An Introduction to Packaging and Recyclability*, November, www.wrap.org.uk/retail/tools_for_change/packaging_and.html

23. Waste and Resources Action Programme (WRAP) (2009) *A Guide to Evolving Packaging Design: A Summary of the Packaging Life Cycle*, WRAP, www.wrap.org.uk/downloads/The_Packaging_Lifecycle.adbffb52.6566.pdf

24. Waste and Resources Action Programme (WRAP) (2009) *A Guide to Evolving Packaging Design: Eliminate, Reduce, Reuse, Recycle*, WRAP, www.wrap.org.uk/downloads/The_Packaging_Lifecycle.adb52.6566.pdf

25. Terracycle available at http://www.terracycle.net/upcycling

26. Ipsos MORI (2008) *Public Attitudes to Packaging*, commissioned by Valpak and INCPEN, London.

27. Ipsos MORI (2008) *Public Attitudes to Packaging*, commissioned by Valpak and INCPEN, London.

28. Ipsos MORI (2008) *Public Attitudes to Packaging*, commissioned by Valpak and INCPEN.

29. Skelton, P. (2007) *Biodegradable and Compostable Packaging: Consumer Perspective*, Green Alliance/WRAP/NNFCC workshop, *Biodegradable and Compostable Packaging: Getting it Right*, 1 March.

30. Ipsos MORI (2008) *Public Attitudes to Packaging*, commissioned by Valpak and INCPEN, London.

31. *Marketing* (2009) 'Magnum Moves Upmarket', *Marketing*, 18 March.

32. Attewill, F. (2010) 'MPs Call for Compulsory Composting', *Metro*, 19 January.

33. *EarthTimes* (2009) 'San Francisco Introduces Compulsory Composting Law', 10 June, www.earthtimes.org/articles/show/272663,san-francisco-introduces-compulsory-composting-law.html

34. De Coverly, E., O'Malley, L. and Patterson, M. (2008) 'Hidden Mountain: The Social Avoidance of Waste', *Journal of Macromarketing* 28: 289–303; Lyons, E., Uzzell, D. and Storey, L. (2002) *Surrey Waste Attitudes and Actions Study*, Surrey University, www.surrey.ac.uk/Psychology/EPRG/files/wastestudy.pdf; Kennedy, P. (2009) 'Bin Brother is Watching', *Solihull News*, 17 July; Smith, L. and Sherman, J. (2008) 'Recyclers are Cashing in on the Fortune in Your Bin', *The Times*, 11 August; Smith, L. and Sherman, J. (2008) 'How a Load of Rubbish is Fast Turning into Green Gold', *The Times*, 11 August; Bridge, S. (2009) 'Rubbish Recyclers on the Scrapheap', *The Mail on Sunday*, 29 March; Hickman, L. (2009) 'The Truth About Recycling', *The Guardian*, 26 February; Kerbaj, R. (2009) 'Recycling Company's Murky Past Emerges', *The Times*, 25 July; Phillips, D., Webster, B. and Burgess, K. (2009) 'Syringes, Nappies and Condoms – Inquiry as British Firms Blamed for Trail of Toxic Waste', *The Times*, 18 July; Sutherland, K. and Gallagher, I. (2009) 'Recycling Fiasco', *The Mail on Sunday*,

4 January; Doughty, S. (2010) 'Spy Chips Hidden in 2.5 Million Dustbins', *The Daily Mail*, 5 March; Local Government Executive (2010) *Bristol City Council to Lead the Way with Waste Incentive Scheme*, 5 March, www.localgovernmentexecutive.co.uk/news/bristol-city-council-lead-way-waste-incentive-scheme-20106801;INCPEN(2008) *Mandatory Deposits on Packaging*, www.incpen.org.

35. Fox, I. (2009) 'London on Parade to Show that Ethical Clothes Can Cut it on the Catwalk', *The Guardian*, 21 February.

36. Gray, L. (2009) '"Primark Effect" Prompts Government Drive to Cut Clothes Sent to Landfill', *The Telegraph*, 20 February; Whitworth, H. (2010) 'Tesco Launches Recycled Clothing Collection', 7 March, centreforsustainablefashion.wordpress.com/2010/03/07/tesco-launches-recycled-clothing-collection/; Carter, K. (2010) 'Tesco Launches Recycled Clothing Collection', *The Guardian*, 2 March; Shields, A. (2009) 'Primark Sales Continue to Soar', *Retail Week*, 9 July; Weir, L. (2009) *Portas: Primark is Destroying UK Indies*, 30 October, www.drapersonline.com/portas-primark-is-destroying-uk-indies/5007578.article; Denby, J. (2009) *Primark Threatening UK Indies, says Portas'*, 2 November, www.retail-digital.com/Primark-threatening-UK-indies--says-Portas-_36947.aspx; Oxberry, E. (2010) *Primark Pledges Further Ethical Initiatives*, 21 January www.drapersonline.com/multiples/news/primark-pledges-further-ethical-initiatives/5009777.article; Creevy, J. (2010) *M&S Loses Clothing Share to Asda, Tesco and Primark*, 23 January www.drapersonline.com/multiples/news/ms-loses-clothing-share-to-asda-tesco-and-primark/5009811

7 Addressing supply chain sustainability

All these supply chains start in the same place –
nature.[1]

Sustainable Development Commission – I will if you will

Chapter objectives

After studying this chapter you should be able to:

1 Understand the potential environmental, social and economic impacts
experienced along the supply chain.

2 Understand the potential of sustainable procurement for improving the
sustainability of the supply chain.

3 Explore the issues of supply and location of resources and production
throughout the supply chain.

4 Explore the alternatives to conventional supply chain management.

Dilemma part 1:   The certification of sustainability

There are at least 100 different eco-labelling schemes in the EU, each competing for the attention of the consumer while serving to validate the sustainability credentials of the products they endorse. Yet such a proliferation of certification schemes, while emphasising the growing importance of sustainability claims as a part of the consumer decision-making process, may only result in confusing the prospective consumer and reducing any potential competitive advantage that the brand could have enjoyed.

Among the many competing accreditation schemes the FAIRTRADE Mark stands out as a cut above the rest. Some consumers believe there are no real differences between the certification schemes, while other consumers perceive that some schemes concentrate more on improving welfare for farmers and supply chain stakeholders in general, while other schemes appear to have a more environmental bias. These perceptions are only partly accurate and are a reflection of the marketing communications of each of the organisations and their participants.

Despite the confusion between the leading certification brands, the FAIRTRADE Mark would still be considered by many to be the market leader with currently over £1 billion in sales, which are growing year on year, and a number of major brand names have been added to its increasing portfolio. Although the figures are encouraging, there is still much room for improvement and growth of Fairtrade as fairly traded goods still only represents less than 1% of global trade.

In March 2010 the supermarket Sainsbury announced it was the world's largest retailer of Fairtrade products, claiming to have sold £218 million worth of Fairtrade goods during 2009. In December 2006, when Sainsbury declared that all its banana supplies would be Fairtrade certified, it was the biggest ever commitment to date by a single company anywhere in the world. In 2007 Sainsbury set up the Fair Development Fund to enable more producers from developing countries to become Fairtrade certified. The fund is run in partnership with Comic Relief and has already helped producers in Uganda, Malawi, Mozambique and Zambia. The impact of just buying a single Fairtrade product can be significant. Now Sainsbury sells 1,200 Fairtrade bananas a minute, creating £4 million in Fairtrade premiums each year. Besides bananas, many of Sainsbury's own label products are Fairtrade, such as roast and ground coffee, sugar and tea. Sainsbury's Red Label tea generates around £1.4 million in Fairtrade premiums each year, benefiting communities in Malawi, Kenya and Southern India. However, consumers are still more likely to identify the Co-operative supermarket as the most ethical supermarket, despite Sainsbury outselling it and its other ethically positioned rivals Waitrose and Marks and Spencer.

Different certification schemes have different aims and objectives and may not be equally attuned to all aspects of sustainable business practice. A close inspection of schemes reveals key differences exist between the rival certifications regarding pricing of commodities and the interpretation of fairer economics in the supply chain, environmental policy, promotion of social policies, working conditions and workers' rights including union membership, qualifying percentage of certified ingredients in products, inspection regimes and overall level of required compliance with regulations.

Another important aspect worth considering is the degree of independence of the certifying body. A certification scheme with industry domination of the standard setting body and in its membership and finance can be expected to have more industry-friendly standards. In contrast, standards can be expected to be stricter where a certification scheme is dominated by an independent environmental and socially responsible organisation.

▶

Consumers now have a range of well-known brands to choose from, which show allegiance to certifying schemes and no doubt they feel they can offset the food miles of many fairly traded products in the knowledge that they are contributing to social change and environmental protection in those places that most need it.

Discuss the following:

Use the list of key differences mentioned in this Dilemma to produce a table comparing the FAIRTRADE Mark against any other two certification schemes. Which organisation appears to be most attuned to economic, social and environmental sustainability issues? Once you have completed the comparison would businesses or consumers be more attracted to one certification scheme than the other?

Addressing supply chain sustainability

Supply chain management has traditionally been preoccupied with maintaining efficiencies of time and cost. For the most part, the timely procurement of raw materials for their use in the subsequent production of goods, in addition to the coordinated movement of such materials, components and goods from upstream suppliers to downstream manufacturers, intermediaries and final consumers in the most cost-effective manner, has not provided a balance between business objectives and sustainability goals.

As with sustainable product design, described in the previous chapter, supply chain management has the potential to have an effect on the sustainability goals encompassed in the Triple Bottom Line, as can be seen in Figure 7.1.

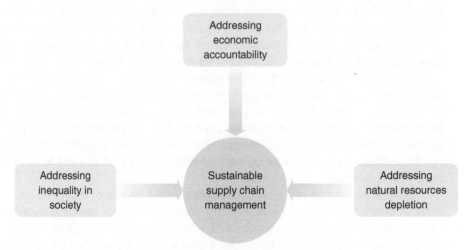

Figure 7.1 Sustainable supply chain management

With sustainability comes the need to shift supply chain management objectives from the narrow, short-term focus on creating more value at less cost for the business, to a broader long-term focus of creating more tangible social, economic and environmental value for all supply chain participants and their dependants, at a lower overall cost to the planet's already restricted and strained resources. Such solutions will entail new forms of supply chain, new forms of collaboration and engagement with stakeholders and even the shortening of lengthy global chains as they currently exist.

This chapter explores the issues surrounding the need to ensure that the supply chain is as sustainable as possible. The global nature of today's supply chains can and do cause obvious tensions in the Triple Bottom Line. The economic, social and environmental impacts of supply are significant but they can be organised to work for the benefit of the sustainability agenda rather than against it.

First the practice of procurement is examined. Sustainable procurement has become the new catchphrase for supply chain management and the organisation of procurement can contribute significantly to sustainability objectives. Second, to understand the impacts along the whole of the supply chain, a typical fashion sector supply chain from the perspective of a single garment, the cotton t-shirt, is investigated. Finally, the localisation of supply is explored from the perspective of the gains to be made by re-localising supply and production closer to point of sale and consumption, an issue that particularly concerns the food sector. In some cases consumers themselves are already becoming suppliers of goods for their own consumption.

Sustainable procurement

Organisations attempt to obtain the materials, goods and services they require essentially at the cheapest price for the best possible quality, maximising their opportunities to make a profit on their activities. Therefore, control of procurement costs is vital in order to get best value for money. Sustainable procurement, sometimes referred to as environmentally responsible or green procurement, aims to balance the procurement needs of the organisation with the broader environmental, social and economic commitments of the Triple Bottom Line, avoiding negative impacts while trying to bring about positive impacts throughout the supply chain at home and abroad. Figure 7.2 highlights the kinds of issues that will have an effect on sustainability impact at different points in the supply chain.

In its 2005 Sustainable Development Strategy, the UK government stated its goal to be a leader in the EU on sustainable procurement by 2009. With the UK government the largest consumer of goods and services in the country, it seemed logical for the government to set an example to industry by becoming a responsible, sustainable procurer. The scale and influence of public sector government spending should not be underestimated, as it accounts for some 13 percent of GDP and more than 50 percent of the impact of public sector procurement arises from its supply chain. As a means of achieving this goal, the government established the Sustainable Procurement National Action Plan, embodied in the 2006 report entitled *Procuring the Future*.[2]

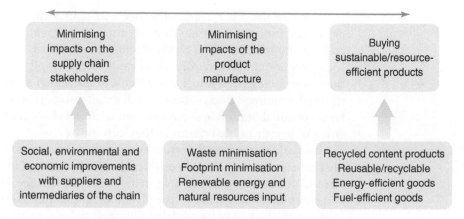

Figure 7.2 The goals of sustainable procurement

One such application of the plan has been to view the government's waste hierarchy as a means of establishing a procurement hierarchy to minimise the negative environmental impacts of waste by buying goods and services more sustainably. In this way, waste is better managed at each level of the hierarchy, sometimes eliminated at source, by modifying the procurement strategy accordingly.

Table 7.1 The waste and procurement hierarchies

Least impact	The waste hierarchy	The procurement hierarchy
↑	Minimisation/ prevention	**Rethink need**
		Eliminate waste at source – no purchase of goods as not really necessary or use a service instead of a product
		Reduce
		Use less material, less quantity, fewer resources
	Reuse	**Reuse**
		Buy goods that may be reused later by customers, suppliers or contractors
	Recycle/compost	**Recycle/compost**
		Negotiate options with contractors for recyclable or compostable versions of goods
	Energy recovery	**Energy recovery**
		Use old goods for energy production such as incineration at power stations
	Disposal	**End of life**
		Negotiate end-of-life management options with suppliers/ contractors for eco-friendly disposal

Source: Defra, p. 13[3]

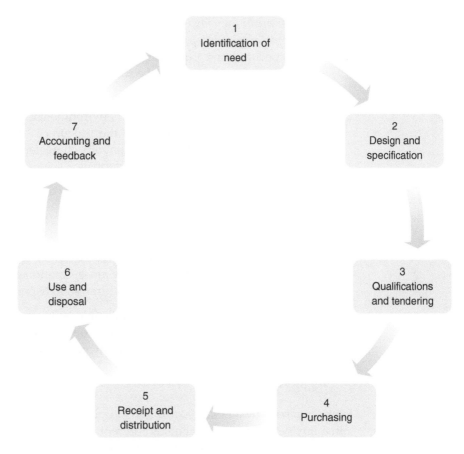

Figure 7.3 The sustainable purchasing cycle

The sustainable procurement process is a cyclical operation, allowing for evaluation of performance at each of its stages and feedback into the beginning of the repeat process, as can be seen in Figure 7.3.

1. *Identification of need* – Is the purchase really necessary or can it be postponed, reduced in quantity or dropped completely? To be sustainable, purchasing less or not at all has to be an option for consideration, especially when purchases carry a high ecological footprint or come at a social cost.

2. *Design and specification* – Can problematic sustainability issues be designed out of the product/supplies from the start? A single ingredient or material may significantly affect the ecological footprint of an organisation. For example, the carbon footprint of the concrete used for construction for the London 2012 Olympics is tracked and managed from quarry to venue as just 1 tonne of concrete involves 4 tonnes of CO_2. The 2012 Olympics aim to be the most sustainable games ever and 60 percent of its 3.4 million tonnes carbon footprint is embodied in construction. A clear specification can facilitate the search and tendering process for potential suppliers who want to control all the aspects of their ecological footprint, e.g. *Copier paper, 90gsm,*

suitable for printing on fax, laser printers and photocopiers, with minimum 75 per-cent content of recycled post-consumer waste. Besides strict environmental product specifications, purchasers may also establish codes of practice for suppliers in order to guarantee the social and economic rights of employees in international supply chains.

3. *Qualifications and tendering* – Supplier environmental, economic and social performance can be requested, and the procurer's appraisal system can take into account both product sustainability characteristics, manufacturing issues and supplier sustainability credentials.

4. *Purchasing* – Purchase can take place after choice of supplier has been made.

5. *Receipt and distribution* – Transport footprint, product handling issues, packaging.

6. *Use and disposal* – Use and maintenance, extension of usable life through upgrade and servicing, possibilities for reuse, component recycling, end-of-life management, retrieval by manufacturer, safe disposal.

7. *Accounting* – Full cost accounting to take into account the cost of the whole life of the product. Feedback should provide an overall assessment of the supplier's and the product's sustainability performance.

Dealing with risk

Every purchase by a business through suppliers represents a risk for the sustainability performance, credentials and reputation of the purchaser. Such risks are likely to increase across lengthy international supply chains where working and living conditions may be poorer, although locating supply closer to point of sale can still be problematic. In November 2010 high street fashion retailer New Look was forced to defend its ethical record after a Channel 4 documentary revealed that one of its UK suppliers of clothing was paying its workers less than half the minimum wage. Other high street stores were found to be linked to the same supplier, including BHS, Peacocks and Jane Norman.[4]

Management researcher and advisor Peter Kraljic is well known for his work on supply chain management. In his seminal paper he presented the Kraljic Matrix as a tool designed to allow the buyer to classify purchased goods and the suppliers involved. By stating 'purchasing must become supply management'[5] Kraljic elevated the strategic value of procurement, highlighting the need to guarantee cost-effective, reliable supplies while guarding against interruptions and dealing with economic and technological change. As can be seen in Figure 7.4, an organisation's supply chain strategy depends on two factors: the potential impact of particular supplies on profit and the ability of suppliers to meet their demand for such supplies; that is, the level of risk that suppliers could fail.

As with many portfolio matrices, the main focus appears to be on differences in power and dependence between buyers and suppliers, with the objective of minimising supply vulnerability while making the most of potential buying power, to the extent that buyers can exploit their dominance over suppliers under certain market conditions, driving down costs.[6]

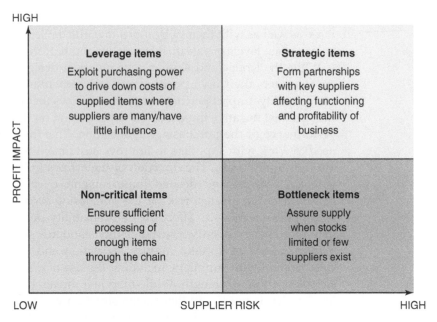

Figure 7.4 The Kraljic Matrix

Source: Adapted from Kraljic, 1983[7]

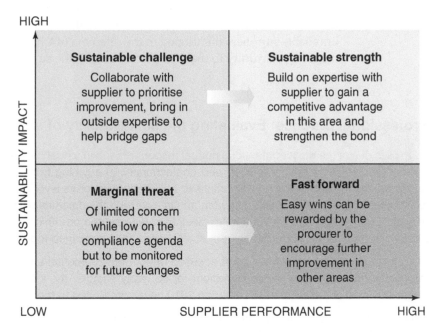

Figure 7.5 Sustainability impact–performance matrix

However, when a similar matrix is created to understand the roles of purchasers and suppliers in the context of sustainability, the considerations are different from those of the Kraljic Matrix. Figure 7.5 compares the level of impact of sustainability performance to the level of expertise of the supplier in sustainable production and management. Sustainability impact involves the likelihood of non-compliance with the purchaser's own sustainability objectives, as well as with their obligations towards the legislation in place to guarantee certain levels of sustainable practice and performance.

While the Kraljic and similar versions seem designed to aid the purchasers to protect their own position and gain advantages where possible, the sustainability–impact performance matrix shows that the priority is to reduce the potential negative impact of the supply chain on the overall sustainability performance of the purchasing organisation. This implies that organisations need to work with suppliers to improve sustainability performance throughout the supply chain. The direction of the arrows in the matrix indicates the potential changes and desired improvements over time. Sustainable challenges carry the greatest risk for the purchasing organisation, as these items or supplies are likely to affect their sustainability performance seriously and may contravene recognised sustainability standards such as ISO 14001 (www.netregs.gov.uk) or specific country legislation and targets. Investment and collaboration with suppliers, including the use of outside expertise, can turn a challenge into a strength. While marginal threats have a low sustainability impact, that is not to say that such a situation would continue in the future. By monitoring the situation organisations can detect if sustainability issues are gaining in significance over time and make appropriate adjustments to their supply chain arrangements.

Marks and Spencer, Waitrose, B&Q, among others, all work with suppliers to improve their sustainability performance. Notably, Primark's decision to ditch unreliable suppliers mentioned in the dilemma of Chapter 6 was criticised as a missed opportunity to make improvements to the supply chain.

Professional practice: Evaluating the sustainability of supply

Palm oil is one of the most contentious natural resources used in a host of different products from sectors as diverse as beauty to food and confectionary. In anything from oven chips to make-up, its production and use is heavily criticised by nutritionists for its level of saturated fat and by environmentalists for the impact of its plantations – causing the destruction of rainforests and the habitat of the orang-utan. By 2008 palm oil already represented one-third of global vegetable oil production and used in about 50 percent of all supermarket packaged food products.

Many producers of palm oil have been accused of poor environmental and labour practices, but the continued importance of the ingredient for so many sectors, the increase in demand from China and India and the rise in price during 2010 have contributed to the growth of the business.

Retailers have also come in for criticism. Between March and September 2009 the World Wildlife Fund (WWF) assessed the progress of 59 European companies on sustainable palm oil sourcing. Companies such as Sainsbury's, Marks and Spencer, Migros and Young's occupied the top positions in the survey.[8]

Rod Taylor, director of the Forests Programme at WWF International, stated that palm oil needed to be sustainably sourced, adding that major palm oil users should be held to account for their procuring practices because certified, sustainable palm oil was available.[9]

As a new head of procurement for a small ethical cosmetics company you have been asked to report on the possibilities of ensuring that its future supplies of palm oil come from totally sustainable sources. Evaluate the extent to which palm oil can be sourced sustainably, identifying producers, locations of production and any relevant environmental, social or economic issues along the whole length of the supply chain.

Getting started

1. Investigate the Roundtable on Sustainable Palm Oil.
2. What can you find out about New Britain Palm Oil?

Impacts along the supply chain

The long and complex supply chains of certain industries are ideal for demonstrating the influence supply chain management can have on environmental, social and economic sustainability. Figure 7.6 shows the environmental, social and economic impacts associated with the supply chain of fashion garments.

In order to properly evaluate all of the sustainability issues, the considerations related to each of the impacts have to be viewed across the whole of the lifecycle of the garment from extraction of raw materials through to disposal of the finished article. As can be seen in Figure 7.6, the most significant impacts tend to occur in the country of production either from the extraction or growth of raw materials and/or the actual manufacture of goods. Over recent years numerous developing nations have become key producers of garments to supply the growing demand for fast fashion in the European countries of purchase and consumption, and they bear the brunt of the impacts. For example, although they are small exporters on a global scale, clothing and textiles account for more than 80 percent of total export earnings for Bangladesh, Haiti and Cambodia, while China and India are the largest exporters.[10]

From cotton fields to t-shirt

Some 75 percent of the world's cotton is grown in developing countries and 99 percent of cotton farmers live and work in the developing world.[11] The story of cotton from cultivation to garment provides a useful illustration of supply chain sustainability issues and the impacts can be seen across all three elements of the Triple Bottom Line.

Environmental

The environmental effects of using oil-based synthetic materials are well known, from the depletion of natural resources to the energy used and pollution created in the production processes and the contaminating disposal issues when sent to landfill.

However, so-called natural fibres can be just as conflictive in environmental terms. Cotton is the largest single fibre in production but standard cultivation relies heavily on the use of pesticides harmful to the eco-system and humans. It is the scale of pesticide use that is difficult to grasp. Cotton accounts for 16 percent of global insecticide applications and in cotton growing countries the proportion is more exaggerated. For example, in India, cotton accounts for 54 percent of all pesticides used annually – despite occupying just 5 percent of land under crops and only 0.15 percent of the world's cotton is guaranteed to be pesticide free.

Cotton cultivation is water intensive. It takes over 3 litres of water to produce just one cotton bud and some 2,000 litres to produce one cotton t-shirt. It has been estimated that nearly half of the water problems in the world are related to cotton growth, and processing can be attributed to foreign demand for cotton products. However, there remains a stark contrast between producing and receiving countries as it has been calculated that 84 percent of the EU's cotton-related water footprint actually lies outside the EU.[12]

Chemical dyeing processes, responsible for more pollution, resource depletion and water usage further add to the ecological footprint of cotton garments.

Economic

Employment opportunities have generally been concentrated at the bottom of the supply chain, low-skilled employment, very often in countries with limited alternative job opportunities. These conditions have contributed towards maintaining wages at relatively low rates.[13]

From a fashion retailer's perspective, two factors drive supply chain decisions: the location of material resources and the location of human resources for production and manufacture. Conventional business practice holds that both of these decisions are governed by the reduction of costs in order to maximise profits. The economics of cotton in developing countries is no exception.

For example, cotton growers have been forced to buy seed, fertiliser and pesticides from agents while being obliged to obtain loans at high rates of interest to do so. This puts farmers into debt even before the crop is planted, let alone harvested, and reduces the amount of profit that can be made, and if the crop fails their economic position is even more precarious. Such predatory lending places many cotton farmers into a cycle of debt from which they cannot escape and the system has been identified as being responsible for the suicides of many Indian cotton farmers.[14]

According to ethical fashion designer Katharine Hamnett, the financing and use of a more expensive but more socially responsible and environmentally friendly cotton should not pose a threat to the fashion industry. She states:

> People say that organic cotton will be too expensive, but the truth is that the value to the farmer of the cotton in a t-shirt is 4–5 percent of the retail value, so if he gets 20 percent more it puts 1 percent on the price of a t-shirt. This is hardly a prohibitive cost, and it can make the difference between survival and the extinction of 11 million farmers in Africa and a further 90 million farmers in the rest of the developing world.[15]

Manufacturing costs are also kept low through low wages to workers, who are often denied a fair living wage. This trend has been described as 'a race to the bottom'[16] in which the competition to obtain contracts from fashion brands drives manufacturing costs down to the extent where workers, factories and whole countries are bent on being the cheapest, quickest and most flexible. The effects of such decisions are felt across all three aspects of the Triple Bottom Line but are more apparent in the economic.

The largest gross profit for the average cotton t-shirt is for the high street retailer, which in part reflects their higher costs but is still proportionally much greater than what is paid to the cotton farmer or the t-shirt manufacturer. With the profit on a cotton t-shirt at 75 percent of its final retail price in comparison to just 2.8 percent in labour costs, it is reasonable to think that the economic returns have not been shared in a mutually beneficial and equitable manner. One study put the labour costs of producing a single cotton t-shirt in Bangladesh at just 3.9 pence at a rate of 900 per day.[17]

Social

Social equity continues to be an issue where lengthy transnational supply chains are involved. Developing nations are not just used because they are cheap; lax labour laws and shoddy governments are also an essential ingredient. Clothing manufacturing workers tend to face long hours as well as poor pay, working in sweatshop conditions with little regard for health and safety. The right to form unions is often ignored, overtime compulsory and child labour condoned. Local communities may be broken up as workers move closer to factories or even live inside them. Indeed, some reports on labour practices within the clothing sector make for grim reading.[18]

By 2006 UK shoppers were buying some 40 percent of their clothes at value retailers, using just 17 percent of their assigned clothing budget. Consumer demand for inexpensive fashion turned cheap into the 'new black', as consumers prided themselves on finding the cheapest bargains. As a result retailers obliged and for the first half of the decade the value clothing retailer market doubled in the UK, to be worth £6 billion.[19]

The taste for purchasing more and more clothes has had a curious effect on supply chains. In one article reporters found that a pair of denim jeans bought in Ipswich in the UK had components and processes which together comprised a journey of about 40,000 miles, including Tunisia, Italy, Germany, France, Northern Ireland, Pakistan, Turkey, Japan, Korea, Namibia, Benin, Australia and Hungary.[20]

Apply it: People Tree

Specialist providers tend to have an even closer relationship with their suppliers such as the ethical clothing firm People Tree. How does People Tree try to mitigate the kinds of supply chain impacts outlined in Figure 7.6?

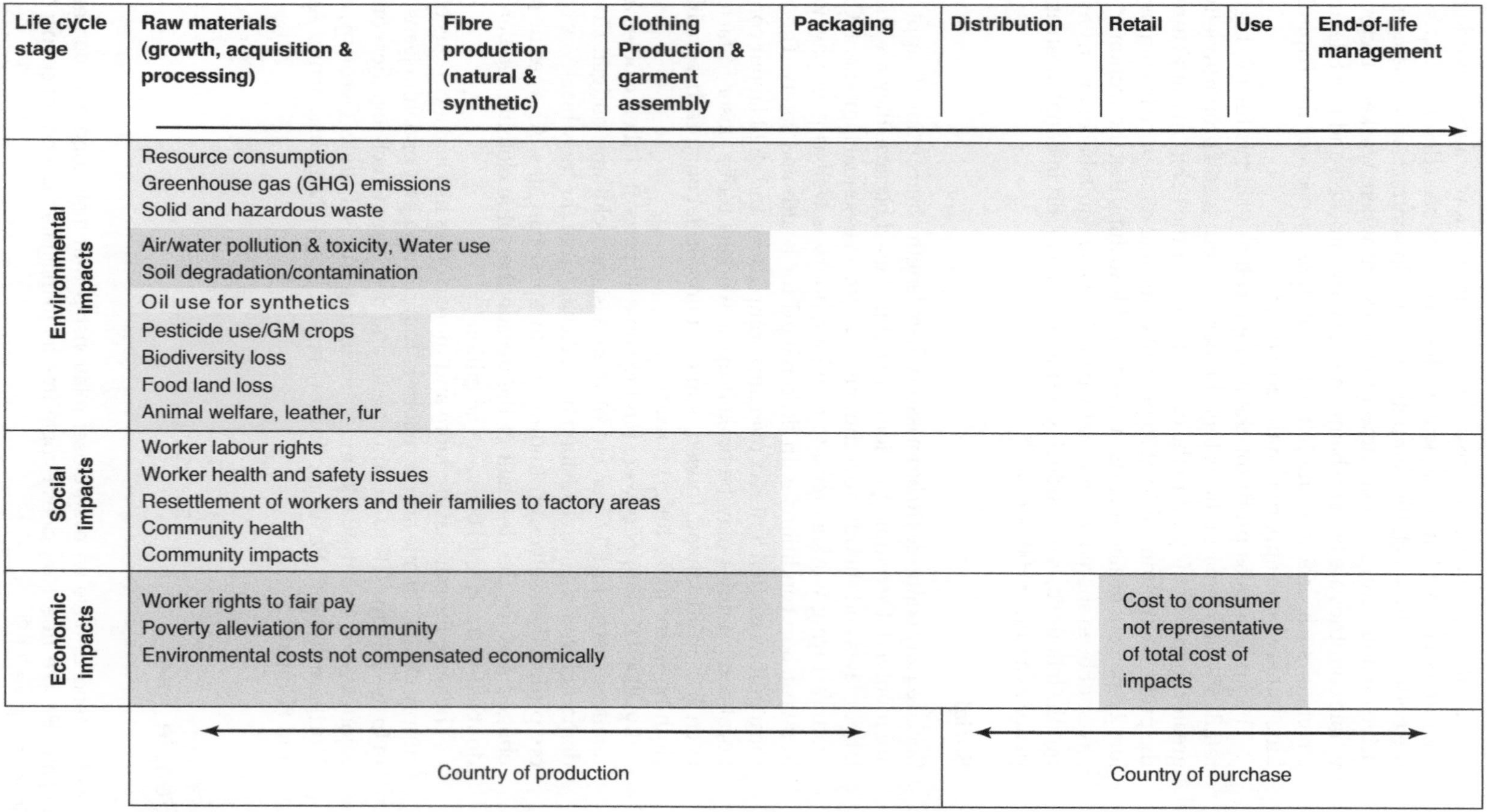

Life cycle stage	Raw materials (growth, acquisition & processing)	Fibre production (natural & synthetic)	Clothing Production & garment assembly	Packaging	Distribution	Retail	Use	End-of-life management
Environmental impacts	Resource consumption Greenhouse gas (GHG) emissions Solid and hazardous waste Air/water pollution & toxicity, Water use Soil degradation/contamination Oil use for synthetics Pesticide use/GM crops Biodiversity loss Food land loss Animal welfare, leather, fur							
Social impacts	Worker labour rights Worker health and safety issues Resettlement of workers and their families to factory areas Community health Community impacts							
Economic impacts	Worker rights to fair pay Poverty alleviation for community Environmental costs not compensated economically					Cost to consumer not representative of total cost of impacts		

Country of production

Country of purchase

Figure 7.6   Supply chain impacts for the fashion sector

Source: Adapted from Defra[21] and Forum for the Future[22]

Researching sustainability: Scenario analysis

A strategy for making supply chains more sustainable is to re-localise supply of materials and/or re-localise the production of goods. To what extent is it feasible to meet the UK's demand for clothing by localising production in the UK? What other changes would be needed to make the manufacturing relocation scenario more feasible, for example, in consumer behaviour or use of materials?

Create a scenario analysis forecasting the implications of relocating clothing manufacturing to the UK indicating the effects of such a decision on the whole of the supply chain. The information in Table 7.2 may help you.

Table 7.2 Supply chain impacts of UK-bought t-shirt

Supply chain from raw material to a single finished t-shirt	Intermediate prices inclusive of gross profit
Retailer UK price to final consumer	£7.00
Wholesale UK	£2.65
Knitted t-shirt China	£1.96
Knitted fabric China	£1.08
Cotton yarn US	£0.55
Production stages	**Actual costs per stage**
Fabric cut and sewn into t-shirt in China	£0.88
Yarn knitted into fabric and dyed in China	£0.53
Yarn spun in US	£0.33
Raw cotton used	£0.22
Total	£1.96
Consumer footprint of one 250g cotton t-shirt	**Waste**
Electricity: washing, drying, ironing	1.7kg fossil fuel/4kg CO_2
Detergent to waste water processing	125g
Incineration	13g
Landfill total waste (inc. fossil fuel extraction)	450g
Employment per 1 million t-shirts purchased in UK	**No. of employees used**
In US	22
In China	234
In UK	57
Total	313

Source: Adapted from Allwood *et al.*, 2007[23]

What techniques are at the disposal of the marketer for analysing potential business scenarios and forecasting possible outcomes?

Snapshot: The story of stuff

Annie Leonard is a well-known campaigner for sustainability and an outspoken critic of excessive consumption. Her most recognised work focuses on the lifecycle of goods and began in 2007 with her *The Story of Stuff*, a 20-cartoon documentary on the wastefulness of uncontrolled consumption which has been viewed by more than 12 million people worldwide, translated into 15 languages and become a book of the same name published on recycled paper with soy ink. Some 70,000 of her supporters are now friends on her Facebook page.

Her success at communicating her messages about sustainability comes from her simple, uncomplicated style, presentation and language. What began as a one-off idea has given way to the *Story of Stuff Project*, a non-profit organisation funded by diverse environmental organisations to extend her work into other areas. Since her first story she has produced other cartoon stories of electronics, cosmetics, bottled water, and cap and trade.

Visit the Story of Stuff website (www.storyofstuff.com) and view the cartoons and other material. What supply chain issues are highlighted?

Forget global, act local

As society has evolved from hunter, gatherer and farmer to FMCG addict, consumers have become divorced from the natural processes on which their lives are based. Our continued consumption and growth has resulted in extensive supply chains around the globe creating numerous sustainability problems in all three elements of the Triple Bottom Line. One means of dealing with overstretched supply chains is to locate production closer to consumption.

The re-localisation of production and supply closer to intended markets is already being proposed as a means of achieving greater sustainability and the food sector in particular is drawing more attention. For many people food comes from supermarkets not from farms, and much of the notion of the seasonality of food has been lost as global supply chains provide the supermarkets of the developed nations with all-year-round summer fruits, even in winter.

With the prospects of lengthy food supply chains becoming too expensive to maintain as a result of increasing transport costs, coupled with the interference of environmental change and soil degradation, national food security has quickly become a cause for concern for many countries. Food supply chain management and the re-localisation of food supply are being seen as a means of ensuring the sustainability of food. The former UK environment secretary, Hilary Benn, has already reserved £50 million for research into food sustainability through the work of Defra including investigation into ways to reduce carbon emissions from soils and rotting waste food, as well as finding ways to grow food with less fertiliser, pesticides and fuel.[24, 25]

It seems that one of the maxims of modern international business – *Think global, act local* – may now be overtaken as attention to local priorities take precedence in order to meet the demands of achieving sustainability.

Turning to local supply

Locavore was 2007 Word of the Year in the *New Oxford American Dictionary* after only two years since its appearance. The term was coined by a group of people in San Francisco who decided to eat only food grown or produced within a 100-mile radius following seasonal availability patterns.[26] The expanding locavore movement encourages consumers to only eat local produce/locally grown ingredients from within a certain catchment area and to grow or pick their own food, arguing that fresh, local products are more nutritious, better tasting and at the same time have a reduced impact on the environment.

Studies in the US (where the average food catchment area is estimated at 1,500 miles – some 2,400 kilometres) show there can be a significant difference in food miles when sourcing ingredients more locally. One study in the state of Iowa showed that the average distance travelled by locally sourced food could be cut to 44.6 miles – just 72 kilometres.[27]

The final stage of the supply chain between food outlet and consumer has also attracted attention. In the UK urban food vehicle kilometres are estimated to have increased by 27 percent since 1992, due largely to an increase in shopping for food by car. This has been driven by an increase in car ownership, together with changes in shopping patterns, as the gradual disappearance of local shops has given way to weekly visits to large out-of-town supermarkets.[28]

Turning to local supply seems to be an effective way of reducing the carbon footprint of food, a simple way of combining healthy eating with concern for the environment, but there are also economic gains to be made too.

Local sourcing of food keeps money in the local economy, whereas conventional agriculture bleeds money out of the region and in many cases would barely break even were it not for government subsidies. Independent Minnesota farm researcher Ken Meter argues persuasively that the development of local food markets makes more economic sense. In Meter's seminal study of south-eastern Minnesota in 1997, farmers made $866 million selling their produce but lost $80 million having incurred $947 million in costs. Nearly half of the costs left the area, as payments to distant suppliers of seeds, fertiliser and pesticides, or to banks in the form of interest on loans. In the meantime the 120,000 households of south-eastern Minnesota spent $500 million on food but just $2 million of that was on food grown within the region. A 20 percent increase in local food purchases would have cancelled out the Minnesota's farmers' loss of that year.[29]

More recently, it is apparent that the local food market in the US is growing significantly as a result of the increased interest in the local movement. The sales of locally grown foods, worth about $4 billion in 2002, are expected to reach as much as $7 billion by 2011. The increased interest in local food supply chains is also apparent in the UK.

The Müller brand, producer of a range of dairy products, proudly announces that 90 percent of its milk supply comes from within a radius of 30 miles of its dairy. Situated in Market Drayton, Shropshire, the company works in partnership with over 150 dedicated local farmers to provide fresh milk twice daily and is prepared to not only pay more for the quality of the milk, but works actively to continuously improve the wellbeing and sustainability of farming practice. Müller's pursuit of more sustainable practices has resulted in an extensive local supply chain beyond just the dairy farmers, to include over 200 local businesses, all located within the 30-mile radius. As a result of working with the agency Good Brand and Company, Müller adjusted its key brand messages on its local sustainability strategy. Müller based its communications for its campaign on three slogans 'made in Shropshire', '90% of our milk comes from within 30 miles of our dairy' and '24 hours from farm to yogurt'.

Waitrose also has a policy of supporting local suppliers, again within a 30-mile radius, and promoting seasonal food. Waitrose holds the annual Small Producers Awards for small producers with fewer than ten permanent, full- or part-time employees, who compete for a £10,000 prize and access to Waitrose business and marketing expertise, including advice on packaging and getting your product to market.[30]

When consumer becomes part-time supplier

Over the last 20 years, food consumers in the US have started to re-establish their links to the natural environment through Community Supported Agriculture (CSA) programmes.[31] Local Harvest, America's leading organic and local food organisation, estimates the number of CSA farms at over 3,000 in 2009 with some areas of the country experiencing more demand than there are CSA farms to satisfy it.[32] This movement, which has been replicated in different guises in other countries, brings consumer and producer together in a closer relationship than the conventional one, to the point where the consumers become part-time suppliers of their own purchases.

In order to participate in the scheme consumers buy a share in a specific farm, which may cost them between $200 and $600. In return each CSA member receives a weekly box of organically grown produce for five to seven months, depending on the growing season of the region, which is collected by the member from a centralised pick-up point. Members can reduce or eliminate the cost of their share by providing five to ten hours of free labour on the farm.

The advantages of this relationship are of mutual benefit to consumer and farmer.

Advantages for the farmer:

- Receive advance payments before crops mature and are sold, improving cash flow earlier in the season.

- Food is marketed early in the year, before farmers begin their more intensive 16-hour days in the field.

- Develop relationships with the local community.

Advantages for the consumer:

- Reconnects the consumer with supply and production and their implications.

- Access to fresh, organic produce direct from farmer.

- Get exposed to new vegetables and new ways of cooking.

- Develop a relationship with the farmer and the other CSA members in the community.

- Extended beyond cultivated produce to include eggs, meat and dairy products.

The programme's fit with sustainability is ideal. The return to local supply rather than global supply chain of food signals the acceptance of the seasonality of food, and the reduction of unnecessary food miles, the reduction of packaging and food waste and the high carbon footprint associated with growing crops out of their natural season. The return to local is also a return to the idea that small is beautiful, the local market becomes the centre of activity, and food quality tends to be better in comparison with mass produced, intensively farmed somewhat tasteless standard produce.

The fact that the risk of farming is shared between community shareholders and farmer is also important. Again it is essential to demonstrate that sustainable food supply depends on environmental factors outside the control of the farmer, and the community shares the good and bad times associated with agriculture.

Snapshot: Incredible Edible Todmorden

In order to drive the UK government's food sustainability plan, it is envisaged that food supply will become more local, that more farmers' markets will appear and that more people will cultivate their own food. According to Defra, one in three people in the UK grow some food and it is hoped that this existing practice can be expanded, fostering greater community spirit, goodwill and developing new or lost skills. Also, the additional benefits for the population in terms of physical and mental health are not lost on the government in its Food 2030 Report. To encourage participation in the general population, the government aims to develop a short-term leasing system for landowners and voluntary groups wishing to set up temporary allotments on land awaiting development. Some localities are already ahead of this initiative.

The town of Todmorden in West Yorkshire provides an excellent example of how progress towards sustainability can be successful when embedded in the locality as a grassroots movement and allowed to develop and spread its influence over time. It is not tainted by the smell of institution or government, and is run for local people by local people, encouraging involvement from all sectors of the community. Again consumers become suppliers in this imaginative initiative.

The aims of the group are:

- To promote and develop a culture and opportunities for growing food, cooking and sourcing local products.

- To build on Todmorden's wealth of voluntary sector engagement to develop new links and partners concerned with the future of food and growing.

- To develop whole community skills in growing and cooking local produce.

▶

Incredible Edible Todmorden[33] has been set up to increase the amount of food grown locally for the townspeople to eat and achieve food supply sustainability. What has captured the imagination of the people was the idea to transform public and private spaces all around the town into herb gardens and vegetable patches to accomplish this. As the movement has gained momentum, now businesses, schools, farmers and the community in general are all involved, making the most of all available areas to grow food to make the town self-sufficient.

The Incredible Edible group facilitates and encourages engagement of the locals by finding land for cultivation, obtaining micro-finance and resources such as tools. The group also helps with training and providing routes to the local market for produce, as well as removing barriers to action such as legal restrictions, public liability issues and soil testing.

Pam Warhurst, one of the founders of the group, describes the local food movement as a door to a sustainable lifestyle because food can be used as a trigger to engage with other issues of sustainability such as carbon footprints, health and enhancing quality of life. Food serves as a common denominator because it has the ability to cut across age, income, race and class barriers, and involve people in an initiative in which they can quite literally see and enjoy the fruits of their labours. Rather than trust in the more abstract and intangible belief of reducing the effects of climate change, the cultivation of fruit, vegetables and herbs provides more immediate tangible benefits. The activity creates jobs and brings people together with shared objectives creating a sense of belonging and community.

Incredible Edible Todmorden was selected by the Sustainable Development Commission as one of its top 19 breakthrough ideas for sustainable lives.[34] The idea has given way to other initiatives from the group such as Every Egg Matters, a scheme to make Todmorden self-sufficient in free-range eggs, and a ten-year programme to *Put the Market Back into Market Towns*. The group is also working with tenants in social housing to show people how to grow food and cook, producing a toolkit to help bring in a range of necessary skill sets, from planning and sustainable design to soil quality expertise.

Since its inception word has spread, nationally and internationally. Now there is the possibility of setting up a national programme to inspire more edible towns and communities. The scheme could be developed in a similar way to *Britain in Bloom* where all of the entrants are winners just for entering, while at a different level it could be competitive with awards available to the best local food producing towns of each region.

Traceability of supply

If businesses are to demonstrate their sustainability credentials across all three aspects of the Triple Bottom Line, being able to trace all the ingredients or components from the entire length of the supply chain and how they are obtained, is necessary. Third-party certification is one means of proving traceability of supply and there is no shortage of organisations offering their services.

The Marine Stewardship Council (MSC) began when WWF and Unilever came together as a result of the collapse of the Grand Banks cod fishery to create a market-based programme to promote and encourage sustainable fishing. The MSC offers certification, including a supply chain traceability and eco-labelling programme to recognise and reward environmentally responsible and sustainable fishing practices. In this way the MSC can empower consumers through the use of its label to make the best environmental choice. The international

Table 7.3   MSC achievements July 2011

	2010 figures	2011 figures
Number of companies worldwide certified for MSC Chain of Custody	1,100	1,805
Number of product lines using the MSC eco-label	3,800	Over 10,000
Number of participating countries	62	80
Estimated retail value	$1.5 billion	$2.25 billion

Source: Adapted from Marine Stewardship Council, 2010[35]

organisation became fully independent, on a not-for-profit basis, in 1999 and has been helping businesses worldwide to demonstrate their sustainability credentials *from boat to plate* and protect the world's fish stock for future generations. The MSC still has work to do as it now accounts for around 12 percent of the annual global wild harvest.

While the environmental benefits of the work of the MSC are evident, the work of the council also provides for social and economic benefits. For example, the ability to demand price premiums for certified catches has allowed the Lakes and Coorong fishery in Australia to command 30–50 percent premiums when selling to restaurants in Sydney and Melbourne in contrast with non-certified seafood. In a community where fishing and related services account for 60 percent of household income, these increased earnings are significant.[36]

The Mexican red rock lobster fishery case demonstrates how MSC certification can contribute to the delivery of wider social benefits through community empowerment. The ten participating villages received increased government support as a result of the MSC involvement, including a $20 million grant for electricity and government help with infrastructure, access roads and drinking water.[37]

'The End of the Line' – the hard-hitting documentary about overfishing, which was inspired by the book by environmental journalist Charles Clover – was premiered in June 2009.[38] Its effect of drawing public attention to how intensive fishing methods are dangerously depleting the world's fish stocks has produced mixed results. Upon viewing the documentary, Julian Metcalf, the CEO of the high street sandwich chain Pret a Manger, withdrew tuna and cucumber sandwiches from all 155 outlets and bluefin tuna from its sushi boxes as well as from its sister outlet Itsu. The Itsu chain signed a deal to use only pole-and-line-caught fish with deliveries that can even be traced to each individual boat.[39]

The decision to stop selling bluefin tuna has also been taken up by supermarkets Waitrose and Marks and Spencer, both of which have added swordfish and skate to the list, and numerous celebrity chefs including Gordon Ramsey have banned bluefin from their restaurants. Overfishing, illegal fishing and the growing demand for high-end raw bluefin as sushi and sashimi has provoked an increase in the number of catches of the bluefin.

However, in March, 2010, at the 15th meeting of the Conference of the Parties to the Convention on International Trade in Endangered Species (CITES) in Doha, Qatar, delegates rejected protecting the severely depleted bluefin tuna together with four vulnerable species of shark. Environmental groups at the conference felt that governments had decided to favour commercial interests, protecting trade above conservation.[40]

On a more positive note, in April 2010 David Miliband, the former British Foreign Secretary, announced the creation of a marine reserve that will double the amount of the world's oceans under protection. The protected area will extend 200 miles around the British Indian Ocean Territory, in the middle of the Indian Ocean, and will include an area where commercial fishing will be completely banned.

Evaluating sustainability through country of origin

'Place matters'.[41] One study recounts how a Puerto Rican shoe manufacturer exported his shoes to New York only to import them again to be able to classify them as New York imports, knowing his prospects for sale in Puerto Rico had automatically improved.[42] A product's country of origin can communicate a range of intangible associations to do with quality and authenticity derived from the consumer's perception of the country itself.

While quality and authenticity have long been associated with product positioning by country of origin, the link between sustainability and country of origin is more recent. Now, the concept of country of origin has developed strong links with environmental sustainability (carbon footprint of transport costs) social sustainability (treatment of workers and the local community) and economic sustainability (degree of support given to local economy). Country of origin can therefore be used by the consumer to evaluate the sustainability credentials of a product and mitigate the risk involved in the purchase.

Deliberately hiding the country of origin removes the ability of consumers to make such judgements. For example, the use of the phrase *'packaged in'* allows retailers to omit true country of origin as in the case of Latvian cheddar cheese, sold in the UK as just cheddar cheese packaged in the UK but without revealing its true origins. Latvian cheddar imports account for some 86,000 kilos, substantially more than the 50,000 kilos made by the Cheddar Gorge Cheese Company, the last remaining business making cheese in the village of Cheddar.[43] If purchasers of cheddar were making their decisions based on food miles and supporting local producers, they might feel disappointed by such an omission of information.

Madagascan vanilla has become a symbol of quality, synonymous with excellence and distinct from synthetic vanilla flavouring in cheaper foods. As an ingredient it can be found in 25 Marks and Spencer products – from candles to cup cakes – and in the main supermarkets a single pod can sell for more than £4. As a country of origin Madagascar has yet to be associated with sustainability. Some 80 percent of the world's supply of vanilla comes from Madagascar but the UN International Labour Organisation estimates that some 2 million children work instead of attending school, particularly on vanilla plantations where they earn on average 8p per day. Vanilla is a labour-intensive crop; the plants have to be hand pollinated on a daily basis and the pods cured in a lengthy process lasting weeks before being readied for export. Since a recent report in the *Sunday Times*, the major UK supermarkets have all stated they would investigate their sources of supply of vanilla.[44]

Geotraceability: Geo Fair Trade Project

In 2009 the World Fair Trade Organisation (WFTO) began a three-year project with a €1.5 million budget due to be completed in March 2012 to develop a geographic data system to provide greater information and transparency on the origin of goods and their supply chain. The Geo Fair Trade Project combines geographical and local data on producers, their working environment and social, economic and environmental indicators, allowing consumers to trace products to their producers and evaluate them. Other relevant indicators such as food safety, product quality and sustainability performance are also included.

The project uses traditional traceability data and links them with geographical information, and online interactive tools will enable consumers to view the supply chain upstream and downstream and see how fair trade initiatives impact the economic, social and environmental conditions of producers and their communities.

The project will benefit consumers and producers mutually. Fair trade producers will be able to present their projects and their outcomes and consumers will be able to see how their support through the purchase of their goods can positively impact sustainable development of producers and their local communities.

Snapshot: Traceable dog food

Even producers of pet food appear to be under pressure to highlight the transparency of their supply chains. In order to gain the trust of pet owners, Mars, the producer of Pedigree Chum dog food, announced it could trace all the meat it used back to the individual farm it came from as part of a new £7 million campaign under the title *Good Honest Food* launched in June 2009.

Summary

The true sustainability impact of any product is not the final product itself but the sum of all its parts. The sustainable management of the supply chain is the means of controlling the different parts that make up the product. The sustainable procurement of the component parts or ingredients of the product is the starting point of the sustainable product followed by control of the individual stages of manufacture, production, distribution, purchase, consumption and post-consumption, whether for reuse, recycle or disposal.

Each of these stages involves a trace, a footprint – a broad ecological footprint or a specific carbon or water footprint. Other impacts may be social, experienced by the workforce at different points in the supply chain or by the local community, or economic such as low wages or abusive prices offered to suppliers. Place of production, geographic source of materials, country of origin are becoming more important as means of evaluating and assessing the sustainability credentials of supply for businesses and consumers.

The drive to make supply chains more sustainable is leading to the creation of alternative strategies of supply. The re-localisation of supply is one means of reducing impacts as the chain becomes shorter and more controllable, closer to its target markets. Consumers are also taking a more active role in the supply chain becoming part-time suppliers of the goods they wish to consume and reconnecting with the origin of goods and products.

Case study: Source4Style

Brainchild of entrepreneur Summer Rayne Oakes, Source4Style is a business-to-business online platform designed to connect fashion designers with suppliers of sustainable materials. The sustainable apparel sector is worth about $6 billion a year and growing annually at an estimated $1 billion, but Oakes hopes to accelerate the growth of sustainable fashion design through her online service. Oakes' market research found that one of the barriers to further expansion of ethical fashion is the difficulty facing suppliers trying to reach the fashion designer marketplace. Trade shows are often too expensive for these small suppliers to attend, and they also lack expertise and funds to set up their own web communications. Oakes also discovered that designers had great difficulty in finding suitable suppliers and spent up to 85 percent of their time sourcing sustainable material when their time would be better spent producing fashion garments. The market is lucrative and, per project, independent designers are spending anything between $5,000 to $100,000 on sustainable materials.

Launched in September 2010, Source4Style effectively bridges this 'sustainable design gap'[45] becoming the world's first online marketplace enabling its users, fashion and interior designers and suppliers, to search and acquire sustainable textiles. The website effectively becomes an all year round online tradeshow linking all the members of the supply chain providing instant access to a vast network of sustainable materials and knowhow for suppliers and designers alike.

Source4Style's mission is to make sustainable design possible through a search and source facility of a network of global designers and suppliers. The design portal allows for a search materials and services, and provides technical data on materials including its sustainability specifications. Designers can obtain swatch samples, connect with suppliers to make orders and calculate lead and shipping times.

After a low key start, Source4Style plans to expand its operations to incorporate some 180 suppliers into its network together with over 20,000 registered users by 2011.

Searches on the site can be made by materiality, location, weave, colour or type of certification. Other services provided include viewing of the stories and photographs of supplier operations, access to supplier reviews from other members, discounts to other affiliated sites, access to competitions and experiential educational workshops.

Source4Style provides a detailed materials guide for designers, and divides the sustainability of the suppliers' products into four broad categories:

- Environmentally preferable – certified organic, rain-fed cotton.
- Environmentally/naturally processed – biomimetic materials.
- Handmade/traditional – craft and culture preservation.
- Fair labour/trade – socially and economically compliant with appropriate standards.

Sustainability of materials to be used and the supply chain that provides them are vital for the overall sustainability of this growing niche within the fashion industry. Materials on offer through the network of suppliers include organic sourced from crops or animals reared by organic methods as well as Fairtrade materials.

Recycled materials may also be accessed by designers. In the fashion industry sustainable designers use both pre- and post-consumer recycled material waste content. Pre-consumer waste refers to the scrap waste materials left over after production and presents designers with a significant opportunity. Ethical clothes designer From Somewhere, mentioned in the previous chapter, specialises in the upcycling of such fashion industry leftovers and highlights this process as an advantage for the consumer who will acquire uniquely-styled articles in limited numbers with their own personal history transformed from unwanted to objects of renewed value. The use of pre-consumer recycled fabric is common practice in other industries and much is re-pulped to be used as filling for furniture and mattresses or the production of insulation products or inferior quality yarns and fabrics. Unwanted off-cuts and surplus rolls of fabric which are often disposed of at the end of each fashion season can be upcycled by sustainable fashion designers and is another means of reducing pressure on landfill sites or pollution through incineration. Source4Style also anticipates demand for hand-made materials. The conservation of traditional production techniques, often linked to the preservation of communities, their culture and way of life also forms a part of sustainable fashion design and is central to some businesses such as People Tree.

By collecting the experiences of suppliers and designers Source4Style create a sense of community among its users, linked in a joint enterprise by a single mission to drive sustainable practice in the fashion industry.

Follow up

1. Research Source4Style and assess how successful it has been to date in establishing a sustainable supply chain.

2. Collect some Source4Style stories from suppliers and designers – how do these examples show you how the supply chain can be managed fairly and sustainably?

Dilemma part 2:   The certification of sustainability

To a certain extent the proliferation of certified labels has left consumers to make their own decisions regarding which organisation assures the fairest supply chains. Although the FAIRTRADE Mark offers the most stringent guarantees; the organisation runs the risk of losing out to brands being attracted to less expensive, less demanding schemes which will give them a short-cut to the image of certified, accredited respectability needed for their marketing communications.

If consumers think all certifications provide the same level of sustainable performance then brands will miss out on the opportunity to differentiate themselves from competitors with similar sustainability badges. Who bears the responsibility for communicating the credentials of schemes to the final consumer to ensure differentiation can take place – the accrediting organisation or the brand that uses the badge? As consumers become more aware of the differences between competing sustainable certifications, but also more aware of the related, competing sustainability issues, such as the choice between fairer economics and the carbon footprint of food miles, how will the consumer decision-making process be affected?

Devise the strategy

The Fairtrade Foundation must differentiate its offerings from its competitors on two fronts in order to maintain its position as market leader and further its agenda to make supply chains more equitable and sustainable.

- business-to-business – to continue to attract brands and suppliers to the Fairtrade certification scheme to be able to extend its work and influence.

- business-to-consumer – to stimulate awareness, knowledge and ultimately demand from final consumers for Fairtrade certified products therefore making it more attractive for brands and suppliers to seek accreditation.

The FAIRTRADE Mark
Source: www.fairtrade.org.uk

As marketing manager for the Fairtrade Foundation what strategies would you recommend to strengthen the Fairtrade position in this situation?[46]

References

1. Sustainable Development Commission (2006) *I Will if You Will*, Sustainable Consumption Roundtable National Consumer Council (NCC) and the Sustainable Development Commission (SDC, London) (p. 8).

2. Department for Environment, Food and Rural Affairs (2006) *Procuring the Future – Sustainable Procurement National Action Plan: Recommendations from the Sustainable Procurement Task Force*, Defra.

3. Department for Environment, Food and Rural Affairs (2006) *Procuring the Future – Sustainable Procurement National Action Plan: Recommendations from the Sustainable Procurement Task Force*, Defra.

4. Wood, Z. (2010) 'New Look Forced to Defend Ethics After Sweatshop Revelations', *The Guardian*, 12 November.

5. Kraljic, P. (1983) 'Purchasing Must Become Supply Management', *Harvard Business Review* 61(5): 109–117 (p. 109).

6. Caniëls, M. and Gelderman, C. (2005) 'Purchasing Strategies in the Kraljic Matrix – A Power and Dependence Perspective', *Journal of Purchasing and Supply Management* 11: 141–155.

7. Kraljic, P. (1983) 'Purchasing Must Become Supply Management', *Harvard Business Review* 61(5): 109–117 (p. 109).

8. World Wildlife Fund (2009) *Palm Oil Buyers' Score Card*, London: WWF, http://panda.org/downloads/wwpalmoilbuyerscorecard2009.pdf

9. Kanter, J. (2009) 'Top Retailers Score Badly on Sustainable Palm Oil Purchasing', *Supply Management*, 28 October.

10. Institute for Manufacturing (2006) *Well Dressed? The Present and Future Sustainability of Clothing and Textiles in the United Kingdom*, University of Cambridge.

11. Trent, S., Executive Director, Environmental Justice Foundation (EJF) (2007) Press Release, *The Deadly Chemicals in Cotton*, EJF, www.ejfoundation.org/page324.html

12. Environmental Justice Foundation (2008) *Water and Cotton*, www.ejfoundation.org/page334.html

13. Institute for Manufacturing (2006) *Well Dressed? The Present and Future Sustainability of Clothing and Textiles in the United Kingdom*, University of Cambridge.

14. Forum for the Future (2007) *Fashioning Sustainability: A Review of the* Sustainability Impacts of the Clothing Industry, www.forumforthefuture.org/files/fashionsustain.pdf

15. Katherine Hamnett (2010) *Clean Up or Die Campaign: Introduction*, www.katharinehamnett.com/Campaigns/Clean-Up-Or-Die/Introduction

16. McMullen, A. and Maher, S. (2009) *Let's Clean Up Fashion 2009: The State of Pay Behind the UK High Street*, Bristol: Labour Behind the Label, www.labourbehindthelabel.org/campaigns/item/828-cleanupfashion (p. 2).

17. Miller, D. (2009) 'What Price a Living Wage?', in Parker, L., Marsha, A. and Dickson, M. (eds) *Sustainable Fashion: A Handbook for Educators*, Bristol: Labour Behind the Label.

18. Environmental Justice Foundation (EJF) (2005) *White Gold: The True Cost of Cotton*, London: Environmental Justice Foundation.

19. Hearson, M. (2006) *Who Pays for Cheap Clothes?*, Bristol: Labour Behind the Label.

20. Abrams, F. and Astill, J. (2001) 'Story of the Blues', *The Guardian*, 29 May, www.guardian.co.uk/g2/story/0,,497788,00.html

21. Department for Environment, Food and Rural Affairs (2009) *Sustainable Clothing Action Plan* (Update September), London: Defra.

22. Forum for the Future (2007) *Fashioning Sustainability: A Review of the Sustainability Impacts of the Clothing Industry*, www.forumforthefuture.org/files/Fashionsustain.pdf

23. Institute for Manufacturing (2006) *Well Dressed? The Present and Future Sustainability of Clothing and Textiles in the United Kingdom*, University of Cambridge.

24. Kinver, M. (2009) '"Radical Rethink" Needed on Food', BBC News, 10 August, http://news.bbc.co.uk/1/hi/8189549.stm

25. Vidal, J. and Meikle, J. (2010) 'Britain Must Grow More Sustainable Food, Says Benn', *The Guardian*, 5 January.

26. Smith, A. and MacKinnon, J. (2007) *The 100-mile Diet: A Year of Local Eating*, Ontario, Canada: Vintage.

27. Pirog, R. (2001) *Food, Fuel, and Freeways: An Iowa Perspective on How Far Food Travels, Fuel Usage, and Greenhouse Gas Emissions*, Ames, IO: Leopold Centre for Sustainable Agriculture, Iowa State University.

28. Smith, A., Watkiss, P., Tweddie, G., Mckinnon, A., Browne, M., Hunt, A., Treleven, C., Nash, G. and Cross, S. (2005) *The Validity of Food Miles as an Indicator of Sustainable Development*, Final Report prepared by AEA Technology for Defra.

29. Meter, K. and Rosales, J. (2001) *The Economics of Food and Farming in Southeast Minnesota*, Community Design Centre, Hiawatha's Pantry Project.

30. Waitrose (2003) *The Small Producers Charter*, www.waitrose.com.

31. Thompson, C. and Coskuner-Balli, G. (2007) 'Enchanting Ethical Consumerism; The Case of Community Supported Agriculture', *Journal of Consumer Culture* 7(3): 275–303.

32. Local Harvest (2010) *Community Supported Agriculture*, www.localharvest.org/csa

33. Incredible Edible Todmorden (2010) www.incredible-edible-todmorden.co.uk

34. Monkhouse, C., Porritt, J. and Lee, A. (2009) *Breakthroughs for the 21st Century*, London: Sustainable Development Commission.

35. Marine Stewardship Council (MSC) (2010) *MSC: Commercial Commitment Growing Worldwide*, London: MSC.

36. Marine Stewardship Council (MSC) (2009) *Net Benefits: The First Ten Years of MSC Certified Sustainable Fisheries*, London: MSC.

37. Marine Stewardship Council (MSC) (2009) *Net Benefits: The First Ten Years of MSC Certified Sustainable Fisheries*, London: MSC.

38. Clover C. (2005) *The End of the Line: How Overfishing is Changing the World and What We Eat*, London: Ebury Press.

39. Leake, C. (2009) 'End of the Line for the Pret Tuna Sandwich', *The Mail on Sunday*, 7 June.

40. Film News (2010) *Commerce Trumps Science at CITES, Threatened Sharks and Bluefin Tuna Still at Risk*, 26 March, http://endoftheline.com/blog/archives/1252

41. Thode, S. and Maskulka, J. (1998) 'Place-based Marketing Strategies, Brand Equity and Vineyard Valuation', *Journal of Product and Brand Management* 7(5): 379–399 (p. 380).

42. Bilkey, W. and Nes, E. (1982) 'Country-of-origin Effects on Product Evaluations', *Journal of International Business Studies*, 13(1): 88–99.

43. Mendick, R. (2009) '"British" Cheddar . . . Made in Latvian Dairies', *The Sunday Telegraph*, 15 November.

44. McDougall, D. (2010) 'Bitter Plight of the Vanilla Trade Children', *The Sunday Times*, 14 March.

45. Jacques, E. (2010) 'Interview: Summer Rayne Oakes', *Sustainable Business Magazine*, August/September.

46. Fridell, M., Hudson, I. and Hudson, M. (2008) 'With Friends Like These: The Corporate Response to Fair Trade Coffee' *Review of Radical Political Economics* 40(1): 8–34; Fairtrade Foundation (2006) www.fairtrade.org.uk/press_office/ press_releases_and_statements/archive_2006/dec_2006/sainsburys_banana_ switch_is_the_worlds_biggest_ever_commitment_to_fairtrade.aspx; Reynolds, J. (2010) 'Brands Divided Over Fairtrade Certification', *Marketing,* 24 February; Batsell, J. (2004) 'Bumper Crop of Coffee Labels', *Seattle Times,* 20 September; Trauben, J. (2009) 'Fair Expectations: Rainforest Alliance v. Fairtrade, Organic Consumers Association', 23 June www.organicconsumers.org/articles/article_18372.cfm; Siegle, L. (2009) 'Is Buying Fair Trade a Waste of Money?', *The Observer Magazine*, 22 February.

8 Communicating sustainability

If sustainability is to become a persuasive vision, it needs a persuasive language[1]

Futerra Sustainability Communications – Words that sell

Chapter objectives

After studying this chapter you should be able to:

1   Identify the reasons behind successful and unsuccessful communications for sustainability.

2   Assess the use of rational and emotional appeal types in communicating sustainability.

3   Examine the issue of greenwash in relation to sustainability claims.

4   Explore consumer expectations of marketing communications.

5   Consider the use of labelling as a means of communicating sustainability credentials.

Dilemma part 1:   Aga and a sustainable future

The Aga cooker is the epitome of cooking luxury and is a brand known and valued for its quality craftsmanship around the world, with some 300,000 owners worldwide. Beautifully enamel painted over three days, made of solid cast iron forged in the UK in one of the most historical sites of the Industrial Revolution where iron was first smelted in 1709, it is a symbol of English heritage, tradition and an opulent country lifestyle. With a design that is uniquely based on the heat-storing qualities of cast iron, Aga cookers are normally left running continuously, so there is instant heat available for cooking whenever it is needed. There are no dials or controls; it requires learning how to cook the Aga way by moving food items around a series of differently heated ovens and burners. The supply of constant heat is not just for cooking, it can be used to warm the kitchen, heat water for the house and warm the surrounding rooms in the house.

Love good food, love warmth, love toast at 3am.
Love one for a lifetime. Call 0845 481 0772 or visit aga-web.co.uk today.

Source: The Advertising Archives

A £3.5 million advertising campaign launched in March 2008 was the largest communications effort in the company's history. The message was about belonging, with the strap line 'Love Aga'. Richard Eagleton, the Aga group marketing director, said 'It is about getting people to remember how much they love their Aga. People form an emotional attachment to them.'

Love certainly seemed to fit the brand as for decades Aga seemed to represent everything that was characteristic of the British lifestyle, the country house, the luxury lifestyle and status. But the agency hired for the campaign, Cogent Elliott, saw that the Aga brand needed to be taken out of that atmosphere and be repositioned as a relevant, contemporary brand in order to engage more meaningfully with a new type of customer. The Love Aga campaign stretched across numerous communications channels including advertising, direct mail, online, retail point of sale and brochures. However, marketing communications were not enough to turn around the Aga brand through the recession-hit years from 2008 onwards.

In March 2009 Aga announced a drop in pre-tax profits to £14.4 million for the whole of 2008 in comparison with £27 million the previous year. Overall sales of Aga, Rayburn and Stanley, the group's cast iron cooker brands, were down 21.5 percent. This position was attributed to the general economic downturn of the global recession and the fact that fewer people were buying houses. As a result, Aga reduced its workforce by 12 percent – some 400 employees – mainly in its US and Irish operations. In the UK, Aga employees agreed to work shorter hours and cost-cutting measures were implemented to save around £6 million a year. By May 2009 its orders had fallen by 20 percent.

Clearly something needs to be done.

Research the Aga brand and discuss the following:

- the brand image built up historically over time;
- consumer perceptions and brand position.

Communicating sustainability

The broad agenda behind achieving the market transformation to sustainability makes the role of marketing communications a significant one. While there is obvious overlap in their use, marketing communications for sustainability are designed to achieve four main objectives:

- To change everyone's behaviour with regard to the sustainability of their lifestyle affecting a variety of habits and practices such as energy use and conservation, recycling, personal travel, consumption reduction and demarketing.

- To change consumer purchase behaviour, encouraging people to lead more sustainable lifestyles through the consumption of sustainable alternatives to conventional products and services.

- To inform consumers and other stakeholders about the sustainable credentials, reputation, practice, performance and achievements of national, regional and local governments, NGOs, charities, businesses and other interested parties.

- To persuade consumers to purchase goods and services from particular companies on the basis of their sustainable features and benefits.

Each of these objectives puts a different emphasis on how marketing communications are planned, designed and delivered.

Marketing communications is an area of sustainable marketing that continues to be criticised. Unfortunately, for many reasons, marketers got it wrong but there are also indications that marketing communications for sustainability are improving and that their persuasive content is gaining ground with consumers.

First, this chapter explores the reasons behind the frequent lack of effectiveness of marketing communications in achieving behavioural change and the duplicity behind some marketing communications when used for commercial gain. Second, the chapter also examines the means marketers have at their disposal to improve their communications. Finally, the chapter reviews the use of sustainability labelling as a methods of communication for providing information and reinforcing sustainability credentials.

Getting it wrong

Marketing communications have not yet been able to deliver a large-scale adoption of sustainable consumption and sustainable lifestyle despite an increasing number of campaigns from varied stakeholders and a significant increase in spending. Despite all the insistence, the communications have not got through to their target markets as they should and in some cases they have simply not been heard. There are numerous reasons for this failure to connect with the target audience over sustainability and the marketing communications sector, and its clients are already learning from their past mistakes and are making up for lost time.

In order to understand how sustainability should be communicated it is worth reflecting on the reasons why marketing communications have not been able to deliver change as successfully as expected. Much of the marketing communications to date from government and business have focused on the environmental issues within the sustainability agenda, more so than issues to do with economic and social sustainability, as will be seen in this chapter.

Doom and gloom fail to appeal

So where have marketers been going wrong?

Imagine selling a series of products and services to adults in mid-life crisis. How would you do it? Would you remind them that they will only be going downhill from this point onwards? Would you point out how their looks, health and fitness will gradually deteriorate and the remainder of their dreams in life will probably never be accomplished? For example, does L'Oreal sell its products aimed at older markets on the strap line '. . . *but you're not really worth it'*? On the contrary, cosmetics companies generally sell hope and optimism, not depression and pessimism.

However, with planet Earth in mid-life crisis, all types of organisations and businesses have decided to market *the end of the world* accompanied by hardship and sacrifice, rather than an exciting and inspiring new way of life through progress to tackle and overcome a series of difficult challenges. Fear, apprehension, guilt, bad consumption, anti-consumption, anti-aspirational messages have all formed the basis of communication appeals to convince people to lead more sustainable lives. But such appeals have only attracted a narrow audience of the already converted and radical few, not the mainstream majority.

Negative emotional appeals can easily be counterproductive when trying to stimulate behavioural change. Many communications, focused on global climate threat through negative emotional appeals, have made the consumer become a mere bystander. The bystander effect is a social psychological phenomenon in which individuals are less likely to offer help in an emergency situation when other people are present. The probability of help is inversely proportional to the number of bystanders; that is, the greater the number of bystanders, the less likely it is that any one of them will help. As we have all become bystanders of environmental sustainability communications because we have all been made responsible for the planet's continued degradation, we all wait for and expect other people to take action. Thus, because we are often branded by communications as being simultaneously bystanders, perpetrators and victims of climate change, we just fail to act out of sheer inertia, perhaps under the impression someone else will take the initiative.

Fear and guilt

Fear has been used with some success when the appeal is directed at the individual with a strong emphasis on self-interest benefits such as drink-driving or anti-smoking campaigns. However, fear, in particular, is more liable to create a feeling of apathy than motivation to act, when there is no immediate tangible link to individual self-interest. For campaigns designed to promote sustainability, appeals based on fear were deemed a natural alternative to rational appeals which had merely aimed to get consumers to understand the situation properly.

For example, fear is often evoked when the enormity of the consequences of global climate change are portrayed, although with little positive effect on mainstream target audiences as they feel the solution is not in individuals' hands. This use of impending environmental disasters to market a product has been criticised as alarmist and unethical.[2] Also, human survival instincts tend to react in minutes when faced with an immediate threat, but messages about the threat of climate change and carbon dioxide levels deal in a timeframe of years, thus nullifying the consumers' impetus to react.

In contrast, guilt is significantly different to fear. Anyone can be afraid or be made to be afraid. Fear can also be taken away relatively easily, either dismissed as irrelevant by the audience or removed by actions of the promoter of fear. But using guilt instead of fear as a means of appeal to change consumer behaviour towards sustainability also has its difficulties. Significantly, the use of guilt is not always well-received by consumers, as they tend to feel blackmailed or manipulated by such messages rather than being allowed to make their own decisions.

Moreover, guilt is a cognitive action that requires consideration. Guilt cannot be forced in the same way as fear because it is something that comes from our understanding of the situation and our role in creating or perpetuating that situation.[3]

Defra's recent study of sustainable consumer behaviour determines that guilt is felt in relation to certain moral standards and personal norms: when these are violated guilt is felt.[4] For example, a person accustomed to living a frugal lifestyle might feel guilty when wasting food, or leaving an electric light on all night. Defra's study found that people were likely to mitigate these feelings of guilt by comparing their own actions against those of others, to leave themselves in a more favourable light. This involves people highlighting that they generally do more towards sustainability than others, more than their friends and more than people in other countries.

The differences felt between three self-identities of the individual (as mentioned in Chapter 3) also reveal where guilt may lie. Guilt is often the result of comparing the actual self and the ought self, with the discrepancy between the two creating the emotion. When the comparison is made between the actual self and the opinions of others, the resulting emotion may be categorised as shame. Yet we only feel guilty *when* and *because* we fully understand the situation in question. Guilt does not come from ignorance. This also means that it is within our power to remove guilt (not with those who provoked our guilt in the first place), but only if we are prepared to assume responsibility for our contributions to the problem and have the opportunity to make a valid contribution to the solution.

According to Klaus Töpfer, former Executive Director of the United Nations Environment Programme (UNEP), 'People are simply not listening. Making people feel guilty about their lifestyles and purchasing habits is achieving only limited success.'[5] As guilt, fear and the full range of more negative emotional appeals have failed to get the vast majority to play their part, rational appeals began to gain more attention.

Rational information overload

Rational appeals have been seen as an alternative to the use of negative emotions in campaigns. There is perhaps a natural assumption that rational, information-based appeals would be appropriate for creating persuasive messages concerning sustainability. The complexity of the issues involved lends itself to rational explanation. However, although information alone may increase awareness, it is unlikely to change the attitudes of the majority or their behaviour. Studies have shown that non-emotional appeals lead to the most negative response and lowest levels of comprehension in comparison with emotional appeals[6] and that few purchases of any kind are made for entirely rational reasons.[7]

The challenge of changing behaviour has not been underestimated. Sustainable communications agency, Futerra, likens it to a complete mindset change and states in its research that 'changing attitudes towards climate change is not like selling a particular brand of soap – it's like convincing someone to use soap in the first place'.[8]

It was thought that information would facilitate choice when in fact consumers now suffer from an information overload regarding sustainability claims, so much so that they feel unable to make a choice and return to their familiar comfort zone of conventional purchase patterns and decision making.

Information-based appeals may be responsible for other counterproductive effects. Information appeals are often accompanied by instructions, telling people what to do or how to behave, and can be made worse when they are accompanied by rules, regulations and restrictions from government or other bodies. No matter how rational the appeal, there is a tendency to reject any impositions that are seen to restrict individuals' personal freedoms. A perceived reduction in personal freedom can produce an emotional state, called psychological reactance, a rejection of the obligation, in order to restore control and autonomy to the individual.[9] Linguistic features in appeals, such as the use of certain words such as *must, need, have to* or absolute assertions, or threats and warnings can provoke the feeling that individual free behaviour is being restricted.[10] Even quite innocent-looking phrases may be misinterpreted. For example, a study into the use of sustainability terminology and its connotative meanings revealed strong psychological reactance to the phrase 'non-essential flying' often used in UK government discourse.[11] People interpreted the phrase as meaning non-business flights and therefore felt it was an attack on holiday flights and visiting friends and family, a personal right which they were prepared to defend.

The misuse of the social norm

An understanding of social norms, already commented on in an earlier chapter, may also shed light on how marketing communications have failed to deliver the correct message. A notable example is that of Chief Iron Eyes Cody, a 1971 television commercial for the *Keep America Beautiful* campaign, in which the Indian chief sheds an emotional tear at the sight of rubbish and litter all around his native land, even seeing rubbish being thrown away in front of him and the scene ends with the slogan *People Start Pollution, People Can Stop It.* Broadcast in the 1970s and 1980s and updated for the 1990s, the advert depicts the descriptive norm, everyone does the same thing, they litter an already littered landscape. Yet the message is more likely to be misinterpreted by the audience than contribute to the avoidance of littering because we are more likely to copy the descriptive norm. Cialdini's path of least resistance leads us to littering an environment we already see depicted as littered and in the process of being littered even more. The injunctive norm, shown as a tear on the face of Iron Eyes Cody, does not provide enough social disapproval to change behaviour.[12]

GET INVOLVED NOW. POLLUTION HURTS ALL OF US.

You can help by becoming a community volunteer. Write:
Keep America Beautiful, Inc.
99 Park Avenue, New York, New York 10016
A Public Service of Transit Advertising & The Advertising Council

People start pollution. People can stop it.

Source: The Advertising Archives

If marketing communications attempt to change behaviour by showing non-sustainable behaviour as the norm, in the hope that people will do the opposite, this appears not to be the case. Recent experiments in the Netherlands by the University of Groningen found that people behaved more responsibly in their surroundings if they were clean and not degraded, but were more likely to behave anti-socially if the area already contained litter or had been painted with graffiti. In one experiment people appeared to be more likely to steal money from an envelope hanging out of a letter box according to the cues they perceived from the surroundings. What was significant was that the portrayal of disorder did not have to be the same as the activity or social norm that was being observed. The presence of graffiti and rubbish, for example, made people more likely to steal from the letter box; that is to say, the violation of one social norm appeared to motivate the violation of others.[13]

Making mistakes in marketing communications is inconvenient but sometimes unavoidable; creating communications that deliberately mislead is unethical and will not further the sustainability cause.

Greenwashing

In the 30th anniversary edition of its annual report, Environmental Data Services identifies that the first cases of greenwashing occurred in 1989, after the Advertising Standards Authority (ASA) upheld public complaints over adverts for Austin Rover for claiming that unleaded petrol was 'ozone friendly' and against British Petroleum for claiming its Supergreen petrol caused 'no pollution'.[14]

The term greenwash has been interpreted in different ways:

● 'the dissemination of misleading information by an organisation to conceal its abuse of the environment in order to present a positive image'[15]

● 'an environmental claim which is unsubstantiated (a fib) or irrelevant (a distraction)'[16]

- 'the act of misleading consumers regarding the environmental practices of a company or the environmental benefits of a product or service'[17]

- 'frequently applied to such approaches that appear to lack sincerity because they suggest an environmentally benign product that may not be benign'.[18]

As the term implies, greenwash normally refers to claims regarding environmental sustainability not social equity or economic sustainability issues. This does not mean that organisations do not make erroneous claims regarding other aspects of sustainability but it seems to indicate that environmental issues are probably more frequently used, are more liable to misinterpretation and misuse and therefore attract more attention. The United Nations Environment Programme (UNEP) does recognise greenwash as a term with broader reference than just the environment and describes it as 'opaque and illegitimate communication practices in the form of misleading or deceitful advertising' in order to 'to minimize or conceal the social or environmental consequences of the main activities of the companies'.[19] UNEP also recognises bluewashing (taken from the blue colour of the United Nations' flag), to describe companies that have signed the Global Compact to adhere to ten universally accepted principles in the areas of human rights, labour, environment and anti-corruption, but fail to do so.

There is evidence to suggest that greenwashing has become common practice. In North America, a recent study by TerraChoice of 1,018 consumer products found that the claims of all but one product were demonstrably false or potentially misleading.[20] In the UK the Advertising Standards Authority (ASA) held a special event in 2008 with industry stakeholders just to deal with the rise in complaints regarding environmental claims.[21] In 2006, the ASA received 117 complaints about 83 adverts making environmental claims. During 2007 the ASA dealt with 561 complaints about 410 adverts and, although complaints went down in 2008, a higher proportion of ASA investigations resulted in upheld rulings, mainly from the motoring, utilities and energy sectors.[22]

Understanding complaints – the sins of greenwash

Complaints about greenwash which have been upheld by the ASA in 2007 fall into the following categories:

- truthfulness

- substantiation

- environmental

- comparative.

Telling lies and not providing enough evidence were the most frequent reasons for upholding complaints about environmental claims according to the ASA.[23] Both of these categories could be equally applied to products that were not making any sustainable claims, as they both relate to consumers' trust, the element which underpins all advertising. Not only consumers complain.

An estimated 10 percent of complaints originate from the competition as they try to take away competitive advantage and invalidate the claims of their competitors.

Marketing agencies have attempted to warn organisations of the sins of greenwashing and the potential pitfalls they face.[24] Mistakes leading to complaints may be made through carelessness or lack of knowledge on the part of the organisation, although unfortunately other aspects of greenwash appear to be intentional, such as fabrication of evidence as well as the use of false third-party accreditation.

Other sources of greenwash complaints involve organisations that want to make too much of one sustainable attribute of their product when other features of the product such as its components, labour costs, lifecycle or disposal are not sustainable. Similarly, organisations have unethically emphasised a 'hero product in a portfolio of villains'; that is, the claims of a sustainable product within a portfolio are highlighted while the remaining unsustainable products are ignored.[25]

Professional practice: Monitoring complaints

You have been asked by the marketing director to prepare a short presentation on your competitors, identifying, classifying and evaluating the complaints of greenwash they have received. Base the study on any sector or product category of your own choice.

The danger of greenwashing

Greenwash is a tag that can be earned overnight, unlike a sustainable brand reputation which has to be built through long-term commitment to sustainable practice in all areas of the business. Greenwashing can permanently damage the hard-earned brand reputation of a business but also has the potential to be more damaging to whole sustainable product categories than communication misdemeanours related to conventional product categories. Conventional products make promises based on their standard benefits and it has long been considered and defended that their claims are prone to fluff, puffery, exaggeration, distortion and embellishment,[26] which is even something expected by the target audience. Moreover, when such claims appear they tend not to be taken too seriously by the consumer; our clothes do not really become whiter than white, nor does our deodorant make us immediately irresistible to the opposite sex.

Greg Nugent, Marketing Director of Eurostar, a company that has communicated its sustainability performance in comparison with other forms of transport, warned marketers to avoid greenwash at all cost. He stated: 'The responsible marketer should be more than diligent about the threat of greenwash. The public do not trust green claims because they have seen people take advantage.'[27]

Literally thousands of adverts for legally produced conventional products which are not sustainable are not denounced as such to the authorities by consumers every year. However, consumer expectations regarding eco-promises are different. There is an explicit promise to be environmentally good, in the case of an eco-promise (if not socially or economically for other aspects of sustainability). Complaints about sustainable claims have increased year on year precisely because consumers have been promised something better than a standard offering. As a result, consumers' expectations are higher, more demanding and they expect easy to understand, verifiable facts and – above all – the truth. When let down by a conventional product, the consumer may abandon that brand for a competing one. When an eco-promise is not fulfilled, the consumer may abandon the environmental product category altogether, moving away from sustainable-based choices back to conventional choices because the two options appear to be exactly the same. In fact the failing sustainable product will appear to be worse than conventional products because it set itself up to be better than its non-sustainable competitors, resulting in undermined confidence, broken trust and an increasingly sceptical consumer. There is some evidence that, because environmental sustainability has become the centre of consumer mistrust and scepticism, businesses are turning to issues of social equity and economic sustainability to avoid further controversy and regain credibility and trust.

Researching sustainability: Writing a research proposal

You work for a government department responsible for the environment which has campaigned for CO_2 reduction among the general population of your country. The government communications campaign was designed to persuade the general public to take a series of measures to reduce their own personal and household carbon footprint. The government department now wants to measure the public's reactions to the campaign and its effectiveness in changing behaviour, and has asked you to plan the research necessary to evaluate the success of the campaign.

You have been asked to write a brief research proposal outlining how you might carry out this research taking into account the scope of work, what kinds of information would be useful for the department to find out, the methodology you think appropriate and how the results might best be presented.

Getting started

1. To find out more on how to write a research proposal go to www.pearsoned.co.uk/emery
2. A recent report from the National Endowment for Science, Technology and the Arts (NESTA) reflects on the inability of policymakers to achieve mass behaviour change in order to reduce

the carbon footprint of the population of the UK and so reduce the risk of climate change.[28] It is calculated that 40 percent of UK greenhouse gas emissions come directly from individuals' behaviour and in order to achieve a reduction on CO_2 emissions there will need to be significant changes in behaviour in residential energy use, road transport use and other forms of travel. There are a number of barriers to behavioural change in this aspect of sustainable living:

● There is often a natural resistance to lifestyle change which compromises individuals' quality of life.

● Residential energy use, car usage and air travel are associated with individual freedoms and are difficult to modify.

● Individuals do not regard climate change as an immediate personal threat but as a possible threat to future generations in far away places.

● Individuals ascribe responsibilities for climate change and CO_2 reduction to businesses and governments, national and global institutions.

As a part of the report NESTA proposed a seven part framework, the 7 Cs, (see Table 8.1) as a means of making communication campaigns regarding reducing CO_2 emissions more persuasive and effective.

3. Look at some CO_2 emissions campaigns from governments from different parts of the world to give you more ideas for the research proposal document, for example *Act on CO_2* in the UK. Try some of the more unusual campaigns from independent organisations such as *Màs osos menos CO_2* (More bears, less CO_2) in Spain (www.masososmenosCO2.com).

Table 8.1   Selling sustainability: the 7 Cs

Clarity of the proposition	What people are asked to do as a result of the communication is clear
Compelling message	Communication works at a rational and emotional level
Connection to the issues	Issues are perceived to be relevant to people's everyday lives
Creativity	Challenge conventional perceptions by saying something new
Communications mix and shape	Media planning is integrated, timely and effective
Consistency	Message is reinforced through wider communication and policy activities
Confidence to act	Use customer segmentation to understand the marketplace and act when the insight is good enough.

Source: Adapted from Bhattachary and Angle, 2008[29]

Getting it right

There is no excuse for the shoddy or deceitful practice that has led to the occurrence of greenwash, nor is there an excuse for not anticipating the kinds of communications and appeals the consumer would most likely respond to favourably. The basic tenet of marketing is the needs and wants of the target market and the reason why marketers have got it wrong in the past is the result of ignoring the starting point of marketing – the consumer. The imperative that is sustainability remains the same for everyone and it is time for marketers to get their communications right.

What do consumers want to know?

According to research into sustainable consumption conducted by Ipsos MORI for the UK retail sector,[30] consumers have quite specific communication needs regarding their potential purchase of products including: health issues, use of chemicals and pesticides, packaging and its recyclability, and product origin, that is, whether it was produced locally or further afield.

Table 8.2 highlights those types of information consumers would most like to see when choosing products and their responses are given in order of

Table 8.2 Which of the following types of information would you ideally like to see when considering whether or not you want to buy products?*

	Information type	Area of concern
1	Health	**Self**
2	Recyclability of packaging	Environment
3	Exposure to chemicals/pesticides	**Self** – health
4	Made/grown locally	Others – local
5	Amount of packaging	**Self** – convenience
6	Fair price given to UK producers	Others – local
7	If supply of product damages future resources	Others – distant
8	Fair price given to overseas producers	Others – distant
9	Employee working conditions with overseas supplier	Others – distant
10	Production and transport impact on climate	Environment
11	Grown in season	Environment
12	Organic	Environment
13	Transported by air	Environment

*Results given in order of importance.

Source: Adapted from Ipsos MORI, 2007[31]

importance. When the areas of concern are identified and analysed it can be seen that consumers' sustainability communication needs are more driven by self-interest in the top five information types. Personal health issues top the ranking in importance. Packaging and the general use of plastic bags in the retail sector has gained more public exposure over recent years. This is coupled with consumers' increasing obligations to recycle more types of packaging and a growing frustration and anger on the part of the consumer when packaging fails to deliver sustainability credentials.[32] Therefore, it is logical that these issues also appear in the top five and they can obviously demonstrate clear links to consumer self-interest through convenience.

As regards altruistic values of social and economic equity, these are placed after considerations of self and there is a noticeable split between a concern for others, which is local community-based (of more importance) and concern for others from further afield, although both sets of others are placed in front of the majority of environmental concerns. Despite the emphasis on environmental sustainability in marketing communications, concern with the environment occupies the bottom places in terms of importance. Thus, issues that physically seem more distant, less tangible or less immediate are rated as less important. These same issues are likely to be less well understood aspects of sustainability and are seen as out of the sphere of control of the individual and therefore less personally relevant.

This poses a problem for marketers who wish to base their marketing communications purely on the more altruistic social, economic and environmental benefits, which are the key foundation stones of sustainability because it would appear that appeals based on consumer self-interest would be more acceptable to such a target audience. It is imperative that marketers find ways to make sustainability issues understood and persuasive and to be valued in their own right. The natural starting point for planning a communications campaign is the communication needs of the target audience[33] and the challenge for marketers is to bring sustainability close to home, close to self-interest, making the remote personally relevant, appealing, inspiring and aspirational.

Matching communications to expectations

Consumer Focus, the UK consumer watchdog organisation set up in 2008 to deal with consumer complaints and defend the rights of vulnerable consumers, also has a statutory duty to lead on issues of sustainable development. Its recent research has focused on the expectations consumers have of the marketing communications related to environmental issues and has resulted in the guiding principles for good practice shown in Table 8.3.[34] The 3 Cs Principle holds that consumers are more likely to be persuaded to act by communications which are clear, credible and comparable with other sustainable claims. While the research was centred on environmental sustainability, it is evident that these guidelines could equally apply to other areas of sustainability.

Table 8.3   The 3 Cs Principle

Clarity	Clear, direct and unambiguous communications, which are easy to understand, without confusing technical terms are favoured by consumers who do not seek more information, just the right information to make a decision.
Credibility	Consumers want realistic, accessible, verifiable claims and judge them on criteria divided into the following four categories:
	• *Advertisement-specific elements:* Consumers dislike small print and footnotes; they engender a lack of trust as it appears the company is trying to hide something. Third-party endorsement from well-known, respected organisations are more valued
	• *Perceptions of brand and brand 'fit' with the environment:* Brands which are well-perceived by consumers can often pass on these positive associations to their environmental policies
	• *Ingrained habits and beliefs:* Consumers rely on previous experience of green products to judge new offers
	• *The wider market and social context:* Consumers have varying levels of confidence in the regulations governing green claims and therefore varying levels of trust
Comparability	Comparison of alternatives is a natural part of the purchase process but competing, complex environmental claims are difficult to evaluate for the following reasons:
	• The lack of mechanisms for like-for-like comparisons
	• The lack of simple comparison points and measures which can be interpreted and evaluated by the target audience
	• The extensive number of competing labelling systems confuses consumers and impedes comparison

Source: Adapted from Yates, 2009[35]

Apply it: Marks and Spencer – half a step ahead

Using the information on Marks and Spencer in the following 'Snapshot' together with your own research on its sustainability marketing communications for *Look Behind the Label* and *Plan A* (original version) and *Plan A 2010–15,* evaluate the extent to which it has followed the 3 Cs Principle.

Snapshot: Looking behind the campaign

The 2006 award winning *Look Behind the Label* campaign invited Marks and Spencer's consumers to look *behind the scenes* of its operations and consider the way products were sourced and prepared. It was the first major campaign by any retailer to focus on and acknowledge the importance of these matters. The challenge to consumers posed by Marks and Spencer to look behind its label was in order to introduce customers to a range of sustainability issues related to *where* whole products and product components came from and *how* they were made. Marks and Spencer had correctly read the growing consumer trend for a more ethical way of living, combined with a healthier lifestyle and used the campaign to deepen consumer appreciation of the issues and move them to behavioural change. The campaign stands out for its holistic treatment of the sustainability agenda as it covered economic and environmental sustainability as well as social equity across its product ranges from clothes and fresh food produce to processed food, raising awareness of fair trade, organic farming, healthy eating, animal welfare and energy consumption.

Communication through full-page advertisements in national daily newspapers accompanied by a host of in-store posters and displays were not only to raise awareness. Some messages were designed to encourage behavioural change such as washing clothes at lower temperatures. Above all, the campaign infused an already respected brand with a whole set of new altruistic values laying the foundations for the wider-reaching *Plan A* sustainability campaign which was launched the following year.

Increasingly sustainability issues are becoming linked to reputation management and brand trust.[36] Marks and Spencer has certainly benefited from its sustainability campaigning since 2006. In the 2008 ImagePower Green Brands survey of the UK, supermarkets occupied five of the top six green brands, and Marks and Spencer was the top green supermarket brand.[37] With the introduction of *Plan A* in 2007, Marks and Spencer embarked on a journey of incremental change over five years on five identified challenges: climate change, waste, sustainable use of natural resources, fair partnership and health. This gradual process, supported by in-store communications in order to convert the Marks and Spencer loyals to sustainability first before taking the message more actively outside the store, has allowed the company to gradually rewrite its DNA and reposition itself as a sustainable brand. The subtle drip-by-drip approach to in-store communications through posters, point-of-sale displays and partnerships (for example with Oxfam for clothes donations) have allowed Marks and Spencer to create a convincing message over time. Believability is the most difficult battle for many brands in their move towards sustainability. Consumers have never been convinced by those brands which preach sustainability after a sudden overnight conversion to the cause, but Marks and Spencer seems to have avoided consumer scepticism. Confirmation of the DNA rewrite can now be seen in the refurbished Marks and Spencer stores, where some of the sustainability promises are no longer displayed on posters but are painted as text directly onto the walls for all to see as a permanent reminder of its sustainable brand values.

For Stuart Rose, CEO of Marks and Spencer, the act of selling sustainability is hard work and consumers have to be guided credibly and in the right way. He stated 'It is no good getting too far ahead of the customer. Half a step ahead is about right. Much more, and you won't sell. Any less, and you won't lead.'[38]

The follow-up to *Plan A, Plan A 2010–15,* has already been unveiled.

Labelling

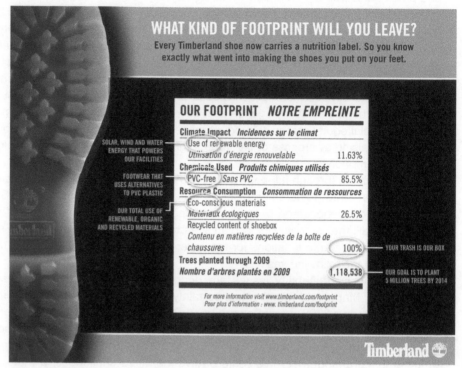

Source: Reprinted with the permission of the Timberland Company

Labelling for sustainability is an important part of communication. The labelling of products provides an opportunity to communicate and clarify sustainable credentials. Sustainability labelling has proliferated in a short space of time and has contributed to the sensation of information overload of the consumer. While allowing for comparison between sustainable brands in theory, in practice the terminology or measurements used are often different and actually impede product comparison taking place on a unified scale or system.

At times producers' own labels run alongside third-party endorsements, which add their own labels and logos to increase the credibility of the product and assist in comparison and decision making.

The International Organisation for Standardisation (ISO) has classified environmental product claims and eco-labels into three types, based on the nature of the claim.

Type 1 claims

Declarations that meet criteria set by third parties and can be based on single product attributes, entire lifecycle impacts such as the EU Ecolabel (see photo) and Green Seal in the USA and may include information on how products are produced, the use of recycled or renewable resources and how they may be

Source: UK Ecolabel Delivery

Source: Federal Environmental Agency, Germany

recycled or disposed of. Dependent on the awarding body, the product must meet independent criteria in order to be able to display their name and logo. Such third-party endorsement can be a significant factor in consumer decision making by mitigating some of the consumer perceived risks involved in the purchase

The Blue Angel label (shown left) was the first national eco-label established in Germany, in 1977, and is now recognised worldwide. Here each is individually tagged with health, climate, natural resources and water.

Other countries established their own labels to be used to establish the environmental credentials of products and services. The EU Eco-label was established in 1992 and is a voluntary scheme. The criteria set to award the label were agreed at European level, following wide consultation with experts, and the label itself is only awarded after verification that the product meets high environmental and performance standards. The label has met with mixed success, as 61 percent of EU citizens stated they had never seen or heard of the label and only 20 percent acknowledged that they had bought products carrying the symbol.

Type 2 claims

Manufacturers' or retailers' own declarations and claims are not verified by independent organisations as in type 1 and follow no set criteria. Therefore such claims may not always be reliable and, from the consumers' perspective, are only as good and trustworthy as the brand itself, although the strength of this technique comes from transparency and honesty of the declaration on the label. Even when it shows there is room for improvement, the open declaration of sustainable performance can win over sceptical consumers. For example, Hewlett-Packard has developed its own eco-labelling system called Eco Highlights.

- Use up to 40% less energy than with color lasers**
- Reduce paper use up to 50% using automatic two-sided printing
- Save paper by viewing and storing faxes electronically

** Majority of color laser all-in-ones < $600, March 2010; for details, www.hp.com/go/officejet. Energy use based on HP testing using the ENERGY STAR® program's TEC test method criteria.

- ENERGY STAR® Qualified Product

www.hp.com/ecosolutions

Please recycle your computing hardware and printing supplies. Find out how at our website.

Source: Daniel J Edelman Ltd.

This Eco Highlights label (see photo) combines Hewlett-Packard's own information regarding sustainability together with Energy Star and SmartWay accreditations as further evidence of sustainable practice. Energy Star was introduced in 1992 by the US Environmental Protection Agency. The label has since been adopted by the EU and covers a variety of electric goods, new homes, and commercial and industrial buildings.

Type 3 claims

Quantified information about products based on lifecycle impacts or Environmental Product Declarations on specific aspects such as energy output. These claims provide relevant, verified information, allowing products to be compared easily on a like-for-like basis and are more useful for public procurement purposes and general business-to-business transactions.

Snapshot: Timberland

The creation of in-house sustainability labels of type 2 is an important recent trend in communication and has allowed some organisations to differentiate themselves from their competitors.

Timberland has developed an in-house label scheme that provides prospective consumers with information on emissions, recycled content and chemical usage known as the Green Index label, as can be seen in the figure.

Source: Reproduced with the permission of
The Timberland Company

The Carbon Trust's Carbon Reduction Label – a chance to compare

There is evidence to suggest that in the near future consumers will increasingly question the credentials of brands that do not label their products.

The Carbon Reduction Label is a certification mark which shows the total greenhouse gas emissions from every stage of the product's lifecycle, including production, transportation, preparation, use and disposal. As it is essential that the footprint calculations take every greenhouse gas into account, the figure is given as their total CO_2 equivalent. Companies that display the label have made a commitment to reduce the emissions of that product over two years. Companies that do not reduce the emissions of that product lose the right to display the label.

The Carbon Reduction Label is underpinned by PAS 2050, a standard developed by the Carbon Trust in partnership with DEFRA and the British Standards Institute (BSI), and

reducing with the Carbon Trust

100g

CO2

per pack

The carbon footprint of this product is 100g and we have committed to reduce it. This is the total carbon dioxide (CO2) and other greenhouse gases emitted during its life, including production, use and disposal

carbon-label.com

Source: The Carbon Trust

Endorsement line

The carbon footprint measurement

The footprint icon

The functional unit

The reduction commitment

Figure 8.1 The Carbon Reduction Label

Source: The Carbon Trust

was conceived with contributions from stakeholders around the world. By applying its own set of comparability rules, the Carbon Trust can certify that measurement is comparable across different products within any particular category, enabling manufacturers and consumers to make quick and valid comparisons. Research of UK consumers in 2011 found that carbon footprinting labels are becoming more widely known and expected. The research found that nearly half of UK consumers (45 percent) said they would be willing to shun their favourite brands if they failed to show a commitment to measuring and reducing the carbon footprint of their products. This compared to 22 percent who stated in 2010 that they would shun brands failing to display carbon footprint labels on products. The Carbon Citizenship research was conducted on behalf of the Carbon Trust by Vanson Bourne during February and March 2011. Opinions were sourced from 1,000 adults across the UK via telephone research in the North West, the North East, the Midlands and East Anglia, the South West, the South East, London, Wales, Scotland and Northern Ireland. Respondents were segmented by gender, age, household income, employment status and region.

As can be seen in Figure 8.1, the Carbon Reduction Label has a set of standard features, endorsement line, footprint measurement, the footprint icon, the functional unit and a commitment to emissions reduction, without which the product would lose its certification. Use of the measurement number within the Label is optional. For further information please visit www.carbontrustcertification.com

The sustainability label still has work to do around the world

A recent Eurobarometer survey found seven out of ten European citizens thought that product labelling should contain a product's carbon footprint and that it should become mandatory to provide this information, in the future, to show the total amount of greenhouse gases emitted during a product's lifetime. However, only 10 percent of respondents felt that greenhouse gas emissions were the most important piece of information on an eco-label. The survey revealed wide variations between different countries, with 90 percent of respondents in Greece and Croatia supporting a mandatory EU scheme, but only around 50 percent of Czechs, Estonians and Dutch in favour. The European Commission is investigating the possibility of introducing such a label.[39]

Certification of sustainability in the US remains complex and confusing for the consumer. In the US the sheer proliferation of eco-labels, with more than 300 for producers (and consumers) to choose from, is actually weakening the entire sector.[40] There is evidence to suggest that the way to make sustainable accreditation more convincing to the consumer is to actually reduce the number of third-party labels that compete for the consumers' attention. After the US Department of Agriculture's (USDA) organic certification was launched in 2002, removing the dozens of competing organic labels, the organic food market started to grow by 20 percent per year. From the producers' point of view, having hundreds of labels to choose from does not necessarily increase the opportunities for business success. While some accrediting labels are free, others (often the best known) are expensive or laborious to adopt but if lesser-known labels are chosen as an easier, cheaper option they may not be recognised or valued by the target market. With such a situation in the US and across Europe, building the brand name and reputation combined with transparent self-declaration on sustainable practice can be just as effective as third-party accreditation.[41]

In August 2009 the UK government launched a proposal for the labelling of food according to sustainability criteria as part of a wider plan for securing a sustainable food system for the future. Food packaging in the UK already carries health and nutrition information in the form of colour-coded indicators of contents together with individual weights and percentages in relation to the recommended daily intake of ingredients. Food sustainability labelling may include air miles, animal welfare, use of fertilisers and pesticides, whether species are endangered and information on pollutants. However, the proposal has not been met with widespread approval from the farming or retail sectors who believe that the consumer is already bombarded with too much information on food packaging.[42,43]

Apply it: Evaluating sustainability communication

According to Futerra,[44] nearly £17 million was spent on advertising containing the words 'CO_2', 'carbon', 'environmental', 'emissions' or 'recycle' from September 2006 to August 2007 in comparison with spending for the same terms of £448,000 in 2003. But just how effective are adverts designed to persuade the public to engage with sustainability?

1. Using the insights you have gained from this chapter so far choose and evaluate a selection of print adverts. To what extent are they examples of good or bad practice?

Getting started

Here are some aspects you might consider.

1. Clichèd images
   London advertising agency Euro RSCG identified that a number of images were being used too often for claims of sustainability after studying over 100 advertising executions.[45] The most used were: polar bears on ice caps, flowers, children playing, exotic animal species and blue skies with green fields. Such reliance tends to make all brands appear the same, fails to engage consumers and only increases the perception of greenwashing.

2. Choice of language
   Eco- has quickly become an over-exploited prefix. The term *eco-friendly* used alone communicates very little; it is neither clear nor specific and therefore fails to accurately indicate environmental impact or improvement. Defra advises that claims with the following words or phrases should not be used for the same reasons: *'environmentally friendly'*, *'green'*, *'nature's friend'*, *'made with care for the environment'*, *'safe for the environment'*, *'ecological'*, *'eco-friendly'*.[46] Words to do with social responsibility and ethics such as *'equality'*, *'fair'*, *'ethical'* can be also contentious and should be used with care.

   Phrases such as *'the* environment' and *'you* should' are not as appealing as phrases using *'our* environment' and *'we* should', which are inclusive and both create personal relevance in messages and show that everyone has a stake in the solution to the problems.

   According to Futerra, we need to find more uplifting terms to describe sustainable behaviour, terms that will be both aspirational and appealing to cater for people's needs to communicate a positive, desirable self-identity and allude to wellbeing and quality of life.[47] The best terminology to use will not be aggressive, authoritarian or political, and will be jargon-free, not unnecessarily technical and easily understood by the layperson.

3. Regulations and guidelines
   Consult regulations and guidelines from appropriate national and international organisations. Greenpeace developed a greenwashing detection kit, other organisations have similar evaluation criteria.

Summary

Marketing communications are expected to play multiple roles in the dissemination of information about sustainability: inform, educate, persuade and encourage behavioural change while serving the varied purposes of a range of stakeholders. However, the approach of many organisations has had more in common with conventional marketing communications and has failed to take into account the particular considerations required by the context of sustainability. At worst this has often led to negative consumer attitudes, a loss of credibility and incidences of greenwash, while at best communication has just failed to convince an already sceptical public.

The planning and execution of marketing communications based on three factors – a better appreciation of consumer behaviour towards sustainability, the communication needs of the target audience and the regulations governing sustainability claims – have improved the effectiveness of many organisations and have pointed to the possibility of future changes, although there remain numerous challenges for the marketing communications professional.

The amount of information still to communicate to consumers, its complexity and variety continue to put a strain on the efforts of marketers who now look to find more appropriate solutions. By learning from previous mistakes, the more rigorous application of sustainability communication guidelines and regulations, the use of third-party accreditations and techniques that aid product comparability, together with the more focused labelling of goods, marketers are beginning to ensure greater consumer engagement through more efficient and credible communication.

Case study: Getting it right and wrong at the same time

In October 2009, the Department of Energy and Climate Change (DECC) showed a television advert on climate change entitled 'Bedtime Story' (see photo below) during a prime-time television programme before the 9pm watershed as part of a £6 million campaign, which was accompanied by four associated nursery rhyme-themed press adverts and two billboard posters, which ran

Source: Lindsey Gardiner: For the Department of Energy and Climate Change

until February 2010. In total the ASA received 939 complaints about the campaign, more than any other campaign for 2009.

The television advert showed a father reading a bedtime story to his young daughter about the effects of CO_2 in the atmosphere and included images of the consequences of climate change depicted in the child's book, such as the rabbit crying because of the heat, causing a drought and plants wilting and dying.

Source: Lindsey Gardiner: For the Department of Energy and Climate Change

The frightening impacts of climate change are emphasised when the dismayed animals look at the dried-up riverbed (see photo above) and later when the father is heard saying that 'some places could even disappear under the sea' and when he adds that 'children would have to live with the horrible consequences'.

At the same time a cartoon image of a kitten floating on an upturned table can be seen next to a puppy that is drowning in the floods. Both of these animals are shown in a village street outside a pub whose sign 'The World's End' (see photo below) is clearly readable.

Source: Lindsey Gardiner: For the Department of Energy and Climate Change

The advert works well on so many different levels. For adult viewers who do not really understand climate change, it allows for the issue to be explained simply without being patronising because the audience is listening to a father telling a bedtime story. While the gloom and doom message is still there the story narrative provides a different packaging to conventional images. The emotional appeal hits the adult audience when the child asks if there is a happy ending to the story, making the message poignant and effective.

Television advert complaints

However, the reaction of some members of the public has not been so positive, with most complaints focusing on the possible effects of children seeing the advert. Some complainants regarded the advert as distressing and scaremongering for children; a Downing Street petition calling on the government to 'stop wasting taxpayers' money on climate change propaganda designed to frighten our children' attracted more than 500 signatures.[48]

The ASA categorised complaints for the television advert into seven types:

1. The advert was political and therefore should not be broadcast.
2. The theme and content could be distressing for children.
3. The advert should not have been shown when children were likely to be watching television.
4. The advert was misleading by presenting human-induced climate change as a fact.
5. The claim 'over 40 percent of the CO_2 was coming from ordinary everyday things' was misleading.
6. The representation of CO_2 as a rising black smog was misleading.
7. The weather-related claims about adverse weather in the UK and imagery used were exaggerated, distressing and misleading.

In its own investigation the ASA did not uphold any of the complaints types 2 to 7 made about the television advertisement. However, because some of the complainants suggested the advert was political, the ASA referred those complaints (type 1) to the Office of Communications (Ofcom), the independent telecommunications regulator. According to the Communications Act, the government is allowed to run advertising of a public service nature, such as warnings about obesity, drink driving or drug addiction, but it is not allowed to run political adverts that aim to influence public opinion on what may be regarded as a matter of public controversy.[49]

Print advert complaints

Of the four print advertisements (two are shown in the following 'Follow up' section) of the campaign (Table 8.4) which used nursery rhymes to warn people of the dangers of climate change and highlight the need to act promptly, the Advertising Standards Authority ruled in March 2010 that two 'should not appear again in their current form'.

Each of the four adverts carried the strap line: 'It's our children who'll really pay the price. See what you can do: search online for Act on CO_2.'

The ASA categorised complaints for the print adverts into three types:

1. For adverts a, b and c, complainants thought them misleading by presenting human-induced climate change as a fact.

Table 8.4   DECC print adverts 'Act on CO_2'

Nursery rhyme theme	Climate change text
a. Rub a dub, dub three men in a tub . . .	. . . a necessary course of action due to flash flooding caused by climate change.
b. Jack and Jill went up the hill to fetch a pail of water . . .	. . . there was none, as extreme weather due to climate change had caused a drought.
c. Twinkle, twinkle little star; how I wonder what you are . . .	. . . looking down at dangerously high levels of CO_2 in the atmosphere.
d. Hey diddle diddle the cat and the fiddle the cow jumped over the moon . . .	. . . on discovering just how easy it was to reduce our CO_2 emissions.

2. For adverts a, b and c complainants thought claims about adverse weather in the UK and imagery used were exaggerated, distressing and misleading.

3. For advert d one complainant thought the claim 'over 40 percent of the CO_2' from heating, lighting and homes and driving cars was misleading.

The ASA upheld complaint 2 with regard to print adverts a and b, stating that they breached three elements of the code (substantiation, truthfulness and environmental) because the climate change claims made in the adverts were still uncertainties and should have been phrased more tentatively to reflect this. These uncertainties included the possible magnitude and timing of climate change as well as regional details, leading to the ASA's assessment of the use of the word *will* rather than a more cautious phrase.

For Ed Gillespie, co-founder of Futerra, the ASA adjudication boils down to the use of the word *will* and not *may* in the main text of both adverts, which affirms that adverse weather conditions such as storms, floods and heatwaves '*will* become more frequent and intense'.[50] Gillespie feels the campaign, or at least the complaints, have damaged the climate change debate, as the forceful style with the threat of uncertain impacts has played into the hands of the climate sceptic lobbyists and allowed them some slim grounds for complaint.

However, the ASA did rule that the images of the UK flooding and of a drought were not in themselves exaggerated or misleading and the television advert had passed a rigorous inspection. The DECC said it was the first time the government had launched a campaign to clearly show that climate change was man-made as a part of its Act on CO_2 initiative and the DECC felt that the reality of man-made climate change had not been challenged by the ASA adjudication, only the degree of certainty of the consequences.

Getting it right and wrong at the same time – marketing communications for sustainability still has some way to go.

▶

Follow up

In March 2010, after a public consultation that received more than 30,000 responses, the overhaul of the Committee of Advertising Practice (CAP) and the Broadcast Committee of Advertising Practice (BCAP) codes were unveiled. Due to come into force in September 2010, they represent the most important changes in a decade, and commentators have signalled the changes to environmental claims to be as far-reaching as the modifications that were introduced to the marketing of alcoholic beverages.[51]

1. Review the code and make a note of the key changes related to sustainability claims.

2. Choose a selection of adverts judged to have adhered to the previous codes of practice; would they still be deemed appropriate by the standards of the new code?

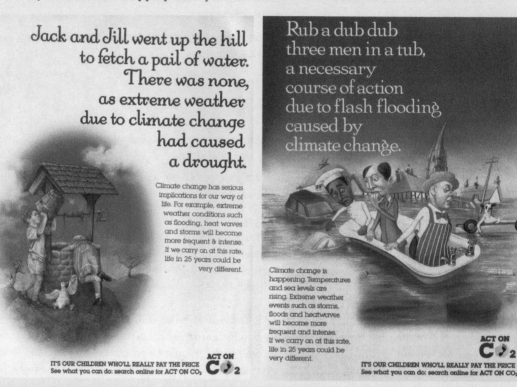

Source: goodillustration.com: Bob Venables for the Department of Energy and Climate Change

Dilemma part 2:   Aga and a sustainable future

The continued bad results for the Aga brand resulted in the Aga Rangemaster Group, the company behind Aga cookers, appointing Ogilvy Advertising to handle a new advertising campaign starting in the final quarter of 2009. The agency was made responsible for creating a strategic campaign for the company, to help raise awareness and increase the popularity of its Aga product range.

Indications in 2010 suggested that Aga sales were beginning to recuperate at least in Europe, although not in the US where the stagnation in the housing market continued to affect new purchases. Overseas markets accounted for some 25 percent of its sales in 2010, with Ireland recording record sales despite the economic problems of that country. However, by now the Aga brand had already come under attack from another quarter, not the recession this time but from a pro-sustainability reporter and campaigner.

It was the campaigning writer George Monbiot, who started a wave of criticism against the Aga cooker for being environmentally unfriendly and forced the Aga CEO William McGrath to defend the brand. From the debate emerged a number of pro- and anti-sustainability arguments for purchasing an Aga, portraying the cooker as either an eco monster or eco-friendly, as shown below.

Eco monster

- Despite different fuel options: kerosene, diesel, biofuel, gas or electricity, fuel consumption is an issue for a system designed to run continuously.
- The smallest Aga, a two-oven gas (without water or central heating), consumes almost as much gas in a week as a standard gas oven/hob does in nine months and an electric four-oven model uses 25 times more electricity than a conventional electric oven. A two-oven can use at least 40 litres of kerosene a week, 2,080 litres a year.
- Aga cookers have a higher carbon footprint from manufacturing compared to conventional cookers.
- Heat energy is wasted as they run when cooking or central heating is not required.
- Leader of the UK Conservative Party, Prime Minister David Cameron, stopped using his Aga to reduce his carbon footprint

Eco-friendly

- A biofuel version is now available.
- Some 55 percent of Aga sales are now for the electric version. Aga is working with energy specialists on wind power, solar power and ground heat as alternative energy sources.
- Aga has produced a programmer that can be fitted to existing cookers so they do not have to run continuously.
- Typically people may buy three or four cookers in a lifetime, whereas an Aga will last a lifetime and longer. In a search for the longest working Aga in Britain in 2008, one was found to have been working since 1932.
- Every Aga is almost completely recyclable. The company also states that 70 percent of each Aga has been made from previously used material.
- Using an Aga removes the need for other domestic electrical appliances (toasters, sandwich makers, kettles, tumble driers, bread makers), reducing consumption of appliances with shorter lives, reducing consumption of natural resources used to manufacture them and saving their corresponding energy consumption.[52]

Devise the strategy

1. An improving position for Aga now seems threatened. How would you reposition Aga cookers in the marketplace as a sustainable product? Devise a communications strategy for this purpose, outlining your decisions by using a standard marketing communications planning framework.

Getting started

1. To find out more on marketing communications planning frameworks go to www.pearsoned. co.uk/emery

References

1. Futerra (2007) *Words That Sell. How the Public Talks About Sustainability,* www. futerra.co.uk

2. Advertising Standards Authority (ASA) (2008) *Environmental Claims in Advertising. Is Green a Grey Area?,* Event Report, London: ASA.

3. Hesz, A. and Neophytou, B. (2010) *Guilt Trip: From Fear to Guilt on the Green Bandwagon,* Chichester: John Wiley.

4. Bedford, T., Collingwood, P., Darnton, A., Evans, D., Gatersleben, B., Abrahamse, W. and Jackson, T. (2010) *Motivations for Pro-environmental Behaviour: A Report to the Department for Environment, Food and Rural Affairs,* London: RESOLVE Defra.

5. United Nations Environment Programme (UNEP) (2005) *Communicating Sustainability: How to Produce Effective Public Campaigns,* UNEP, www.uneptive.org/ shared/publications/pdf/DTIx0679xPA-CommunicatingEN.pdf (p. 13).

6. De Pelsmacker, P. (1998) 'Advertising Characteristics and the Attitude Towards the Ad – A Study of 100 Likeable, TV Commercials', *Marketing and Research Today* 27: 166–179.

7. Ogilvy, D. and Raphaelson, J. (1982) 'Research on Advertising Techniques That Work and Don't Work', *Harvard Business Review,* July/August: 14–18.

8. Futerra (2005) *The Rules of the Game: Evidence Base for Climate Change Communications Strategy,* Futerra, www.futerra.co.uk/downloads/RulesOfTheGame.pdf (p. 2).

9. Brehm, J. W. (1966). *A Theory of Psychological Reactance,* New York: Academic Press.

10. Quick, B. and Stephenson, M. (2008) 'Examining the Role of Trait Reactance and Sensation Seeking on Perceived Threat, State Reactance, and Reactance Restoration' *Human Communication Research* 34: 448–476.

11. Futerra (2007) *Words that Sell. How the Public Talks About Sustainability,* Futerra, www.futerra.co.uk/downloads/Words-That-Sell.pdf

12. Cialdini, R. (2003) 'Crafting Normative Messages to Protect the Environment', *Current Directions in Psychological Science* 12(4): 105–109.

13. Ahuja, A. (2009) 'Supermarket Trolleys Make Us Behave Badly', *The Times,* 22 January.

14. Environmental Data Services (2008) *How Green Has Britain Gone Since 1978?,* Environmental Data Services, May, www.ends.co.uk.

15. Hugen-Tobler, L. (2008) *Measure, Manage Then Communicate – The New Mantra for Green Advertisers,* WARC, www.warc.com

16. Futerra (2008) *The Greenwash Guide,* www.futerra.co.uk

17. TerraChoice (2007) *The 'Six Sins of Greenwashing™' A Study of Environmental Claims in North American Consumer Markets*, Philadelphia, PA: TerraChoice Environmental Marketing Inc. (p. 1).

18. Kilbourne, W. (2004) 'Sustainable Communication and the Dominant Social Paradigm: Can They be Integrated?', *Marketing Theory* 4: 187–208 (p. 190).

19. United Nations Environment Programme (2007) *Sustainability Communications A Toolkit for Marketing and Advertising Courses* UNEP (p. 77).

20. TerraChoice (2007) *The 'Six Sins of Greenwashing™' A Study of Environmental Claims in North American Consumer Markets*, Philadelphia, PA: TerraChoice Environmental Marketing Inc.

21. Advertising Standards Authority (ASA) (2008) *Environmental Claims in Advertising. Is Green a Grey Area?*, Event Report, London: ASA.

22. Advertising Standards Authority (ASA) (2008) *Annual Report 2008*, www.asa.org.uk

23. Futerra (2008) *The Greenwash Guide*, www.futerra.co.uk

24. TerraChoice (2007) *The 'Six Sins of Greenwashing™' A Study of Environmental Claims in North American Consumer Markets*, Philadelphia, PA: TerraChoice Environmental Marketing Inc.; Futerra (2008) *The Greenwash Guide* www.futerra.co.uk

25. Business for Social Responsibility (BSR) (2008) *Eco-promising: Communicating the Environmental Credentials of Your Products and Services*, BSR (p. 13).

26. Levitt, T. (1970) 'The Morality (?) of Advertising', *Harvard Business Review*, July/August: 84–92.

27. *Marketing Week* (2008) 'Beware Lure of Making Green Claims' *Marketing Week*, 17 April.

28. NESTA (2008) *Selling Sustainability Seven Lessons from Advertising and Marketing to Sell Low-carbon Living*, London National Endowment for Science, Technology and the Arts.

29. NESTA (2008) *Selling Sustainability Seven Lessons from Advertising and Marketing to Sell Low-carbon Living*, London: National Endowment for Science, Technology and the Arts (p. 6).

30. Ipsos MORI (2007) *Sustainability Issues in the Retail Sector*, Ipsos MORI, www.ipsos-mori.com

31. Ipsos MORI (2007) *Sustainability Issues in the Retail Sector*, Ipsos MORI (p. 29), www.ipsos-mori.com

32. Futerra (2007) *Words that Sell. How the Public Talks About Sustainability*, www.futerra.co.uk

33. Shimp, T. (2000) *Advertising, Promotion: Supplemental Aspects of Integrated Marketing Communications*, 5th ed., New York: Dryden Press.

34. Consumer Focus (2009) *Green Expectations: Consumers' Understanding of Green Claims in advertising*, London: Consumer Focus.

35. Consumer Focus (2009) *Green Expectations: Consumers' Understanding of Green Claims in advertising*, London: Consumer Focus (p. 4).

36. Charter, M., Peattie, K., Ottman, J. and Polonsky, M. (2002) *Marketing and Sustainability*, Cardiff: Centre for Business Relationships, Accountability, Sustainability and Society (BRASS).

37. Landor Associates, Cohn & Wolfe and Penn, Schoen & Berland Associates (2008) *2008 ImagePower® Green Brands Survey UK Analysis*, www.cohnwolfe.com

38. *The Economist* (2008) 'The Good Consumer', *The Economist*, 19 January, 386 (8563): 16.

39. Euractiv (2009) *Carbon Labelling Finds Favour with Europeans*, 31 July, www.euractiv.com/en/sustainability/carbon-labelling-finds-favoureuropeans/article-184550

40. Stroud, S. (2009) 'The Great Eco-label Shakedown', *Sustainable Industries*, 27 July.

41. Ottman, J. (2009) *Alternatives to Eco-labels*, www.sustainablelifemedia.com/content/column/brands/alternatives_to_ecolabels

42. Oakeshott, I. and Ewart, S. (2009) 'Green Labels to Show Foods' Eco-credentials', *The Sunday Times*, 9 August.

43. *Farmers Weekly Interactive* (2009) *DEFRA Moots Green Labelling Scheme for Food*, 10 August www.fwi.co.uk/Articles/2009/08/10/117095/defra-moots-green-labelling-scheme-for-food.html

44. Futerra (2008) *The Greenwash Guide*, www.futerra.co.uk

45. Open PR (2008) *Polar Bears, Melting Ice Caps, Flowers and Fields: Advertisers Risk Clichè Meltdown in Rush to Go Green*, www.openpr.com/news/39942/Polar-bears-melting-ice-caps-flowers-and-fields-Advertisers-risk-clich-meltdown-in-rush-to-go-green.html

46. Department for Environment Food and Rural Affairs (DEFRA) (2003) *Green Claims – Practical Guidance How to Make a Good Environmental Claim*, London: DEFRA.

47. Futerra (2007) *Words That Sell. How the Public Talks About Sustainability*, www.futerra.co.uk

48. Khan, U. (2009) 'Climate Change Ad Showing Drowning Puppies to be Investigated After 300 Complaints', *The Guardian*, 22 October.

49. Sweney, M. (2010) 'Ofcom to Investigate Government Climate Change TV Campaign', *The Guardian*, 24 February.

50. Gillespie, E. (2010) *Climate Change Adverts Help Take Debate Among Public Back Several Years*, www.guardian.co.uk/environment/blog/2010/mar/17/climate-change-advertising-standards-authority

51. Charles, G. 'Don't be a Code Breaker', *Marketing*, 17 March.

52. www.aga-web.co.uk; *Campaign* (2009) 'Ogilvy Advertising Picks up Aga Brief', 30 July, www.campaignlive.co.uk/news/search/923858/Ogilvy-Advertising-picks-Aga-brief/; Cogent Elliott www.cogent.co.uk/client/aga; Goodman, M. (2009) 'We're Not Eco Monsters, Says Embattled Aga Chief', *The Sunday Times*, 9 August; Rosen, C. (2006) 'Are We Worthy of Our Kitchens?', *The New Atlantis* Number 11: 75–86; Brewer, A. (2008) 'Can Aga Win Over Environmentally-Conscious Customers?', *The Sunday Times*, 20 April, property.timesonline.co.uk/tol/life_and_style/property/interiors/article3721176.ece; Hawkes, S. and Rossiter, J. (2008) 'Sex-appeal Makeover Fails to Halt Aga Fall in Sales', *The Times*, 10 May, http://business.timesonline.co.uk/tol/business/industry_sectors/consumer_goods/article3905006.ece; Wallop, H. (2009) 'Agas and Bentleys: Slow-tech Solutions for An "Overwound World"', *The Telegraph*, 12 June, www.telegraph.co.uk/technology/news/5515268/Agas-and-Bentleys-slow-tech-solutions-for-an-overwound-world.html; Hornby, G. (2009) 'Help Aga Owners, Not Just the Car Industry', *The Telegraph*, 16 March 2009, www.telegraph.co.uk/comment/personal-view/5002446/Help-Aga-owners-not-just-the-car-industry.html; Monbiot, G. (2009) 'How Did Marxist Class Warriors End Up Fighting for the Bosses' Right to Fly?', *The Guardian*, 13 January; Woods, J. (2009) 'Is this the End of Aga's Saga?', *The Telegraph*, 15 January, www.telegraph.co.uk/comment/personal-view/4240508/Is-this-the-end-of-Agas-saga.html; Walesonline (2010) *Aga Confident as Volumes Increase in Seasonal Sales Rise*, 20 November, www.walesonline.co.uk/business-in-wales/business-news/2010/11/20; Costello, M. (2010) 'Irish Sales Head for Record to Give Aga a Warm Glow', *The Times*, 20 November.

PART

4

Implementation

9 Managing sustainable change

Now is absolutely a perfect time to be able to start to grasp the nettle of how we make that transition to a lower carbon economy. This is the time when we should be investing in the green infrastructure that we need for this century.[1]

Caroline Lucas – Leader of the Green Party, First member of the Green Party to be elected to the House of Commons in the general elections of 2010.

Chapter objectives

After studying this chapter you should be able to:

1 Understand the role of business, government and the community in achieving sustainable change.

2 Explore the nature of holistically designed solutions for sustainable change.

3 Examine frameworks for change proposed to manage the implementation of strategies for sustainable change.

4 Design and apply frameworks for sustainable change.

Dilemma part 1:   Bad for business, good for you

In the finale to season four of the American television series *Mad Men*, produced by Lionsgate Television, the character Peggy Olson, who plays a copywriter in the series, successfully pitches to Topaz, a small company that produces pantyhose. Peggy says that the pantyhose are so good, so comfortable that it will be the one item of clothing that she does not need to change before going out for the evening. Her strapline impresses the Topaz representative: 'Topaz, the only pair of pantyhose you'll ever need ... bad for business, good for you'.

There has been a logical focus on recycling and its contribution to sustainability, and manufacturers use the words *recyclable* and *recycled* as a claim to better sustainability credentials. Recycling is fashionable and marketable. Governments have also been set recycling targets and these have been passed on to regional and local authorities, and when consumers are encouraged to contribute to these efforts by recycling the goods they have bought, the circle is complete and it makes everyone feel virtuous. But something has been lost in the growing *recycling, recyclable, recycled* frenzy: product durability.

Market research indicates that the average life of consumer durable goods has decreased over the years. Product durability is an excellent way of achieving more sustainable consumption patterns. The longer the product lasts the better for the environment. Durability is the best way to improve resource efficiency as even when products are recyclable it takes more natural resources to make those recyclable components into something else, as well as energy and water, compounded by the ecological footprint associated with putting them back into the marketplace. Keeping and using goods for longer is therefore good sustainable practice.

Discuss the following:

Why would businesses be reluctant to extend the life span of products? Is product durability bad for business? How could durability be made to be good for business?

Managing sustainable change

The chapter opening quotation from the leader of the Green Party, Caroline Lucas, highlights the need for infrastructure to be in place in order to be able to initiate a move towards a more sustainable economy. Infrastructure is certainly necessary but it is only one of the elements needed that can be provided by the stakeholders involved in change.

Simple knowledge and awareness of issues has also proven to be insufficient alone. Only a small proportion of pro-environmental behaviour can be directly linked to environmental knowledge and awareness. One study points to 80 percent of the motives for pro-environmental or non-environmental behaviour as being centred on situational or other internal factors.[2]

The triangle of change is often mentioned as a means of demonstrating the three vital ingredients required for change towards sustainable consumption

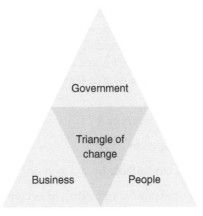

Figure 9.1 The triangle of change

and lifestyles to take place.[3] The triangle places each of the three major stakeholders – government, business and people – in separate corners of the triangle, as can be seen in Figure 9.1.

Each group has a part to play in the move towards sustainable living but no one, or even two groups, can successfully lead on sustainable consumption alone over the long term. Different corners might lead at different times by doing what they can do best, often in individual, one-off activities, but in actions which are not coordinated with the other groups.

Unilateral action by any of the groups is not necessarily detrimental, but it may lack sufficient impetus to convince others and not produce a long-lasting change. What is significant is that no single solution serves as a remedy for the challenges presented by sustainability. Interventions have to be tailored to the issues, sector, products, target markets, and their levels of motivations and perceived barriers. Securing change is also not achieved through a single event or action; it is likely that interventions need to be planned and implemented over the long term for behavioural change to be firmly established.

This chapter explores the management of sustainable change. First it examines the roles of each of the parties placed in the three corners of the triangle of change – government, business and people – highlighting where they might be able to influence change for the benefit of sustainability. Second, the four Es framework for change, first proposed in the government sustainability strategy *Securing the Future*, is presented and explained. Finally, the four Es framework is applied to sustainability contexts in order to understand how intervention programmes can be planned and implemented involving all of the relevant stakeholders in the process.

The people corner

The barriers to people participating in establishing more sustainable lifestyles are well documented in preceding chapters. What is needed is a means of mobilising the majority in such a way as to make sustainable behaviour desirable and even contagious. Focusing on the simple things in people's everyday lives can be a starting point, such as household energy and water management, food consumption, daily travel and holiday travel, which can account for some 80 percent of the impact of households on the local and global environment.

For change towards such a sustainable lifestyle to be feasible it has to be seen by people as:

- Fair for everyone.

- Not open to fraud.

- Not exploitable by the rich or privileged.

- Not excessive or unduly coercive.

- A collective response from consumers.

- A collective response from society, i.e. government, business, internationally.

- A social norm to be followed.

- A highly visible norm.

- Being part of something bigger, better and uplifting.

- A personally rewarding experience – tangibly and intangibly.

- Regaining control over a difficult situation, making progress to a solution.

- Making a real difference.

- Consistent, structured and organised in approach.

These issues are going to be difficult to deal with at times. Fair for everyone is a noble objective but, as has been demonstrated by the economic austerity measures of the UK government in 2010, there are many people who would disagree that governments act fairly in the interests of everyone. Dealing fairly with the rich and privileged is a more contentious topic and perhaps not resolvable even through tax measures. Bill Gates, regarded as the richest man in the US, is well known for all his altruistic campaigns financed by his great fortune, although he also has a carbon footprint that is 10,000 times more than the average American.[4]

Feedback is essential to combat people's scepticism about the value of their contributions to sustainability, particularly when they feel there is no direct link between their actions and the problems, or when they feel their actions are too small to have any positive effect. For many, sustainable behaviour may only mean one thing, such as recycling, to be more environmentally friendly; feedback on other issues is therefore vital to maintain progress towards sustainable lifestyles in other areas.

Rewards are important, even the intangible reward of a thank you from an organisation or public institution. However, while committed sustainable consumers may be content with the intangible, a warm feeling inside from having *done good*, many will require something more material and substantial. Tangible rewards are also important, such as vouchers for having recycled or tax breaks for buying less polluting vehicles. In the case of tangible rewards, highlighting what people will miss out on as a result of their inaction rather than what they might gain by acting may be more effective in marketing communications.

When people lead the way

On occasions consumers alone can lead a change in consumption patterns, forcing businesses to follow their demand. For example, by the end of 2009 the number of free-range eggs sold in the UK was expected to rise to 2 billion following a sharp decline in battery-farm sales. Free-range egg sales by volume rose to 53 percent of the market between March 2009 and March 2010.[5] Egoistic, biospheric and altruistic values all contributed to this turnaround in sales and a willingness to accept a price premium. Positive attributes of quality, taste and health, combined with a growing concern for animal welfare, stimulated demand from the public, which increased still further after television documentaries denounced caged-hen production techniques. Logically retailers who sold eggs reacted. Waitrose and Marks and Spencer were the first to stop stocking caged-hen eggs and were followed by Sainsbury's in 2009, but such has been consumer pressure that businesses that use eggs as ingredients also switched to free range, including Starbucks and Fox's Biscuits, which use over 4 million eggs a year between them.[6]

In other cases, such as the consumer switch to dolphin-friendly tuna or Fairtrade coffee, the more sustainable solutions available involved no compromise on quality and the price was the same or the price differential was within the acceptable norm. However, in cases where the price or quality differential is too high, consumers are unlikely to provide the driving force behind change.

People can also lead the way when motivated by purely altruistic values. Year on year in the UK people get together for a worthy cause such as Children in Need, Comic Relief, Sport Relief or Race for Life. Essentially, all of these campaigns which achieve mass participation and media coverage are designed to help others, improve their quality of life, even save their lives. Participants tend to enjoy taking part; they are intrinsically motivated and form extensive networks socially and at work in order to be more effective fundraisers and beat previous campaign results.

Pledges and procrastination

Cannot similar altruism-based techniques be used more frequently to drive sustainable behaviour in order to help save us from ourselves? Supporters of those charities make a pledge, a promise to raise money for their cause. In a similar way the 10:10 campaign asks individuals and businesses to pledge to reduce their carbon emissions. On 20 October 2010 the University of Virginia in the US launched its own sustainability pledge campaign, encouraging its students to make the following pledge and state what actions they would undertake to fulfil the pledge.

> I pledge to consider the social, economic and environmental impacts of my habits and to explore ways to foster a sustainable environment during my time here at UVa. and beyond.

Encouraging people to make a pledge to engage in sustainable behaviour helps to overcome one of the main barriers to action: inertia. When faced with making a commitment about the future, people tend to procrastinate, even when those actions may be to our long-term benefit.[7] By making a commitment public, particularly when it is written down for others to see, people are more likely to fulfil their promise in order to avoid damaging their reputation and falling down in the opinion of others.[8] Therefore pledging can be more effective than exhortation to achieve behavioural change, as pledging increases the social and ego risks of failure, something that most people will want to avoid.

Carillion plc is one of the UK's leading support services and construction companies, employing around 50,000 people. The company carries out numerous sustainability activities including a sustainability week. The company gives opportunities to employees to make a sustainability pledge and shows how much they can save if they continue their pledge beyond sustainability week for a whole year, as shown in Table 9.1. The table also shows how much can be saved if all the employees who made each particular pledge kept their promise for the year. In this way Carillion wants to demonstrate how the smallest lifestyle changes can have a significant impact on the environment and produce cost savings for the participants.

These pledges are made public throughout the company, underlining the collective nature of the activities being undertaken and the sacrifices being made. By doing this, combined with showing the cumulative impact of the activities, the system appears to be more robust and is able to satisfy many of the employees' key feasibility concerns mentioned earlier. Also the public nature of the commitment contributes to portraying pledging as the social norm within the organisation, leading to greater levels of participation and fewer dropouts on year-long pledges.

The business corner

It is logical to assume that because the niche green consumer was unable to force the complete reshaping of the marketplace during the 1980s and 1990s that something else is needed to tip the scales in favour of sustainable consumption

Table 9.1 Example of a sustainability pledge

Pledge	Sustainability impact	Number of employees taking on this pledge	Cumulative impact over a year
Turning biodegradable waste into compost	Each person dumps 194kg of organic waste a year. Equivalent 12,900 apple cores	7	1,358 kilos 90,300 apple cores

Source: Adapted from Carillion plc, 2005[9]

Figure 9.2   The sustainable business network

now. While deep greens have had an important role in setting examples as early adopters, the contribution of business is vital to achieve a more consistent change towards sustainability.

Figure 9.2 shows the business in a dominant position of influence within its own sustainable network. The sustainable business should be able to act as an agent of change by placing itself in the centre of its network of stakeholders, acting as a hub of communication and coordination between the various parties to maximise the sustainable outcomes of business activity by influencing and utilising their contributions.

The dominance of supermarkets in the UK retail sector places them in a privileged position to influence the growth and practice of sustainable business. Supermarket chain Waitrose, part of the John Lewis Partnership, has responded to the challenge and is using its position of responsibility to extend sustainability considerations across all aspects of the business (Table 9.2).

Choice-editing and sustainable supply chain management (covered in Chapters 6 and 7 respectively) are means at the disposal of businesses to enhance the sustainability of their operations. The systematic use of those methods combined with an appreciation of other relevant factors such as changes in the external environment, legislation and regulations, socio-cultural change and new technology issues allows businesses to produce a roadmap for their products and identify all the key points and milestones where sustainability has to be taken into account.

Table 9.2   Waitrose's sustainable business network

Engagement with consumers	Research with consumers highlighted three sustainability issues they wanted Waitrose to tackle: • packaging, waste and recycling • improving the nutritional value of their food • responsible sourcing, both in terms of labour standards in the supply chain and the sustainability of products Consumers are regularly consulted on sustainability and other issues
Engagement with employees	Democratic systems of employee involvement and representation with management. All employees are referred to as *partners* in the business, owning a share in the business and receiving a proportion of the profits. In 2007 the Partnership returned £324 million to employees in the form of a bonus, pensions and other benefits. Annual surveys are used to gather employee input on sustainability issues as well as on the general management of the chain
Engagement with suppliers	Conferences, forums, partnered projects, workshops, open days are used to engage suppliers. Local and small producers are showcased at the three-day Waitrose Spring Food Festival at the company's Leckford Estate Suppliers (food and non-food) must adhere to Waitrose's Responsible Sourcing Code of Practice and register and complete information requirements on Sedex, the Supplier Ethical Data Exchange. Supplier forums are held to share best practice on issues such as energy efficiency and carbon reduction As well as developing a special relationship with local suppliers, the Waitrose Foundation provides for a unique partnership with South African fruit farmers, investing to improve community welfare. It has supported more than 19,000 farm workers on 32 farms in South Africa through 58 different community projects. The projects cover training in literacy, IT, technical and life skills to help workers to earn a living outside the fruit growing season
Support of local community	'Meet the Buyer' or 'Meet the Farmer' events, which introduce customers to local producers. Public consultation in local communities before new building or refurbishment programmes
Industry-related partnerships	Support for organisations such as Linking Environment and Farming (LEAF), the Marine Stewardship Council, and Greenpeace on issues such as soya, palm oil and sustainable fishing. Senior managers attend training conferences with Forum for the Future on sustainability issues
Government collaboration	Ensure compliance with central government and local authorities and engage with policy-makers over legislation on sustainable issues such as waste and packaging

Product road mapping

A broad, all-encompassing approach, product road mapping provides businesses with the opportunity to envisage and plan ahead combining choice-editing decisions with legislation change, supply chain considerations and business environment changes, marking milestones and showing planned adjustments in product development over time.

Product roadmaps represent a planned product policy approach, particularly useful for addressing the difficulties posed by high-impact products. The roadmap permits the planner to look forward over the timescales of product development – including sourcing of materials, design, manufacture, storage and distribution, packaging, use and end-of-life – and foresee where the business and other parties can respond to the sustainability concerns that may arise. It therefore can be used to plot the current and future trajectories of the product and how it improves its sustainability performance in each reincarnation.

The roadmap helps businesses to identify areas for improvement and might include sustainable procurement mechanisms, deadlines and stages for achieving sustainability targets, the entry point of new legislation and regulations, standards to be met, incentives for increased sustainability, cross-support/participation mechanisms and tools from government, local government or NGOs.

Figure 9.3 shows a product roadmap template from The Hub, a web project funded by the Australian Federal Government to provide a consolidated space for engagement, interaction and connectivity to help build communities of responsible business practice in Australia. Visit its website at http://thehub.ethics.org.au.

A product roadmap becomes a powerful management tool when combined with other available data such as quantitative analyses of greenhouse

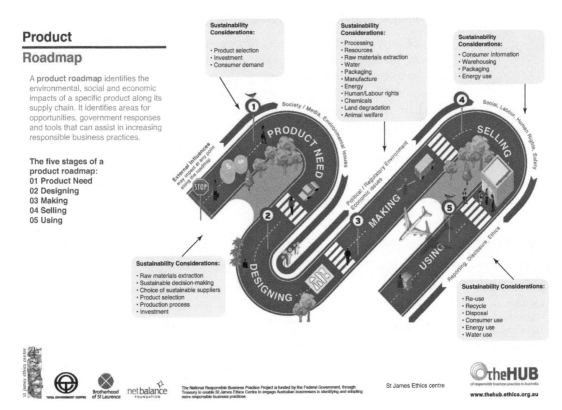

Figure 9.3   A product roadmap

Source: St James Ethics Centre, Australia

gas emissions at particular stages together with other footprint considerations. The map reveals the complexities and interdependencies between procurers, suppliers, manufacturers and consumers so they can be better understood and managed throughout the product lifecycle. It assists in identifying cost-saving points from implementing sustainability policies to gain resource efficiencies and helps to resolve conflicting interests between parties.

The government corner

The government has a significant influence over the product lifecycle through legislation, regulations, incentives and voluntary agreements, and has the ability to lead by example, as with its own sustainable procurement policies.

Figure 9.4 shows that different policy interventions from UK and EU bodies result in a variety of initiatives that affect the product at different stages in its lifecycle. Such an interpretation would have to be specific to each industry sector and, although the figure does not represent a particular industry-product context, it helps to identify the kinds of issues that might be relevant at different stages for numerous business types.

For example:

Responsible sourcing of materials

BES 6001 (www.netregs.gov.uk) has been published to enable construction product manufacturers to ensure and then prove that their products have been made with constituent materials that have been responsibly sourced. The standard describes a framework for the organisational governance, supply chain management, and environmental and social aspects that must be addressed in order to ensure the responsible sourcing of construction products.

Environmental impact

ISO 14001 (www.netregs.gov.uk) is an internationally accepted standard that sets out how businesses can put in place an effective Environmental

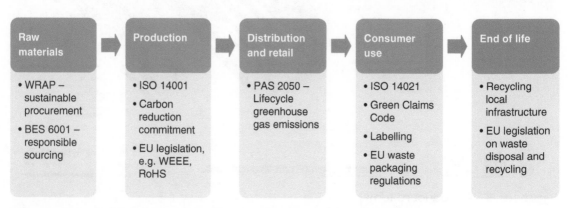

Figure 9.4 Policies for sustainable change during the product lifecycle

Management System (EMS). The standard is designed to address the delicate balance between maintaining profitability and reducing environmental impact, and requires the commitment of the entire organisation to be successful on both counts. ISO 14001 assists the business in identifying all those aspects of their operation that may impact on the environment and understand those environmental laws most relevant to deal with them.

Lifecycle greenhouse gas emissions

On the recommendations of Defra and the Carbon Trust, BSI Standards Solutions has developed PAS 2050, a Publicly Available Specification (PAS) to establish a method for measuring the embodied greenhouse gas (GHG) emissions from goods and services. The method can be used by all sizes and types of organisations and considers all lifecycle stages along the supply chain – from raw materials to end of life – and includes the six GHGs identified under the Kyoto protocol.

Hazardous substances

RoHS stands for the restriction on the use of certain hazardous substances in electrical and electronic equipment. It is a European directive aiming to control the use of certain hazardous substances in the production of new electrical and electronic equipment runs in conjunction with the WEEE Directive (Waste in Electrical and Electronic Equipment) that controls the disposal and recycling of such equipment. The RoHS directive is applicable to producers that manufacture or assemble electrical or electronic equipment in the UK, or that import electrical or electronic equipment from outside Europe or those businesses that re-badge electronic products as their own.

No single policy initiative alone is enough. What is needed to secure sustainability is a coordinated package of policies and interventions for each of the desired outcomes, including marketing communications that address each of the core motivations of the parties involved and the barriers to change.[10] The following Snapshot on the sustainable challenge presented by food waste serves as a good example of the managing role of government attempting to achieve sustainable lifestyle change.

Snapshot: Waste not, want not

For example, in order to tackle the issue of food waste and to meet targets for the reduction of food waste being sent to landfill, the government relies on a number of different initiatives including UK and EU regulations, incentive schemes and voluntary agreements, and public awareness campaigns to help achieve the changes required of local authorities, food manufacturers and retailers, food service providers and consumers.

Food waste is a significant sustainability issue. The greenhouse gas emissions associated with avoidable food and drink waste is the equivalent of approximately 20 million tonnes of carbon

▶

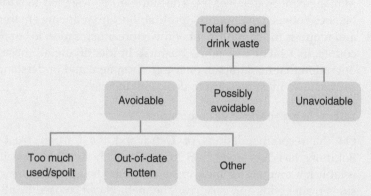

Figure 9.5   WRAP's classification of food and drink waste

Source: Adapted from WRAP, 2009[11]

dioxide per year. This is roughly 2.4 percent of greenhouse gas emissions associated with all consumption in the UK. Kitchen food waste accounts for about 17 percent of household waste.

A 2009 study by Waste and Resources Action Programme (WRAP) identified three types of food and drink waste according to how avoidable they were, as shown in Figure 9.5. Much of avoidable food waste is still edible when it is thrown away, while possibly avoidable waste is food that might have been eaten by someone else who liked it or might have been eaten if it had been prepared in a different way. Unavoidable food waste is inedible under normal circumstances, such as orange peel, meat bones or spent coffee grindings.

The avoidable proportion is also made up of three different types. Too much food is bought or prepared and then the remainder thrown away or food is spoilt and discarded during the cooking process. Some food might have gone rotten before consumption or gone beyond its use-by date. The avoidable portion of the food and drink waste is worth some £12 billion per year, that is, an average of £480 per household per year. The food industry is also responsible for food waste. For example, it is estimated that up to 50 percent of raw vegetables and salad by weight are rejected at some stage of the production line before reaching the shopper.

A series of policy interventions and initiatives has sought to address the issue of food waste for the last decade. The Food Industry Sustainability Strategy, published in 2006, was first to set out directives to deal with food waste with a requirement to decrease food waste from manufacturing by between 15–20 percent by 2010.

The EU Landfill Directive (99/31/EC) came into force in 1999, and the UK had two years to incorporate the requirements into its legislation. The Directive's overall aim is to prevent or reduce as far as possible any waste-related negative effects on the environment, including the greenhouse effect, from the use of landfill disposal, during the whole lifecycle of the landfill. The Directive sets demanding targets to reduce the amount of biodegradable municipal landfill waste, with strict deadlines to be met by 2020.

In order to help local waste disposal authorities (WDAs) meet the landfill targets of the Landfill Directive in the most cost-effective way, the Landfill Allowances Trading Scheme was established for England to allow WDAs to trade, bank or borrow against their own capacity or the surplus capacity of others.

Various agreements between the government's WRAP and food retailers have also been designed to drive a reduction in food waste. For example, the Courtauld Commitment Phase 2 is a voluntary agreement between WRAP and the food and grocery industry, a follow-up from the original commitment launched in 2005. It aims to achieve more sustainable use of resources over the entire lifecycle of products, throughout the whole supply chain, including to reduce UK household food and drink waste by 4 percent and to reduce traditional (both solid and liquid) grocery product waste and packaging waste in the grocery supply chain by 5 percent, using 2009 data and working to a 2012 deadline. The commitment has already received the support of 29 major retailers.

Individual retailers are continuing to contribute to reducing food wastage in the supply chain, such as Waitrose which works with farmers and growers in the UK and abroad to improve their packaging and transport practices. After working with a group of 100 banana growers in the Windward Islands to look at how their fruit was cultivated and transported, wastage from shipped fruit has reduced from an estimated 40 percent in 2002 to less than 3 percent in 2008. Fruit and vegetables are often rejected for sale by the retailer, not because they are inedible, but because they do not look perfect and as a result will not be purchased by the consumer. This practice has also come under scrutiny and is as much the responsibility of the retailer as the consumer who has come to unrealistically expect perfection every time. Waitrose now accepts cosmetically imperfect fruit and vegetables from suppliers but explains this practice to consumers. For example, in 2007, much of the UK apple crop was damaged by hail, but was accepted for sale by the retailer and this was communicated to its customers so they would not be rejected by them (the consumers).

Also, after criticism from the government in its review of food sustainability in 2009, supermarkets Tesco and Sainsbury's reviewed their *Buy One Get One Free* policies and started to pilot and then introduce *Buy One Get One Free Later* schemes. Critics felt that *Buy One Get One Free* schemes increased food waste as consumers did not have enough time to consume the extra free food products before their use-by date.[12,13]

As can be seen already, consumer engagement is vital to reduce food waste. WRAP also engages consumer actions to reduce food waste such as changing food purchase and preparation practices and piloting home composting schemes. WRAP's *Love Food Hate Waste* campaign aims to raise awareness of the need to reduce food waste with the final consumer. The campaign shows that by doing some easy practical everyday things in the home people can all waste less food, save money and benefit the environment.[14] Food waste avoidance has also trickled into the popular media. Television chef Nigel Slater regularly demonstrates how to make appetising meals from leftovers on his BBC programme *Simple Suppers*.[15]

Towards a framework for consolidated change

Figure 9.6 illustrates how the change might be profound if it were coordinated between all three stakeholders by blending together their actions in a more synchronised approach to produce the conditions necessary for sustainability to take a greater hold of society.

As can be seen in Figure 9.6, all three players need each other in order to stimulate the conditions necessary for change. Government has to establish the right infrastructures and incentives to provide a platform for businesses to build upon. For their part businesses have to understand the sustainable marketplace and the demand for sustainable products and services, and develop

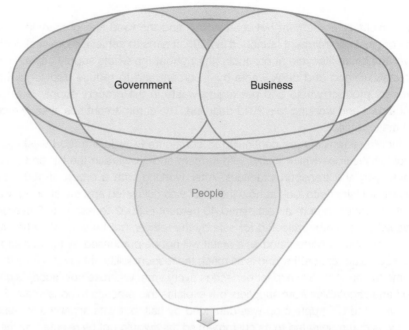

For people to access and use sustainable products and services:
Government – infrastructure, legislation, incentives, agreements
Business – new market/product development, demand creation
People – behavioural change, new demand, lifestyle change

Figure 9.6   A synchronised approach to change

these in accordance with legislation and the terms of the Triple Bottom Line. Finally, consumers, have to be prepared to accept and adopt any necessary behavioural changes to their consumption patterns and demand that more sustainable products and services be made available to them. All of this needs to be timely; the right sequence of events and initiatives directed by the right agencies in the right way to the most appropriate target markets.

The 4 Es framework for managing change

In 2005 the UK government published its updated strategy for sustainable development entitled *Securing the Future*, in which it laid out its plans for a sustainable future focusing on four priorities: sustainable consumption and production, climate change, natural resource protection and sustainable communities.[16]

The UK government's 4 Es framework (Figure 9.7) recognises that interventions that drive change need to be carried out as part of a mutually reinforcing package involving different stakeholders delivering those actions they are best placed to provide.[17] In the strategy document, the 4 Es framework provides a design template for interventions to promote sustainable behaviour among target audiences. The framework sets out a coordinated approach in order to

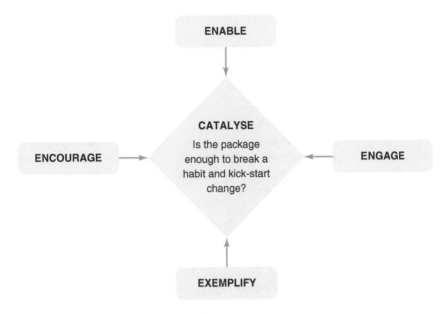

Figure 9.7 The 4 Es framework

Source: Adapted from HM Government, p. 26[18]

engage, encourage and *enable* the general public to adopt sustainable behaviours, combined with efforts to *exemplify* appropriate sustainable behaviour in order to help people make better choices with regard to leading a sustainable lifestyle.

The four headings help to identify and categorise the contributions that can be made by coordinating a certain number of actions, as shown in Table 9.3. With an overall aim to establish sustainable practice as the norm, elements of the framework resonate with aspects of consumer behaviour already discussed in previous chapters. For example, injunctive norms are reflected under the heading *encourage,* with the recognition of progress, social pressure and penalties, and the use of opinion formers as role models echoes aspects of the social learning theory in the *engage* stage, as does leading by example in the *exemplify* stage. The framework also owes its design to social marketing practice as its focus is on the replacement of undesirable behaviour with desirable behaviour.

Actions from the four areas working together should be enough to function as a catalyst for change to sustainable behaviour. The framework aims to provide a comprehensive and consistent structure for whole communities to approach sustainable practice, including all the relevant stakeholders with an interest in or influence over the initiative. All-encompassing, it allows for local and national government, businesses, families and communities, the public sector, voluntary and community organisations to participate.

Involving the general public in designing sustainable interventions and developing policies jointly, an approach known as co-production, gives

Table 9.3   The 4 Es for change

Enable
- Remove barriers
- Give information
- Provide facilities
- Provide viable alternatives
- Educate, train, provide skills
- Provide capacity

Engage
- Community action
- Co-production
- Deliberative forum
- Personal contacts/enthusiasts
- Media campaigns
- Opinion formers
- Use of networks

Encourage
- Breaks in tax system
- Grants
- Reward schemes
- Recognition
- Social pressure/league tables
- Penalties and fines*
- Enforcement action*

Exemplify
- Lead by example
- Policy consistency

*Sometimes accommodated under a fifth E – Ensure – in order to differentiate disincentives from the incentives under Encourage.

Source: Adapted from HM Government.[19]

credibility and community ownership of projects, by improving their acceptance and success. Deliberative forums used to engage people allow for more in-depth discussion about options than standard means of collecting opinions, such as survey or questionnaire. Forums also allow for greater opportunities for everyone to voice their opinions and listen to others' opinions, at the same time providing a more spontaneous comparison of opinions and ideas both for and against from all interested parties, including expert advisers.

Apply it: The 4 Es of household food waste

In this chapter and in previous chapters there have been references to issues of waste management and the changes in attitude and behaviour towards waste, which are desirable in order for sustainable progress to be made. Reducing household food waste requires a number of behavioural changes likely to clash with many well-established consumer habits. By applying the 4 Es framework, marketers are able to explore these potential barriers to behavioural change and source appropriate solutions.

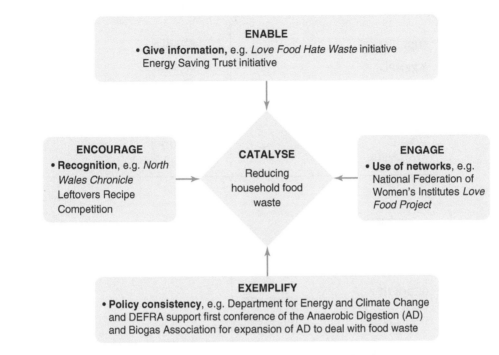

Figure 9.8   A 4 Es framework for household food waste

Figure 9.8 applies the 4 Es framework to the issue of household food waste by taking a single bullet point from each of its sections, as shown in Table 9.3, and finding examples of how initiatives are being put into practice.

1. Using the remaining actions for each of the 4 Es from Table 9.3, find examples of current or past initiatives designed to deal with each of these aspects in order to complete the figure. As a result you should be able to provide a more comprehensive view of how the issue of household food waste is being tackled by the various stakeholders involved.

Interventions become segment-specific

A fundamental change in consumer behaviour may take a considerable amount of time. It may only take place as a result of frequent interventions, legislation and campaigns or by experiencing some of the more drastic consequences of continuing with the current unsustainable system (e.g. massive price increases in petrol). For many consumers it is probably too early to perceive a need to change or perceive a real threat to their lifestyle and they feel that life will go on regardless. Those who dabble in sustainable practices without leading a fully sustainable lifestyle may feel that what they do is enough and that they are relieved of their responsibility to make any more significant changes to their lifestyle.

Therefore, what is clear is that different segments of the population will need different intervention mixes to cater for their levels of willingness, understanding

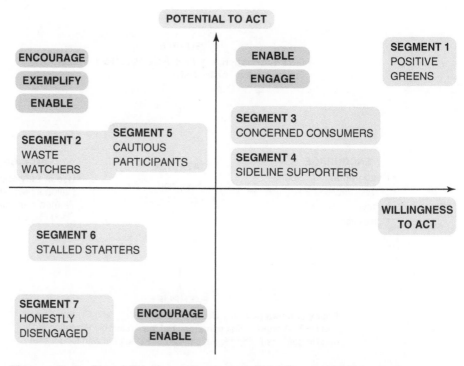

Figure 9.9 The 4 Es elements appropriate for each of the Defra segments plotted against their ability and willingness to act

Source: Adapted from Defra[20]

and ability to act sustainably. The 4 Es framework can be plotted against Defra's segmentation model (commented on in Chapter 4) to identify the potential to make further progress in each of the segments through the application of its different elements, highlighting those areas where more emphasis might need to be placed in each intervention.

As can be seen in Figure 9.9, interventions that concentrate on enabling and engaging may be more suitable for segments 1, 3 and 4 and the continued engagement of segment 1 may further aid the conversion of the other two segments in that quadrant. The lack of willingness to act of segments 2 and 5 requires encouragement and examples of good practice to be used in interventions, while segments 6 and 7 need encouragement and enabling processes to remove specific or perceived barriers to get them started towards sustainable lifestyles.

Snapshot: A gentle nudge

Consumers *unable* or *unwilling* to make sustainable lifestyle choices need to be *enabled* or *nudged* respectively so they can engage in more sustainable behaviour. Waiting for everyone to act out of individual personal choice and personal responsibility with little or no stimulus or support to do so will not help achieve the country's sustainability goals. The idea of *nudging* has been made popular by best-selling book *Nudge* from behavioural economists Richard Thaler and Cass Sunstein.[21] Behavioural economics suggests that people are more likely to change their behaviour if they feel they have chosen to do so rather than having been coerced into it.

The theory proposes that people's decisions are affected by their choice architecture, that is, the way in which choices are presented to them. The key to success for nudge marketing would be to design the choice architecture in such a way that consumers feel they are making their choices freely.

There is still some scepticism about its use and effectiveness, although its advocates point to a number of successes. For example, one of its more well-known applications is the use of an embossed fly 'target' on the porcelain urinals in Schipol Airport toilets in Amsterdam. The irresistible temptation to use the fly as a target has reduced urine spillage by 80 percent and cut the cost of cleaning products at the same time. The nudge tactic has been much more effective than simply using posters asking consumers to be more careful and hygienic!

Apply it: A gentle nudge

1. Collect what you might regard as examples of nudge marketing tactics, either from everyday marketing activity or from sustainable initiatives. What can be learnt from these? Have they been effective? Are there more opportunities for nudge marketing to promote sustainable behaviours? What do you think would be the effect on consumers if they found out they were being nudged?

Intervention design evolves

Recent research has seen the modification of the original 4 Es framework. The MINDSPACE report built on the existing framework by adding *explore*, for gaining insight, and *evaluation* for reviewing results and outcomes before feeding back into the process again to improve and evolve the intervention or design a new one.[22] Within the modified framework a series of tools have been included for influencing behaviour known as MINDSPACE. MINDSPACE is an acronym for *Messenger, Incentives, Norms, Defaults, Salience, Priming, Affect, Commitment* and *Ego*, which have been identified as those elements that have been found to have strong impacts on behaviour and often, although not always, can have an automatic effect (Table 9.4).

Not all the MINDSPACE elements are necessary for every intervention, only those relevant for the target audience – context and behavioural goals – need be used. Many of these elements have been covered in previous chapters, although the role of the messenger and the use of incentives are worth further comment.

People's reactions to the deliverer of marketing communications for planned interventions depend greatly on their perceptions of the messenger. The source of the message may communicate authority (government), expert opinion (Sir David Attenborough, the world-famous naturalist) or attractiveness and aspirational value (Julia Roberts, actress and sustainability campaigner). Choice

Table 9.4   MINDSPACE

Messenger	people are heavily influenced by who communicates information
Incentives	human responses to incentives are shaped by predictable mental shortcuts
Norms	people are strongly influenced by what others do
Defaults	people tend to 'go with the flow' of pre-set options
Salience	people's attention is drawn to what is novel and seems relevant to them
Priming	people's acts are often influenced by subconscious cues
Affect	people's emotional associations can powerfully shape their actions
Commitments	people seek to be consistent with public promises and reciprocate acts
Ego	people act in ways that make them feel better about themselves

Source: Adapted from Dolan et al., 2010[23]

of messenger may therefore affect the effectiveness of communications of an intervention.

The use of incentives to drive sustainable change during interventions is a double-edged sword that can work in favour of change or against it. There is a danger of economic rewards diminishing the worthiness and value of adopting sustainable lifestyles, as if some element of sacrifice or difficulty provides credibility to the lifestyle change. When economic rewards are influential there tends to be a consumer preference for smaller, quicker rewards favouring short-term, more immediate gain instead of the more distant promise of longer-term gains.

The addition of *explore* and *evaluate*, as shown in Figure 9.10, closes the loop in the intervention framework. It permits better planning by gaining insights beforehand and provides feedback to judge the effectiveness of the intervention.

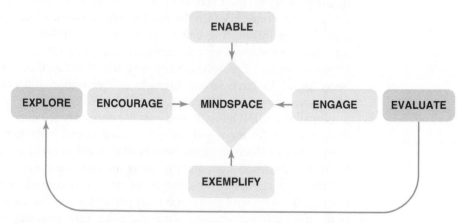

Figure 9.10   The 6 Es framework for change with MINDSPACE
Source: Adapted from Dolan et al., 2010[24]

Snapshot: Defra checklist of best practice principles to encourage pro-environmental behaviour

All interventions are designed to impact on behaviour in some way and the desired behavioural changes need to be seen as an outcome in the longer term and not as an intervention for the sake of it. The interventions have to overcome a difficult barrier that is the disconnect people face between the current benefits of their behaviours and lifestyles and the longer-term negative impacts they have on the environment and society. Defra provides the following advice to organisations wishing to try to change consumer behaviour:[25]

1. There is no single solution that will motivate a mainstream audience to live a greener life. It requires multiple, integrated interventions.

2. Draw on all the interventions available to you. Develop an intervention mix combining tools from across the policy and communications spectrum.

3. Build an understanding of the public and societal trends. Consider public attitudes, beliefs, motivations, barriers, and current and desired behaviours. Review your options for interventions against these insights. Use key insights and segmentation models to develop targeted approaches.

4. Understand the behaviours you are asking people to adapt or adopt. Tackling habits, choices or purchasing behaviours may need different tactics.

5. Be clear what your organisation and programme can do as well as what others are doing. Consider the role of government, business and the public – the Triangle of Change.

6. Work across sectors in designing and implementing programmes – evidence shows this makes interventions more successful.

7. Accept that outcomes of behaviour change interventions are difficult to predict; you need to take risks and pilot activity.

8. Recognise securing behaviour change is a long-term process not a single event.

9. Demonstrate consistency.

10. Address both internal and external motivations and barriers.

11. Optimise common motivations and barriers. Use non-environmental motivations.

12. Recognise the role of social norms, identity and status for moving towards greater adoption of pro-environmental behaviours.

13. Use 'opinion leaders' and trusted intermediaries to reach your audience.

14. Recognise the value in joining up environmental issues for people, as well as joining up organisations' work and messages.

15. Give feedback on progress made. Consider when we can ask people or organisations to make commitments to being more pro-environmental.

Professional Practice: Intervention design

You are a junior assistant in the sustainability department of your Regional Council and have just been given the information provided in Table 9.5 on micro-generation from your department head. The first thing you noticed was that the table was incomplete; this is not the first time this has happened and you are getting used to it. The second thing you noticed was the handwritten note at the bottom of the page.

The note read as follows:

Can you draw up a draft intervention aimed at improving the uptake of micro-generation in domestic households? I need to have ideas to take to the Management Away Day next week. I have made a start and written out my own ideas for you but I am too busy to do much more as I have fire safety training and interactive whiteboard induction this week. Please use the 4 Es framework – it seems to me that lots of other people are using that one. Must dash. I'd like it as a PowerPoint presentation. Leave a hard copy on my desk and send me the file as an email attachment by Monday morning 9.00 am.

Investigate the area of micro-generation using the cues in Table 9.5 and the knowledge gained through this chapter to help you. Prepare a short presentation to demonstrate how an intervention might be organised to stimulate the micro-generation market in domestic households. Be prepared to present your findings back to the rest of the group.

Table 9.5   Micro-generation . . .

Behavioural goal	Increase uptake of micro-generation in domestic households
Examples of micro-generation	. . .
Benefits	Lower GHG emissions
	Conservation of non-renewable sources of energy
	. . .
Target markets	. . .
Behaviour type	One-off purchase of system
Barriers to adoption	. . .
Current schemes and initiatives and (dis-)incentives	. . .
Current providers of micro-generation productions	. . .
Other stakeholders	. . .

Researching sustainability: Reviewing performance indicators

The University of Winchester rose a total of 38 places in the People & Planet Green League in 2010 to reach 28th out of 137 institutions. The Green League is the only league table that ranks the environmental performance of British universities. Significant areas of improvement at the University of Winchester this year include recycling, student engagement, and energy and carbon emissions. In addition, Winchester Student Union was ranked by the National Union of Students as the greenest in England in the Sound Environmental Impact Awards, and received the Ecologist Communications Award 2010 for a short awareness-raising film about students and their environmental impact.

Tommy Geddes, Deputy Vice Chancellor of the University of Winchester stated: 'Sustainability has become a pressing concern on campus and the university has made significant progress in reducing its environmental impact over the past couple of years.'

Waste recycling at Winchester University rose from 14 percent in January 2009 to 56 percent in May 2010, and a target of 70 percent is planned for 2012. Additionally, more than £180,000 has been invested in energy efficiency measures and 90 percent of the university's electricity is now supplied from green sources. Energy saving campaigns are being held campus-wide and students in university accommodation can compete with each other in an energy saving competition by reducing the energy consumed in their flats. No surprise that sustainability programmes are available for students at both undergraduate and postgraduate levels and their MSc Sustainable Development prospectus material states the programme is 'available to students across the globe without impacting on the learner's carbon footprint'.[26]

The Carbon Reduction Commitment (CRC) Energy Efficiency Scheme is the UK's mandatory climate change and energy saving scheme. The scheme started in April 2010 and is administered by the Environment Agency (EA).

The CRC is a mandatory scheme aimed at improving energy efficiency and cutting emissions in large public- and private-sector organisations. These organisations are responsible for around 10 percent of the UK's emissions.

The scheme features an annual performance league table that ranks participants on energy efficiency performance. Together with the reputational considerations, the scheme encourages organisations to develop energy management strategies that promote a better understanding of energy usage.

The scheme is designed to tackle CO_2 emissions not already covered by Climate Change Agreements and the EU Emissions Trading Scheme.

Organisations are eligible for CRC if they have at least one half-hourly electricity meter (HHM) settled on the half-hourly market. Organisations that consumed more than 6,000 megawatt-hours (MWh) per year of half-hourly metered electricity during 2008 qualify for full participation and register with the EA, which is the administrator for the scheme.

Organisations that do not meet the 6,000MWh threshold will have to make an information disclosure of their half-hourly electricity consumption during 2008. Participants include supermarkets, universities, water companies, banks, local authorities and all central government departments.

▶

Qualifying organisations will have to comply legally with the scheme or face financial and other penalties.

In October's Spending Review (2010) the UK government announced that the CRC would be simplified to reduce the burden on businesses, with the first allowance sales for 2011/12 emissions now taking place in 2012 rather than 2011. Revenue from the sale of CRC allowances, totalling £1 billion a year by 2014/15, will be used to support the public finances, including spending on the environment, rather than recycled to the participants.

The implications of this announcement for CRC are:

- In order to clarify the price signal to participants and support the public finances, revenue from allowance sales will not be recycled back to participants by the UK government.

- The first sale of allowances will take place in 2012 instead of 2011, postponing the financial requirements of the scheme for participants. Participants will therefore be able to purchase allowances to cover their 2011/12 emissions at the end of the 2011/12 compliance year.

- The Performance League Table will be retained as the main reputational driver within the scheme, with the metric weightings and publication dates as envisaged in the current legislation including the October 2011 table.[27]

The Higher Education Funding Council for England (HEFCE) requires institutions to have carbon management plans in place after 2011.

The university sector in England has also been devising its own carbon reduction targets. A joint consultation between HEFCE, Universities UK and Guild HE on developing a carbon reduction target and strategy for higher education in England was published on 29 July 2009, with the final strategy published in January 2010

1. Investigate the sustainability plans of your university. What performance indicators are being used? How are their plans progressing in relation to the targets set by the CRC? How are students being engaged with the project? How does your university compare with others?

Summary

Communities, businesses, and local and national government have the potential for delivering sustainable change alone, although initiatives are more likely to succeed in collaborations. Businesses have the opportunity to close the loop on their operations by taking a holistic approach to the sustainability issues of all aspects of their operations from the design of their installations, their use of natural resources and their energy requirements, to the management of waste and recycling and attention to legislation, regulatory requirements and voluntary agreements must be paid throughout the product lifecycle.

Effective strategies for societal change require that a package of activities combined into interventions be delivered consistently and that they involve the three main players: people – society in its broadest sense – businesses and government. There is no single solution for sustainable change nor can a single event cause change. Multiple interventions need to be put into effect and have to be designed to address the core motivations for lifestyle change and the potential barriers that impede change, and therefore should be tailored to the characteristics of the target audiences.

It is the accumulative effect of holistic interventions that is more significant, particularly when working with other appropriate delivery partners such as third-sector organisations, community groups, and opinion leaders and influencers. Infrastructure, facilities, legislation, incentives all have to be in place and the 4 Es framework provides a suitable structure for organising and implementing planned interventions.

Case study: Adnams – sustainable brewing for the 21st century

Adnams brewery stands out as a company prepared to act on the sustainability agenda in all aspects of the business. Tackling sustainability on all fronts at the same time is an ambitious goal but Adnams' holistic approach is already reaping dividends.

Britain's greenest warehouse

Regarded as Britain's greenest warehouse, Adnams' purpose-built distribution centre located in Southwold, Suffolk, was designed to minimise its environmental impact while maximising its ability to function sustainably. Set in a former gravel pits site, Adnams spent time to restore the natural environment around the installations: planting trees, re-establishing existing ponds and encouraging the return of native wildlife. Placing the building itself in the hollow of one of the pits allows much of the development to be shielded from public view, minimising the impact of noise and nocturnal light on the local community.

The building showcases Adnams' commitment to sustainability, a tangible, visual calling card to its clients. The structure incorporates numerous sustainable construction techniques. For example, a range of hemp, quarry waste and lime-based products from the sustainable construction company Lime Technology have been used in the construction of the walls of the building. Hemp is a renewable resource – in just 14 weeks 1 hectare will grow enough to build five houses. The use of hemp allows for this part of the construction to be better than carbon neutral because the cultivation of the hemp captures CO_2, locking it into the construction of the walls, rather than emitting it as in the production of standard concrete products. The Adnams distribution centre has therefore made a potential net saving of over 500 tonnes of CO_2 by using this method.

The attention to detail on the part of the company is key to achieving the maximum level of sustainability. Adnams worked closely with the manufacturer of the lime and hemp blocks, and invested £20,000 to ensure the technology was viable on a large scale. Over 90,000 blocks were used in the construction, making this the largest building in the UK to use this material. Timber (not steel) beams hold up the largest green roof in Britain of 0.6 hectares in size. The roof is planted

▶

to create a growing meadow and blend the building into the landscape as most of the building is hidden in the base of the pit. The roof vegetation also serves to insulate the building and create an area for wildlife.

Constructed for energy and water efficiency

● Natural daylight to the warehouse is provided by special windows and natural roof lights.

● Excessive heat gain and solar glare through the office windows have been minimised by the use of overhanging eaves and screens at the south-facing end of the main building.

● Two collector solar panels on the roof provide 80 percent of the centre's hot water requirements.

● Movement sensors control lighting.

● The special construction allows for the building to be naturally maintained at the temperature of 11°C–13°C ideal for the storage of beer, without the need for extra heating, refrigeration or ventilation.

● The roof, other surface areas and the whole building design allows for the collection of rainwater which is reused for toilet flushing, vehicle washing and maintenance of the ponds. It is estimated that some 650,000 litres of rainwater can be collected each year. An additional waste water system passes dirty water through a septic tank and through reed beds before being returned to nearby ponds.

With so many sustainable elements, the building received an 'Excellent' rating under the Building Research Establishment Environmental Assessment Method (BREEAM) rating system. The £14 million building was 15 percent more expensive than one produced by conventional methods without any built-in water, energy or environmental efficiencies. However, the new distribution centre is already paying its way. Adnams has cut its gas bill by 56 percent a year, its electricity bill by 67 percent, and refrigeration costs by £56,000 a year. Mains water bills are now minimal.

Nitesh Magdani, the project architect, stated: 'A unique combination of features means that Adnams' distribution centre is a landmark development. It provides an ideal illustration of the importance of sustainable design and commitment to green issues at every level.'[28]

Carbon-neutral beer

Adnams' pursuit of sustainability does not stop at its distribution centre. Its response to the challenge of sustainability is a coordinated reaction to the problems facing the brewery and its desires to engage in a long-term strategy to ensure a sustainable future. Ageing production equipment and reduced capacity of limited facilities caused Adnams to rethink its strategy and seek better equipment as well as a new distribution centre.

Resource efficiency was the priority behind choice of production machinery. For example, 100 percent of the process steam used for brewing is reused, resulting in 90 percent of the heat from one brew able to be used to produce the second. The new production equipment reduced gas bills by 31 percent despite rising production volumes, and uses over 60 percent less water per pint produced. The production of an average pint of beer takes 4.5 litres of water, Adnams has reduced this to 1.8 litres and intends to reduce it further. Adnams has also reduced the energy used to produce each barrel of beer from 51.4kWh in 2007 to 46.3kWh in 2008.

East Green is Adnams' first carbon-neutral beer. In addition to production savings, Adnams also worked with its supplier to reduce bottle weight by a third, and has continued to use high-yield local crops to reduce pesticide use and transport of raw materials. In conjunction with the University of East Anglia CRed carbon reduction scheme and the Carbon Trust, Adnams reduced the carbon footprint of East Green by 25 percent and, by offsetting to the value of 0.004p per bottle, East Green beer was certified as carbon neutral to the distribution centre.

Table 9.6 East Green carbon emissions

	High emissions scenario pre-2006 gCO_2 eq per bottle	High emissions scenario post-2006 gCO_2 eq per bottle
Barley production	43g	43g
Malting process	19g	19g
Brewing process	81g	66g
Transport	39g	31g
Bottling process	66g	54g
Bottle Manufacture	334g	219g
TOTAL	583g	432g
tC_e	$159gC_e$	$118gC_e$

Source: Adapted from Adnams, 2008

The offsetting is carried out by Climate Care, which has been involved in emissions reduction projects since 1998. Not all Adnams products are carbon neutral though; some such as Adnams Bitter, Broadside and Explorer have a lower than average carbon footprint due to the savings made in the production of the bottle, the use of local raw materials and energy-efficient brewing processes.

Completing the circle

The end of 2010 has seen Adnams close the circle by inaugurating an anaerobic digestion plant at the same site as its distribution centre to produce biogas from brewing by-products and local food waste. By using waste from the brewery and food waste collected locally to generate biomethane, the plant will prevent the release of methane to the atmosphere, eventually saving 50,000 tonnes of CO_2 equivalents from landfill.

In partnership with British Gas and with support from the Royal Bank of Scotland and grants from the European Regional Development Fund, East of England Development Agency and the

Department of Energy and Climate Change, the facility has started injecting renewable gas into the grid, generating up to 4.8M kilowatt hours a year – enough to heat 235 family homes for a year.

This industrial ecology project combines three anaerobic digesters for the production of bio-methane, together with solar thermal panels permitting Adnams to produce its own renewable energy supply for its facilities and run its delivery lorries, while still leaving around 60 percent of its gas output to be sold back to the national grid. Just converting its distribution lorries to run on gas will reduce Adnams' carbon footprint by 26 percent. Using its own waste to produce energy part-way completes Adnams' cradle-to-cradle, closed-loop approach. The final touch comes from the production of the biomethane itself as one of the by-products of the process is a liquid organic fertiliser, to be given back to the farmers who grow the grain to make the beer. Nothing is wasted, not even the waste.

More to digest

Anaerobic digestion seems to be the ideal partner for the alcohol distilling sector and the practice seems likely to expand. Bruichladdich Distillery on the Scottish island of Islay hopes to solve several sustainability problems in one go by installing a new type of anaerobic digester. The technical solution in this case has been provided by Northamptonshire firm Biowayste. Until recently, AD plants were only available on an industrial scale, but a new generation of affordable compact bio-digesters are practical and viable for small companies to install and operate on site.

Islay distilleries have been required to transport their industrial wastewater to a pumping station on the island where it is piped out to sea, paying for the privilege of dumping 800,000 litres of pot-ale waste water each year, a by-product of the distillation process. But the liquid is far from being ordinary waste; its yeast content makes it ideal for anaerobic digestion. The only by-product would be pure water, which could be used to clean the production units, or added to the whisky for dilution to commercial strength. The plant is expected to generate 80 percent of the distillery's electricity, with the remaining 20 percent sourced from the often unreliable mains supply from the Scottish mainland. The system will reduce the company's reliance on diesel backup generators and when a second unit is installed surplus energy produced will be sold back to the grid.[29]

Follow up

1. Alongside its extensive range of beers, Adnams recently added three more riverside pubs to its pub portfolio. Adnams also has three hotels and the Adnams Cellar and Kitchen Stores offer a range of quality wines, stylish kitchen utensils and gifts.

2. Anaerobic digestion has allowed Adnams to reduce the throughput of resources shifting from a linear to a circular strategy so that inputs of virgin raw material and energy and outputs in the form of waste requiring disposal decline. The supermarket sector is also investigating the potential of using anaerobic digestion. Investigate how the supermarket sector is developing these opportunities.

3. Review the other business interests of Adnams and assess the extent to which they also follow the company's sustainability values.

Dilemma part 2:   Good for business, bad for you

There are various design strategies that may contribute to product durability and longevity based on design for:

- reliability and robustness
- repair and maintenance
- upgradeability
- product attachment
- variability.

Most of the reasons point to the technical features of the product and its ability to maintain its optimum performance over time. Yet despite the efforts of business to design for longevity, increased product durability will not improve sustainability if the attribute is not valued by the consumer. Many products are thrown away when they are still in full working order and, although many may be purchased for reuse through charity shops and second-hand markets, it still means that the donors of the goods will be going on to consume more new products. The reasons for this aspect of consumer behaviour are understandable. The product may appear old-fashioned after a long period of time, may no longer be compatible with other products or be overtaken by new products that offer more features and benefits, increasing consumption which is good for business but not so good for achieving sustainability.

So is product durability bad for the consumer? Is it incompatible with the psychology and behaviour of the consumer?

One solution to increase consumer acceptance of product durability could be to design them in such a way as to induce product attachment. Product attachment refers to the level of emotional attachment the consumer has with the durable product and the strength of the bond of that relationship. One possible strategy to slow down product lifecycles is by increasing the attachment people experience towards the products they use and own. If the strength of consumer-product attachment is high, the product is likely to be handled and used more carefully, repaired when it breaks down and its replacement postponed as long as possible.

Devise the strategy

Choose any durable product category and assess the length of its lifecycle. Consider the reasons why consumers dispose of the products even when they still function properly. Devise a five-point plan to lengthen the product lifecycle by increasing the attachment a consumer could feel towards the product. Present your findings to the rest of the group.

References

1. Caroline Lucas (2010) *Now is the Time to Invest in a Green Economy*, Interview for Green Futures, part of the Guardian Environment Network, 26 July, www.forumforthefuture. org/greenfutures/articles/interview_caroline_lucas and http://www.guardian. co.uk/environment/interactive/2010/jul/26/green- economy-caroline-lucas

2. Kollmuss, A. and Agyeman, J. (2002) 'Mind the Gap: Why Do People Act Environmentally and What Are the Barriers to Pro-environmental Behaviour?', *Environmental Education Research* 8(3): 239–260.

3. Sustainable Development Commission (SDC) (2006) *I Will if You Will*, London: Sustainable Consumption Roundtable National Consumer Council (NCC) and the Sustainable Development Commission (SDC) (p. 7).

4. Rogers, S. (2010) *Bill Gates has 10,000 Times the Carbon Footprint of an Average American*, http://earthfirst.com/bill-gates-has-10000-times-the-carbon-footprint-of-an-average-american/

5. Casey, S. (2010) 'Over-supply Threatens High-welfare Egg Market', *Farmer's Weekly Interactive*, 30 April, www.fwi.co.uk/Articles/2010/04/30/121051/Over-supply-threatens-high-welfare-egg-market.htm

6. Booth, R. (2009) 'Free Range Cracks the Egg Market', *The Guardian*, 15 May.

7. O'Donoghue, T. and Rabin, M. (1999) 'Doing it Now or Later', *The American Economic Review* 89(1): 103–124.

8. Cialdini, R.B. (2007) *Influence: The Psychology of Persuasion*, New York: HarperBusiness.

9. Carillion (2005) *Making Personal Sustainability Pledges*, www.carillionplc.com/sustain_2005/assets/documents/2005pecent20casepecent20recordspecent20inpecent20PDF/CR_2005_Roads_pledges_warickshire_sustwk.pdf

10. Rowland, D. (2010) *Towards Pro-environmental Behaviour Change: Defra's Framework Approach*, Sustainable Behaviours Unit, London: Defra.

11. WRAP (2009) *Household Food and Drink Waste in the UK*, London: WRAP.

12. Webster, B. (2009) 'Buy One Now, Get One Later as Tesco Joins the Fight to Cut Food Waste', *The Times*, 17 October.

13. *Daily Mail* (2009) 'Sainsbury's Launches First "Buy One Now, Get One Later" Campaign to Cut Down on Waste *Daily Mail'*, 19 November.

14. Waste and Resources Action Programme (WRAP) *Love Food Hate Waste*, www.lovefoodhatewaste.com/

15. Nigel Slater *Simple Suppers* http://www.nigelslaterssimplesuppers.com/ and http://www.bbc.co.uk/programmes/b00mql0v

16. HM Government (2005) *Securing the Future: Delivering UK Sustainable Development Strategy*, www.defra.gov.uk/sustainable/government

17. Sustainable Development Commission (2010) *House of Lords Science and Technology Select Committee Call for Evidence: Behaviour Change Submission*, London: SDC.

18. HM Government (2005) *Securing the Future: Delivering UK Sustainable Development Strategy*, www.defra.gov.uk/sustainable/government

19. HM Government (2005) *Securing the Future: Delivering UK Sustainable Development Strategy*, http://www.defra.gov.uk/sustainable/government (8 November 2008).

20. Department for Environment, Food and Rural Affairs (Defra) (2008) *A Framework for Pro-environmental Behaviours – Report*, London: Defra.

21. Thaler, R. and Sunstein, C. (2008) *Nudge: Improving Decisions about Health, Wealth and Happiness*, New Haven, CT Yale University Press.

22. Dolan, P., Hallsworth, M., Halpern, D., King, D. and Vlaev, I. (2010) *MINDSPACE: Influencing Behaviour Through Public Policy*, Institute for Government, www.instituteforgovernment.org.uk.

23. Dolan, P., Hallsworth, M., Halpern, D., King, D. and Vlaev, I. (2010) *MINDSPACE: Influencing Behaviour Through Public Policy* Institute for Government, www.instituteforgovernment.org.uk

24. Dolan, P., Hallsworth, M., Halpern, D., King, D. and Vlaev, I. (2010) *MINDSPACE: Influencing Behaviour Through Public Policy*, Institute for Government, www.instituteforgovernment.org.uk

25. Department for Environment, Food and Rural Affairs (Defra) (2008) *A Framework for Pro-environmental Behaviours – Annex E*, London: Defra.

26. The University of Winchester (2010) www.winchester.ac.uk/studyhere/Pages/MScpecent20Sustainablepecent20Development.aspx

27. Department of Energy and Climate Change (DECC) (2010) *CRC Energy Efficiency Scheme: What is the CRC Energy Efficiency Scheme?*, www.decc.gov.uk/en/content/cms/what_we_do/lc_uk/crc/crc.aspx

28. Corus (2009) *Adnams Brewery Distribution Centre: Corus Panels and Profiles Structural Case Study*, Corus, Panels and Profiles (p. 2).

29. Corus (2009) *Adnams Brewery Distribution Centre: Corus Panels and Profiles Structural Case Study*, Corus Panels and Profiles; Rainharvesting Systems (2007) *Case Study: Adnams Distribution Centre, Suffolk*, Rainharvesting Systems Ltd; Lime Technology (2009) *Case Study: Adnams Brewery*, Lime Technology Ltd; Resource Efficiency East (2009) *Improving Your Resource Efficiency in Adnams, Suffolk*, www.businesslink.gov.uk/east/resource; *Sustainable Business Magazine* (2010) *Putting the AD into Adnams*, www.sustainablebusinessonline.com/news/news.asp?id=97&title=Putting+the+AD+into+Adnams; Suffolk County Council (2010) Adnams Distribution Centre, www.greensuffolk.org/case_studies/business_case_studies/adnams_distribution_centre; Adnams (2008) *East Green – the First Carbon Neutral Beer From the Coast*, http://adnams.co.uk/news/environment/east-green-pecente2pecent80pecent93-the-first-carbon-neutral-beer-from-the-coast; Rowe, D. (2010) *Biowaste Plant for Greener Scotch*, Green Futures 11 May, www.forumforthefuture.org/greenfutures/articles/biowaste_plant_greener_scotch.

10 The future for sustainability:
Raising the game, changing the game

When the cost of an activity outweighs the benefit, we should stop.[1]

Herman Daly – Professor of Ecological Economics at the University of Maryland

Chapter objectives

After studying this chapter you should be able to:

1 Understand the key issues that drive the sustainability agenda.

2 Reflect on the challenges of the future in the light of current sustainable practice.

3 Explore your own attitudes towards sustainability and your own sustainable behaviour.

Dilemma part 1:   Nine billion sustainable lifestyles

Hypothesising about future lifestyles is fraught with difficulty, and much of the sustainability debate may seem to be based on an unsteady mixture of certainties and uncertainties. True focused debate on how sustainable lifestyles may be achieved in the future and what form they may take is often stifled. Consumers do not want to talk about it because they feel it might restrict rather than enhance their lifestyles. Governments are divided in their strategies and political expediency often gets in the way of concerted national and international action, as with the recent climate change agreements. The business response has often been quick when adopting money-saving sustainability strategies but somewhat slower on encouraging lifestyle change considering their position of influence in society.

If we imagine what modern sustainable lifestyles we might have achieved by 2050 what would they be like? What would be the most significant differences between then and now?

The SDC has proposed its own scenario for 2050, with a population of 9 billion people following a one-planet living lifestyle. Its proposal highlights ten key differences between the lives we lead now and the lifestyle of society in 2050.[2] According to the scenario someone from 2050 would describe these differences in the following way:

1. I manage my own self-esteem and health.
2. I live within my financial limits.
3. The products I buy help local and international trade.
4. I only use clean and renewable energy.
5. I am active in a vibrant community.
6. I live in a high-trust society in which I talk with, rather than at, people.
7. I have found the right balance between technology and simplicity.
8. My political and business leaders have courage.
9. The true value of nature is protected by economics.
10. I use much less stuff, but get the same level of service from the stuff I buy and use.

Discuss the following:

1. To what extent do you agree with these principles? Are they viable future principles? Can they be applied to the total population of the world in the future?

Raising the game, changing the game

> The acquisition of wealth is no longer the driving force in our lives, we work to better ourselves and the rest of humanity.[3]   (Jean-Luc Picard, Captain of the Starship Enterprise)

The quotation above refers to a scene in the film *Star Trek: First Contact* in which Captain Jean-Luc Picard has travelled back in time to a period of Earth history before space travel was commonplace. When he takes one of the inhabitants of

Earth of that time period, Lily Sloane, back to the Starship Enterprise, she asks him how much his spaceship of the future cost. To her surprise he explains that money does not exist in the 24th century and that human activity is centred on improving the quality of life for all instead of continuous economic growth.

It appears that human development of the fictional future is focused on *being* more rather than *having* more, and points to a significant change in the motivations of humanity. Far from being a Hollywood-inspired utopian vision of society, such a distinction was first proposed by psychoanalyst and social theorist Erich Fromm in 1976 in his last major work *To Have or To Be?*[4] Fromm argued that these two modes of existence – *having* based on the accumulation of material possessions through greed, in contrast to *being*, based on love – the improvement of self and of others through shared experience and productive activities were in direct competition with each other. Fromm suggested that to continue on the *having* path would eventually cause the social, economic and psychological failure of society.

Reliance on a conventional world economy based on growth has not provided for quality of life and happiness for everyone; it has only motivated continued consumption. Achieving a solution that balances people, planet and profit will take time and more radical change than many people imagine. On reflection, perhaps profit is an inappropriate word in the light of Fromm's ideas, despite it being the third member of the Triple Bottom Line it still smacks of *having* more. Replacing profit with the term prosperity might be more appropriate as it would not only apply to economic prosperity but also to improving individuals' quality of life in other ways . . . to *being* more.

In order to develop and progress sustainably, the mechanisms of government, business and society will need to be different and we will have to significantly improve how we do things – raising our game by doing things better, as well as changing our game by doing things differently.

This chapter revisits a number of the themes from earlier sections of the text in order to appreciate them from a more knowledgeable perspective. It looks at the present but looks to the future for sustainability at the same time. The decade to come is a make or break decade for sustainable development and it is fitting that this chapter takes stock of some of the key issues, and looks to how much progress has already been made and the changes required for the future.

First the chapter explores issues from the last decade; in particular it revisits the contentious issue of economic growth which lies behind sustainable development and looks at what progress has been made towards sustainability for all. The second part of the chapter looks forward to the next decade, the make or break decade that will drive sustainability forward if the right decisions are made and the right actions taken. This chapter explores some of the more positive moves towards sustainability and indicates that there are many examples of initiatives that will contribute to improvements in society. Other issues mentioned are quality of life, happiness and wellbeing as they move up the political agenda as a means of encouraging more sustainable and fulfilling lifestyles. The chapter also challenges the reader to explore his/her own attitudes towards sustainability now he/she has come to the end of the text and asks how he/she might adopt a more sustainable lifestyle and pursue a career in sustainability.

Not nice at all

As the world struggles out of a growth-induced recession, it should seem obvious to everyone that an economy based solely on continuous economic growth is not sustainable economically, socially or environmentally. Yet the first decade of the 21st century has also been referred to as the 'nice' decade, despite the numerous unsustainable effects it created and its culmination in recession.

Non-Inflationary Constant Expansion (NICE) was a term coined by the governor of the Bank of England Mervyn King to describe the ten years of growth until 2008.[5]

The much desired goal of growth without negative consequences appeared to have been achieved, with increasing demand being opportunely met by cheap increasing supply neutralising the threat of inflation from higher prices. However, the negative consequences of growth were only momentarily masked, as can be seen in Figure 10.1. Growth under those conditions has been flawed and the issues of sustainability have been placed in the spotlight for all to see.

The catalogue of failures makes for a long list. Developed and emerging markets combined to demand more than could be supplied; consumer access to cheap credit surpassed their capacity to repay the debt; the banking industry took increasingly risk-filled investments in financial markets and were unable to recoup their inevitable losses on unwise bets; price increases accompanied the rise in demand and commodities (such as oil and food). As the bubble burst the chain reaction caught up with all of the stakeholders involved and caused the world recession in 2008 from which we have not quite recovered.

But the collapse of 2008 has also allowed for a pause, a moment of reflection to understand the nature and challenges of becoming a sustainable society. So the recession-filled last years of the first decade of the new millennium have seen the sustainability debate intensify, particularly the challenge to ensure prosperity without incurring unsustainable growth.

Future growth: novelty or necessity?

Despite the need to make sustainable development the norm, the recession has indicated that there are many countries that are not performing within sustainable parameters. In simple terms they have grown too much, too quickly and they no longer fit into a resource-constrained, sustainable world where one size must fit all. It is clear that finding a solution to growth is essential; growth has to be made compatible with sustainable development.

In finding a means of achieving sustainable development it is necessary to separate the perfect couple that is made up of business and the consumer. Business and the consumer make the perfect couple because of their matching motivations. Business is motivated to make a profit through growth and achieves this through its continual search for and production of newer, better, cheaper, more exciting products; that is, business engages in the production of novelty. Meanwhile, the consumer's restless desire for quality of life, status,

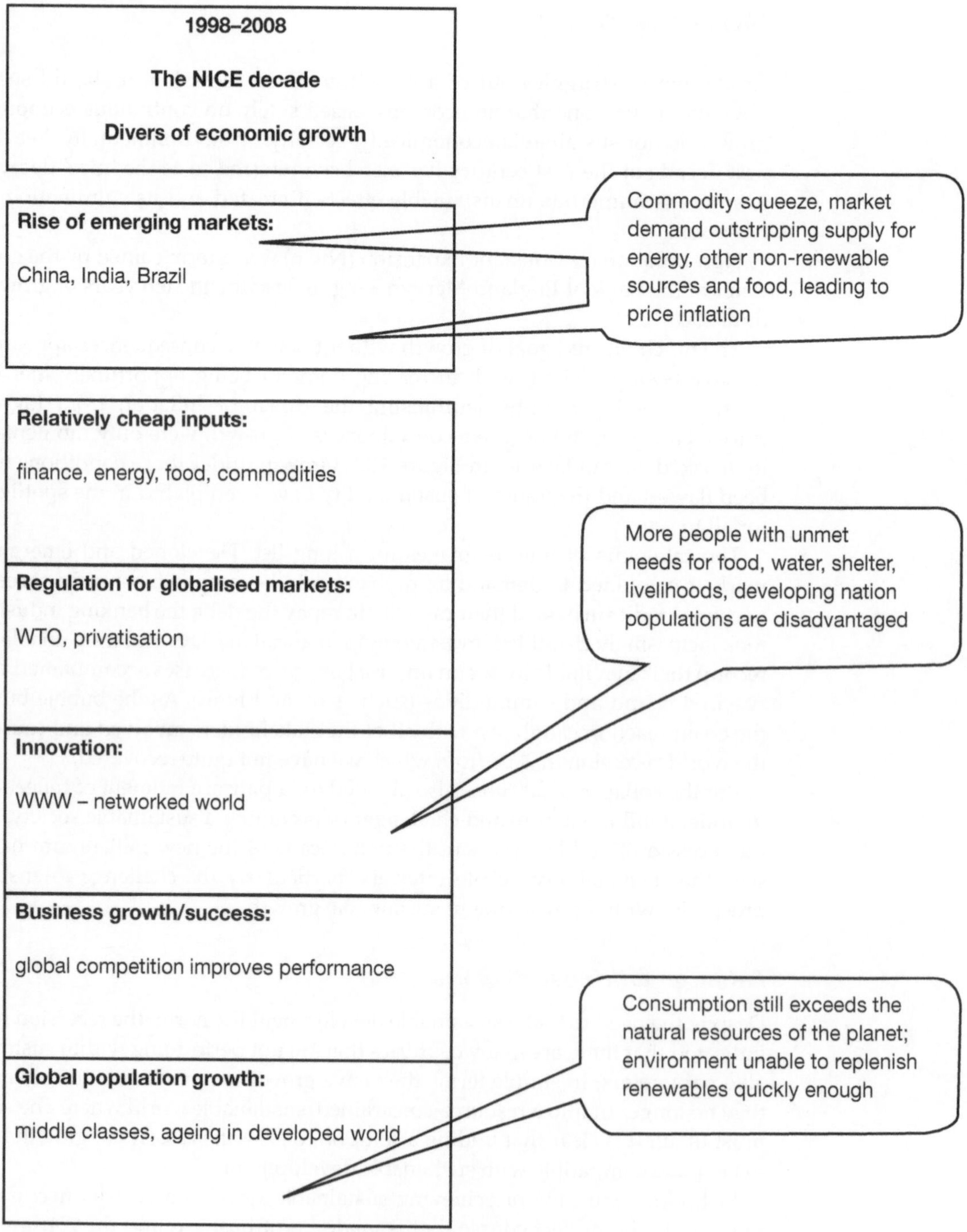

Figure 10.1   Consequences of globalised growth

Source: Adapted from Forum for the Future and Capgemini[6]

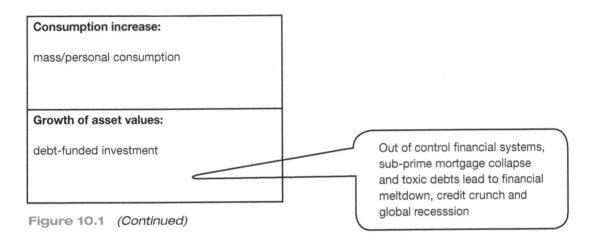

Figure 10.1   *(Continued)*

identity, social affiliation and aspiration to acquire material goods and services results in continual consumption; the consumer seeks to satisfy his/her desires for novelty through consumption.[7]

Thus, the production and purchase of novelty make business and consumers perfect partners and drive growth in a circle that is not broken as long as business can continue to produce novelty at the right level and price, as long as the consumer is still willing and able to purchase novelty, and as long as substitutes for both of the parties involved are not found.

A possible steady future

In Chapter 2 it was suggested that one possible solution to the growth dilemma was the setting up of the steady-state economy. Its main proponent Herman Daly, once a senior economist of the World Bank and one of the founders of the field of ecological economics, proposed that the way to avoid an economic and environmental collapse would be to switch the focus from quantitative growth to qualitative development.

De-growth is a term used to described the planned reduction of economic output. A possible solution to reconciling the problem of sustainable growth may be to follow a system of both growth and de-growth. The consuming public should be weaned off growing for novelty and encouraged only to grow for necessity. A slowing of growth in the developed countries responsible for over-consumption could be balanced by an increase in growth in underdeveloped nations where social and economic equality has not been achieved.

Sustainable growth: decoupling

One of the suggested means for achieving greater sustainability is decoupling. Decoupling environmental pressures from economic growth is one of the main objectives of the Organisation for Economic Co-operation and

Development (OECD) Environmental Strategy for the First Decade of the 21st century, adopted by OECD Environment Ministers in 2001. The OECD describes the term *decoupling* as breaking the link between *environmental bads* and *economic goods*.[8] Decoupling is therefore a means of reconciling economic and environmental objectives, by decoupling economic growth and environmental impact.

Relative decoupling

In short, decoupling is about driving efficiency without the footprints. Relative decoupling is about doing more with less: more economic activity with less environmental damage; more goods and services with fewer resource inputs and emissions.

Relative decoupling refers to a situation where resource impacts decline relative to the GDP. Impacts may still rise, but they do so more slowly than the GDP. Evidence of this type of decoupling is easy to identify, although its overall contribution to sustainability remains inconclusive.

For example, while the energy required to produce a unit of economic activity has declined by a third over the last 30 years, this saving through resource productivity is cancelled out by increases in the amount produced over the same period of time.[9] OECD countries, in particular, have seen a significant reduction in the use of energy, which has been reduced by 40 percent in the US and UK since 1980. However, country statistics on decoupling have proved unreliable as they often do not take into account resource use and waste from importing finished and semi-finished products from abroad.[10] In this way, countries are effectively exporting their ecological footprint to developing countries while enjoying the benefits of a reduced domestic footprint.

Absolute decoupling

When resource impacts decline in absolute terms, while the economy is growing, it is referred to as absolute decoupling. While resource efficiencies must increase at least as fast as economic output does in order to move towards sustainable growth, it is clear that achieving absolute decoupling is not straightforward.

Evidence suggests that absolute decoupling is not taking place and is unlikely to occur while demand for goods from developed countries goes unabated. This is compounded by the desires of the emerging economies to reach the same level of development as the most advanced countries of the planet, increasing the demand for commodities such as iron ore, bauxite and cement in order to invest in their physical infrastructures.

The forecast of the world ecological footprint from the Global Footprint Network (www.footprintnetwork.org) in Figure 10.2 shows that even moderate *business as usual* does not reduce the global overshoot, and only a significant and timely reduction in consumption will have any beneficial effect on the environment. A report from the Chartered Institute of Purchase and Supply (CIPS) makes for depressing reading. It highlights that the availability of critical elements and metals used for many key products and technology applications is already severely limited with consumption at present rates and if

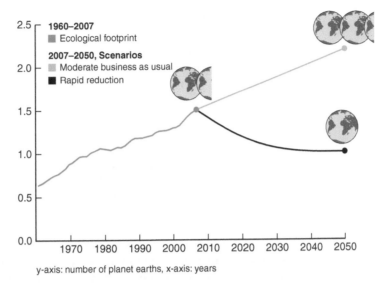

y-axis: number of planet earths, x-axis: years

Figure 10.2 World ecological footprint

Source: Global Footprint Network, 2010

consumption increases to 50 percent of US rates then some natural resources have less than a decade remaining.[11] This kind of data suggests that absolute decoupling is a myth.

Decoupling theory and the extent to which it is used to produce greater sustainability can lead to the creation of a whole set of new problems. These problems have been referred to as wicked problems.[12] Wicked problems arise because there is a lack of willingness to compromise or change, so the solutions to wicked problems are clumsy and as a result tend to perpetuate old unsustainable practice with even more negative consequences.

For example, growing corn to produce plastics and biofuel as a substitute for oil-based products has raised food prices by diverting corn from the food chain, creating a significant ecological footprint associated with the production of these corn-based substitutes. The rapid investment in carbon capture and storage technology encourages the continuing burning of finite fossil fuels to produce electrical energy, when the money would be better invested in zero carbon renewable energy sources instead of looking for ways to keep the old systems running. It makes little sense to initiate a policy of reducing waste to landfill while encouraging a policy of dumping carbon waste underground, particularly when there is no guarantee the carbon dioxide will stay underground and, like landfill, the space will eventually run out.

Historically, the mistake has been to ignore the link between economic activity and the environment and society. This was an error that now cannot be undone by conventional thinking determined to maintain unsustainable systems. Data from the United Nations Environment Programme (UNEP) indicates that from 1981 to 2005 the global economy more than doubled, but at a cost of the degradation or over-use of 60 percent of the world's ecosystems.[13] The truth is that there is as yet no credible, socially just, ecologically sustainable scenario of continually growing incomes for a world whose population is due to increase to 9 billion people.

According to Michael Braungart, Chemist and Co-Founder of McDonough Braungart Design Chemistry and proponent of cradle-to-cradle product design, thinks that while we focus on strategies designed to minimise impacts and decouple impacts from growth we are following the wrong path. He stated:

> We should not be aiming to 'minimise' or be 'low-carbon', this is not enough for the amount of people on the planet – we should aim to be beneficial to our environment, not simply minimise our impact. We should be like trees and give back as well as take from our surroundings; we should clean the air, not aim to reduce how much we pollute it. We need innovation that brings about products and services that are good, not less bad.[14]

From another perspective, it is possible to say that, in order to conserve natural resources and reduce environmental and social impacts of growth-related consumption, what needs to be decoupled is improvement in people's quality of life and their overall level of life satisfaction from increases in consumption.

This kind of decoupling requires that we should do things differently in order to achieve a greater level of sustainability; we need to change the rules of the game.

Snapshot: *Ferraris For All*

Ferraris For All: In Defence of Economic Progress is the full title of a book by Daniel Ben-Ami, in which the author advocates increased growth to overcome the challenges faced by humanity.[15] To use his words: 'The conventional green-tinged view is that we need to limit economic growth to stop us destroying the planet. . . . Such an approach could not be more wrong.'[16] His opinion is that growth can continue to deliver real progress and its much reported environmental, social and economic ills present a narrow view of economic progress. Ben-Ami proposes that the problems of development should be solved by more growth, more resources and better technology such as building higher sea walls to prevent flooding.

The reaction to the text from Jonathon Porritt, founder director of Forum for the Future, was not unexpected.[17] He describes Ben-Ami's vision of the world as surreal and points out that he fails to deal properly with the issue of climate change, finite natural resources, the damage to the planet's biodiversity or soil depletion. Porritt's criticism of Ben-Ami underlines that *Ferraris For All* sees humanity at its peak with the ability to control nature. Proposing to build walls to prevent flooding of low-lying coastal areas is an attempt to deal with the consequences of environmental degradation but fails to address the causes.

Make or break

John Elkington, exponent of the Triple Bottom Line and founder of SustainAbility, the consultancy agency, has commented that the decade ahead, 2010–2020, is the make or break decade for sustainability. In an interview for Sky Business News, Elkington points out that the impact of the global financial crisis has changed the way companies are approaching sustainability and that while progress is being made the largest transformative changes are yet to come over the next decade.[18]

The next section looks at the kinds of developments we are likely to see in the future at this critical stage in our progress towards more sustainable development. As plans to move sustainability initiatives forward begin to take effect, we will see more governments establishing and achieving more ambitious targets in key areas such as energy and transport. Technological advances will continue to help improvements in energy consumption and resource efficiency. The next decade is also likely to be marked by attempts and initiatives aimed at changing consumer lifestyles in order to reign in unsustainable consumption in favour of quality of life and wellbeing.

Over the next decade

Sustainable development involves multiple and complex issues that will need to be addressed in the future by governments in their policies, businesses in their practices and consumers in their choices.

The United Nations Commission of Sustainable Development (CSD) stated that future sustainable development would be focused on what was referred to as the 3D vision of the future: demographic, development, and de-coupling.[19]

These 3Ds of sustainability refer to a stable, non-growing population, a high level of human development for all people and all countries, and a complete de-coupling of economic growth from materials use.

The United Nations CSD points to several indicators of change at an international level. For example:

- In 2009, OECD countries adopted a Declaration on Green Growth, tasking the OECD with developing a Green Growth Strategy bringing together economic, environmental, technological, financial and development aspects into a comprehensive framework.

- The proportion of Denmark's energy consumption from renewable energy is expected to be 30 percent by 2030. In the course of the past 30 years Denmark's wind energy sector has increased and now delivers the bulk of renewable energy in the country. There are around 5,200 wind turbines in Denmark, a country of just 5 million people.

Some countries have ambitious energy efficiency and renewable energy targets:

- New Zealand has a renewable energy target of 90 percent by 2025.

- Mexico aims to reach a 26 percent renewable energy target by 2012 and a halving of carbon by 2050.

- Several countries have pledged carbon neutrality – the Maldives by 2020, Costa Rica by 2021, Norway by 2030 and Sweden by 2050.

- California (led by its 38th state governor Arnold Schwarzenegger, a pioneer in sustainable policymaking) has a target of 33 percent renewable energy and reduction of 20 percent in per capita water use by 2020 as well as zero net energy use for all new residential buildings by 2020 and commercial buildings by 2030.

One-planet living

In the *One Planet Business Report* of 2007, produced in collaboration with sustainability consultancy SustainAbility, the World Wildlife Fund (WWF) set out its ten-point One Planet Living Initiative designed to make sustainable living easy, affordable and attractive.[20] The initiative itself is run in conjunction with BioRegional, an entrepreneurial charity whose aim is to promote and facilitate sustainable living solutions, and some of their initiatives have already been mentioned in Chapter 6.

As can be seen in Table 10.1, the One Planet Living Initiative provides a series of suggestions for improvements that can be made to achieve a more sustainable lifestyle for individuals and a more sustainable operation for businesses and organisations. Many of these initiatives are already contained in plans and projects from other organisations, both governmental, such as Defra, and non-governmental, such as Forum for the Future.

Table 10.1   One Planet Living Initiative

Zero carbon	Making buildings more energy efficient and delivering all energy with renewable technologies
Zero waste	Reducing waste, reusing where possible, and ultimately sending zero waste to landfill
Sustainable transport	Encouraging low-carbon modes of transport to reduce emissions, reducing the need to travel
Local and sustainable materials	Using sustainable healthy products, with low-embodied energy, sourced locally, made from renewable or waste resources
Local and sustainable food	Choosing low-impact, local, seasonal and organic diets and reducing food waste
Sustainable water	Using water more efficiently in buildings and in the products we buy; tackling local flooding and water course pollution
Natural habitats and wildlife	Protecting and restoring biodiversity and natural habitats through appropriate land use and integration into the built environment
Culture and heritage	Reviving local identity and wisdom; supporting and participating in the arts
Equity and fair trade	Creating bioregional economies that support fair employment, inclusive communities and international fair trade
Health and happiness	Encouraging active, sociable, meaningful lives to promote good health and wellbeing

Source: BioRegional and WWF

Researching sustainability: Where to from here?

Progress against One Planet Living targets is being made, although there is still much to be done. No one single initiative over the next decade is liable to tip the balance definitively in favour of sustainable development but their cumulative effect may well be enough to balance the scales.

1. Many of the One Planet Living aspects have already been mentioned earlier in the text but can you bring them up to date?

2. What can you find out about any initiatives that would contribute to the ten different aspects of One Planet Living, either taking place in 2011–2012 or planned for the more distant future? Find at least one example for each aspect. You might like to consider a variety of initiative types according to whether they are driven by government, local/regional government, business or NGOs or whether they are delivered in collaboration.

Getting started

Here is an example to inspire you.

Zero waste

Zero waste to landfill remains an ambitious and fragile One Planet Living objective. Gaps between total waste produced and waste still currently allowed to go to landfill need to be bridged by more and more recycling, recovery and composting schemes. In the UK, targets for the reduction of biodgradable waste to go to landfill indicate a 65 percent gap between the reduced amount that may be sent to landfill and the sum total produced of this type of waste. This means that 65 percent of biodegradable waste will have to be recovered and diverted from landfill by the year 2020 to meet established EU targets.[21]

WRAP continues to drive food waste reduction through favouring prevention at source rather than just diversion of waste away from landfill. As part of its World Without Waste programme (shown in Figure 10.3), WRAP is developing resource maps for different sectors to identify where waste occurs along thier supply chain. In February 2010 WRAP announced its intention to produce a resource map to calculate the amount of waste in the UK retail supply chain for pre-prepared food for the first time and to identify how this can be reduced in order for businesses to make cost and environmental savings.

Covering four representative products – sandwiches, pizza, quiche and ready meals – the research will develop detailed resource maps to highlight the amount of food and packaging waste generated for each product type at key stages in the chilled and frozen supply chains. It will also calculate the associated carbon emissions and economic impact, and detail the amount of water used and disposed of during the manufacture of the selected products. The research will also include data on individual ingredients as well as levels of packaging and food waste from households, so that a whole chain from component ingredients through to final

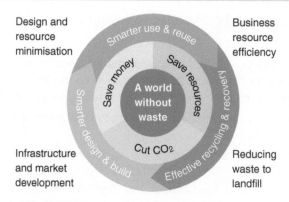

Figure 10.3 A world without waste

Source: WRAP, 2010[22]

consumer can be analysed and the most critical points where waste occurs be identified, so strategies to minimise it can be implemented. Meat, fish, fruit and vegetables are other food categories that will be covered by resource maps to be researched later in 2010 and published in 2011.[23]

Measures of success

One way of ensuring that progress is being made over the next decade is to measure change and compare and contrast data. If sustainable development initiatives are to be successful there needs to be a reliable measure of their impact, so that performance may be improved over time.

Tangible products can be compared for their sustainability performance by their carbon and water footprint labelling and by third-party accreditation. The evaluation of businesses and their products is not without difficulty despite measurements such as carbon and water footprinting. In order to clarify the situation for businesses and consumers, in May 2010 the consultancy group SustainAbility launched a new research programme entitled *Rate the Raters* through which it intends to better understand the means and use of corporate sustainability ratings and to influence and improve the quality and transparency of such ratings. The work is due to be completed during 2011. The complexity of the task is underlined by the rapid increase in sustainability measuring and rating mechanisms. Of the 108 rating mechanisms in the inventory to be carried out by SustainAbility, only 21 of those existed ten years earlier in the year 2000.[24]

Different measures are needed to allow for comparison between countries and their inhabitants, between past and present trends and for projections of the future. GDP has provided the benchmark for evaluating and comparing the economic growth of countries for some 80 years but does not give a clear indication of sustainable growth. In order to get a better picture of the state of sustainable development, other indicators need to be included.

The most widely used indicator for development is the UNDP Human Development Index (HDI), which combines income, life expectancy and educational attainment to compare the social and economic development of different countries. The UN defines the threshold for a high level of development as an HDI value of 0.8 and statistics for the UK in 2010 put the HDI index at 0.849 in comparison with a world average of 0.624.[25]

However, ecological footprinting also provides vital insights and UNDP statistics indicate that as development increases beyond a certain level, so does the ecological footprint per person, to such an extent that a small increase in HDI can result in a very large increase in ecological footprint. Also noticeable is the breakdown in connection between wealth and wellbeing above a certain level of GDP per capita, suggesting that a high level of consumption is not necessarily required for a high level of development or wellbeing.[26]

Looking back at the two key parts of the definition of sustainable development given in Chapter 1 – 'meeting the needs of the present' and 'without compromising the ability of future generations to meet their own needs' – it is possible to establish a standard international measure of success for both of these criteria.

An HDI of 0.8 sets the lower limit for meeting the needs of the present, while an ecological footprint of less than 1.8 global hectares (gha) per person sets an upper limit for living within the Earth's ecological capacity in order not to compromise future generations. In 2007 only one country, Peru, matched both of these criteria with an HDI score of 0.806 and an ecological footprint of just over 1.5gha per person.[27]

The New Economics Foundation released its latest version of its Happy Planet Index in 2009. The index, often referred to as HPI 2.0, has been calculated with new improved data sets for 143 countries. Each country is scored from 0 to 100 by the degree to which they meet three targets embodied in the index, which are high life expectancy, high life satisfaction and a low ecological footprint. Countries achieving all three targets will obtain a higher HPI score.[28]

Costa Rica boasts the highest HPI score of 76.1 out of 100. As well as reporting the highest life satisfaction in the world, Costa Ricans also have the second-highest average life expectancy of North and South America, scoring second only to Canada for life expectancy. However, with a footprint of 2.3 global hectares they are slightly over the criteria for one-planet living in terms of their use of natural resources.

The highest-placed EU country is the Netherlands, which comes 43rd out of 143 nations. People in the Netherlands live, on average, over a year longer than people in the US, and have similar levels of life satisfaction, but their per capita ecological footprint is less than half the size of the US at 4.4gha in comparison with 9.4gha, making them over twice as ecologically efficient at achieving good lives.

Apply it: How do we measure up now?

Look for HDI, HPI and ecological footprint data for 2010. Compare and contrast a selection of countries from the developed, emerging and less developed economies against the minimum criteria. How do they perform? Which countries are closest to meeting the criteria for sustainable development and which have the most improvement to make?

An innovative sustainable future

Jonathon Porritt, founder director of sustainable development organisation Forum for the Future and one of the judges of the Design Directions awards from the Royal Society for the encouragement of Arts, Manufactures and Commerce (RSA), underlined the importance of innovative design for future sustainability. He stated: 'Design and innovation have a vital role to play in creating a low-carbon future. We need designers who can imagine how our world will change and create sustainable products and services which bring environmental and social benefits.'[29]

Innovation is no longer about creating new material wants. Innovative designers are looking for solutions to sustainability issues and creating imaginative and attractive ways to live more sustainably and acquire a lifestyle that is desirable and aspirational, without the sacrifice that is often associated with giving up the material for the sustainable. The focus on successful design for sustainability should be on people and how they use the products, on their usage and behaviour, not solely on the product itself as the intention is to modify behaviour and not just create a new or substitute product for the sake of it. Following are some examples which show that small inventions can be just as effective as the larger developments such as wind farms and biogas generators.

E-on offers its customers a hand-held monitor to help them manage their household energy consumption (see photo). However, no matter how simple, devices to inform consumers about their energy usage can be too technical, too number-driven and difficult to understand and interpret, just like the energy bills that accompany them. The hand-held gadgets themselves can be less than user-friendly and unattractive in design, relying on the motivation of the user to utilise them efficiently and consistently.

Digital Growth is the brainchild of graphic designer Joe Harrison (www.joeharrison.co.uk), who combines digital knowhow and technology, visual communication simplicity and a desire to nurture living things into a highly imaginative and decorative means of monitoring energy behaviour and consumption on the home, and aiding people to modify their energy consumption behaviour.

Digital Growth was runner-up in the Design Directions Awards from the RSA for sustainable designs aimed at encouraging people to live sustainable and environmentally friendly lifestyles.

Source: Courtesy of E-on[30]

The focus of Digital Growth is the plant that grows and develops on a wall of the household as a piece of electronic wallpaper. The growth rate, colour and shape of the leaves of the plant are directly linked to the efficiency and lifestyle of its residents. Digital Growth works by taking data using wireless communications from different appliances; it converts these data into a visual format on a section of electronic wallpaper. Water and electricity usage, and the efficiency of particular appliances, affect how the plant will look. Each leaf represents a different appliance; its stems represent water, gas and electricity.

Source: www.joeharrison.co.uk

Digital Growth copies patterns of plant growth and mimics how healthy or dying plants behave. Brown and drooping leaves indicate low efficiency; when they appear, the user can find out what is causing this using touch-screen technology in areas of the digital plant to get detailed pop-up information. The invention also allows people to experience plants from different locations and by tending the plant they are managing their energy needs more sustainably.

Another award-winning design from the same competition makes for the ideal partner of Digital Growth. A selection of light switches, called Flick my Switch, has been designed to encourage children to turn off lights and appliances. They are very varied in texture – some are wobbly ridged rubber, others sponge pyramids or bristles that tickle. When the switch is turned off, it mimics pleasant sounds such as pebbles plopping into a puddle, the hiss of a fizzy drink can opening or the popping of a champagne cork. Rather than forgetting to turn off appliances and lights you actually look forward to it. Conversely, switching things on again is not as rewarding, to reinforce the need to save energy not use it. In order to reactivate the switch the user has to wind a little handle for a whole minute before it reacts and kicks into action with a loud groan! With the slogan 'we're always touching things, but not being touched in return', Flick my Switch proposes to provide its users with energy-saving satisfaction. Rather than family arguments about who left everything turned on, the arguments are likely to be about who wants to turn them off.

Professional practice: Pitching to investors

First launched in Japan, the television programme *Dragons' Den* is now an international brand, with versions on television channels in countries all around the world. In the UK, *Dragons' Den* has completed its fifth series on BBC2 and gains a dedicated audience each year. In the programme entrepreneurs pitch for investment in their prospective business in the Den, where five Dragons (five venture capitalists) decide whether they are willing to invest their own money in exchange for a share of equity in the entrepreneur's new business.

Inventors are good at inventing but often do not have the marketing skills to take their invention to market and make a real business of their big idea. Prepare a five-minute pitch to potential investors in the style of Dragons' Den for either Digital Growth or Flick my Switch. Go to www. thersa.org/_data/assets/pdf_file/0020/204842/Design-Directions---sustainability-PN.pdf for more information to prepare your pitch.

Getting started

1. Go to the Dragons' Den website and watch and evaluate successful and unsuccessful pitches www.bbc.co.uk/dragonsden.

2. Plan the different sections of the pitch; keep it structured around all the vital information the Dragons will need to know to be able to decide whether it is worth investing in the invention.

3. What do you think the company will be worth? How much money do you think you will need to get the business off the ground? How much equity are you prepared to give away?

Gadgets, inventions, green and clean technology will no doubt help to improve the quality of our sustainable lifestyles over the coming decade, but what about quality of life itself? Re-evaluating what really contributes to a feeling of contentedness and quality of life is already on the political agenda and is increasingly being seen as a means to driving lifestyle change towards sustainability. Happiness and wellbeing are the new buzz words and are proposed as alternatives to materialism and over-consumption.

Alternative hedonism and routes to sustainable happiness

Kate Soper, a British philosopher, offers an alternative to the pursuit of consumption as a means to its own end in a search for materialistic happiness. She refers to this concept as alternative hedonism. She believes one of the main reasons why a change to more sustainable lifestyles has been impeded is that it was an error to portray sustainable development as lifestyles of restraint, sacrifice and lacking in satisfaction in comparison with conventional ones.[31] Sustainable development has too often been depicted as unattractive and likened to a return to the Stone Age, implying that sustainability will mean *less is less* rather than *less is more*.

Also, it has been suggested by exponents of alternate forms of pleasure and happiness that much of what is done towards sustainability at present actually perpetuates consumption. The array of labelling on ingredients, footprints, supply chains and recyclability seems to assuage the guilty consciences of consumers while at the same time reassuring and encouraging them to consume as often as they want.[32]

Alternative hedonism is meant to combat the ills of consumption, of stress, traffic congestion, overwork, pollution and exhaustion of resources by presenting a rationale for consuming differently.[33] In this way Soper suggests alternative hedonism can have a stronger appeal to consumers rather than a simple exhortation not to shop and a rage against the weekend exodus to the shopping centre. The roots of alternative hedonism are not in over-consumption *per se*, but in the ills we experience from over-consumption, the stress and the fatigue of consumption and the anxiety of having to work more, having less quality time, having to earn more and borrow more to maintain the cycle.[34]

Alternative hedonism is also meant to provide the more simple pleasures lost, forgotten or prevented by the current continuous cycle of work and consumption, with people working more and producing more in order to consume more. Soper's premise is based on the idea that even if consumerism were sustainable it would not enhance happiness beyond a point already reached.

The startling facts of our current relationship with work, production, growth and consumption have been highlighted by Juliet Schor, Professor of Sociology at Boston College. She pointed to the evidence that when comparing 1948 to 1991, productivity of US workers had more than doubled during that time. She went on to argue that if Americans had settled for the standard of living of 1948 in terms of marketed goods and services, every worker could work just four hours a day or even take every other year off with pay.[35]

Pursuing this kind of alternative lifestyle may be a result of altruistic or biospheric concerns for the social and environmental impacts of consumerist consumption. But it is also increasingly being seen as a reflection of consumer self-interest due to feeling discontent with the demands and negative effects of a work-growth-consumption lifestyle. Consumers are beginning to realise that due to their desire for the acquisition of material possessions, they are missing out on activities and lifestyle alternatives that would provide greater satisfaction, pleasure, quality time to pursue interests and relaxation and above all a better quality of life.

Wellbeing: the new watchword

The happiness and wellbeing of citizens is now explicitly on the political agenda. But this interest has been gaining momentum for some time within the political sphere and think tanks such as the New Economics Foundation have provided the fuel for political debate and the emergence of UK Prime Minister David Cameron's Big Society. The UK coalition government has already announced its intentions to measure the happiness of the country and define what makes us happy and unhappy, with the Office for National Statistics (ONS) charged to devise measures of progress by leading a debate called the National Wellbeing Project, which will seek to establish the key areas that matter most to people's wellbeing for a quality of life survey to start from April 2011.

Interest in wellbeing is not new. The concept has been debated by economists, politicians and social theorists for many years. More recently, wellbeing is seen as a means to help create a more sustainable society. A lifestyle based on the principles of wellbeing is more likely to avoid over-consumption and be more based on cooperation, collaboration, community spirit and solidarity – closer to *being* more than *having* more from the perspective of Fromm.

In general terms, the concept of wellbeing is comprised of two main elements: feeling good about oneself and functioning well. Feelings of happiness, contentment, enjoyment, curiosity and engagement are characteristic of people who have a positive experience of their lives. It is also important to function properly in the world. Experiencing positive relationships, having some control over one's life and having a sense of purpose are all essential attributes of wellbeing.[36]

Autonomy	Self-esteem		In control
Quality of life	Family	Fear of crime	Community
Feeling good	Feeling loved	Feeling safe	Feeling connected
Neighbourhood	Friends	Violence	Networks
Formal education	Education and skills		Skills and training
Comfort	Keeping fit	Employment	Recreation
Decent housing	Good health	Satisfying work	Having fun
Spirituality	Slow time		Virtue
Reflection			Work–life balance

Figure 10.4   The components of wellbeing

Source: Adapted from Porritt, 2007[37]

Wellbeing is a more profound concept than happiness; it is more inclusive and relies on a series of stakeholders working in collaboration. Figure 10.4 shows the complexity of the notion. The figure shows self-esteem and slow time as the key framing themes and indicates the importance of community, friendships, network and relationships as central to achieving a society which is more sustainable.

Summary

The decade 2000 to 2010 has been the most significant to date for the sustainability agenda. The NICE decade, built on unlimited growth, exposed the ills of economic growth that was not founded on sustainability and this helped to focus the attention of governments, business and society in general on the need to do things differently. The issue of growth is far from resolved. Its incompatibility with the sustainable agenda still presents significant challenges.

The sustainability agenda is wide and complex, and progress is being made on several fronts. Programmed improvements, targets and deadlines accumulate in the next decade and provide business with multiple opportunities to be profitable and sustainable at the same time, and opportunities for different types of employment in different industries.

Society may also be on the verge of change. Consumerist consumption may be overtaken by more sustainable values: quality of life, happiness and general wellbeing.

Case study: Unilever and global sustainability

The next decade appears to be make or break for Unilever and its efforts to incorporate sustainable practice in all aspects of its business operations. November 2010 saw Unilever overtly announce its plans for sustainability. Under the bold headline in one of its press releases, the multinational company states its intention to decouple its environmental impact from growth as one of its main objectives. Unilever has organised its plans to deal with greenhouse gases, water, waste, sourcing raw materials and smallholder farmers and distributors in developing countries. Most aspects of the plan have time-bound targets for 2020, although it is stated that this is just the beginning of a longer-term plan.

The overall plan centres on three main objectives intending to:

- halve the environmental footprint of its products by decoupling growth from environmental impact
- help 1 billion people to improve their health and wellbeing
- source 100 percent of its agricultural raw materials sustainably and enhance the livelihood of thousands of people in the supply chain.

Unilever's *Sustainable Living Plan* had a truly global launch to match its sustainable initiative, and the message rang out simultaneously from London, Rotterdam, New Delhi and New York. CEO Paul Polman explained: 'We have ambitious plans to grow the company. But growth at any price is not viable. We have to develop new ways of doing business which will ensure that our growth does not come at the expense of the world's diminishing natural resources.'

Unilever has plans to achieve other objectives by or before 2020 including:

- sourcing 100 percent of its agricultural raw materials sustainably including, by 2015, 100 percent sustainable palm oil
- changing the hygiene habits of 1 billion people in Asia, Africa and Latin America so that they wash their hands with Lifebuoy soap at key times during the day – helping to reduce diarrhoeal disease (the world's second biggest cause of infant mortality)
- making safe drinking water available to half a billion people by extending sales of its low-cost in-home water purifier, Pureit, from India to other countries
- improving livelihoods in developing countries by working with Oxfam, Rainforest Alliance and others to link over 500,000 smallholder farmers and small-scale distributors into its supply chain.

The plan is subtitled *'small actions big difference'* but the inclusion of partnerships with governments, NGOs, suppliers and other stakeholders show this is a much more elaborate and holistic

Figure 10.5   An example of Unilever's GHG footprint across the lifecycle
Source: Adapted Unilever Sustainable Living Plan, p. 12

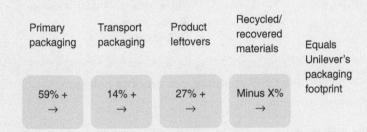

Figure 10.6   Unilever's waste footprint
Source: Adapted from Unilever Sustainable Living Plan, p. 16

plan of action, in the style of Marks and Spencer's *Plan A*. With over 50 initial specific targets to be met, the plan takes a sweeping look at all of Unilever's product categories.

For example, Unilever has committed to reducing its greenhouse gas (GHG) emissions across the breadth of the organisation and the entire length of the supply chain through to consumer use and post-consumer disposal, as can be seen from Figures 10.5 and 10.6. As mentioned earlier in the chapter, measuring success is vital to provide a baseline for current performance and a means of indicating how and where improvements are being made.

Unilever's specifically designed metrics have been used to calculate the greenhouse gas emissions associated with the lifecycle of a product on a per consumer use basis, e.g. the GHG impact of drinking a single cup of tea. This was done for 1,600 representative products on an absolute basis as well as per consumer single use across 14 different countries, covering 70 percent of Unilever's total volumes.

In this way Unilever is able to map its GHG emissions across all its product categories in order to evaluate which categories require the most improvement in performance. As can be seen in Figure 10.7, certain categories, such as soaps, detergents, etc., have the highest footprint.

When calculating its overall packaging footprint across product categories and taking a lifecycle perspective, Unilever discovered that food packaging and shower gel bottles were the biggest contributors to its waste footprint. The sustainability plan recognised that waste reduction would have to occur in all product categories in order to meet waste reduction targets, through a combination of reducing, reusing, recycling and eliminating packaging materials. In the calculation of waste, Unilever included the amount of product that may be left over.

▶

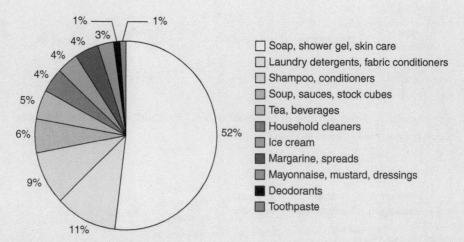

Figure 10.7   Unilever's GHG footprint per product category

Source: Unilever Sustainable Living Plan, p. 12

Not everyone loves a *Plan A*

It may come as a surprise that not everyone is an advocate of exposing the general public to sustainability planning in advance in such detail. It is suggested that creating forward-looking promises, such as Marks and Spencer's *Plan A*, creates a gap between intention and the actual position of the business in reality. This gap may immediately deposition the brand, as it highlights all the sustainable actions the organisation does not actually carry out. Alternatively, it can create a reputational risk for the brand if subsequent actions do not match promises. The plan may also be interpreted as greenwash by the public; the more ambitious the plan and the more widespread the publicity, the greater the risk to the brand.

There is also the suggestion that Unilever has not become a hostage of its own plans. If Unilever can deliver on those plans its success will attract investors and consumers alike, if Unilever fails it runs the risk of being rejected by both. Marks and Spencer's *Plan A* is rightly regarded as a milestone in corporate sustainable practice but Unilever's strategy is even more ambitious. Unilever is setting in motion a ten-year sustainability strategy which, by its nature, has a long-term return on investment, which is likely to be incompatible with the investors seeking short-term returns for their financial support.

Most chief executives report a lack of interest in sustainability activities from investors and analysts, according to a survey of 766 CEOs by Accenture for the 2010 United Nations Global Compact. Only 12 percent regard pressure from investors as being a factor in driving them to take action on sustainability issues. By comparison, 72 percent cite brand, trust and reputation as key deciding factors for action for investment.

Almost in anticipation of investor issues, CEO Paul Polman decoupled the assessment of stock market performance from quarterly earnings, and replaced it with topline revenue growth when he took over at Unilever. In addition, Polman placed the marketing function in centre stage to deliver the strategy for sustainability. Polman promoted Keith Weed to the post of chief marketing officer and gave him a place on the Unilever board, making him responsible for communications and sustainability in addition to the more conventional aspects of marketing.[38]

Follow up

1. Read the full sustainability plan of Unilever. How is Unilever performing to date on its own sustainability strategy?

2. In its introduction to its own sustainability strategy Unilever states its intention to grow and double its sales. Is this objective compatible with its aim to become a sustainable business?

Dilemma part 2: One sustainable lifestyle

Source: BioRegional Development Group

Devise your own strategy

At this stage in your learning it seems appropriate that you devise a strategy for yourself to improve your own sustainability credentials.

Review the sustainable lifestyle differences for 2050 in the first part of the dilemma. How many of them do you already adhere to? What evidence do you see from government initiatives, regional or local projects, business initiatives that these sustainable lifestyle goals are being encouraged?

Take the One Planet Challenge set up by Bioregional (http://calculator.bioregional.com) to calculate your own carbon and ecological footprints (see photo above). On completing the survey Bioregional provides immediate feedback indicating your carbon footprint and

▶

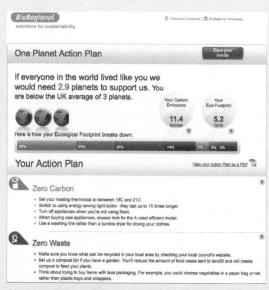

Source: BioRegional Development Group

ecological footprint together with a personalised action plan (see photo above) dealing with each of the relevant behaviours of the ten initiatives with practical suggestions on how to reduce impacts.

All things considered, what will be your own plan to lead a more sustainable lifestyle?

Epilogue

A decade of reluctant or whole-hearted engagement?

Although there is gathering momentum behind the sustainable movement, will the next decade be one of reluctant or whole-hearted engagement of sustainability? The challenges of the next decade are many. Following are three representative ones.

Low- and zero-carbon (LZC) homes

By 2010 regulations come into force which cut the permissible emissions from new-build houses by approximately 25 percent when compared to the average home built to 2006 Building Regulations standards. This reduction will be set at 44 percent when compared to 2006 standards. The year 2016 will bring the greatest step change, when the net emissions from a new-build home must drop to zero. This is a bigger step change than any other because for the first time the unregulated emissions from activities such as cooking, watching television and using a computer will be included in the emissions calculation.

The greatest difficulty for house builders (other than meeting the LZC standards) will be to persuade consumers to pay a higher price for a new home and overcome their unwillingness to pay for LZC features which are perceived as expensive and unproven possibly unreliable technology, requiring a level of understanding and maintenance not required from older properties. These perceived barriers from the part of the consumer will be in addition to a stagnant home-buying market with falling prices of current stock and fewer mortgages being granted by financial institutions.

Electric cars

2011 is the year of the electric car, or at least it is the first year that models of electric car start to become available for the general public. Leaving the debate about performance to one side, price will be a significant barrier. Despite the offer of £5,000 off the price tag of a new electric car by the UK government, the general public is likely to remain lukewarm to the idea of purchasing one. Even with the price reduction, the final cost will still be higher in relation to its petrol partners. The problem, though, is very *chicken and egg*. While people play a wait and see game, waiting for rising demand and improving technical engineering expertise to bring down prices, demand will be low and prices will continue to be high. Also, while demand is low providers of recharging facilities and infrastructure will be reluctant to invest in such systems; unfortunately leaving the early adopters of electric cars with nowhere to go. Finally the issue of home recharging of the electric car remains unresolved. How would the National Grid cope with demand and what will be the carbon price of all the recharging? Many countries currently have a cheaper off-peak, night-time tariff for electricity, but if everyone waits until then to recharge their car, off-peak may become the new peak.

The rise of the nimby

Nimby is an acronym for *not in my backyard* and refers to someone who objects to siting something in their own neighbourhood but does not object to it being sited elsewhere. A nimby resists change and this can work for sustainability or against it. Nimbys have consistently complained about the setting up of new ecotowns, so much so that by September 2009 only four out of the original ten sites were still proceeding.[39] Protests against windfarms have become commonplace, as people criticise them for spoiling the natural beauty of the places where they are to be installed. Such has been the movement against windfarms in the countryside that planners are granting permission for wind turbines to be set up closer to towns.[40] The number of groups objecting to plans for wind farms, wave turbines and waste-to-energy plants appears to be increasing. In Scotland there are more than 12 separate pressure groups protesting against the development of renewable energy sources and that number rises to over 100 throughout the UK.[41]

Marketing and sustainability – ideal partners

September 2010 saw the launch of another sustainability awareness, marketing and engagement campaign known as the Start Initiative, which began with a nine-day conference hosted by IBM and attended by business leaders, public sector figures and sustainability pioneers.

In a survey of expert opinion making the most of the opportunity of the conference, CRM online magazine MyCustomer.com asked where the responsibility for sustainability should be placed in the business organisation. Keith Weed, Unilever's new marketing chief, was of the opinion that marketing should lead the development of sustainability, as Unilever announced a major business overhaul to drive sustainable practice through the multinational. Mark Stuart, head of research for the Chartered Institute of Marketing, agreed that marketing was best suited for sustainability for its key role in communications.

Jo Kenrick, brand director of the Start Initiative and chair of the Marketing Society Green Alliance, also believes that marketing is best placed to deliver on sustainability initiatives, but highlighted that sustainability, like the marketing function itself, should be integrated across the whole organisation as sustainability needs an holistic vision and treatment.

Kenrick added:

> By providing consumers with new ways to be sustainable through product innovation, incentivising and monetising them, or simply by exciting them we can ensure that sustainability is not only an easy choice to make but a painless and even a fun choice too.[42]

Employment opportunities

There exist many opportunities for employment within the sustainability sector and these opportunities are likely to increase according to UNEP.[43] A report by UNEP highlighted the following:

- 2.3 million jobs in renewable energy currently to grow to 20 million by 2030.

- EU and US: green buildings to create 2–3.5 million jobs.

- Organic agriculture to provide 30 percent more jobs per hectare.

- China: 10 million jobs in recycling.

References

1. Daly, H. (2008) 'On a Road to Disaster', *New Scientist*, 18 October.

2. Knight, A. (2009) *Sustainable Lives: What Will Sustainable Lives Look Like? A Provocation by Alan Knight SDC Commissioner*, London: Sustainable Development Commission.

3. Dialogue extract from the film *Star Trek: First Contact* (1996) between the character Jean-Luc Picard, Captain of the starship Enterprise and the character Lily Sloane.

4. Fromm, E. (1976) *To Have or To Be?*, London: Continuum Publishing Group (Rev. ed. 2005).

5. Stepek, J. (2007) 'Has Independence Changed the Bank of England?', *MoneyWeek*, 17 May, www.moneyweek.com/news-and-charts/economics/has-independence-changed-the-bank-of-england.aspx

6. Forum for the Future and Capgemini (2009) *Acting Now for A Positive 2018, Preparing for Radical Change the Next Decade of Business and Sustainability*, London: Forum for the Future/Capgemini.

7. Jackson, T. (2009) *Prosperity Without Growth? The Transition to a Sustainable Economy*, London: Sustainable Development Commission.

8. Organisation for Economic Cooperation and Development (OECD) (2002) *Indicators to Measure Decoupling of Environmental Pressure from Economic Growth*, OECD, www.oecd.org/dataoecd/0/52/1933638.pdf

9. Jackson, T. (2009) *Prosperity Without Growth? The Transition to a Sustainable Economy*, London: Sustainable Development Commission.

10. Sustainable Development Commission (SDC) (2009) *Where We Are Now? A Review of Progress on Sustainable Development*, A support document for Breakthroughs for the 21st century July, SDC.

11. Chartered Institute of Purchase and Supply (CIPS) (2009) *A Cynic's Supply to Sustainable Procurement*, London: CIPS.

12. O'Riordan, T. (2009) 'Reflections on the Pathways to Sustainability', in Adger, W.N. and Jordan, A. (eds), *Governing Sustainability*, Cambridge: Cambridge University.

13. United Nations Environment Programme (UNEP) (2008) Press Release on the launch of the Green Economy Initiative, 22 October, London.

14. Green Futures (2009) *New Ideas that Work: How Sustainable Innovation is Changing Our World*, www.greenfutures.org.uk

15. Ben-Ami, D. (2010) *Ferraris For All: In Defence of Economic Progress*, Bristol: Policy Press.

16. Ben-Ami, D. (2010) 'Prosperity Without Growth: A Contradiction in Terms?', *The Independent*, 20 October, http://blogs.independent.co.uk/2010/10/20/prosperity-without-growth-a-contradiction-in-terms/

17. Porritt, J. (2010) *Ferraris For All Versus Limits to Growth: Jonathon Porritt Makes the Case For Sustainability at a Time When Many Still Regard the Planet's Resources as Limitless*, www.forumforthefuture.org/greenfutures/articles/jp-learning-to-prosper-within-limits

18. Elkington, J. (2010) *Make or Break Decade for Sustainability*, 13 October, www.volans.com/uncategorized/make-or-break-decade-for-sustainability/

19. United Nations Commission of Sustainable Development (2010) *More People, More Consumption, Finite Planet: Demographics, Development and Decoupling*, Press Release 3 May.

20. World Wildlife Fund (WWF) (2007) *One Planet Business: Creating Value Within Planetary Limits*, London: WWF/SustainAbility.

21. Corin, M. (2010) *Can We Get it in Perspective, Please? Sustainable Exports From the UK*, Presentation by Mary Corin Directorr, Value Resource Development.

22. Millar, J. (2010) Resource Efficiency Support from WRAP: Slaughtering and Animal By-products Industries EBP, Seminar: 29 September, presentation by Josephine Millar Project Manager–Retail Supply Chain Team.

23. WRAP (2010) *New 'Waste Mapping' Research Across the Pre-prepared and Chilled Foods Supply Chain,* Press release 26 February www.wrap.org.uk/media_centre/press_releases/new_waste_mapping.html

24. SustainAbility (2010) *Rate the Raters: Phase Two Taking Inventory of the Ratings Universe*, London: SustainAbility.

25. United Nations Development Programme (2010) *Human Development Report 2010*, http://hdrstats.undp.org/en/countries/profiles/GBR.html

26. World Wildlife Fund (WWF) (2010) *Living Planet Report 2010 Biodiversity, Biocapacity and Development*, London: WWF.

27. World Wildlife Fund (WWF) (2010) *Living Planet Report 2010 Biodiversity, Biocapacity and Development*, London: WWF.

28. New Economics Foundation (NEF) (2009) *The Happy Planet Index 2.0*, NEF, www.happyplanetindex.org/public-data/files/happy-planet-index-2-0.pdf

29. Royal Society for the Encouragement of Arts, Manufactures and Commerce (RSA) (2009) *Sustainable Designs Win National RSA Award*, Press release, 8 May.

30. E-on (2008) 'Installing Your Energy Saving Monitor', *Consumer Guide Book* (p. 10).

31. Soper, K. (2008) Paper from Kate Soper to Sustainable Development Commission Meeting on *Living Well (Within Limits) – Exploring the Relationship Between Growth and Wellbeing*, April, London.

32. Ashley, J. (2006) 'A New Campaign by Those Disaffected With Our Shopping Culture Could Be a Cure for Anxiety and Low Self-Esteem', *The Guardian*, 17 April.

33. Soper, K. (2007) 'Re-thinking the "Good Life": The Citizenship Dimension of Consumer Disaffection with Consumerism', *Journal of Consumer Culture* 7(2): 205–229.

34. Soper, K. (2009) *Beyond Consumerism: 'Alternative Hedonism' and Cultural Politics*, Presentation for RESOLVE at Surrey University, www3.surrey.ac.uk/resolve/ocs/Conference/K%20Soper%20PowerPoint.pdf

35. Schor, J. (1991) *The Overworked American: The Unexpected Decline of Leisure*, New York: Harper Collins.

36. Huppert, F. (2008) *Psychological Well-being: Evidence Regarding its Causes and its Consequences*, London: Foresight Mental Capital and Wellbeing Project.

37. Porritt, J. (2007) *Capitalism: As If the World Matters*, London: Earthscan (p. 255).

38. Unilever (2010) *Unilever Unveils Plan to Decouple Business Growth From Environmental Impact*, Press release, 15 November, www.unilever.com/mediacentre/pressreleases/2010/Unileverunveilsplantodecouplebusinessgrowthfromenvironmentalimpact.aspx; Unilever (2010) *Unilever Sustainable Living Plan: Small Actions, Big Difference,*

Unilever; Hesz, A. and Neophytou, B. (2010) *Guilt Trip: From Fear to Guilt on the Green Bandwagon*, Chichester: John Wiley and Sons; Smith, S. (2010) 'Is Unilever's Sustainability Drive a Hostage to Fortune', *Marketing Week*, 9 December, http://stuartsmithsblog.wordpress.com; Skypala, P. (2010) 'Sustainability's Stumbling Blocks', *Financial Times*, 28 November.

39. Hewitson, J. (2009) 'Not in One's Back Yard', *The Sunday Times*, 16 August.

40. Leake, J. (2010) 'Wind Farms Blow into Town as Rural Protests Grow', *The Sunday Times*, 14 March.

41. Kelbie, P. (2009) 'Nimbys "Thwart Plans" for Cheap Green Energy', *The Observer*, 26 April.

42. Mycustomer (2010) www.mycustomer.com/topic/marketing/should-sustainability-sit-under-marketing/113362.

43. Scanlon, J. (2010) *The Green Economy and International Environmental Governance*, Presentation by John Scanlon – Principal Adviser to the Executive Director of the United Nations Environment Programme.

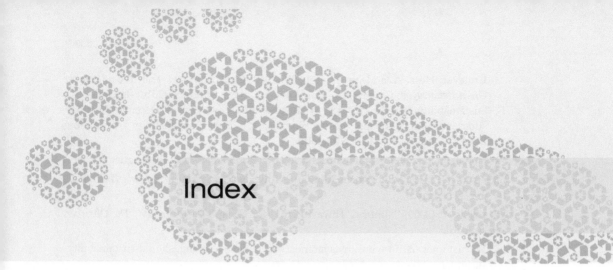

Index

absolute decoupling 286–8
Acorn 100
actual self 75
Adnams Brewery 263–76
advertising and consumption 78
Advertising Standards
        Authority 223, 224
Affluenza 77
Aga 217–18, 242–3
Ajzen, Icek 146–7
Albrecht, Terrance 141
Aldi 93
alternative hedonism 297–8
altruistic behaviour 138
altruistic values and
        behaviour 134, 229
Anderson, Gillian 146
Andreasen, Alan 140
Annan, Kofi 104
Apledorn, Paul 69
Arnold, Chris 20
aspirer consumer type 102
Attenborough, Sir David 267
attitudes towards consumption 70–1
    not matching behaviour 78–85
attitudes towards
        sustainability 70–1, 79
    conflict of interests 81–3
    and consumption 78–85
    contradictions in 84–5
    self-interest 83–4
    trade-offs 83–4
    trust, lack of 84–5
Austin Rover 223

bananas 261
Bandura, Albert 136
Bangladesh 197, 199
Baudrillard, Jean 74
behaving responsibly 4

behaviour
    and attitudes towards
        consumption 78–85
    influence of values on 134
behavioural beliefs on
        sustainability 146
behavioural change
    framework for 140–8
        participants 144–5
        social marketing 140–4
        sustainability 146–7
    methodology for 146–7
    motivating 129
    negative models for 137
    normative information for 135–6
    norms of 131–40
        descriptive norm 132, 133
        do as others do 132
        injunctive norm 132–3
        and social learning theory 136–7
        social norms 133–6
        thinking of others 138–9
        thinking of ourselves 139–40
    positive models for 137
    transitional models for 137
    vicarious motivators for 137
believability in selling
        sustainability 231
Bellamy, Julian 82
Belz, Frank-Martin 11
Ben-Ami, Daniel 288
benefits, evolution of 9
Benn, Hilary 202
Benyus, J. 168
Berry, Leonard 5
BHS 194
Biel, Jessica 104
biomimicry 167–8
biospheric values and behaviour 134
Blue Angel label 233

bluefin tuna 207
Body Shop 12, 182
bottled water 119–21
Bottletop 104
B&Q 162–3, 196
Braungart, Michael 165, 288
Brazil 6
British American Tobacco
        (BAT) 30–1
British Petroleum 223
British Retail Consortium 152
British Standards Institute 235
Brundtland Report 20–1
Business Enabler Survey Tool 4
Business in the Community 4, 30
business not as usual 41–58
    carbon footprints, impact
        of 43–7
        ecological footprints 43–4
        ecological overshoot 44
        water footprint 45–6
    costs, externalising or
        internalising 47–8
    polluter pays 48
    technology, contribution of 56–8

California 289
Cambodia 197
Cameron, David 243, 298
Canada 293
Capgemini 283–4
car usage
    consumer behaviour on 115
    reduction of 142–4
    thresholds of 129–30
carbon
    as new global currency 49–53
    as new household currency 51–2
carbon emission trading scheme 37,
        49–53

carbon footprints 37
  of consumers 63–4
  impact of 43–7
    ecological footprints 43–4
    ecological overshoot 44
    water footprint 45–6
  reduction of 227
Carbon Reduction Commitment 271
Carbon Reduction Scheme 234–5, 258
Carbon Trust 12, 259
  Carbon Reduction
      Scheme 234–5, 258
Carillion plc 254
Carrier Bag Consortium 152
cars, electric 305
cautious participants 107, 266
certification of sustainability 189–90,
      212
Charter, M. 16, 17
Chartered Institute of Marketing
      (CIM) 19
Chartered Institute of Purchase and
      Supply 286
checklist for product
      sustainability 170
Cheddar Gorge Cheese Company 208
Children in Need 253
China 6, 197
choice-editing 255
Cialdini, Robert 132, 222
circle of consumption 74–6
citizen's act of faith in
      sustainability 88–9
clarity in selling
      sustainability 227, 230
clichèd images 237
climate change 106, 107, 108
Clinton, Bill 104
closed-loop economy 165
Clover, Charles 207
Clownfish 20
Co-operative Bank 9, 19, 90
Coddington, W. 16
Cogent Elliiott 218
Columbia Forest Products 167
Comic Relief 253
Commission of Sustainable
      Development (CSD) 289
communicating sustainability 218–19
  evaluation of 236–7
  greenwashing 223–6
    dangers of 225–6
    sins of 223–5
  labelling 232–7
    Carbon Trust's Carbon
        Reduction Scheme 234–5
    evaluation of 236
    sustainablility label 235–6

type 1 claims 232–3
type 2 claims 233
type 3 claims 233
language used 237
problems with 219–27
  fear and guilt 220–1
  greenwashing 223–6
  lack of appeal 219–20
  social norm, misuse of 222–3
success in 228–31
  consumers' information 228–9
  matching expectations 229–30
communication, consumption as 74
communication mix in selling
      sustainability 227
Community Supported Agriculture
      (CSA) programmes 204
comparability in selling
      sustainability 230
compelling messages in selling
      sustainability 227
compost in waste hierarchy 192
composting 178
concerned consumers 107, 109, 266
confidence in selling
      sustainability 227
conflict of interests in
      sustainability 81–3
connection to issues in selling
      sustainability 227
consistency in selling
      sustainability 227
consolidated change 261–72
conspicuous bags 104
constructive effect of normative
      information for behavioural
      change 135
consumer as part-time supplies 204–5
consumer behaviour goals 54–5
Consumer Focus 229
consumer perceptions pro-
      environmental
      behaviours 111
consumers' information in selling
      sustainability 228–9
consumption
  and advertising 78
  attitudes towards 70–1
    not matching behaviour 78–85
  circle of 74–6
  as communication 74
  continued 75
  habitual 72–3
  hedonistic 73
  and inequality 40–1
  infectious nature of 76–7
  nature of 71–8
  rational 72

self-identity 73–4
sociological 73
continued consumption 75
contradictions in attitudes towards
      sustainability 84–5
control beliefs on sustainability 146
Convention on International Trade
      in Endangered Species
      (CITES) 207
conventional marketing 5, 7–10
  and sustainable marketing,
      compared 24–5
corporate governance
  sustainable future for 21
corporate social responsibility
      (CSR) 11–14
Costa Rica 289, 293
costs, externalising or
      internalising 47–8
cotton 197–8
country of origin in supply chain
      sustainability 208–9
Courtauld Commitment
      Phase 2 260, 271
cradle-to-cradle design 165, 169–71
creativity in selling sustainability 227
credibility
  in attitudes towards
      sustainability 79–80
  in selling sustainability 230
Crouch, Peter 146
Cumbria County Council 152–3
Curtis, Richard 145
cynical attitudes to sustainability 80

Daily Mail 164
Daly, Herman 280
decoupling 285–6
denial as attitude to
      sustainability 80
Denmark 289
Department of Energy and Climate
      Change (DECC) 238–42
Department of Environment,
      Food and Rural Affairs
      (DEFRA) 184
  future of sustainability 290
  on guilt 221
  information overload 221–2
  on labelling 235
  on pro-environmental behaviours
      108–13
  on sustainable change 259, 266
    checklist 269
descriptive norms of behaviour 132
  influence of 133
  misuse of 222
designer shopping bags 104

designing sustainable product 161–71
  biomimicry 167–8
  B&Q 162–3
  choice editing 161–2
  closed-loop economy 165
  design checklist 170
  energy efficiency 162
  light bulbs 163–4
destructive effect of normative
        information for behavioural
        change 135
Diderot, Denis 76
Digital Growth 294–6
disinterested attitudes to
        sustainability 80
disposable nappies 128
disposal in waste hierarchy 192
divided ethics 113–16
do as others do as norm of
        behaviour 132
Dolan, P. 268
dominant social paradigm (DSP) 39

Eagleton, Richard 218
ecocentrism 41
ecological awareness 116
ecological footprints 43–4
ecological overshoot 44
economic growth and
        sustainability 288
economic impacts along supply
        chain 198–9
ecopreneurship 18–19
Ecover 17
EDF Energy 9
Edible Todmorden 205–6
eggs, free-range 253
ego risk of sustainability 86
egoistic values and behaviour 134
Elaboration Liklihood model 72
electric cars 305
Elgin, Duane 116
Elkington, John 21, 288
enable
  of household food waste 265–6
  for managing sustainable
        change 263–4
encourage
  of household food waste 265–6
  for managing sustainable
        change 263–4
end-of-life options for goods 166
end-of-pipe products 165
energy efficient fridges and
        freezers 162
energy recovery in waste
        hierarchy 192
Energy Star 233

engage
  of household food waste 265–6
  for managing sustainable
        change 263–4
environmental costs, externalising or
        internalising 47–8
environmental impacts along supply
        chain 197–8
Environmental Management
        System 258–9
environmental marketing 15–20
  ecopreneurship 18–19
  measuring pro-environmental
        tendencies 42
  variants 17–18
ethical banking, perceptions of 111
ethical fashion 158–60, 183–4
EU Eco-label 232
EU Landfill Directive 260
Eurostar 225
evaluate for managing sustainable
        change 268
evaluation of labelling 236
exemplify
  of household food waste 265–6
  for managing sustainable
        change 263–4
expectations, matching in selling
        sustainability 229–30
explore for managing sustainable
        change 268
explorer consumer type 102

Fairtrade 11, 63, 183, 189, 209, 212
fatalist attitudes to sustainability 80
favourable attitudes towards
        sustainability 79–81
fear in communicating
        sustainability 220–1
fed-up attitudes to sustainability 80
feedback for sustainable change 252
Fenchurch 104
financial risk of sustainability 86
Finisterre 169
Fisk, G. 16
focus groups 87
Food Industry Sustainability
        Strategy 260
food waste 259–61
Forest Stewardship Council 12
Forest Stewardship Council
        (FSC) 162–3
Forum for the Future 283–4, 290
Fox's Biscuits 253
France 106
free-range eggs 253
From Somewhere 183–4
Fromm, Erich, 282

Futerra 222, 236
future for sustainability
  absolute decoupling 286–8
  alternative hedonism 297–8
  changing the game 281–2
  consequences of growth 283–9
  decoupling 285–6
  innovative sustainability 294–7
  non-inflation expansion 283
  relative decoupling 286
  steady-state future 285
  success, measures of 292–4
  wellbeing 298–9
  Zero waste 291–2

Gates, Bill 252
Geddes, Tommy 271
Geldof, Peaches 104
geotraceability through supply
        chain 209
Germany 108, 233
Gillespie, Ed 241
Ginola, David 146
Global Footprint Network 286
global warming 106
Green League 271
green marketing 17
Green Party (UK) 6, 249, 250
Green Seal (USA) 232
Greencycle 180
greenhouse gas emissions 258, 259
Greenpeace 13, 99
greenwashing 223–6
  dangers of 225–6
  sins of 223–5
growth, consequences of 283–9
guide in biomimicry 168
guilt in communicating
        sustainability 220–1
guilty as attitude to sustainability 81

habits of a lifetime 38–41
  dominant social paradigm 39
  inequality and consumption 40–1
  recession and sustainability 40
  usual suspects 39–40
habitual consumption 72–3
Haiti 197
Hamnett, Katherine 198
Hans Merensky 11, 28–30
Happy Planet Index 293
Harrison, Joe 294
Harveys brewery 117
Havas Media 106, 107, 108
Hawken, Paul 23, 39
hedonistic consumption 73
Henion, K.E. 16
Hewlett Packard 233

Higgins, E. Tory 74
Hindmarch, Anya 104
H.J. Berry 11, 12
honestly disengaged 107, 266
Hosking, Rebecca 149
human needs, evolution of 101–4
human scale behaviour 116

IBM 306
ideal self 75
ignorant attitudes to sustainability 80
Imbruglia, Natalie 104
India 6, 197, 198
Industry Council for Packaging
    and the Environment
    (INCPEN) 175
inequality and consumption 40–1
infectious nature of
    consumption 76–7
information on packaging sustainable
    products 229
Ingwersen, Peter 183
injunctive norms of behaviour 132–3
Innocent 9
innovative sustainability 294–7
intervention design for sustainable
    change 267–8, 270
Iron Eyes Cody, Chief 222–3
Issak, R. 16

Jack, Michael 178
Jackson, Tim 36
Jane Norman 194
John Lewis Partnership 255

Keep America Beautiful campaign 222
Keep Britain Tidy campaign 179
Kelloggs 26–7
Kenrick, Jo 306
Keogh, P.D. 16
Kern, Georges 98
Kevlar 168
King, Mervyn 283
Kinnear, T.C. 16
Kiuchi, Masao 62
Knight, Alan 127
Knightley, Keira 104
Kotler, Philip 13, 16
Kraljic, Peter 194–6
Kraljic matrix 195
Kruger, Barbara 73
Kyoto Earth Summit 37

labelling 232–7
    Carbon Trust's Carbon Reduction
        Scheme 234–5
    evaluation of 236
    sustainablility label 235–6

type 1 claims 232–3
type 2 claims 233
type 3 claims 233
lack of appeal of sustainability 219–20
Lazer, W. 16
leather, popularity 99
Lee, Nancy 13
Lennox, Annie 104
Lenoir 9
Leonard, Annie 202
Leopold, Aldo 41
Levy, S.J. 16
Lidl 93
life cycle technology
    sustainable future for 21
life product cycle 258
lifecycle greenhouse gas
    emissions 259
lifecycle management in
    packaging 171–2
lifestyle sacrifice threshold 130
light bulbs, editing 163–4
Lime Technology 273
Lloyds TSB 84
local supply chain 203–4
Locavores 203
Lovins, Amory and Hunter 23, 39
low- and zero-carbon (LZC)
    homes 304–5
Lucas, Caroline 249, 250

McDonald, Seonaidh 111
McDonough, William 165, 288
McGrath, William 243
Mackay, David 46
macromarketing 15
Mail on Sunday 164
mainstream consumer type 102
Maldives 289
Marine Stewardship Council
    (MSC) 206
marketing
    corporate social responsibility
        (CSR) 11–14
    definitions 8
    right direction 11–15
    with social norms of
        behaviour 133–6
    and sustainability 306
Marketing Society Green Alliance 306
markets, sustainable future for 21
Marks and Spencer 19, 93, 149, 159,
    196, 207, 230–1, 253
Maslow, Abraham 101–3
material simplicity behaviour 116
materialism versus simplicity 113–18
    divided ethics 113–16
    voluntary simplifiers 116–17

meat production and
    consumption 144
Menon, A. and A. 16
mentor in biomimicry 168
Metcalf, Julian 207
Meter, Ken 203
Mexico 289
micromarketing 15
Migros 196
Milliband, David 51
Mineralwaters 119–21
minimisation in waste hierarchy 192
Monbiot, George 243
MOSAIC 100
Muji 62–3
Mulberry 104
Müller Brand 203–4

nappies, disposable 128, 152–3
National Endowment for Science,
    Technology and the Arts
    (NESTA) 226–7
National Wellbeing Project 298
need 7
negative models for behavioural
    change 137
Nestlé 176–7
Netherlands 293
New Ecological Paradigm 139
New Look 194
New Zealand 289
    emissions trading scheme 50
New Zealand: Merino
    Company 122–3
nimby, rise of 305–6
Non-Inflation Constant Expansion
    (NICE) 283
normative beliefs on
    sustainability 146
normative information for
    behavioural change 135–6
norms of behavioural change 131–40
    descriptive norm 132, 133
    do as others do 132
    injunctive norm 132–3
    and social learning theory 136–7
    social norms 133–6
    thinking of others 138–9
    thinking of ourselves 139–40
Norway 289
Nugent, Greg 225

Oakes, Summer Rayne 210–11
Oates, Caroline 111
O'Connor, Erin 104
offsetting, irresponsible 52–3
Oliver, Jamie 137–8
One Planet Challenge 303

One Planet Living Initiative 290
Organization for Economic
    Cooperation and
    Development (OECD) 41,
    285, 289
Oslo Symposium on Sustainable
    Consumption 71
Ottman, J.A. 16
ought self 75

Pachauri, Dr. R. 144
packaging sustainable products 171–8
    best practice, framework for 173–5
    information on 229
    lifecycle management 171–2
    options 174
    public perceptions of 175–7
    roles of packaging 172–3
palm oil 196–7
partnerships, sustainable future
    for 21
Peacosks 194
Peattie, Ken 11, 16
People for the Ethical Treatment of
    Animals (PETA) 99
People Tree 183, 199–200
performance indicators for
    sustainability 271–2
performance risk of sustainability 86
Persil 9–10
personal growth behaviour 116
pets, environmental footprint
    of 46–7, 209
physical risk of sustainability 86
polluter pays principle 48
Polman, Paul 302
Polonsky, M.J. 16
population, offsetting 60–1
Porritt, Jonathon 40, 60, 288, 289
Portas, Mary 183
positive greens 107, 109, 266
positive models for behavioural
    change 137
practising as attitude to
    sustainability 80
Primark 158–60, 183, 196
pro-environmental behaviours 107
    DEFRA on 108–13
        building profiles 110
        concerns 112–13
        consumer perceptions 111
product durability and
    sustainability 277
product road mapping 256–8
product sustainability 160–1
    designing sustainable product
        161–71
        biomimicry 167–8

B&Q 162–3
    choice editing 161–2
    closed-loop economy 165
    design checklist 170
    energy efficiency 162
    light bulbs 163–4
    goals 160
    packaging 171–8
public perceptions of
    packaging 175–7

quantitative data on
    sustainability 108

Race for Life 253
Radiohead 146
Ramsey, Gordon 207
Rangan,V.K. 141
rational consumption 72
recession and sustainability 40
reciprocity in attitudes towards
    sustainability 79–80
reconstructive effect of normative
    information 135
recycling
    managing 250
    (mis)behaviours 179–83
    in waste hierarchy 192
reform oriented route to
    sustainability 59
reformer consumer type 102
relative decoupling 286
resigned consumer type 102
reuse in waste hierarchy 192
risk
    of sustainability 85–6
    in sustainable procurement 194–6
Roberts, Julia 267
roles of packaging sustainable
    products 172–3
Roper Green Gauge 2008 105–6, 107
Roper Starch Worldwide 105
Rose, Sir Stuart 159, 231

sacrifice in attitudes towards
    sustainability 79–80
Sainsbury's 72, 104, 150–1, 189, 196,
    253, 261
Schor, Juliet 298
Schwartz, Shalom 138
Schwarzenegger, Arnold 289
segmentation see sustainable
    segmentation
self-determination behaviour 116
self-identity consumption 73–4
self-interest 83–4
Selfridges 73
Sharkah Chakra 22–3, 183

shopping bags 104
    reducing use of 148–52
sideline supporters 107, 266
simplicity versus materialism 113–18
    divided ethics 113–16
    voluntary simplifiers 116–17
simplifiers, voluntary 116–17
Slater, Nigel 261
small and meduim-sized
    companies 11
SmartWay 233
soap operas and social learning
    theory 136–7
social cognitive theory 136
social impacts along supply
    chain 199
social learning theory 136–7
    and Jamie Oliver 137–8
social marketing and behavioural
    change 140–4
    promoting sustainable
        behaviour 142–4
social norms of behaviour 133–6
    misuse of 222–3
social risk of sustainability 86
societal marketing 17–18
sociological consumption 73
solidarity in attitudes towards
    sustainability 79–80
Soper, Kate 297–8
Source4Style 210–11
South Korea 106
Spain 108
Sport Relief 253
stakeholder 7
stalled starters 107, 266
Starbucks 253
Start Initiative 306
status quo oriented route to
    sustainability 59
steady-state future 285
stealth taxes 85
Stern, P. 139
Stern Review 20
Stibbe, Arran 58
sticky behaviours 132
struggler consumer type 102
stuff, story of 202
succeeder consumer type 102
success, measures of 292–4
Sun 164
Sunstein, Cass 267
supply chain sustainability 190–1, 255
    evaluating 196–7
    impacts along 197–202
        economic 198–9
        environmental 197–8
        social 199

local, not global 202–9
    consumer as part-time
        supplies 204–5
    country of origin 208–9
    edible Todmorden 205–6
    local supply 203–4
    traceability 206–9
management 190
scenario analysis 201
SustainAbility 288, 290, 292
sustainability
    as act of faith 88–9
    attitudes towards 70–1, 79
        conflict of interests 81–3
        and consumption 78–85
        contradictions in 84–5
        self-interest 83–4
        trade-offs 83–4
        trust, lack of 84–5
    backdrop to 38
    certification of 189–90, 212
    communicating see communicating
        sustainability
    future for see future for
        sustainability
    and marketing 306
    methodology for behavioural
        change 146–7
    performance indicators 271–2
    and product durability 277
    quantitative data on 108
    and recession 40
    researching 14–15, 87
    risk of 85–6
    routes to 59
    and segmentation 104–8
    selling 227
    seven revolutions to 21
    of supply chain see supply chain
        sustainability
    thresholds 129
        challenges beyond 129–31
sustainability crunch 93–943
sustainability impact-performance
    matrix 195
sustainability label 235–6
sustainable business network 255
sustainable change,
        managing 250–1
    business corner 254–8
    consolidated change 261–72
        intervention 265–6
        intervention design 267–8
    framework for 262–4
    government corner 258–61
        environmental impact 258–9
        hazardous substances 258–9
        responsible sourcing 258

people corner 251–4
pledges and
        procrastination 253–4
product road mapping 256–8
triangle of change 250–1
sustainable consumption 71
Sustainable Consumption
        Roundtable 158, 160
sustainable development
    approaches to 58–61
    population, offsetting 60–1
    routes to 59
    steady-state economy,
        towards 59–60
Sustainable Development
        Commission (SDC) 60,
        188, 281
Sustainable Development
        Strategy 191
sustainable happiness, routes
        to 297–8
sustainable lifestyle 303–4
sustainable marketing 5–7
    and conventional marketing,
        compared 24–5
    defining parameters 23–7
    sustainable transformations 26
sustainable procurement 191–7
    goals 192
    hierarchies 192
    risk in 194–6
sustainable purchasing cycle 193
sustainable segmentation 99
    evolution of 100
    and human needs 101–4
    simplicity and materialism 113–18
    and sustainability 104–8
sustainable transformations 26
Sweden 289

Tanaka, Ikko 62
Taylor, Rod 197
teach in biomimicry 168
TerraChoice 224
TerraCycle 174
Tesco 93, 159, 184, 261
Thailand 106
Thaler, Richard 266–7
thinking of others as behavioural
        norm 138–9
thinking of ourselves as behavioural
        norm 139–40
360 Vodka 91–2
thresholds of sustainability 129
    in car usage 129–30
    challenges beyond 129–31
Timberlake, Justin 104
Timberland 234

time considerations in sustainable
        futures 21
time risk of sustainability 86
Töpfer, Klaus 221
traceability through supply
        chain 206–9
trade-offs in sustainability 83–4
transformation oriented route to
        sustainability 59
transitional models for behavioural
        change 137
transparency, sustainable future
        for 21
Triple Bottom Line 19, 21, 22, 190, 191,
        202, 262
trust, lack of 84–5
Twiggy 104
type 1 claims in communicating
        sustainability 232–3
type 2 claims in communicating
        sustainability 233
type 3 claims in communicating
        sustainability 233

UK household expenditure, greening
        of 90
UN Environment Programme
        (UNEP) 221, 224, 287
UN Food and Agricultural
        Organisation 144
UN Human Development
        Index 293
UN Intergovernmental Panel on
        Climate Change 144
unfavourable attitudes towards
        sustainability 79–81
Unilever 9–10, 12, 206
    on global sustainability 300–3
United Kingdom, climate change
        in 106–7, 108
United States, climate change
        in 106, 108
unwilling participants in behavioural
        change 144–5
usual suspects: habits of a
        lifetime 39–40

Vale, Robert and Brenda 46
value-belief-norm model 139
values
    influence of on behaviour 134
    sustainable future for 21
Van dam, Ynte 69
van der Rohe, Ludwig Mies 62
Vanson Bourne 235
Varadarajan, P.R. 16
Veblen, Thorstein 76
Verde Nieto, Diana 20

vicarious motivators for behavioural
          change 137
voluntary simplifiers 116–17

Waitrose 9, 196, 204, 207, 253, 255, 261
    sustainable business network 256
Walker, David 27
want benefit 7
Waste and Resources Action
          Programme (WRAP) 172,
          177, 258, 260, 261
waste disposal authorities 260
Waste Electrical and Electronic
          Equipment
          Directive 166–7, 259

waste food 259–61
waste hierarchy 180, 192
waste watchers 107, 109, 266
water footprint 45–6
Watson, Emma 183
Weed, Keith 302
wellbeing 298–9
wicked problems 287
Wiebe, G. 16
willing participants in behavioural
          change 144–5, 266
wool marketing 122–3
World Business Council for
          Sustainable Development
          13–14

World Commission on Environment
          and Development 20
World Wildlife Fund 20, 196, 206

Young and Rubicam 101–2
Young's 196

Zaltman, G. 16
Zero waste 291–2